Love Analyzed

Love Analyzed

EDITED BY
Roger E. Lamb

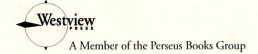
Westview PRESS
A Member of the Perseus Books Group

William Butler Yeats, "For Anne Gregory," taken from *The Collected Poems of WB Yeats*, reprinted by permission of Simon & Schuster and A P Watt Ltd on behalf of Michael Yeats.

Published in 1997 in the United States of America by Westview Press, 5500 Central Avenue, Boulder, Colorado 80301-2877, and in the United Kingdom by Westview Press, 12 Hid's Copse Road, Cumnor Hill, Oxford OX2 9JJ

Library of Congress Cataloging-in-Publication Data
Love analyzed / edited by Roger E. Lamb.
    p.   cm.
Includes bibliographical references and index.
ISBN 0-8133-8891-0 (hc)—0-8133-3223-0 (pbk.)
1. Love.   I. Lamb, Roger E.
BD436.L68 1996
128'.4—dc20   96-38902
                                                                                     CIP

The paper used in this publication meets the requirements of the American National Standard for Permanence of Paper for Printed Library Materials Z39.48-1984.

10   9   8   7   6   5   4   3

for

Laurie Gaffney

Contents

Preface   ix
Acknowledgements   xiii
About the Contributors   xv

1   **Love and the Individual: Romantic Rightness
     and Platonic Aspiration**
     Martha C. Nussbaum   1

2   **Love and Rationality**
     Roger E. Lamb   23

3   **The Right Method of Boy-Loving**
     Deborah Brown   49

4   **Union, Autonomy, and Concern**
     Alan Soble   65

5   **Love and Human Bondage
     in Maugham, Spinoza, and Freud**
     Barbara Hannan   93

6   **Love and Autonomy**
     Keith Lehrer   107

7   **Love and Solipsism**
     Rae Langton   123

8   **Love and Its Place in Moral Discourse**
     Philip Pettit   153

9   **Jealousy and Desire**
     Daniel M. Farrell   165

10 Love Undigitized
Ronald de Sousa   189

11 Is Love an Emotion?
O. H. Green   209

12 Love and Intentionality: Roxane's Choice
Sue Campbell   225

13 Love's Truths
Graeme Marshall   243

Index   257
About the Book and Editor   268

Preface

This is a collection of articles on love. More specifically, the topic is romantic and erotic love, even though *agape* and *philia* receive the occasional mention. For the most part, the articles have been especially commissioned for this volume, and hence are previously unpublished.[1]

My aim has been to show the style of thinking that a subclass of contemporary philosophers, sometimes broadly designated as 'analytical', are likely to engage in, in thinking about love--and, by showing it, to reveal its value. I will not here argue that that value is considerable, although I believe it to be so, but will let the chips fall where they may in the evaluative judgment of the average curious reader. For, in general, I do not think the deliverances of my analytic colleagues get much better than this. And if, in the judgment of readers, this kind of thinking about love satisfies a part of--or revealingly reflects an illuminating capacity to be found within--our complex and deep human nature, I will not be surprised.

In saying this, I do imagine and believe there to be many other illuminating, and at the same time typically human, ways of cognitively approaching the topic--not the least of which is via the myths, literature, poetry, and drama of many diverse cultures. There are also naturalistic and, differently, phenomenological approaches; their respective methodological protocols may, as well, yield much that is illuminating.

Still, in my view, there is something fundamental about the issues being raised and, *mirabile dictu*, discussed with clarity and care here. Moreover, the questions are natural ones. These two points together mean we are naturally given to raising fundamental questions about love. This itself is not unnatural, for love is a momentous, and consequential, phenomenon in the lives of an

---

1. The foremost and, indeed, complete exception to this rule is Martha Nussbaum's 'Love and the Individual: Romantic Rightness and Platonic Aspiration' which originally appeared in 1986, and appeared again in 1990. It is such a fine piece that it deserves the widest possible circulation. As well, distinct ancestral versions of Alan Soble's 'Union, Autonomy, and Concern' have previously seen the light of day in two Hungarian journals, one version appearing in Hungarian, the other in English. And an earlier version of Keith Lehrer's 'Love and Autonomy' has made an appearance in German. But, for the linguistically-challenged English reader, Soble's and Lehrer's pieces are as new.

extraordinary number of people. Curious creatures that we sometimes are, we seem bound to raise questions, even fundamental questions, about love's character and significance. Its presence amongst us is made all the more remarkable, we recognise, by the measure, even the violence, of its contrast with that part of us which answers, in circumstances arising in every generation, to brutality and coarseness. Sidgwick is therefore right to remark that

> ...it seems that most persons are only capable of strong affections towards a few human beings in certain close relations, especially the domestic: and that if these were suppressed, what they would feel towards their fellow-creatures generally would be, as Aristotle says, "but a watery kindness" and a very feeble counterpoise to self-love: so that such specialised affections as the present organisation of society normally produces afford the best means of developing in most persons a more extended benevolence, to the degree to which they are capable of feeling it.[2]

Yet, a common inquisitiveness about uncommon benevolence is only *one* of the things that drives our interest in love.

Another is surely the very intensity of feeling, joyful to jealous, that escorts love; and the related intensity of desire which may establish or constitute it. In lives which may otherwise be rather dull, love can remind us of how alive we are, or itself re-invigorate us; and that has a natural interest for us.

Other stimuli come from the fact that in reflection upon our experience, we find ourselves approaching puzzles about love, certain intrigues, which challenge views we may have earlier assumed to be natural and unavoidable. Bradley writes: "Our pleasure in any one who in some way resembles those we love should warn us that love is in its essence not individual".[3] Is there truth here and, if so, what--less aphoristically expressed--is it? Or is there, instead, deep confusion; and how might that be shown?

Again, do loving and being loved pose kinds of challenge to the 'autonomy' of lover or beloved and, if so, why is this; and how is it to be dealt with? Do certain widely held views *about* love, just because they are held, pose problems for autonomy, and are such views coherent? Are all views about what love *really* is, inherently suspicious? Is love, itself, of epistemic value?

These questions and many others are addressed in what follows. Although addressed with clarity and care, there is speculation here too. In this, Plato's example turns out to have been an indication of what was to come in thinking about love. In both description and argument, this fusion of care, with speculation and critique, about a phenomenon close and consequential in the lives of most of us, is a heady brew indeed.

---

2. Henry Sidgwick, *The Methods of Ethics*, 7th edition, Macmillan & Co., 1907, p. 434.

3. F. H. Bradley, *Aphorisms* (Oxford, 1930), No. 18.

As to the order in which the papers appear here, I say only that the first three clearly belong together and might profitably be read in the sequence in which they appear. The third of these makes reference to the views of Robert Nozick, thus mandating that Alan Soble's piece, with its extensive and scholarly criticism of Nozickian-like views, appear next. After that, the topic-threads begin to interweave in complex patterns that allow for a number of sensible orderings. I hope the arrangement I have chosen is one of these.

Roger E. Lamb

Acknowledgements

There are many I wish to thank for assisting, in witting and unwitting ways, in the production of this collection of (in my view) fine essays on love. First of all, there are the contributors who, to a person, most patiently waded through my voluminous and, I suspect, sometimes incontinent comments on their early drafts. Indeed, more than exhibiting mere patience, there seemed to be a welcoming of that critical dialogue which their early drafts had initiated. But then, that is what philosophy and philosophers are properly noted for. Secondly, there are those I daily live, and converse, with. These include my immediate family, and my colleagues. They have in their various ways, with dialogue, apt questions, raised eyebrows, studied silence, and (so I have experienced it) warm regard, assisted in manners without which there would not be this collection. Thirdly, there are those at Westview Press who were helpful at every turn.

In the first group, I would like especially to thank Keith Lehrer and Alan Soble for their encouragement in this project throughout its duration. Indeed, it was Keith who first put the idea in my head over a glass of red in some downbeat bistro on a surreal autumn afternoon in Tucson. I also especially thank Martha Nussbaum for allowing the reprint of her excellent article.

In the second group, Laurie Gaffney, without whom this would be a much poorer world and to whom this volume is dedicated; and Uschi Sterf, Grace Dunn, André Gallois, Gary Malinas, Graham Priest, and Michelle Walker.

In the third, Cindy Rinehart, Spencer Carr, and Lynn Arts.

Finally, there are family and friends abroad, who have assisted in ways they may not have appreciated, especially Phil, Joan, and Bernice Lamb, and Simin Karimi.

Thanks.

R. E. L.

About the Contributors

Deborah Brown is an assistant professor of philosophy at York University, and works in metaphysics and the philosophy of mind and language. She has published on the topic of mental representation in the *Canadian Journal of Philosophy* and the *Philosophical Quarterly*, and on the semantics of William Ockham in the *Review of Metaphysics*. She is co-editing an anthology of humourous philosophy.

Sue Campbell, assistant professor of philosophy and women's studies at Dalhousie University, has previously contributed to *Hypatia* on the politics of emotional expression, and has a book, *Interpreting the Personal: Expression and the Formation of Feelings*, forthcoming from Cornell University Press.

Ronald de Sousa, professor of philosophy at the University of Toronto, has written on a variety of philosophical topics including knowledge, belief, natural kinds, emotion, and desire, with articles in many journals including the *Journal of Philosophy*, *Canadian Journal of Philosophy*, *Mind*, *Review of Metaphysics*, and most recently *Dialogue* and *Metaphilosophy*. He is the author of the frequently cited *The Rationality of Emotion* (MIT Press, 1987).

Daniel M. Farrell, professor of philosophy at Ohio State University, has written on civil disobedience, punishment, Mill on liberty, coercion, jealousy, Hobbes, deterrence, and immoral intentions, with articles in a variety of journals including *Ethics*, *Pacific Philosophical Quarterly*, *American Philosophical Quarterly*, *Social Theory and Practice*, *Nous*, *Philosophical Review*, *Philosophical Studies*, *History of Philosophy Quarterly*, *Philosophical Quarterly*, and *Philosophy and Public Affairs*.

O. H. Green is associate professor of philosophy at Tulane University, and the author of *The Emotions* (Kluwer, 1992). He has published in *Mind*, *American Philosophical Quarterly*, *Analysis*, *Southwestern Journal of Philosophy*, *Personalist*, *Philosophia*, *Metaphilosophy*, and *Philosophy and Phenomenological Research* on the expression of emotion, killing and letting die, emotions and belief, materialism, intention, speech acts, obligations concerning emotions, action theory, metaethics, Wittgenstein, and the fear of death.

Barbara Hannan is associate professor of philosophy at the University of New Mexico, and the author of *Subjectivity and Reduction* (Westview Press, 1994). She has argued against eliminative materialism in her articles in *Mind & Language* and *Behavior and Philosophy* and has discussed determinism and identity theory in *Inquiry* and intentional stance theory in *Mind*.

Roger E. Lamb is a lecturer in philosophy at the University of Queensland. He has written several articles on the emotions for *Philosophy and Phenomenological Research*, and on topics in legal philosophy, and the semantics of fictional names, for the *Bulletin of the Australian Society of Legal Philosophy* and the *Australasian Journal of Philosophy*, respectively. He claims to have enjoyed the editing of this volume.

Rae Langton is a research fellow in philosophy at the Australian National University (on secondment from Monash University). She has written on pornography and liberalism, on Kant on duty and desire, and on feminist critiques of reason for *Philosophy and Public Affairs*, *Philosophy*, and the *Australasian Journal of Philosophy*. A companion piece to her article in the present volume, entitled 'Sexual Solipsism', appears in *Philosophical Topics*. She is the author of a book on Kant's metaphysics forthcoming with Oxford University Press.

Keith Lehrer is a Regent's Professor of philosophy at the University of Arizona, a past Chair of the Board of Officers for the American Philosophical Association, and a recipient of a Guggenheim Fellowship and of a grant from the National Endowment for the Humanities. He is author or co-author of at least six books and the editor or co-editor of at least four others. In the former group, there are *Philosophical Problems and Arguments* (Fourth Edition, Hackett, 1992), *Theory of Knowledge* (Westview Press, 1990), *Metamind* (Clarendon Press, 1990), *Thomas Reid* (Routledge, 1989), *Rational Consensus in Science and Society* (D. Reidel, 1981), and *Knowledge* (Clarendon Press, 1974). He has been the editor of *Philosophical Studies* (1974-1980, 1988-1991), and is the editor of the Philosophical Studies Series. His views are the subject of two books, *Keith Lehrer* (D. Reidel, 1981), edited by Radu J. Bogdan; and *The Current State of the Coherence Theory: Critical Essays on the Epistemic Theories of Keith Lehrer and Laurence BonJour* (Kluwer, 1989), edited by John Bender. He is a frequent contributor to many philosophical journals with a concentration in *Grazer Philosophical Studies*, *Synthese*, *Journal of Philosophy*, *Analysis*, and *Monist*.

Graeme Marshall is a reader in philosophy at the University of Melbourne. He has a long standing interest in Wittgenstein and in the philosophy of mind with a special concern for problems associated with the will. He has been a contributor to *Mind*, *Philosophical Quarterly*, the *Australasian Journal of Philosophy*, and *Dialogue*.

Martha Nussbaum is professor of law and ethics at the University of Chicago, and has taught at Harvard and Oxford Universities. She is the author of *The Therapy of Desire: Theory and Practice in Hellenistic Ethics* (Princeton, 1994), *Love's Knowledge: Essays on Philosophy and Literature* (Oxford, 1990), *The Fragility of Goodness: Luck and Ethics in Greek Tragedy and Philosophy* (Cambridge, 1986), and *Aristotle's De Moto Animalium* (Princeton, 1978); and is the editor or co-editor of at least nine other books. She delivered the Gifford Lectures in 1993 under the title, Need and Recognition: A Theory of the Emotions. She is a frequent contributor to learned journals with some concentration of her work to be found in *Apeiron*, *Ethics*, *Philosophy and Literature* and the *Proceedings of the Boston Area Colloquium in Ancient Philosophy*.

Philip Pettit is professor of social and political theory at the Australian National University. His work is concentrated in the foundations of the social sciences, and in moral and political theory. He is the author of *The Common Mind: An Essay on Psychology, Society and Politics* (Oxford, 1993), *Judging Justice: An Introduction to Contemporary Political Philosophy* (Routledge and Kegan Paul, 1980), *The Concept of Structuralism: A Critical Analysis* (Gill and Macmillan, 1975). He is a co-author of *Not Just Desserts: A Republican Theory of Criminal Justice* (Oxford, 1990), of *Rawls: A Theory of Justice and its Critics* (Polity Press, 1990), and of *Semantics and Social Science* (Routledge and Kegan Paul, 1981). He is the editor or co-editor of at least six other volumes. He is a frequent contributor to many philosophical journals with some concentration of his articles in *Analysis*, *Mind*, and *Synthese*.

Alan Soble is professor and research professor of philosophy at the University of New Orleans. He is the author of *Sexual Investigations* (New York University Press, 1996), *The Structure of Love* (Yale University Press, 1990), and *Pornography: Marxism, Feminism, and the Future of Sexuality* (Yale University Press, 1986). He has edited *The Philosophy of Sex* (Rowman and Littlefield, 1st edition, 1980; 2nd edition, 1991) and *Eros, Agape and Philia* (Paragon House, 1989). He is currently at work writing an introductory text, *The Philosophy of Sex and Love* (Paragon House), and editing the 1977-1992 Proceedings of the Society for the Philosophy of Sex and Love, to appear as *Sex, Love, and Friendship* (Rodopi). He is a frequent contributor to the journals with articles most recently in *Philosophy of the Social Sciences*, *Monist* and *The Journal of Value Inquiry*.

Love Analyzed

1

Love and the Individual:
Romantic Rightness and Platonic Aspiration

Martha C. Nussbaum

Veritas
motto, Harvard University

In Deo Speramus
motto, Brown University

Last month, while I was worrying about how to write a paper on this impossible topic, I was moving all my books and papers from Harvard down to Brown. The movers carried my files and boxes of papers into the Philosophy Department building, storing them in a closet under the stairs where I had been given permission to leave my things for the year. There in this closet, on the floor, I noticed a strange document: a manuscript of some 38 pages, typewritten. Its title was 'Love and the Individual: Romantic Rightness and Platonic Aspiration. A Story'. Now this was a remarkable coincidence; for I had just chosen this title for my presentation at Stanford. I sat down right there in the closet and read it through. It was an odd document indeed, a strange hybrid of fiction and philosophy. But it was on my topic, a topic on which I myself had found nothing at all to say. I began to consider taking it and reading parts of it at Stanford. But I could not figure out who its author was. I strongly suspected that it was a woman, and a philosopher. The setting is a real place, a philosopher's house; I've even been there. I thought immediately of my one female colleague in philosophy; but, I reasoned, she works on completely different topics. This author is clearly familiar with Plato and Aristotle, Proust and Henry James. Her interests, in fact, lie very close to mine. What's odder still, she introduces as a sentence allegedly written by one of her characters (the one called "she") a sentence that I wrote and published in an article on Plato's

1

Symposium.[1] Her other character (the one called "I") claims to have written my article on Henry James.[2] Well, I thought, sitting on the closet floor, whoever she is, if she can lift my words, I can lift hers. So I have decided to do that here.

A STORY

Or incomincian le dolenti note
a farmisi sentire; or son venuto
là dove molto pianto me percuote.

Now the sounds of misery have begun
to reach my ears. Now I come to a place
where many cries of anguish beat against me.
Dante, *Inferno* V.25-27

Late one January night, in that winter of 1982, when it snowed all over Florida, blighting the orange crop, she found herself wide awake in Tallahassee, thinking about love. And, not surprisingly, about an individual who was the object of hers. Her guest room looked out over a white-blanketed golf course whose genteel contours, enduring with Protestant dignity the region's prospective loss of millions, offered a polite reproof to her more disorderly experience of loss. The insouciant smile of the country club moon, floating above natural disaster as clear and round and single-natured and unaffected as a Platonic form --or a resurrected orange--seemed to her to express the Platonic thought that loved individuals, like orange crops or even like oranges themselves, always came along one following the other in due succession, essentially undistinguishable from one another in their health-bringing and energizing properties. A loss of one could be compensated fully and directly by the coming-into-being of the homogeneous next. One had only, therefore, to endure a brief interstitial period of whiteness, snow, and clear light.

Finding this hygienic Diotiman optimism impossibly at odds with her messier ruminations, finding it, indeed, not to speak genteelly, absurd as a consolation addressed to real personal loss (for it was in those days a point of honor with her to accept no replacements, to insist that any willingness to be so

---

1. Martha C. Nussbaum, 'The Speech of Alcibiades: A Reading of Plato's *Symposium*', *Philosophy and Literature* 3 (1979), 131-72; also chap. 6 of Nussbaum, *The Fragility of Goodness: Luck and Ethics in Greek Tragedy and Philosophy* (Cambridge, Eng., 1985). See also chap. 7 of *Fragility*, an interpretation of Plato's *Phaedrus*.

2. Martha C. Nussbaum, 'Flawed Crystals: James's *The Golden Bowl* and Literature as Moral Philosophy', *New Literary History* 15 (1983), 25-50.

consoled was a falling off from grace), she rejected it and considered other possibilities. As she leaned out the window, feeling the preternaturally calm starry air on her eyelids, she saw that the appropriate next step would be to break up that calm; to demonstrate somehow her complicity with Diotima's opponent Alcibiades and his more accurate view of love. Perhaps by going out and smashing several sacred statues; or by doing violence to the seventeenth green. But the truth was that she was a gentle character, for whom the consolation of violence was a constitutional impossibility. And besides, wasn't her own real view the view she had found and described in writing about the *Phaedrus*, namely, that personal love was not necessarily linked with disorder, but was actually constitutive of the best sort of orderly life, a life dedicated to understanding of value and goodness? That madness and sanity, personal passion and rational aspiration, were, in their highest forms, actually in harmony with or even fused with one another? That we do not really need to choose between Socrates and Alcibiades? It was just this, indeed, that she saw as her problem; for if only disorder were gone one might even contrive to be pleased.

That afternoon when she first saw him, years before, he was walking down the sun-streaked hallway, laughing and talking, his whole body fiercely illuminated from behind by the light from the door, so that he looked to her like Turner's Angel Standing in the Sun. Or, better, like some counterpart good angel, equally radiant but entirely beneficent in power. Like what the *Phaedrus* calls a "form truly expressing beauty and nobility". It is not necessary to choose between Socrates and Alcibiades. Under the right circumstances.

At odds, then, with both Diotima's order and Alcibiades' violence; feeling not like Turner's fishermen, irradiated by that angel's light; or even like the lover of the *Phaedrus*, awestruck by the splendor of some beautiful boy; feeling more like Plato's Stesichorus, blinded by the gods, groping for the verses that would restore his sight, she turned for help and light to the only help that occurred to her. Nothing dramatic, or even Platonic. Aristotelian rather. She turned into the room and began looking through the books.

There are too many individuals, and all of them are married. This is the only piece of general wisdom I have to offer on this topic about which I so rashly agreed to write. Socrates said in the *Symposium*, "I understand nothing --with the exception of love". This preposterous statement tips us off, of course, that something funny is going on. For, sure enough, it turns out that the claim to have grasped and understood the nature of love is part and parcel of an enterprise that is busy converting loved persons into instantiations of a universal, and so into proper objects of (scientific) understanding, all in order to repudiate and transcend the phenomenon of love as ordinary mortals experience it. The sight of the knowing intellect is incompatible, Diotima tell us, with the sight of the human body. Uttered about ordinary passion by an ordinary mortal, the claim to have a general understanding of love is as good an example of the self-refuting proposition as anything philosophy has to offer. More: like Socrates' claim, it is also some sort of denial or refusal of love's dangers. As Alcibiades, telling his love story, shows. ("Oh love. I know all about that." I'd say that in the same tone of voice I used for my opening "general truth". For similar reasons.) The question, then, becomes how to write about love of the individual, if one does not wish, even tacitly, to make the Socratic claim to general understanding. How to limit and undercut one's claims, making it clear that they are not guilty of Socratic "overweening". How, at the same, to authenticate such limited statements as are made, showing where they come from and what gives them any claim to be telling human truth. Thinking of what I had written about Alcibiades, about Henry James, above all about Proust, I could not avoid the conclusion that I would only be entitled to speak about love in the form of a narrative.

This will, to be sure, be a conspicuously philosophical narrative. Most of its "plot" will be a story of thought and work. Its title sounds like the title of an article. Part of it will be an article, or a sketch for one. It will tell you at length about this lady's general reflections; how she thought and even wrote; how she interpreted the *Phaedrus*; how she marshaled objections and counterexamples. For thought is one of the things that occupies space in a life, especially this one. It is also a major device by which this life tries to keep itself in line. A love story should not fail to show this.

And her story is philosophical in yet another way--in the way in which Aristotle said poetry was philosophical and history was not. For it is, like Alcibiades' narrative, like Proust's, not simply the record of some idiosyncratic things that in fact happened. (You should doubt whether any of it happened as told.) It is, rather, a record, addressed to the reader, of "the sort of thing that might happen" in a human life. And if the reader is not determined to conceive of himself or herself as radically individual, sharing with this lady no relevant responses and possibilities, the reader can take it to be, *mutatis mutandis*, his or her own love story.

But it will be, this philosophical story, quite unlike a philosophical treatise or article on the same topic. For it will show her thoughts arising from pain, from hope, from ambition, from desperation--in short, from the confusion in which thought is born, more often than not. It will present them, these off-spring, all wrinkled and naked and bloody, not washed and dressed up for the nursery photographer. You will be in no doubt as to their provenance, and also their fragility. And you will be encouraged to ask how their characteristics are explained by the particular desires and needs that engendered them. This should by no means make you dismiss the question of truth or treat them as mere subjective reportings. But when you entertain them as candidates for truth, you will be able to ask hard, suspicious questions about background conditions that might have biased the inquiry, questions about what bias is in such an inquiry, and what objectivity. While you are made suspicious, however, you are to feel in another way reassured. For seeing the blood and hearing the cries, you are to know that these babies did come out of somewhere real, that they are live, ordinary children of human life and action, not some philosophical changelings simply masquerading as children. For changelings never go so far as to masquerade the pain of being born.

I shall embark, then, on this rather confused lady's philosophical love story. I am not certain that I am entitled now to write it. It is not 1982 now. Though once again it is cold and white and silent, and oranges (grapefruits, I believe, as well) are dying all over Florida. It is not 1982; and I am not, like her, mourning. In fact, I have been happily sitting in my kitchen this afternoon drinking tea and reading Dante. Just now I was in the middle of writing a love letter to somebody else. The title 'Love and the Individual' is, I now see, ambiguous. I took it as a question about the individuality of the object of love. But it also forces me to raise questions about my own individuality and continuity from one love to the next. As Wittgenstein said, the world of the happy man is different from the world of the unhappy man. Can the inhabitants of two such different worlds really be the same person?

My discontinuity from her is not, however, total. For the radio's mournful announcement, last night, of the demise of fruit, the solemnly intoned tale of moribund grapefruit and of orange juice cut off before its prime, pulled me oddly back inside her old tale of the demise of a love. And today the newspaper photograph of a young orange wrapped in a sheath of ice reminded me of a sentence she once wrote: "When the light of Socrates 'appears all at once' for Alcibiades, it is the sort of light that, radiantly poured round the aspiring body, may seal or freeze it in, like a coat of ice. That is its beauty". I don't altogether approve of that, but it moves me. Now, in spite of my lack of sympathy with her more apocalyptic and self-indulgent responses, despite my desire to treat the topic playfully and not to weep over it at all, I find myself once again in her presence, seeing her and seeing the image of him that she then saw, that image more like a lightning bolt than a sun (as Alcibiades knew) in its power to strike, even as it brings illumination.

You shall have her story, then--but as I tell it. And you must, therefore, be on your guard. For you can see by now what an interest I have in making it come out one way rather than another. So that it will be both true and morally acceptable that I survived and am here cheerfully replacing. That, loving a different individual, I am myself the same one, and not too bad either. For I have an interest in being her heir and continuant, rather than a mere two-year old. And if I shall say, further, that to survive the death of love is not just logically possible but also morally best, if I even contend that the best conception of love is one that permits some sort of replacement of individuals, you must remember that these arguments, though placed in her mouth, may be shaped by the fact that I have just been writing a love letter to somebody else. It is not only in the context of war that survivor guilt is a useful explanatory concept.

Now, guarding against her and yet pulled by the power of her love, half toughly warding her off, half longing to know her passion, in the manner of cautious Dante before the spirit of Francesca, I approach her. What can I do but what he did: call her "by the love that leads" her? And like some mad, disorderly dove, through the dark air of that malignant winter, she comes before me, "directed by desire", quite gentle in her grief. I'm not like that.

I said that her search through the books was Aristotelian. This was inexact. Augustine's *Tolle lege* was, far more, the motivating hope. She wanted to have, right then, a text that would change the course of her life from damnation to salvation, a text that would set her on the path to beatitude, lifting her above the winds of longing onto a promontory from which she could survey all the world and her own place in it. She was not quite but almost *nel mezzo dal cammin*, as they liked to conceive of it in those unhealthy times, so it seemed about right that some salvation should come her way.

But there are no sacred books in Tallahassee. So what could she do but see what was in fact in the guest room, taking a book at random and reading her fate in its pages? (And how clear it was in any case that she desired the salvation not of religion but of love.)

Her hosts had filled this particular guest room with books by and about members of the Bloomsbury group. This did not seem promising. She would have preferred Proust. She knew little about the people of Bloomsbury, but she thought they were probably well suited to their Diotiman surroundings. She knew enough, at any rate, to suspect them of excessive gentility of feeling and a strong interest in the replacement of one person by the next. It was, then, with no very high expectations that she selected from the shelf nearest the windows a large volume of Dora Carrington's letters and diaries and turned (hoping against hope, I suspect, for something tragic enough to suit her) to the end, though ignorant, as yet, of the nature of Carrington's.

There she came upon the following entry. (She memorized much of it at once involuntarily and carried it about with her for some months as a ready source of tears, but I have had to get hold of it from the library. And when I read it I find that very little of it is even familiar. This makes me wonder.)

No one will ever know the special perfectness of Lytton. The jokes when he was gay. "The queen of the East has vanished." I believe you eat my nail scissors and then at lunch pretending to play a grand fugue before we got up. And the jokes about the coffee never coming because I stayed so long eating cheese. Sometimes I thought how wasteful to let these jokes fly like swallows across the sky. But one couldn't write them down. We couldn't have been happier together. For every mood of his instantly made me feel in the same mood. All gone.... And now there is nobody, darling Lytton, to make jokes with about Tiber and the horse of the ocean, no one to read me Pope in the evenings, no one to walk on the terrace. No one to write letters to, oh my very darling Lytton.

...What point is there now in what I see every day, in conversations, jokes, beautiful visions, pains, even nightmares? Who can I tell them to, who will understand? One cannot find such another character as Lytton and curious as it may seem to G.B. these friends that he talks of as consolers and substitutes for Lytton cannot be the same, and it is *exactly* what Lytton meant to me that matters.

One cannot live on memories when the point of one's whole life was the interchange of love, ideas, and conversation.

She felt that she had written this entry, so directly did it express her own mourning. She sat there, somewhat absurdly weeping into the book, and the phrase "special perfectness" conjured up an image so concrete that she shuddered at its nearness and wept again. (I find it difficult to describe this.)

Here, she thought, was something worth reading about love. Call it the view of Alcibiades. Call it (right now) her own. For she too knew those consolers and their games. She knew, and all too well, that what she loved and did not have was, as this woman said, a special perfectness, an exact, nonrepeatable thing that could not be found again. There was a value and a knowledge that were inseparable from this particular relation. To try to recapture or replace them would be as futile as to go hunting for a joke after it has gone by. And she thought of their jokes.

Well, what was this individuality? In what did it consist, according to Carrington? (You now begin to see how this lady is: she goes on thinking at all times. She won't simply cry, she will ask what crying consists in. One tear, one argument: that's how her life goes on.) Carrington had, in this passage, several distinct, though related, quarrels with her consolers. Three, to be exact. First, the friends do not seem to grasp the fact that unique, nonrepeatable properties are essential to love. They talk of others who could be substitutes. This implies that they believe that there are certain general features of Lytton that could be instantiated in someone else--perhaps in someone with similar values and character. But Carrington knows that, in the sense that counts for loving, there is not such another character as Lytton. That nobody else makes those wonderful jokes or has the power to transform the ordinary by that precise sort of magic. Sameness of species might be good enough for Aristotle; it is not what she wants. It is that exact thing, unique and (as she too well knows) transient. ("Death", she writes on the same page, "is unfortunately *not* incomprehensible. It is all too easy to understand." The end of an affair brings similar epistemic problems, with less dignity.)

Beyond this, second, she knows that some of the things she most loves in Lytton are not in him at all; they are properties of his relation to her. There was a special affinity of mood, a rightness of humor, a mutuality of understanding, that are themselves nonrepeatable values, not to be searched for by any rational method, but just found--as when one of Aristophanes' jagged people suddenly comes upon the jagged other half that perfectly fits his or her own odd shape.

Surely, surely, part of what so moved her in Carrington's diary was that so much of it was private and unintelligible to her; it gestured toward a density of intimate communication that no person outside the relation could altogether grasp. For she knew, like Carrington, the dreadful isolation that comes with the knowledge that nobody will laugh with her in just that way or respond with that special rightness to her responses. It occurred to her to remember many things. These thoughts took some time. She did not find it possible to include them in a numbered list of any kind.

And beyond all this, she thought--pulling herself back to the list, for she had said there were three items, and in her stubbornness of character she was not going to let anything stop her before she reached three--beyond all this, there is their history. Even if there might have been in the first place more than one person who could have aroused the same dimension of love in Carrington (a fact that in her own case she very much doubted), such another person could not possibly step in as a substitute now. For now the relationship had been enriched by years of intimacy, of conversation, of letters written and received. One could say that the love is in large measure constituted out of this history, out of the habit, for example, of telling every experience and of finding a fresh joy from each experience in the telling. Their relational rightness may have been in part a matter of initial fit, but history and its intimacy is a large part of what constitutes it as this deep, this irreplaceable.

Nobody else will ever know his special perfectness. One cannot find such another character. And if I chose to describe the images that filled her as, her list of three points exhausted, she reached Carrington's uncompromising conclusion, you would perhaps understand her better, and the love that was so great a part of what she then was. I do not so choose. I plan that you shall know nothing of the concrete individuality of her beloved, of their relation, their history, the immediate reasons for her grief. There are many reasons for this. Some I won't mention; some are connected with the Aristotelian point about what makes a story philosophical. But not least among the reasons is the thought that if I allowed myself to become the full companion of her wanderings through memory and pain and wonder, if I allowed the power of that individuality to overwhelm me as it then intermittently overwhelmed her, I would not, perhaps, go on with the letter I am writing. And, equally clearly, I would not continue writing this paper or story, whichever it is. There is a price, I think, for writing about love's fragility; this is a certain refusal of a certain sort of knowledge or recognition of that fragility. Could it be that to write about love, even to write humbly and responsively, is itself a device to control the topic, to trap and bind it like an animal--so, of necessity, an unloving act? And if I could set him down in writing, every movement and look and virtue translated into words, if I could do this without in fact ceasing to write, would I not have most perfectly, most finally controlled him and so banished the power of that love? Seen this way, my inability to do so looks like an accidental grace.

What I am after, it seems, is a noncontrolling art of writing that will leave the writer more receptive to love than before. That will not be guilty of writing's usual ruthlessness toward life. For the fashionable idea that writing is a form of creative play, and that everything is, after all, writing, seems to me to ignore the plain fact that much of human life is not playful at all, or even creative. And writing's relation to that nonplayful side of life is deeply ambiguous. Writing records it, to be sure. But even as it does so it goes to work fixing, simplifying, shaping. So it seems difficult for it not to be the enemy and denier of mystery and of love. Overwhelmed by the beauty of some landscape, the power of some emotion, I run for my pad of paper; and if I can put it into words, set it down, I breathe a sigh of relief. A kind of humble passivity has been banished. Writing, then, seems not to be everything, but to be opposed to something--say, waiting. Beckett tries to find a way to use language to undo, unravel the simplifications and refusals of language, undermining stories with a story, words with words. If I were not so determined to survive, I'd try to write like that.

These are thoughts she might have had. They don't entirely suit me. She probably reads Heidegger too, heaven help her. I'm getting too close to her, like Dante. But for me, there's only one angel in the picture, and the only salvation might be to be as thoroughly damned as possible. Now, as I watch her weeping, uncontrollably at this point, into the pillow on which she has placed her book, I feel with her what it is to love an individual and to be loved, as well, by one. And for fear of saying something individual of my own--for it would describe him and thus violate the canons I have laid down--I simply say:

> Oh lasso,
> quanti dolci pensier, quanto disio
> meno costoro al doloroso passo!

> Alas,
> how many sweet thoughts, how much desire
> led them to this miserable condition.

But even as she wept, she began to wonder whether Carrington had really had the last word against her consolers. It was a terrible last word; she had read far enough to see to what conclusion it led. She wanted to know, so did it frighten her, whether Carrington had been altogether fair. (For fairness in argument seemed a possible way of evading that conclusion.) It was clear as one read on that one of the consolers' arguments did precisely address the conception of individuality relevant to her love and blamed her for in effect misunderstanding the very thing on which she herself laid most stress. She seems to find all of Lytton's individuality, all of what he really is, in the unique, the evanescent, the relational. And yet, they argue, Lytton was a person with a definite moral and intellectual character and a definite set of values, commitments, and aspirations. How could she claim to love Lytton if she did not love and see the central importance of these elements, which are a far deeper part of him than the fact that on a particular day he talked about cheese? All of this had promising implications for mourning and the continuation of life. But for now, what began to impress her was this idea that the extreme romantic view of love (or Aristophanic, since we can trace it back at least to those unique jagged other halves), this view that holds that love is above all a matter of contingent particular fit, may not contain a deep enough conception of the individual, precisely because it slights these repeatable elements.

These elements are, of course, really at the heart of Carrington's love. (So, clearly, at the heart of her own.) For consider her talk of the exchange of ideas and conversation. Or consider even her sentence "One cannot find such another character as Lytton". One does not, she thought, use such a sentence of someone whom one does not admire, and admire on account of certain virtues and values. What one means in saying it (what she herself meant when she thought it especially apt for her case) is that this person is exceptionally good in ways in which one believes it important to be good. Alcibiades said it of Socrates, not confining his love to the (repeatable) virtues, but insisting that they were a very central and essential part of what he loved when he loved Socrates. In loving he was aspiring; he was not simply seeking his other half. He could not have said the same thing of Agathon, except as a joke. How could Carrington claim to love Lytton without understanding how central it was to his being Lytton that he had and lived by certain values, that indeed he built his life around a certain picture of value?

But now something intriguing seemed to follow. For in that case, as the consolers correctly argue, there is something that has survived his death, something that she can continue to love and cherish although it is no longer realized in that particular life. Listen to how she answers them. "They say one must keep your standards and values of life alive. But how can I, when I only kept them for you? Everything was for you. I loved life, because you made it so perfect, and now there is no one left to make jokes with, or to talk about Racine and Molière and talk of plans and work and people." They ought to reply, she thought, excited, that this utterance reveals a deep confusion about love and about Lytton. For it is crucial to his being him that he is a person who does have values and standards, who loves valuable things for their own sake. How can she claim it is Lytton that she loves, if she has not tried to share the sense of what Racine means for him, if she makes of Racine just a jagged idiosyncrasy, a piece of contingent fit? These consolers, she began to think, had a point. For, clearly, she herself did not love the man she loved just as someone who was in arbitrary ways right for her, but more because he was an angel. This is to say, radiantly good and fine in ways in which it was important to her also to be good and fine. That is to say, uncompromised in his pursuit of standards to which she also aspired, loving them for their own sake. (You think you don't know anything about him. Knowing that, you could pick him out from ten million.)

She was by now not weeping but pacing about the room, excited. For it seemed to her that it would be an excellent result for her grief if a richer love of the individual, a love that was most truly a love of the individual, her love let us say, turned out to be based upon an acknowledgment that certain things have intrinsic value which, being repeatable and not idiosyncratic, will survive the death or departure of the individual. That the better one loved this individual the more one would see that there was, in fact, something to live for beyond that person, something connected with the commitments and aspirations on which the love is itself based. And this something could be sought in someone else, even pursued on its own, apart from love. (For like many a recalcitrant pupil of Diotima, this lady, who thought of herself as a hopeless romantic, and was so on Mondays, Wednesdays, and Fridays, also liked to look about for the morally acceptable ways to satisfy her longing for stability. The way of Diotima was not acceptable. But if the truest value of the unique and uniquely loved could turn out also to impart stability to the life that loved it--this would be the best conjuring trick of all. As I warned you, I'm trying a variant of that trick now: trying, by doing justice in writing to love's fragility, to make that very fragility a source of stability for myself.)

The hope of bringing off this argument against Carrington excited her beyond tears. It would require a lot of probing, of debating back and forth --since the powerful appeal of that implacable grief made her deeply suspicious of any such *consolatio philosophiae*. And to be convincing it would have to be done in writing, for she was never convinced by her own thoughts until she saw them fixed.

Where would she begin this assault on Carrington (also, as you see, an assault on the moral superiority of her own death)? She envisaged a statement of the view about value and the superiority of a love based upon repeatable features of commitment and aspiration, followed by a series of objections by Carrington and replies to those objections. For the initial statement she might have thought only of her own love, but so much was she a lover of the general that she could not even try to understand something so particular without holding it up against some philosophical account that would illuminate it, and be illuminated by it. The text that had always seemed to her to describe better than any her own views about love, the text that seemed to her to argue effectively both against Diotima's banishment of individual passion and against Aristophanes' extreme emphasis on other halves was, of course, Plato's *Phaedrus*. She got out a pen and a pad of yellow paper (with which she was always equipped, even in despair), sat down at the desk, and began to write, for herself, the following.

I feel no pity for her now. For she is a very tough lady, as she sits there writing objections and arguments. No longer a timorous dove, but a self-assured, agile professional. Far more like me.

"*A la guerre comme à la guerre*, then", I say to her, as James's Prince, so ambiguously, to Charlotte Stant. "But I am charmed by your courage and almost surprised by my own."

Loving an Individual: Romantic Rightness
and Platonic Aspiration

I. The 'Phaedrus': the best view of love bases it on a view of the individual as essentially constituted by values and aspirations.

This is not a description of what passionate love in general is like. It is a description of the best type of passion. Socrates argues that this sort of "mad" passion for another individual is an essential part of the best human life and the way that passion best figures in a good life. This is also supposed to be the best way in which love loves an individual. Against Lysias, who argues that the person in love never gets to know who the beloved really is, Socrates argues that it is in passion (not all sorts, but this high sort) that one person is most truly able to know and to love another--to love what the other most truly is.

It begins with the recognition of values. Souls are individuated by what they most deeply care about. For example, the Zeus-like type cares most about philosophy and moral value and pursues these two together. To care about these values is the essence of such a soul. We could imagine these people losing their money, their reputation, their youthfulness--and still being essentially the same. We couldn't in the same way imagine them ceasing to care about knowledge or justice. Aristotle says this succinctly: the character and value commitments (as opposed to superficial pleasantness or advantageousness) are what each person is *kath' hauto*, in virtue of himself or herself. To love a person himself or herself, and not the accidental features of a person, is to love that.

The values are recognized in a way that truly involves, even requires, passion. And being passive. The first thing that happens is that the lover is simply, mysteriously, struck by the splendor of the other, the "form truly expressing beauty and nobility". He is dazzled, aroused, illuminated. His soul is compared, in its arousal, to the gums of a teething child. He is also compared to a plant, watered and nourished by the presence of the other's beauty and excellence. What he experiences is nothing like cold respect or mere admiration. And yet, it is crucial that in the beauty that arouses him he sees a sign of the values that he cherishes and pursues. What he is always doing is "following the trace of his god". The beauty of the other is not, even in the beginning, seen as mere superficial attractiveness but as the radiance of a committed soul. Awe and wonder are essential components of his love.

The point is, he wouldn't be in love really if the other didn't answer to his aspirations. Love and sexuality (at least in good people) are themselves selective and aspiring. What excites the passion, makes him shudder and tremble, is the perception of something that answers to the desires of his soul. Passion loves *that*: it demands an object that is radiant with value. What it wants from the person, ultimately, is a mutual exchange of love and ideas that will be a seamless part of each one's pursuit of their central aspiration.

Aspiration, on the other hand, becomes in this account something not detached and self-sufficient, but needy, vulnerable, bound up with motion and receptivity. They cannot pursue their values without the inspiration and nourishment of love. In order to be moved toward value, each soul must, first of all, be open and receptive. The crucial first step toward truth and knowledge comes when the stream of beauty that enters in at the eyes is allowed to moisten and melt the solid dry elements of the soul. Only then does the soul begin to have insight into itself and its aims. And as time goes on, with "unfeigned passion", both touching and conversing, they "follow up the trace", each in the other, of their own god, coming to know one another, themselves, and true value at the same time.

And where, in all this, is the individual? The essential individuality of each is to be found in the fineness of soul, the character and commitments that make each the follower of a certain god. Since these patterns of commitment are repeatable and not idiosyncratic, the account implies that there might have been, at least at the beginning, more than one person of the appropriate soul type who might have answered to the lover's inner needs. It is also plausible that a single life might (in the wake of a death or a departure) come to contain a plurality of similar loves. And yet there are limits. First, such people will not be easily found. Then, the person must also have a more mysterious attractiveness that compels and overwhelms. Next, there is, too, the evident importance of history: the deepening of the relationship over time is clearly one of the sources of its value as a source of knowledge, self-knowledge, and motivation. The accidents in this way draw close to the core. Finally, against Carrington's consolers we must notice that Plato's account does not allow the bereaved person to go on pursuing the loved one's values alone, in the total absence of love; at least, they cannot be pursued nearly as well. The bereaved person has to wait to be struck again.

Still, there is room both for personal survival and for replacement. The lover will not feel that he is nothing at all without the love, has nothing to live for, can't go on being the same person. For his love was based on things that endure --that are, we might say, "bigger than both of us". To have a new love is crucial to the continued pursuit of philosophy, or whatever, and if what the lost love loved was that, it is natural that the bereaved person should try to perpetuate and further the goals of the relationship.

　　She paused, relatively satisfied. Here was a challenge to Carrington subtle enough that even that hopeless romantic ought to take it seriously. But she was not really convinced, as she reread what she had written, that it did justice to the things that had moved her in Carrington's account of Lytton. For didn't this view imply, after all, that one could in principle advertise for a lover, say, in the *New York Review of Books*? (Zeus-type soul, committed to philosophical and ethical values, seeks excellent man with similar aspirations...) And if the list could be complete enough, and if there were in addition some reliable way of making sure that the applicant really had the virtues he purported to have, then didn't the view imply that the successful applicant would be her passionate lover? And wasn't this absurd? Plato is less crude than the advertisement on the epistemological issue, for he insists that real knowledge of habits and ways requires a context of intimacy. You cannot tell beforehand: you go by that trace; you allow yourself, in considerable ignorance, to be melted. But it looked as if the real presence of these general traits was, in his view, sufficient for passionate love and sufficiently defined love's object. And this seemed bad or absurd enough. It was not only epistemology, surely, that prevented her from taking out such an advertisement.

I tend to agree with her here. When I first said that I would write on this topic, I tried to draw up a list of the repeatable properties I admired and aspired to; I rated against this list of properties men I had loved, and also men that I plausibly might have but hadn't. Not surprisingly, the men I had seriously loved came out with the highest rating. But I knew that I had made up the list by thinking about them. Like Aristotle's flexible ruler, this list looked posterior to the perception of concrete particulars. Though it might summarize these, it "bent to the shape of the stone, and was not fixed". It was quite clear that a new lover who lacked some of the properties on this list and had others would not, just on the account, be rejected. If I loved him I'd change the list. The question then would be, was I discovering something about myself that had been true all along (a kind of Platonic inner list), or was I really changing the list? I saw no clear reason to prefer the first alternative.

Her sketch, she saw, had not gone far enough. She was left still feeling the absurdity of Platonism, the dignity and truth of Carrington's repudiation. She would have to go on with the second part of her plan: a real debate between Carrington and the *Phaedrus*. She would imagine the romantic objections one by one, giving Plato in each case the strongest possible reply. The scholastic and numerical look of what she then wrote testifies to the violence of her confusion.

(When, much later, I first felt desire for another man, she became violent in a different way. I hadn't realized she was still there; or I thought that she had by now become me. She, or the he that she carried around inside her, the internal person who had, like Proust's Albertine, walked down into her heart and taken up residence there, a jealous and disturbing guest, kept me awake all night for several days with what felt like a series of kicks to the head and stomach. It was later diagnosed as viral labyrinthitis. But I knew.)

II. Romantic objections and Platonic replies.

The romantic opponent has several different types of objections to make to Plato. Some are objections to the particular contents of a Platonic list of valuable properties; some pertain to his use or construal of that list; some, finally, are objections to the entire idea of basing love on a list of properties.

A. *Objections to the content of Plato's list.*

Objection 1. The Platonic list enumerates the individual's commitments and aspirations. But a lot of the valuable properties of an individual are not values. Intelligence, a sense of humor, warmth: these are not commitments and aspirations, and yet they are very valuable, arguably central, to the individuality of the person who has them.

Objection 2. Furthermore, the properties on the list are all high-minded moral and intellectual properties. But some of the repeatable features that will be pertinent to my loves will not be of this sort. They may be morally (aspirationally) irrelevant, such as a certain coloring, or height, or ethnic background. They may even have a negative relation to aspiration. Carrington's persistent choice of men who belittled her artistic ambitions and treated her like a child surely worked against her aspirations, and yet it is a salient pattern in her loves and an important part of the individuality of those she loves.

Objection 3. The Platonic list stresses shared aspiration and similarity of commitment. But some of the properties that will be most valued in a beloved person are properties that are not shared; often they are valued precisely because the lover lacks them. Carrington, not well educated in literary matters, values Lytton's eloquence and knowledge. A shy and nervous person, she values someone who has the ability to tell marvelous fantastic jokes.

Objection 4. There are far too few properties on Plato's list. He says that there are twelve types of souls, correlated with twelve forms of aspiration. But in fact the properties that are relevant to aspiration are much more subtly demarcated, more numerous, and susceptible of more varied combination.

Reply to Objection 1. It is indeed striking how many valuable properties do have to do with a person's values and commitments. We don't value a person's kindness, or courage, unless we believe that the person is in some sense committed to behaving in that way, values that way of behaving. If it's just accidental or sporadic, it won't be valued in the same way, and it won't enter in the same way into an account of what that person really is.

Reply to Objection 2. Plato does not want to insist that all loves fit his account. This is a normative, not a descriptive, view of human love. Of course there are people who are repeatedly attracted to some arbitrary property, or even to evil. Aristotle points out that the first is characteristic of immature people, of whatever age; the second is clearly an illness, though the Greeks have little to say about it. Furthermore, if we find a repeated feature in our loves that seems aspirationally irrelevant but is ubiquitous and rather deep, it may turn out that its deep meaning for us is, after all, not unconnected with our aspirations and values.

Reply to Objection 3. These diversities, if we press them, are rooted in a similarity. Their different careers are complementary ways of pursuing a commitment to artistic creation. Bloomsbury is nothing if not a community of aspiration based upon shared values. It would have been a different matter had the commitments been altogether unrelated, or even antithetical. Then, however, we would feel that the difference was a disadvantage to the love; we would doubt whether they could fully love one another for what each one really was. Plato's soul types are very general forms of aspiration. He nowhere rules out complementary differences of this sort, and the differences in age and experience between the lover and beloved make some such differences inevitable.

Reply to Objection 4. Here Carrington seems to have a point. Being a philosopher is, for example, far too coarse a property to explain the shape of my aspiration and therefore my aspiring love. It all depends on what kind of philosopher, and what the view of philosophy is. Furthermore, the combination of values that I will go for in making up a plan for a good life will almost surely be heterogeneous enough not to correspond to any one of Plato's types. But we should be wary of pressing this specificity too far, for one thing Plato's approach does permit is an informative account of the unity among the loves of a single person.

So far, she saw, Plato had not had to give very much ground before the objections. His essential conception remained untouched. Carrington, however, had barely begun to state her case.

B. *Objections to the use or construal of the list.*

Objection 5. The list, insofar as it suggests that I can go out into the world looking (or advertise in the *New York Review*) for someone with, for example, justice or wisdom, fails to capture the most characteristic ways in which the deeper aspiration-properties present themselves to our awareness. They do not march up to us wearing placards; they make themselves known through other related and more obvious properties, through images, masks, and disguises. Often I will know only that this person is beautiful and exhilarating in some way I cannot yet describe.

Reply to Objection 5. This point was not ignored by Plato. Indeed, he insists on it. It is in fact one of his main reasons for thinking that you can't understand values like justice or wisdom in yourself or in the world without personal love. For only personal love draws a person into the exchange of choices and thoughts that will suffice to reveal, over time, the nature of these values. Love itself begins not so much with these values, which are hard to discern, as with the experience of being struck by a mysterious kind of beauty. (She tried not to think of the way the sunlight from the doorway flamed at the edges of his shoulders and ringed his head.) Even if the values are apprehended through these indirect traces, they are still what is loved. A more serious point lurks here, however, a point about how beloved properties are really individuated and which the really relevant ones are. What's to say that looking a certain way in the sunlight is merely a mode in which brilliance and beneficence make themselves visible?

Objection 6. A list of value properties is something fixed, fixed in advance of the discovery of the loved one. I am a Zeus-like soul, and what I want is to match up with another similar soul. I may as yet not know what type I am, but according to Plato I am already one type or another. It is there for me to discover, partly by following up the traces of my god in the soul of the person I love. But in real life my aspirations and values are not this fixed. I operate with an open-ended, revisable list, and I frequently must decide to commit myself to one thing or another, to pursue one value rather than another. When I love in the aspiring way, it is as much a matter of decision as of discovery. The choice between one potential love and another can feel, and be, like a choice of a way of life, a decision to dedicate oneself to these values rather than these. The choice to devote myself to that love is a choice to love and cultivate those elements in myself.

Reply to Objection 6. This objection has force, but it is not an objection to the list per se, or even to the idea of regarding the list of value properties as normative for particular choices of lovers. It just points out that not all my norms and values are set; some are still evolving. If we think about how this evolution works, we find that it has very much the same shape as rational deliberation elsewhere in life. In neither case does the deliberation proceed in a vacuum. When I think about what, for me, will count as living well, I hold certain commitments firm in order to deliberate on others, or I hold the general conception of one element firm while I ask, more concretely, what will count as realizing that. Even so, in making choices in love I recognize and hold firm some general values while deliberating about others. So the objection does not even show that an antecedent list is a bad guide; it just warns us about holding too fixedly to it. We have, then, a friendly amendment.

She paused. Plato was enormously strong. She was surprised at the strength of the replies she was finding on his behalf.

And here she noticed, all at once, that this well-ordered scholastic questioning, this probing scrutiny of love with its numbered objections and replies, could not claim to constitute an external and neutral investigation of the phenomenon that resided in her heart (and in the obscure connections between that organ and other portions of the world distant, perhaps, in space, but dwelling in close proximity). For as she investigated, the investigation was effecting a change in her heart, was calming its grief and loosening its connections. It was opening a clear, high space over and around her ribs, a space that, being empty of the internal presence of the loved person, was filled with air and light. She thought of Proust's narrator, trembling before the equanimity of his own heart as before a deadly snake; for he knew that a life in which his love and his suffering for Albertine no longer existed would be a life in which he no longer existed. She too felt panic. Am I really myself right now? she asked herself, hoping that some tears would come to prove it.

How clear it is to me that there is no neutral posture of reflection from which one can survey and catalogue the intuitions of one's heart on the subject of love, holding up the rival views to see how well they fit the intuitions--no activity of philosophizing that does not stand in some determinate relation to the love. The relations can be of many kinds; they are not always, as here, inhibitory and consoling. For the *Phaedrus* shows, precisely, that a certain high type of philosophical activity may be called into being by, and in turn express and nourish, the energy and beneficence and subtle insight of happy love. And the insights gained in passion can best be pursued collaboratively, in the context of the love. (As in Phaedrus's fantasy, in the *Symposium*, of an army composed of pairs of lovers, a fantasy made reality in the Sacred Band. We might by analogy imagine a philosophy department similarly constructed, dedicated to the understanding of love. I wonder what the Thebans did when they broke up.) On the other hand, as in her case, the philosophy might, as here, emerge from and reinforce the desire for distancing and safety; it might effect and express a transformation of the perceptions and intuitions of love, and even of the lover, inasmuch as the relation seems to her to be partly constitutive of her identity.

The object of my scrutiny, Heraclitean (or rather Cratylan even) is never the same the minute you begin to step into it, even once.

In addition to the question who shall write about love, we have still on hand our old question how. I gave you some reasons for thinking that a narrative might be truer than a treatise or article on the subject. I can add to these now the argument that narrative writing, more than standard philosophical writing, seems to express the author's own acknowledgment of the power and importance of particular love and to elicit from the reader a similar response. (My experience right now is different from hers; as she is moving further from her love through scholastic argument, I risk being quite immersed. I can't write this story, however abstract it is and however much concerned with thought and argument, without launching myself into those currents.)

But the point is not simple, as I see it. For stories too impose their own simplifications. They demand that something happen, that there be a plot with a beginning and a middle and an end. They demand singleness where in life there is multiplicity, statement where there is indeterminacy, description where there are indescribable, undepictable things. So they do not escape the general suspicions I have expressed about writing. In some ways philosophy might fare better; for it follows the inquiry wherever it leads, without insisting on drama, or interest, or endings. Proust's idea was that only through the focusing and sharpening power of narrative art could the messy matter of life assume a shape, become really real and true. I feel the force of that. But I see even more clearly the other side, and here I turn to Beckett: art, especially narrative art, forces life to assume a shape rather than letting it be in its formlessness; forces it to demand an ending where one way of loving might be to forbear to do that. This forces us to ask, not just who should write about love, not just how, but also whether.

As she took note of her own forgetfulness, her heart shivered. And as it shivered, it cracked like the ice on top of a stream, and the currents of her feeling, like the liquid in one of Plato's melted souls, welled up. Outside, oranges were dying, wrapped in their coats of ice. Inside, she could not find ice enough to halt her own demise. For she knew, and with certainty, that Carrington was right. There was no life for her without that love, no continuation of its meanings without that particular person, radiant and separate. Carrington's diary goes on: "Human beings seem to me divided into those who can say 'I live for myself alone' and those who know that 'without this person or thing I could not live'". Once Plato's souls were melted, how could they help dying of a loss? She knew, and with certainty, that she was not one of the self-sufficient ones.

What do I mean by writing "She knew, and with certainty"? Not that she had come up with new and clever arguments destined to refute the skeptic on the plane of intellect. Argument, indeed, had led her to the opposite conclusion. I mean that she felt her stomach rising up into her mouth. That she felt like one of those Greek tragic unfortunates to whom someone has given a poisoned cloak that causes the wearer to sweat blood. The half of her had gone out, the next minute, into the empty space where he was and was floating around with him in the still moonlight above the golf course, lightly carried on the wind. For she saw how beautiful he was, and she did not want to be apart from him. All this is knowledge of love. And all this is happening now to me.

"Amor ch'al cor gentil ratto s'apprende", love that quickly takes hold in the gentle heart, is taking hold in mine as I watch, showing it to be more gentle than hard. I am, I tell you, the visitor and watcher of her grief, and yet as I record her knowledge I begin to have it. Francesca says:

> Amor, ch'a nullo amato amar perdona,
> mi prese del costui piacer si forte,
> che, come vedi, ancor non m'abbandona.

> Love, who absolves no beloved one from loving,
> seized me with such a strong desire for him
> that, as you see, it has not left me yet.

I want only to watch. But she is seeing him. Her watcher sees him too. I can hardly distinguish the spectator I am from the one she is. She wants Carrington to win the debate now. She wants to get all the way to that conclusion, so she won't be happier than love is.

I'm very tired, and I'm shaken by all this. I haven't finished my letter. What's strangest is that I'm more worn out than she is. I'll tell you what's going to happen now. She's going to write some more. Can you believe it? She will go all the way back to her original list of three objections, calling them, now, Objections 7, 8, and 9; she writes them out, putting Carrington's case with new force. She adds two more she has just thought up to help her. One charges the Platonist list with making love seem more determinate and reason-based, less mysterious, than it is; the other with making it too active and will-governed. I don't feel like reproducing them; you know the sort of thing she will say. And I suppose you expect that now she will get exhausted and go to sleep despairing. Not this lady. Her father died putting his papers into his briefcase; shriveled by cancer to half his former weight, he never lay down once. Her father's father once served on a jury. After ten days of deliberation he came home: the jury couldn't agree; they had ordered a new trial. He walked into the house and said to his wife, "Those were eleven of the stubbornest men I have ever seen". Now you know what you're dealing with. Do you think a lady from that background --and a philosopher on top of it all--is going to give up the argument just because it is 3:00 A.M. and most of the oranges are dead? Do you suppose, furthermore, she is going to let Carrington, and death, have the last word? No, she's going to fight it out to the end, fighting against that love with Platonist replies about value, pen in her hand and a stubborn foot in his face.

This is love she's dealing with. Can't she ever stop writing?

I won't reproduce it all. I'll give you the last paragraphs. Then I'll go to sleep, or faint like Dante.

> I propose, then, a new construction of the individual as object of love. We can, I think, combine the best elements of the *Phaedrus* with several concessions to the strongest romantic objections. We begin by insisting with Plato that the best kind of love, the kind that loves the individual for what he or she really is, is a love of character and values. But we make some alterations in the way the *Phaedrus* presents the search for character. To the first six objections we make the concessions already noted, concerning variety of properties and flexibility of choice. The final five require us to make a more substantial modification. We say something like this: in any love that is based upon character, the lovers will also see in one another, and truly love, many relational and nonrepeatable properties. They will not love these in a merely incidental way; they will come to see one another as wholes, not as composites of essence and accident, so that the nonrepeatable will be just as intrinsic to the love as the repeatable. The history, too, will come to have more than an enabling and extrinsic value; they will love it for its own sake too, rejecting even a substitution that could (*per impossibile*) preserve the same trust and knowledge. Carrington will love Lytton's character and standards, she will also love his jokes, their letters, their years of intimacy.
>
> We can still maintain, however, that the *Phaedrus* elements take priority, in the following way. We know that to be a good object of love, a person must have these repeatable character traits and not these--for example, be committed to justice and not injustice. We don't in the same way care which lovable accidents the person has. There have to be some; but insofar as they are morally neutral, it seems not to matter what they are (whether he makes jokes about cheese or some other jokes).
>
> This construction permits of real mourning; for there has been a real loss of an intrinsic value that will never come again. But it also entails that not everything is lost when a particular love is lost. The *Phaedrus* elements will sustain the person and provide continuity from one love to the next. Because both lovers love the values for themselves, it will not be disloyal to engage in such a search.
>
> This proposal has not made things altogether easier for the bereaved person. In one way, it has made them harder--by insisting on the felicitous combination of two elements that are hard enough to find singly. A few people are really good; a few are truly pleasing and 'right'; very few indeed are both. The romantic can take comfort from the thought that Platonism, so modified, has actually made things worse.

Now she's going to sleep at last, feeling victorious. She's not going to die, not her. Me? As Dante says, and Virgil's Dido before him, "Conosco i segni de l'antica fiamma". "Agnosco veteris vestigia flammae." I recognize those traces.

It's morning now. When morning came in Florida, she went running on the golf course. For even when she had been thinking of death it never occurred to her not to be healthy. The cover of snow was thawing under a cheerful Florida sun. She ran, as often, to the tune of the March to the Scaffold from Berlioz's *Symphonie Fantastique*, which she could conjure up in her head when she wished to go on, but in a tragic way. She ran from one fairway to the next, aware that she did not know the way back to her hosts' house but convinced that the numbers would bring her back in safety. She noticed the opulent ugliness of the bordering houses and remembered true beauty. She did not want to go on. She went on. And as the frozen ground began to thaw beneath her feet, the Berlioz march paused briefly. A head, flaming in the doorway. The unhappy lover heard once more from a distant place, tender and absent, the music of his only beloved. It came and hovered over the guillotine. The angel standing. And then the rapid cymbal clashes came to end it. She went on, as she thought she might. Someone went on; she thought that it was her.

When I first saw him, he was walking down the sun-streaked hallway, laughing and talking, his whole body fiercely lit up from behind by the light from the door. He looked to me like Turner's Angel Standing in the Sun, or like a counterpart good angel, victorious but tender, beneficent in power. And was there, within that remarkable and dangerous radiance, a division to be found between repeatable value properties and idiosyncratic accidents? Or was it all one seamless "perfectness"? In spite of all her constructing, there still seems to me to be no clear answer to this question. So much depends on the use you intend to make of it. And now I don't want to use it to forget. I would like to want that, but I don't. "Amor, ch'a nullo amato amar perdona"--love who lets no loved one off the hook--"mi prese del costui piacer sì forte, che, come vedi, ancor non m'abbandona". I'm in the story now, floating around. "Amor condusse noi ad una morte. Caina attende chi a vita ci spense." Love brought us to one death; Caina waits for the one who took our life.

Who am I, then, truly? Am I Francesca, the dead one, carried on the winds, dead of her love and loving on in death? Or am I, as seems more likely, the one who was responsible for her death and the death of her love, for whose callousness, for whose happiness, the icy pit of traitors is the just reward? I used to be able to distinguish myself from her, my narrative voice from hers. I was the bright, wary, slightly tough, optimistic one, the one who made jokes, who was happy, who was writing a love letter, who had survived to love again through her Platonic commitment to general values. She was the fragile one, in mourning for her loss, tossed on the currents of confused desire. Then I, sympathizing, came like Dante close to her, and the intensity of her devotion put my salvation to shame. And now: haven't we changed places? There she goes, running along the melted fairway, listening to heaven know what romantic music. But she goes quite toughly on, thinking and running. She has survived. She is well on her way to being me. I, now, am mourning, now I feel the force of the past upon me, I am no different from her; I will not finish a love letter to somebody else; I'll be the individual constituted by her love.

I refuse to be happier than love is.

I didn't expect the story to end like this. My writing didn't have the same result for me as hers did for her, clearly. Perhaps because it was a different kind of writing. There is much more to be said about the connection between these experiences and ethical objectivity. But I am too immersed to say it. I'm seeing a "form truly expressing beauty and nobility". It's like being one of those fishermen in their light-drowned boat.

Did I find what I wanted, then, the noncontrolling art of writing?

I write only what occurs to me now. It won't look this way tomorrow. Tomorrow I'll see my current lover. Who is an individual. With many repeatable (and even repeated) properties, and some that are unique. We'll have dinner in a good restaurant, and I'll tell jokes about this paper and its strange effect upon my mood. I'll say how happy I am. It will be true.

"Caina attende chi a vita ci spense."

What ending did you expect? Did you think I would collapse, or die? Remember, I'm the one who wrote this down. Remember, this is writing you're reading.

"Love, and be silent."

Reprinted from *Reconstructing Individualism: Autonomy, Individuality, and the Self in Western Thought*, edited by Thomas C. Heller, Morton Sosna, and David E. Wellbery, with the permission of the publishers, Stanford University Press. Copyright 1986 by the Board of Trustees of the Leland Stanford Junior University.

A slightly different version appears in Professor Nussbaum's *Love's Knowledge: Essays on Philosophy and Literature*, Oxford University Press, 1990.

2

Love and Rationality

Roger E. Lamb

"Love bade me welcome: yet my soul drew back,
Guiltie of dust and sinne."
George Herbert
The Temple

I.

It is relatively uncontentious that when we adopt attitudes towards others, we typically do so either *in virtue of* certain properties (replicable within a world[1]) which those others manifestly have or else in virtue of our belief that they have such properties. Thus, it is because she manifestly resisted, or else because you believe she resisted, the temptations proferred, and did not succumb

---

1. Some properties are not replicable within a world. It is usual, for example, to think that only you can have the property of being identical with yourself (in this world). And perhaps we sometimes do adopt attitudes towards others because, as we might say to them, 'You are you'. (It is not always clear what this is supposed to mean, but that is another point.) As well, we sometimes adopt attitudes towards others because it was they who stood in special historical relationships with us--did certain things with us, lived through certain things with us, and so forth--and, given it was they who stood in those relationships with us, no one else could have. For example, suppose someone has the property (if it really is one) of being *the only one* who stood up for me at some critical time. Given that that person does have that property, no one else could *actually* have it *as well*, and in that sense it is not replicable--not replicable within a world (although someone else could have had it *instead*, and thus the property is replicable in another non-actual world).

From this point forward when I use the cognate notions of 'property', 'feature', 'trait', etc. in the '*in virtue of*'-context, read *intra-worldly replicable property* (etc.).

to the subsequent threats, that you *respect* her. And it is because he has been forced to listen to his children being tortured in the next cell by agents of the generals' junta that you *pity* him. Less alarmingly, but similarly, it is in virtue of the students having done efficiently and without complaint what was reasonably required of them, that their lecturer *approves* of them. And so on. Another way of putting this kind of very general point is to say that our taking up of attitudes towards others is typically a function of various properties, features, or traits which those others manifestly have, or are believed to have.

An apparent consequence of this rather unremarkable fact is that attitudes are *universalizable*. This is to say that if we adopt some attitude towards someone we know, in virtue of the fact that that person either manifestly has or is believed by us to have a certain property or set of properties, then *we* (I do not say others) are *constrained* to extend the same attitude-type towards *others* manifesting, or believed by us to have, the same (or relevantly similar) properties.

It is not just that, in such circumstances, we generally will extend the same attitude-type but instead, as I say, that we are under a constraint to do so. However, the constraint at issue is not always a socially sanctioned one, nor is it necessarily one with moral credentials (though in particular cases either social or moral constraints could obtain). Rather, if Smith adopts some attitude towards Jones in virtue of Jones' evidencing some property, *F*, then Smith is *rationally* constrained, *ceteris paribus*, to extend the same attitude-type towards others similarly evidencing the property.[2] If she fails to do this, then Smith's rational credentials are under threat. How, we will want to know, can she--*in consistency*--adopt some attitude towards Jones in virtue of Jones' having property *F*, but fail to extend the same attitude-type towards another plainly having the same property? Surely if the property in question is, as stated, the one in virtue of which Smith has the attitude in the one case, it ought to suffice as a property in virtue of which the same attitude-type is extended towards others possessing it. For example, if Smith pities someone nearby in virtue of the fact that that person is malnourished, diseased, and a child, then, *ceteris paribus*, as a rational being Smith pities others exhibiting just those features.

I said above, however, that this universalizability of attitudes[3] was "appar-

---

2. It is important to understand that if this is so, it is so even if Smith's original adoption of the attitude towards Jones (in virtue of the fact that Jones has the property, *F*) is itself irrational (provided, of course, that Smith is unaware of the irrationality of the original adoptive act).

3. I need to say something at this point about my use of 'attitude' in the foregoing and in what is to come. Following a clue left behind by Irving Thalberg in his important article,
...*continuing*...

ent". The fact is that not all attitudes are uncontentiously universalizable. For *love*, at least, is not *uncontentiously* universalizable.[4]

One way of discussing the issue of love's putative non-universalizability or--as I will sometimes refer to it--its *'particularity'*, is by considering the following sort of case. You love S. Furthermore, you love S in virtue of the fact that S manifestly has properties $F_1, ... F_n$.[5] Now as it happens there is someone else who also manifests properties $F_1, ... F_n$. Call this other person 'J'. *J now appears on your scene.* The question for us to consider is not whether you do (for at this point you do not)--nor, indeed, whether you ever will--love J. You may, but you may not. Rather the question to consider (in its initial formu-

---

'Emotion and Thought' (*APQ*, I, 1964 at pp. 47-48a), I require of any state which is an 'attitude' to be such that *all* of its possible intentional tokens take *non*-propositional objects. The following states appear to meet this condition: *pity*, devotion, disdain, admiration, contempt, compassion, detestation, loathing, abhorrence, adoration, *respect*, despisal, dislike, esteem, *approval*, reverence, scorn, spite, sympathy, veneration, friendship, erotic love, and hatred. And I am inclined to regard them all as attitudes. On the other hand, by way of example, neither anger (as opposed to hatred), nor fear, nor suspicion, nor amazement will count as attitudes, since some of each of their respective possible intentional tokens do take *propositional* objects. (In 'Emotion, Attitude, and Mind', forthcoming, I distinguish between 'attitudes' and 'emotions', requiring of any state-type--e.g., fear, anger--which is an emotion to be such that some of its possible intentional tokens take *propositional* objects, and inquire as to the consequences and merit of such a differential perspective on attitude and emotion. Having an attitude towards someone will, as one can plainly see from the list of attitude-types above, frequently manifest itself in emotion--as well as in behaviour, belief, etc. I will not pursue these more fundamental matters in this paper, however.)

4. Roger Scruton, for example, has recently claimed that it is not:

"Although there is, no doubt, some feature of James which is a reason (perhaps even *the* reason) why I love him, I am not obliged to love William as well, just because he shares that feature." [*Sexual Desire* (1986), p. 96.]

Compare Max Scheler, who observes approvingly that,

"It is...noticeable that though other objects may have value-qualities identical to those alleged as reasons for love or hatred, no such emotions are addressed to them." [*The Nature of Sympathy* (1st edition 1913), tr. P. Heath (1954), p. 149.]

5. I suspect that, usually, such properties are reasonably widely distributed. It is possible, of course, for A to love B in virtue of B's possession of certain properties which, as it happens, are only rarely instantiated. Mostly, however, it seems reasonable to suppose this is not typical.

lation[6]) is whether, all other things remaining equal, you are under any rational constraint to love J (as well as S). And thus, the question is whether, under such circumstances, you must, as a rational being, love J.

Contrast that case with a structurally similar case. You respect A. You respect A in virtue of the fact that A manifestly has properties G_1, ... G_n. As it happens there is someone else who manifestly has properties G_1, ... G_n. Call this other person 'B'. B now appears on your scene. The question to consider is whether, all other things remaining equal, you are under any rational constraint to respect B (as well as A). And thus, the question is whether, under such circumstances, you must, as a rational being, respect B.

Now, it seems that in the second case, the case involving respect, the obvious answer to the question is 'yes'. That being so, we say that *respect* is universalizable. I believe the same holds for admiration, pity and approval (already mentioned illustratively), as well as veneration, loathing, and so on.

But let us return to your problem. Here is the lovable J, possessing those properties in virtue of which you love your beloved S. Are you under any rational constraint to love J too? Accepting the legitimacy of the question, there are really only two ways to go on this. We could say that you are *not* under any such constraint and that hence, while all other attitudes may be universalizable in the sense specified, love, at any rate, is not. If we should go that way, we would have the job of explaining how it can be that love is different in this respect to all other attitudes. Alternatively, we could say that you *are* under a rational constraint to love J.

Of course, there may be enormous *practical* problems for you (posed, for example, by a miserable and jealous S) if the latter is what we all decide, and you wish always to do the rational thing. Still, any adequate account of what is rational here would ultimately have to take such practical problems into account. Thus the *ceteris paribus* clause may be invokable in your case so as to make your life (and S's) less problematic. In this way, under appropriate forms of pressure from S, you may be able, rationally, to let yourself off the hook, since then the rational constraint to love J is only a potential or *prima facie* constraint.

Still, in the rational society, the society in which people (*especially* including S) do not needlessly make it difficult for one another to do *the otherwise rational thing*, the constraint will verge on being an actual or absolute one.

These remarks suggest, however, that our topic is being delimited in a way that ought to be made explicit. In speaking about you loving S, I am not concerned with the case in which S remains unaware of that fact. Nor, I realise, am I speaking of the case in which your love is unrequited. Let me, then, take as the *standard* case a love you have for S which in some way you have made known to S, and which S returns to you in such a way that you know of it.

---

6. But see the last paragraph of this section.

Now, I wish to avoid one line of objection that might be raised to the universalizability-option, the basic idea of the objection being that no one could ever be under a rational constraint to love anyone since the general idea of a 'commandment' *to love* (whether religiously, morally, or rationally inspired) does not make any sense (or is impossible to obey, or... etc.). I am not sure whether this is correct, but I do not think we need address such an objection and the issues it raises, for the following reason. In the case of you and J, where J possesses just those properties in virtue of which you love S, allow me to suppose what is a natural supposition, namely, that you will already have an understandable *inclination* to love J. You can go along with such inclination or impulse, but you are also able to resist. So, in this governing context, we can take the universalizability-thesis as simply requiring the rational-you *not* to resist: 'Succumb!' whispers reason. And there certainly is sense in *this* commandment. So, the question to consider in what follows is whether, all other things remaining equal, you are under any rational constraint *not* to resist going along with your understandable inclination to love J. The universalizability-thesis is the affirmative answer to this question.

II.

There is at least one common argument, with a distinctly moral profile, for *not* accepting that love is like other attitudes in being universalizable for rational beings. The argument I have in mind relies heavily on some notion of *commitment*. A basic statement of the argument is that: if (counter-factually) your love for S were universalizable, then the rational-you would not be committed *to S*. But a putative 'love' *of S* without commitment *to S* would not be love at all. Therefore, the rational-you, *contra hypothesi*, would not love S. More simply, the idea is that if the universalizability-thesis were applicable in the case of love, then love would be out of bounds, i.e., impossible, for beings devoted to rationality. This might understandably be viewed as both a theoretically-inspired disaster for rational beings on the one hand, and for loving beings on the other--and thus as something to be avoided at all costs. And to avoid it, one only need *deny* universalizability regarding love. Presumably, that course might prove to have its own hazards, but it is hard to see how they could be so considerable as the ones just mooted.

Well, is there any merit in such a line? More particularly, is commitment an essential component of love? What is commitment? And does universalizability really violate it? These are large and difficult questions and I cannot do more here than outline one kind of response to them. To take the first of the 'more particular' questions first, viz., 'Is commitment an essential component of love?', personally, I am inclined simply to give this one to the particularist--and I suspect that even dedicated universalists can risk generosity here as well. It is not yet clear, of course, what is being conceded, and particularists may suspect that initially apparently generous universalists are likely to withdraw, in what ultimately will prove to be insipid analyses of commitment, that which they conceded, nominally, at the outset. In any event, I propose to allow the battle lines to be drawn further down the dialectical path, supposing that nearly all parties will accept that commitment is an essential component of love.

We are therefore left with the questions, 'What is commitment?' and 'Does universalizability violate it?'. It is fairly clear that these questions cannot be answered independently, i.e., that an answer to one is likely to commit us to an answer to the other. Still, we can begin with only one of them.

As to *what commitment is*, it may seem that the sense of 'commitment' which is of interest here is a sense referring to our *obligations* as lovers.[7] It is doubtless a logical tragedy that something as grave as obligation should tap the shoulder of the lover. Yet it may be difficult to avoid acknowledging the fact of such intrusion. To agree, then, that there can be no love without commitment, on any account of commitment requiring reference to the special obligations of lovers, is simply to agree that there can be no love free of obligation. On the assumption that such obligation as love might impose on the lover is owed to the beloved *qua* beloved, we should need to ask what it is that one, as lover, is obliged to do, not do, or (perhaps) be. What would the content of such obligation be? Remember that in trying to answer this question, we will be looking for obligation essentially involved in being S's acknowledged and beloved lover.

It will be helpful at this point to take a side-long look at *friendship*.[8] Here, too, it seems that without commitment, friendship, like love, is essentially defective. If you are friend to someone, then (we may suppose) you (to) have a *commitment* to that person in the sense that he or she can, as we say, 'count on' you, that is, can count on you to be concerned for their welfare; and thus, for example, can count on your attending to any requests they might make (say, for assistance) from that concerned perspective. Amoralists aside, sharing a friendship with someone, you *feel specially obligated* to assist that person. In know-

---

7. As opposed, for example, to that different sense of 'commitment' which is such that committing myself to another is entrusting myself *to the care of* another.

8. This is a comparison which would be natural to Aristotle: "...loving seems to be the characteristic excellence of friends...." [*N.E.*, Bk. VIII, 1159a34, Ross translation as revised by Urmson]. (It should be borne in mind that the Aristotelian discussion of love in Books VIII and IX, with few exceptions, is a discussion of *philia*--not *eros*. So, the passage at 1159a34 reads: "...*philon arete to philein eoiken*". One of Aristotle's few comments on *eros* in Book VIII is cited and remarked upon in footnote 26 below. On the general nature of the Greek distinction, see 'The Individual as an Object of Love in Plato', *Platonic Studies*, G. Vlastos (1981), note 4, p. 4.)

ingly inaugurating and maintaining a friendship one sets up trust[9], and trust so constituted is one of the things we feel committed, i.e. (once again), obligated, to defend. Probably, you will also *want* to assist--at least most of the time; yet even if this should be an occasion when you do not want to, and even if you decide not to, the felt obligation will have left its calling card. For, at least one kind of excellence in friendship answers to such descriptions as 'reliability', 'dependability', 'constancy', and 'steadfastness'. None of this means that someone who is staunch friend to you will always in fact assist you, nor even that they will, minimally, always want to assist you; but it does mean that they will always be concerned for your welfare. Can they really be concerned for your welfare when there is an occasion when they do not even want to help? Of course. For they always feel under a special obligation to help.

Having said this, it nevertheless needs to be said as well that in friendship the degree of this commitment, this obligation, can be (and usually is) *limited*. That is not a point about human psychology. Many factors can limit it. But one of the more interesting of them from the point of view of this discussion lies in the fact that friendship is clearly *possible with more than one*.[10] That friendship with more than one--indeed, that friendship with *many*--is, as well,

---

9. Thus Aristotle remarks, "...nor can [men] admit each other to friendship or be friends till each has been...trusted by each". [*N.E.*, 1156b30, Ross-Urmson]

10. Aristotle does not disagree, though it is true that he thinks that friendship of the highest kind is not possible with *many*. "One cannot be a friend to many people in the sense of having friendship of the complete type with them...." [*N.E.*, Book VIII, 6, 1158a11, Ross-Urmson] His major discussion of this interesting topic is, however, in Book IX, 10. Briefly, having earlier urged, plausibly, that "Nothing is so characteristic of friends as their fondness for each other's society" [1157b19, Thomson tr., *cf.* 1158a9], in this place he claims that "it is obvious that one cannot associate closely with a large body of people, dividing oneself among them". [1171a3, Thomson] A reason given for this is that the practical probability that one will have (what *we* might call) contrary obligations rises with the number of friends one has (for an Aristotelian example of this, see footnote 12 below).

The 'impossibility' to which Aristotle is here sensitive is of a practical, rather than a logical, sort, though it is true that it partly arises out of what is--in my view--a logical feature of friendship, viz., the fact that it involves commitment.

Another general difficulty with having large numbers of friends, he says, is that if the fondness for the society of one's friends is to be realised, then "It is also requisite that one's friends be friendly with one another, if they are all to pass the time in each other's company; but for a large number of people all to be friends is a difficult matter". [1171a3-5, Thomson/Rackham]

uncontentiously *desirable*[11] gives the following point some real force. That point is that giving effect to an obligation to one friend may prevent you from carrying out an obligation to another. Thus, the extent or degree of your commitment to a friend can be limited in practice--limited by (among other things) your commitment to *another* friend or *other* friends.[12] With this fact in mind, we can see that commitment in friendship is self-limiting.

Now the fact that, generally, commitment is the kind of thing that quite clearly can be legitimately limited, might suggest that the commitment which all parties accept as logically parceled up with love is itself *similarly* limitable. And if it is thus limitable then the thesis of universalizability ought to be sustainable against the 'argument from commitment'. So, an important question to be addressed is: 'Is the commitment involved in loving someone like that involved in being a friend to someone, viz., limitable in degree, or extent, and limitable in a way *analogous* to the way it is limitable in friendship--by the *desirable* possibility of having more than one lover?'.[13] If the universalist is correct, it seems it *must* be so limitable and, in fact, limited in your case (if you are a *rational* lover), since--given that (i) J is $F_1 ... F_n$, and that (ii) you love S in virtue of S's possession of the same properties--you are under a rational con-

---

11. In Aristotle's time also, it is "...thought to be a fine thing to have many friends". [*N.E.*, 1155a30, Ross-Urmson] And Aristotle agrees with this common view, for in spite of being properly impressed with the practical difficulties involved in having many friends--difficulties which lead him to suggest that "Perhaps therefore it is a good rule not to seek to have as many friends as possible" [1171a8, Rackham]--he nevertheless supposes that if these difficulties are surmountable, then the having of many friends is clearly desirable: "For if it is possible to live with and share the perceptions of *many* at the same time, it is most desirable that these should be as numerous as possible". [*E.E.*, 1245b21-24, Ross-Urmson]

12. This general logical point can lead to (or, perhaps, is actually constituted by) particular intractable practical problems of the sort Aristotle draws our attention to. For example, "...it may likely happen that one has at once to be merry with one friend and to mourn with another". [*N.E.*, Book IX, 1171a7, Ross-Urmson]

13. That the commitment of love is limitable *in general* is plain. Giving effect to the obligations we owe our children, our employers, our parents, our friends, and so forth, may sometimes prevent us from giving effect to the obligations we have towards our (one) beloved. This may be a disappointment to them, but it is simply a fact of moral life that they do not invariably come first in every matter. What may not be immediately plain is the answer to the question whether the commitment one has to one's beloved (just in virtue of the fact that that person is one's beloved) is limitable by the desirable possibility of having more than one lover.

straint, *ceteris paribus*, not to resist extending love to J.[14] But this appears to give us an answer to the last of the three questions, viz., 'Does universalizability really violate commitment?'. The answer is neither a simple 'yes' nor 'no'. The answer is that universalizability necessarily *limits the extent* or degree of commitment that you can have to S as S's lover.[15]

Now, we are all presumed to have accepted that love involves commitment, but there is no universal agreement as to *what degree of* commitment is involved, or more exactly, under what kinds of circumstance such commitment may be bounded. And it is at this point that one becomes aware of the passionate drawing of swords in love's history--as well as that phenomenon's very sublimated cousin, the earnest unsheathing of philosophical pens.

A side-long look at a second phenomenon, plainly related to friendship, is natural at this point. Suppose I *like* A in virtue of A's manifest or believed properties $H_1, \ldots H_n$. Everyone acknowledges this. B comes along, manifesting those same properties. I am, and will remain, utterly indifferent to B. Others who take an interest in me wonder why I am indifferent. 'Why don't you like B', they will ask, 'when B is like A in all the relevant respects?' Suppose I agree that B *is* like A in all the relevant respects, but insist that it is only A whom I like. No one, of course, will say, 'Well, you *must* like B', or 'You're just mistaken, you really *do* like B'. (Though, wishing to save my rationality in this matter, they might well want to reconsider, and say, 'We were all mistaken in thinking that you like A in virtue of A's being $H_1, \ldots H_n$'.) If having a liking for someone in virtue of that person's manifest or believed properties is universalizable, it is nevertheless not always universalized. However, to say that an attitude is universalizable is to put rational constraints on withholding the same attitude to some others regarded under certain relevantly similar descriptions. So, while it doesn't follow that I am in error about the putative fact that I do not like B, it does seem that in failing to extend the favorable attitude-type to B (whilst acknowledging that I like A in virtue of A's being $H_1, \ldots H_n$) I have put some kind of question mark over my rationality in the matter. Upon consideration, reflective people will ask, in tones of rising logical indignation, 'How *can* you like A in virtue of A's being $H_1, \ldots H_n$, yet refrain from liking B, when you acknowledge both that B is $H_1, \ldots H_n$ and that all other things are equal?'. They are not after my *technique* in this affair. They mean to ask, 'How can you *in consistency* like A... [*etc.*]?'. Their questions indicate that in the matter of

---

14. Or, more carefully put: if the universalist is correct, you are under a rational constraint, *ceteris paribus*, *not* to resist going along with your understandable inclination to love J.

15. But as already pointed out in footnote 13 above, many sorts of human relationships limit it.

liking someone in virtue of that person's being H_l, ... H_n, concerns about consistency, and hence rationality, can and do arise.

On the assumption that this brief account of liking someone is on the right track, it is natural to ask: Is loving someone like liking someone, in respect of the latter's universalizability? If not, why not?

One final lateral glance, this time at *patriotism* (of all things!). We have already seen that the commitment of friendship is self-limiting, i.e., that one's commitment to one's friend is limited by one's commitments to one's friend*s*. We have wondered whether an analogous point must not hold regarding love. For if love is universalizable then one's commitment to one's lover may be limited by one's commitments to one's lover*s*, *that is*, the lovers *that one may have* owing to one's *rationality*. We have also seen that liking someone in virtue of that person's manifest or believed properties apparently invites an uncontroversial line of questioning indicating that 'inconsistency' in these matters is possible and is conceived to be some kind of intellectual vice. Again, we have wondered, 'If it is like this with liking someone, mustn't it be the same with loving someone?'. But now consider patriotism. My uncle, Sam, has a love for his nation. He is a great patriot. Suppose he loves his nation in virtue of its having certain properties, properties he is able to specify. Now, of a certain second nation, he comes to believe that it also has such properties, having no countervailing ones either. As a patriot nevertheless striving to be a rational being, must he be patriotic with respect to the second nation?[16] Is patriotism, like admiration, universalizable? Well, I confess that my own intuitions need a certain measure of manufacture here.

Still, one can perhaps imagine someone of firmly delivered intuitions about such matters (a particularist-traditionalist, in fact) forcibly arguing that: 'While Sam may be under a rational constraint to, say, rather admire the second nation, he cannot be under a rational constraint to be *its patriot as well*. For if he were really under such a rational constraint, his patriotic nature would be put under destructive *logical* stress when his two favored countries fell out and threatened war on one another. As "*their* patriot" (the very idea!), would he have to approve such mutually threatening behavior, and if it came to a fight, perhaps fight for both sides--in order to preserve his "rational" patriotism?! But clearly', so the argument might conclude, '*rationality* itself can not require such incoherence'.

-'On the contrary', might come the universalist reply. 'Such an objection goes through only on the assumption that the commitment universally acknowledged to be essential to any genuine patriotism is not self-limiting. A "logical" stress can arise only if we assume that Sam's patriotic commitment to country is

---

16. That is, must he (as a rational being) not resist going along with any patriotic stirrings he may understandably have towards the second nation?

never limited by patriotic commitment to a second country. Yet this is surely precisely what is at issue. The stress is, in fact, mis-characterised as "logical". Sam's generous patriotism is not *incoherent* at all. His stress is simply the familiar kind of stress that comes from having contrary obligations. His situation is analogous to the situation in which two of one's friends, both of whom one likes for much the same reasons (and continues to like), are currently behaving hostilely towards one another. That this situation can arise without posing a *logical* threat to the universalizability of the attitude of *friendship* is obvious. And so it should be equally clear that the analogous situation poses no logical threat to the universalizability of patriotism.'

Well, whichever of these incompatible lessons about patriotism we are individually inclined to support, and although the model is in many ways rather unattractive, we might nevertheless wonder whether love of another is, in respect of one's favored contrary lesson on offer here, like love of nation.

Much more important, however, is the fact that it is (by now) becoming increasingly clear that I have thus far been skirting two issues throughout this discussion, increasingly clear because the issues in question come very close to the surface in the phenomenon of patriotism. They are the related issues of *loyalty* and *exclusivity*. Now an undoubted element in a traditionally conceived patriotism is *loyalty*. And *divided* loyalty is *defective* loyalty--at least from the point of view of its recipients. From that perspective, loyalty to one's nation which is not defective is not divided, and is *therefore* exclusive. In wondering whether love of another is like love of country we should mostly be wondering whether love is like patriotism *in respect of* the exclusivity attaching to *traditionally conceived* non-defective instantiations of the latter.

III.

I have been exploring some issues originating in an argument "with a distinctly moral profile, for not accepting that love is like other attitudes in being universalizable". I am now going to set considerations of this argument to one side in order to discuss a second argument, one without any distinctly moral profile, which reaches the same conclusion--the conclusion, that is, that we should not accept that love is universalizable. 'Argument', however, is an honorific term, and it may be thought that the series of considerations that I am about to put in the mouth of your beloved S are better regarded as 'protests' than genuine arguments. We shall see.

So, I return to your love for S, a love you have in virtue of S's being $F_1, \ldots F_n$. Let it be that you accept that love is universalizable. That is, you accept that *if* someone loves someone else in virtue of lover-specifiable properties of the one loved, *then* the lover is constrained *as a rational being* (not to resist any natural inclination he or she may have) to extend the same attitude-type towards others having those properties. S discovers this fact about you. Actually, you have made no secret of it. Why should you? But, surprisingly, S protests. She asks, somewhat inquisitorially, 'Do you mean that if you met someone who was like me in respect of being F_1, ... F_n, that you would love her too?'. Believing yourself to make a pretty good fist of being a rational being, and obviously not fathoming what all the fuss is about (perhaps you wrongly supposed that the *ceteris paribus* clause had been met), you respond bravely, 'Of course'. We can imagine that you are now going to have to deal with a series of protestations in which first personal pronouns will heavily feature, protestations such as,

> 'But what about *me*? Where do *I* fit in to all this? Am I *just* some... some "place-holder of predicates"[17], some cipher who happens to have the right char-acteristics, such that anybody else with the same characteristics *will do* just as well? For you, am I just an exemplification, an instantiation, of some favoured set of properties? -In what way could you experience *my* death as a *loss* if I am thus *replaceable*?'[18]

We imagine as well that these protestations are followed by what can only be described as accusations, such as,

> 'You don't really love *me*, you know; you value some set of properties, and therefore, derivatively, *any* instantiation of those properties. What is there that is *personal* in all that? The difference between love and, for example, admiration, is that love is a personal attitude in a way that admiration is *not*. It is a relation between subjects, between *you* and *me* and is unmediated by characteristics in the way that admiration is mediated.'[19]

-----

17. Compare Vlastos ['The Individual as an Object of Love in Plato', *Platonic Studies*, G. Vlastos (1981)], who says, "What Plato's theory is really about is love for place-holders of the predicates 'useful' and 'beautiful'...." (p. 26) Also, compare one of Martha Nussbaum's philosophical characters, a narrator, who is given the lines,

> "For, sure enough, it turns out that the [Socratic] claim to have grasped and understood the nature of love is part and parcel of an enterprise that is busy converting loved persons into instantiations of a universal...." ('Love and the Individual: Romantic Rightness and Platonic Aspiration', this volume, p. 3.)

18. *Cp.* Nussbaum's narrative character who writes about "...the Platonic thought that...a loss of one [loved individual] could be compensated fully and directly by the coming-into-being of the homogeneous next". (This volume, p. 2.)

19. Perhaps S has been reading McTaggart:

> "...the emotion [love] is directed to the person, independently of his qualities, and...the determining qualities are not the *justification* of that emotion, but only
> *...continuing...*

All this to be capped by,

> 'I see now that you don't love me in particular nor, in spite of what she might mistakenly think, will you ever love the unsuspecting J in particular. And if you don't love me *in particular*, you don't really love *me* at all!'[20]

Reeling from such unbridled haecceity, you retire to consider your position. What can you suppose? 'Clearly', you say to yourself, 'there is something rather mad, or at least terribly *unfair*[21], in S's response'. You soliloquize:

> 'For just as no one would think of denying that people *admire* others in virtue of the way those others are believed to be, just so, it cannot be denied that one can also *love* others in virtue of the way those others are believed to be. And thus, if

---

the means by which it arises. ... We come, then, to the conclusion that love... involves a connection between the lover and the beloved which is of peculiar strength and intimacy, and which is stronger and more intimate than any other bond by which two selves can be joined. ... Qualities and relations can only prevent love by preventing the union, or the sense of it, and can only destroy love by destroying the union, or the sense of it. Love is for the person, and not for his qualities, *nor is it for him in respect of his qualities*. It is for him." [*The Nature of Existence*, Vol. 2 (1927), pp. 153-4. The italics are mine.]

20. In all of this, S seems to regard your attitude towards her as belonging to the chilling type described by Bernard Williams in a discussion of what he calls the 'reduplication problem':

"If someone loved a token-person *just* as a Mary Smith, then it might well be unclear that the token-person was really what he loved. What he loves is *Mary Smith*, and that is to love the type-person. We can see dimly what this would be like. It would be like loving a work of art in some reproducible medium. One might start comparing, as it were, performances of the type; and wanting to be near the person one loved would be like wanting very much to hear some performance, even an indifferent one, of *Figaro*--just as one will go to the scratch provincial performance of *Figaro* rather than hear no *Figaro* at all, so one would see the very run-down Mary Smith who was in the locality, rather than see no Mary Smith at all.

Much of what we call loving a person would begin to crack under this...." ['Are Persons Bodies?', in *Problems of the Self* (1973), C.U.P., p. 81. All the italics are Williams'.]

But you may seriously question whether there is any reason to think that: because you (admittedly) love S in virtue of her being $F_1, ... F_n$, and are an avowed universalist, it follows that you love her "*just* as an" $F_1, ... F_n$.

21. This idea is further discussed in section IV.

admiration can, as a consequence of this feature, give an account of itself, if one who admires another can answer questions which, left unanswered, might impugn one's judgement--for example, questions such as "Why, for God's sake, do you admire *him*?"--by citing various relevant characteristics *he* has, then surely it ought also to be possible to respond to questions asking for a similar account of why one loves the people one does love. If someone asks "Why do you love her?", is one always supposed to be able to say only, "I just do, that's all", or perhaps, "I love her *for herself alone*"?[22]   One might as well be confined to "We were made for each other". *Must* we then remain mute in the face of such questions? What nonsense! I *may* not know, of course, why I love her[23]; but that, clearly, is a different matter. The point is that there is surely nothing in the nature of love that *prevents* me from knowing what it is about that person in virtue of which I love her, nothing in the nature of love that prevents me knowing that I love her in virtue of her being $F_1 ... F_n$. And these will be the characteristics I should cite if someone should ask me "Why, for God's sake, do you love *her*?"'

The tension between you and your beloved is very considerably heightened, however, when the parallel between admiration and love is *continued* by you. For you go on to suppose that just as the occurrence in Y of properties, in virtue of whose occurrence in X you admire X, constrains you as a rational being to extend admiration to Y, so equally the occurrence in J of properties, in virtue of whose occurrence in S you love S, constrains you as a rational being to extend love to J.[24]

And if you give in on this one, *that is*, if you give up the universalizability of love, doesn't irrationality enter your life in unprecedented measure?

Not long ago, I suggested that the issue of exclusivity was being skirted. Now, of course, it is center-stage. For anything, however, there are various

---

22. For an extended sceptical discussion of this notion, see the long endnote commencing on p. 46.

23. And if *that* was Montaigne's implication when he wrote (in 'Of Friendship', *Essays*):

"If someone were to urge me to say why I loved him, I should feel it could not be expressed except in the reply: 'Because it was he; because it was I.'"

then (but only then) it ought to pass unchallenged.

24. Again, this is intended in the sense that: you are constrained not to resist any natural and understandable impulse you may have to extend love to J. This qualification continues to be stressed only to meet objections of the sort mentioned earlier, viz., that no one could ever be under a rational constraint to love anyone since the general idea of a 'commandment' *to love* (whether religiously, morally, or rationally inspired) does not make any sense (or is impossible to obey, or...etc.).

descriptions, and it is no different with properties of human relationships. What is frequently referred to as 'exclusivity' is sometimes thought to be equivalently referred to as 'uniqueness' (or even 'specialness')[25]. In some ways these are happier descriptions.

Suppose we stipulated that instances of some kind of relationship (which I will refer to as '*luv*') could only count as such if they had the 'property' of intentional exclusivity. That is, we proposed that, necessarily, for any two people to stand in the *luving* relationship, it was the case that they did not wittingly stand in that relationship to anyone else.[26] Suppose we also thought that when A

---

25. Ilham Dilman uses both of these notions as well as others in his discussion of exclusivity and 'love as a sexual passion'. Exclusivity, he argues, requires what such love requires, viz., uniqueness, specialness. I think he is correct both about the requirements of exclusivity and of love. What one ought to be *very* doubtful about, however, is whether exclusivity is required for the uniqueness and specialness appropriate to a loving relationship. (See the interestingly titled section, 'Exclusive Love and Regard for the Beloved: Are They Compatible?', in his *Love and Human Separateness*, Basil Blackwell (1987), pp. 84-86.)

Amelie Rorty ('The Historicity of Psychological Attitudes', *Midwest Studies in Philosophy* X, 1986) discusses uniqueness as a requirement of lovers (without confusing it with exclusivity). A taste of her discussion is given in this passage (p. 402):

"...both [Ella] and her successor Gloria might be aggrieved that Louis always brings the same love, a love that is contained within *his* biography, to be given as a gift. Presumably Gloria does not want to inherit Louis's love for Ella: she wants Louis to love her in a wholly different way, defined by the two of them."

26. 'Wittingly', to take care of tricky twin-cases, clone-cases, etc.

Aristotle seems to have some such view of *eros*, yet he appears not to regard what he takes to be the 'natural' exclusivity of *eros* as a point in its favor:

"...one cannot be in love with many people at once (for love is a sort of *excess*, and it is the nature of such only to be felt towards one person)." [*N.E.*, Book VIII, 1158a11-12, Ross-Urmson]

Alan H. Goldman ('Plain Sex', *PPA* 6, p. 273) takes a similar view of love when he writes of it as

"...more or less exclusive. A normal person cannot deeply love more than a few individuals even in a lifetime. We may be suspicious that those who attempt or claim to love many love them weakly if at all."

It is not entirely clear what Goldman thinks about loving *more than one* individual *at any given time*. If he should take the 'narrow' view, then the universalist will be interested to know why, and probably tempted to ask him what he thinks of families with

...*continuing*...

luved B it was the case, frequently at any rate, that A *luved* B in virtue of some sub-set of B's (intra-worldly replicable) properties. It would seem to follow for us that the proposed exclusivity of the relationship between A and B could not be a function of properties uniquely possessed by B. More generally, the guaranteed exclusivity of the *luv*-relationship certainly could not be a mere *reflection* of a guaranteed uniqueness of possession of the relevant properties by the *relata*. The guaranteed exclusivity of the relationship would have to be the result of a 'creative' act, e.g., a decision. The exclusivity could not be guaranteed to be the result of a responsive or reflecting act. For, given that you live out a normal life-span, nature may simply not cooperate in providing you with a *luver*, S, who is relevantly unique. Around any corner, there 'she' may be, 'again'! (well, not really)--only, this time, in the person of J.[27]

Where does this leave us? Well, simply to say of one kind of relationship--characterized essentially by exclusivity--that it must be the result of a 'creative' act is clearly not to say that the act is, on that account, any the more rational. The question will remain, 'How to salvage the rationality of a

---

more than one child. If he takes the broader view, supposing that one can perhaps love more than one individual at any given time, but still not *many*, well, there is probably something in that view (depending, I suppose, on how many 'many' is). There are only twenty-four hours in a day, and love places its demands on the lover. It might be thought that this thought (or admission) shows the universalist's position to be, ultimately, mistaken. But this is doubtful. For even though one may admittedly meet uncontentiously *many* people who exemplify properties, in virtue of whose occurrence in X one loves X, all things will ultimately not be equal: the *ceteris paribus* clause will come into play, for one will simply not be *able* to love them all. A similar and well-known phenomenon is at work in hospitals in the case of health care workers *vis a vis* their patients--with respect to pity; and in the case of social workers *vis a vis* their clients, etc. This does not mean that pity is not, in the sense specified here, universalizable.

Amelie Rorty ('The Historicity of Psychological Attitudes', *Midwest Studies in Philosophy* X, 1986) adopts the following perspective on love's putative exclusivity, one which would probably be accepted by most universalists:

> "The account I sketch does not assume that...there is a strict economy of love, such that its expansion to others automatically constitutes a diminution or loss elsewhere. Nevertheless, although such love is by no means exclusive, it cannot include more people than the lover is able to attend closely." (400)

27. Of course, J may--and almost certainly would be--in many respects a very different sort of person than S. And this could prove to be important in making a loving (not, of course, a *luving*) relationship with J especially attractive, and unique. After all, there might not be much point in a series of relationships with numerous members of a set of clones, when one of them 'would do just as well'--a phrase that will get a work-out later on in a different context.

wholly non-universalizable attitude?'. Notice, by the way, that an attitude which one took towards only one other, but utterly whimsically--that is, that one took *not* in virtue of some set of characteristics of the other but, say, in order to amuse oneself with the consequences of taking the attitude--could not, on the basis of that description, lead to similarly-based concerns about one's rationality. What appears to threaten our rationality as lovers is the *conjunction* of our loving *in virtue of* properties believed by us to be possessed by those loved, yet *refusing to extend* this most important of attitude-types towards others who admittedly have just the same (or relevantly similar) properties. If such refusal is detected in a less important attitude, e.g., in liking, or admiring, we are commonly and rightly open to criticism. How, then, can we be less open to correct criticism where a similar refusal is meted out in the case of a much more important attitude?

Perhaps another way of approaching the issue is to ask *what work* the phrase 'in virtue of' is doing when one owns that one loves S *in virtue of* her being $F_1 \ldots F_n$.

Suppose your S, as seems to be the case, wishes to defend the particularity of love, but concedes that even she loves you *in virtue of* some sub-set of your intra-worldly replicable properties. What work can 'in virtue of' be doing as S employs it? You challenge her to provide an account of that labour. She counters in this way: 'Well, if I were to have met someone other than you, but with those properties, I suppose I should have loved him (*instead of* loving you)'.[28] That is, she counters with a counterfactual.[29] Her understanding of the work of 'in virtue of' is that part of that work takes place in various counterfactual situations or 'possible worlds'. Your properties are important to her alright, so important that, instead of you, had she met someone else with just those characteristics, then, *ceteris paribus*, she would have loved him, i.e., she would have loved him in virtue of his possession of those same characteristics. She claims that there is, then, a sense in which love is 'universalizable' even for her. It is universalizable across various possible worlds, but not universalizable within the actual world (indeed, not universalizable within *any* possible world).

---

28. This could move you to inquire, somewhat gleefully, 'Ah yes, and he *would have done* just as well, then?'. But this, *too*, would be unfair--wouldn't it?

29. Roger Scruton, who appears to be more like S than S herself, seems not to allow even this limited sort of universalizability:

> "I am interested in this school because it is *my* school.... But we can envisage, here, a kind of counter-factual substitution. Had another school been mine, then it would have been an object of just this interest. ... As I shall argue, ...certain forms of love are characterised by the fact that even this counterfactual substitution is ruled out." [*Sexual Desire*, 1986, p. 81]

She also urges that (i) this sense of 'universalizability' is all that is necessary to establish her rationality in the matter, while allowing that (ii) perhaps she would be violating rational constraints if she judged that she loved you in virtue of your being F_1', ... F_n', but would not concede even that she would have loved someone else possessing the same characteristics had she met him instead of you. So she maintains that if rationality does require that an attitude held 'in virtue of...' cannot be wholly non-universalizable, then she has provided a kind of universalizability. It operates across possible worlds, but not within a world.

Developing something of a head of steam she goes on to claim that this alone provides for the possibility of specifically *personal* attitudes; and that if the universalizability-requirement were thought of as applying not only across possible worlds, but within the actual world as well, the consequent loss of such provision would be too great. Specifically 'personal' attitudes would no longer be possible. All attitudes would become like admiration, respect, liking, and so forth--admirable enough in their own way but less than fully satisfying.

She argues that this move allows for the possibility of a kind of commitment that is not *self*-limiting, thus further enriching the affective and behavioural world. The commitment of friendship is admirable, she says, but self-limiting. She asks, 'Can rationality really demand that all commitment be self-limiting, and that we live in a thus impoverished world?'; and concludes that her own perspective allows her the possibility of a *reason* for loving the one she loves, but allows her as well a reason for regarding that reason as having limited intra-world applicability.

Of course, even if you grant that there is something attractive about her perspective, you remain unconvinced by her argument. Perhaps you will begin your reply by questioning her central claim to having salvaged her *rationality* as lover with this move, pointing out that had she not allowed herself even this anemic species of 'universalizability', the constraints she would then have inevitably violated would have been better characterized as ones governing *intelligibility*. The intelligibility of her judgment that she loves you in *virtue of your* being F_1' ... F_n' may have been salvaged by her concession to this counterfactual 'universalizability', but the rationality of herself as lover remains under suspicion.

Doubtless, however, these are only opening salvos between you and S.

IV.

It would be good to produce a comprehensive and universally convincing solution to these difficulties, but the problems run too deep for that. The most we can reasonably hope for in what remains is that our discussion can be slightly advanced.

I want to return to the universalist's feeling that S has been unfair to him.

Some of what is behind this feeling has already come out in his soliloquy. But there is more. For our universalist is not specially likely to accept any of the metaphysical and evaluative perspectives that S attributes to him. For example, he is not likely to accept that for him, S is "*just* some 'place-holder of predicates'". Nor is he likely to accept the related charge that somebody else "will do just as well", that S is "replaceable". He believes he would experience her death as a loss, even if J were still about. And he supposes that it is really *she* 'in particular' that he loves. In general, then, he does not accept that: merely because he (i) loves her in virtue of her being $F_1, ... F_n$, and (ii) thinks that he is under a rational constraint, *ceteris paribus*, not to resist extending love to the similarly-propertied J, such awful consequences follow. We may imagine him fulminating as follows:

> It is as obvious to me as it is to anybody else that S is a ('particular'!) individual, plainly qualitatively different from J.[30] And it is this 'particular' individual, S, whom I love, not something else--"*just* some place-holder of predicates", or "exemplification", or whatever. If S were to contract a life-threatening illness, I would do everything I possibly could to see that her medical treatment was sufficient to save *her* ('particular'!) life. If I failed in this, *of course* I would experience her death as a loss. Universalists can grieve! Since I do not regard--and am not rationally constrained by any of my previous cognitive commitments to regard--S (in Bernard Williams' phrase) "*just* as" an $F_1, ... F_n$, as a *mere* instance of that kind, J (whom I also do not and need not regard as a *mere* instance of the kind) could never be a 'replacement' for S.
>
> After all, and importantly, *the situation in respect of these issues is no different than that prevailing between friends.* If I have two dear friends, each of whom I very much like in virtue of their both being (as it happens) $G_1, ... G_n$, and one of them dies, or so much as turns against me, I will feel keenly the loss of that particular friendship. Or anyhow, the mere fact of my being a universalist with respect to the attitude of liking is hardly sufficient to prevent me from feeling loss.

1. Universalizable Attitudes and Particular Objects:

It seems fair to say that S is operating under the assumption that if an attitude is universalizable, then it cannot be the case that the intentional object of such an attitude is an individual, *simpliciter*--that it must be that the object of a universalizable attitude is something rather more complex, something like "the individual *only as an* instance of a kind," where what happens in such a case is

---

30. That this is so--that is, that S and J are differently propertied, and observably (discernibly) so--is why the spectres of Leibniz and Goodman do *not* essentially haunt *this* discussion.

that "a *universal*...enters into [the] intentional object and provides the true object of attention".[31]

In brief, the rather curious idea appears to be that if an attitude is *universalizable*, then its object is in some way a *universal*!

S is not alone in operating under this kind of assumption. As is indicated by the foregoing citations, it is shared by Roger Scruton, who has also recently written (somewhat incoherently):

> If I feel contempt for James it is because of some feature of James: had William possessed that feature, I should have felt contempt for William as well. The object of contempt is the particular--James--as an instance of the universal (coward, selfish oaf or whatever). ... What I despise is James' cowardice or selfishness, and I would feel just the same towards anyone else who showed the same defect.[32]

The assumption is mistaken, however, and our universalist is quite right to object to its application to himself. Perhaps the manifest slippage (the 'to-ing and fro-ing') in the way Scruton, himself, seems forced to describe the object of the despisal is symptomatic of the problems there are with the assumption: for on the one hand the object is someone ("James", "William", "anyone else..."), but on the other hand the object is either someone "as an instance of [a] universal", thus, James as coward, or else (as Scruton also, and differently, suggests) someone's "cowardice".[33]

Of course, it *is* perfectly possible to despise some aspect of someone's character without 'following through' and despising the person him- or herself. After all, the person may have considerable, redeeming features. In such a case,

---

31. The quoted phrases are drawn from Scruton, *Sexual Desire*, p. 96. My italics.

32. *Sexual Desire*, 1986, p. 96. Compare his remarks on the same page about love, hatred and sexual desire:

> "Attitudes like love, hatred and sexual desire have particular objects. They impose on the subject no obligation to respond likewise on like occasions. Although there is, no doubt, some feature of James which is a reason (perhaps even *the* reason) why I love him, I am not obliged to love William as well, just because he shares that feature."

There is the strong suggestion in both this and the passage cited in the text that Scruton supposes that the particularity of the objects of love is possible only on condition that love is not universalizable.

33. *Cf.* Alan Soble's able discussion on pp. 225 *ff.* of his *The Structure of Love* (New Haven & London: Yale University Press, 1990), in which he demonstrates "the cost of conflating the basis and the object of love" in another writer.

we might say, 'Well, I don't despise James, you understand, but I do find his cowardice completely contemptible'. On the other hand, it is obviously just as possible to despise *James* (himself), in virtue of his cowardice. And here, it is not that I despise some complex, e.g., '*James as a coward*'. It is quite simply that I despise James. And this situation is untouched by my being a universalist.

2. *Universalizable Attitudes and Replaceability:*

The notion of the 'replaceability' of the object of an attitude is connected with the notion of the 'transferability'[34] of the attitude itself. This is most easily appreciated by attending to the bridging-role of the relationship marked out by the phrase, 'will/would do just as well'. If some intentional object, A, is replaceable by some other intentional object, B, without loss (from the point of view taken in the original intentional act), then B *will do just as well* as A. And if this is so, then the self-same intentional state can be redirected or transferred onto B. More exactly, what is claimed here is that the same intentional state, *relevantly characterised*, can be transferred from A to B. In the case of 'Nagel's omelette'[35], for example, what one wants (and what one accordingly orders) is *an* omelette. Given this usual starting point, omelette A (which I am about to devour, and which I want because I want *an* omelette and A is the one which has been placed before me) can be replaced by omelette B. For omelette B will do just as well as A. I am indifferent between A and B with respect to my originating want because that want is simply my want for *an* omelette. It is true that my derivative and subsequent desire for omelette A (once A has been placed in front of me) is not transferable to omelette B. Any subsequent desire for omelette B will be a different desire with respect to my earlier desire for omelette A. But the point is simply that my desire for *an* omelette *can* be transferred from A to B--given that B will do just as well as A, that is, given that A is replaceable by B.

Now, it is certainly true that the love of one person for another does not have this structure. Love is not a transferable attitude.[36] But if we supposed that love were universalizable, that would *not* commit us, S and Scruton to the

---

34. On transferability, see Robert Nozick, *Anarchy, State, and Utopia* (1974), pp. 167-8; T. Nagel, 'Sexual Perversion' in *Mortal Questions* (1979), C.U.P., p. 43; and Roger Scruton, *Sexual Desire*, pp. 103-107, esp. p. 104.

35. Nagel, 'Sexual Perversion', in his *Mortal Questions*, p. 43.

36. To say this is not to say that sexual desire is not (ever) transferable. See Alan Soble's discussion of omelettes and sexual desire on pp. 293-297 of his *The Structure of Love* (New Haven & London: Yale University Press, 1990).

contrary, to regarding love as a transferable attitude. For, as we noted at the very outset, there are other attitudes that are uncontentiously universalizable, and this does not commit us to regarding these other attitudes as transferable. Much earlier, for example, I wrote that "if Smith pities someone nearby in virtue of the fact that that person is malnourished, diseased, and a child, then *ceteris paribus*, as a rational being Smith pities others exhibiting just those features". But, accepting this, nobody would (nor should anybody) suppose that this means that pity is a transferable attitude. Your pity for one unfortunate child is not transferable to another child. No sense can be given to the idea that a second similarly unfortunate child 'would do just as well' with respect to your (genuine) pity. There is no way to understand the notion that the first child is 'replaceable' by a second in the case of your pity.

And this is because you do not ever pity, simply, *some* child or *a* child, in the way that you do sometimes desire, simply, *an* omelette. Instead, you always pity *that* child. (Necessarily, pity is 'definitely directed'. In another, related vocabulary, pity is always a *de re*, and never a *de dicto*, attitude.[37]) And, just as the universalizability of pity is not sufficient for the transferability of that attitude, neither would the (putative) universalizability of love be sufficient for love's transferability.

V.

I am inclined to think the universalist has got much the better of the argument over the non-universalist (the 'particularist') throughout the above discussion, and that the discussion shows universalists have available to them plausible analyses of what motivates particularist moves at several crucial points in the dialectic--analyses which show those motives to involve confusions of various sorts. I therefore conclude (for the time being) that love *is* universalizable, *i.e.*, that if someone loves someone else in virtue of lover-specifiable properties of the one loved, then the lover is under a rational constraint, *ceteris paribus, not* to resist any natural inclination he or she may have to extend the same attitude-type towards others having those properties.

Others may disagree with this, my principal, if tentative, conclusion, but any further argument will have to be taken up elsewhere. Before ending, however, I want to draw a practical corollary from this conclusion. It takes the

---

37. On the notion of the 'definitely directed', see D.W. Smith and R. McIntyre in *Husserl and Intentionality* (1982), Synthese Library, v. 154, D. Reidel, p. 18 and elsewhere. That all 'attitudes' (see the third footnote of this paper), including love, must be definitely directed, referring *de re*, and never *de dicto*, is a point I develop at some length in 'Emotion, Attitude, and Mind'.

form of a lesson for those who believe they are in S's social circumstance as that has been represented in this paper. To the extent that they come ultimately to agree with the logic of the universalist's position then, in my view, they are *themselves* under a constraint not to let their own jealousy get in the way of the newly developing loving relationship.

Why should this be? The matter is relatively simple. What they agree *to* (in one of its less guarded formulations) is that there is, for their lover, a *prima facie* rational constraint to love J as well. Now it may happen that the only thing standing in the way of the *prima facie* constraint becoming an absolute one is their own affectively-driven intransigence.[38] When we find that we are *this sort* of fly in an otherwise obligatory ointment then, as a general rule, we ought to do what we can--provided the emotional cost to ourselves is not too heavy--to cease occupying that role. True, if there is *nothing* we can do to cease being that which blocks the satisfaction of the *ceteris paribus* clause, then we are part of nature and that is that. But if this is not so, then we ought (again, if the cost to ourselves is not too great) to have regard to a point made earlier, viz., that

"...in the rational society, the society in which people (*especially* including S) do not needlessly make it difficult for one another to do *the otherwise rational thing*, the [lover's] constraint will verge on being an actual or absolute one."

Merely having regard to this point will not be sufficient to carry the argument through to the practical corollary. There are principles that require articulation and assent before such movement becomes rational. Their identification and arguments for them are, however, beyond the scope of this paper.

And, of course, S will not feel rationally compelled even to attempt vacating the role of fly-in-the-ointment unless she (or he) agrees in the end that the universalist has got the better of the argument in this paper.

---

38. I accept that 'intransigence' is not a sympathetic description of what they may be going through. Jealousy is not always an easy thing, and certainly not something that any sane person would will upon themselves. In that sense, it is a 'passion'. Nevertheless, it is something that is ordinarily subject to a certain degree of control after the fact. Arguments of the sort put forward in this paper may rationally motivate some people to control it.

Endnote

On loving her *for herself alone* (*cf.* footnote 22), compare Yeats' droll 'For Anne Gregory':

'Never shall a young man,
Thrown into despair
By those great honey-coloured
Ramparts at your ear,
Love you for yourself alone
And not your yellow hair.'

'But I can get a hair-dye
And set such colour there,
Brown, or black, or carrot,
That young men in despair
May love me for myself alone
And not my yellow hair.'

'I heard an old religious man
But yesternight declare
That he had found a text to prove
That only God, my dear,
Could love you for yourself alone
And not your yellow hair.'

Amelie Rorty ('The Historicity of Psychological Attitudes', *Midwest Studies in Philosophy* X, 1986), commenting on the yellow-haired woman's concern, suggests that it is about love's "constancy or endurance" (399). Equally (but entirely distinctly), it is about its exclusivity.

On the yellow-haired woman's desire that she be loved for herself alone, D. W. Hamlyn dryly remarks that "there is a good deal of difficulty in that idea". ['The Phenomena of Love and Hate', *Philosophy* 53 (1978), no. 203, p. 12.] As a universalist, you will, of course, agree with Hamlyn. There is, however, a sense of the phrase 'for herself alone' which *is* acceptable. This is the sense in which it means 'for *her* sake'--though even this rendering has to be heard in the right way for the acceptable sense to appear. We can detect the sense at work as early as Aristotle:

(A)   "...it is those who wish the good of their friends *for their friends' sake* who are friends in the fullest sense, since they love each other *for themselves* and not accidentally." [*N.E.* 1156B10-11, Rackham]

The necessary ethical (i.e. 'other-interested') context of this sense appears above, and is also plainly given later when Aristotle writes:

(B)   "They define a *philos* as one who wishes and acts for the good, or the apparent good, of one's *philos*, for the sake of one's lover; or as one who wishes for the existence and life of one's lover for that man's sake." (*N.E.* 1166A2-5, trans. Vlastos, in his 'The Individual as an Object of Love in Plato', *Platonic Studies*, 1981, p. 3)

Aristotle does not suppose that this means that the beloved's qualities are not the reason for the love (i.e., do not sustain it), for he immediately continues the earlier passage at 1156B11 by writing:

(A+)   "Hence the friendship of these lasts as long as they continue to be good; and virtue is an enduring quality."

Here, the possibility of (the beloved's) concern with the constant or enduring nature of love, mentioned above by Rorty, is intimated. For while human virtue is an enduring quality, it is certainly not essential for any individual, nor even for any temporal portion of some individual (e.g., the good man after he becomes good). Thus, in the *Categories* Aristotle writes:

"By a quality I mean that in virtue of which things are said to be qualified somehow. But quality is one of the things spoken of in a number of ways.

One kind of quality let us call states and conditions. A *state* differs from a condition in being *more* stable and lasting *longer*. Such are the branches of knowledge and *the virtues*. For knowledge seems to be something permanent and hard to change if one has even a moderate grasp of a branch of knowledge, unless a great change is brought about by illness or some other such thing. So also virtue; justice, temperance, and the rest seem to be not *easily* changed." [8 b, 25-35, trans. Ackrill. My italics.]

It should be clear, then, that the legitimacy of the ethical sense of the phrase 'for herself alone' (viz., 'for her sake', and compare the Kantian notion 'as an end in herself') does not in any way sanction the haecceitistic sense employed by Yeats' yellow-haired woman, and the latter sense should not be confused with the former. Equally, the legitimacy of the ethical employment of 'for her sake' would not sanction its haecceitistic employment.

- - -

Ancestors of this paper were presented to the Annual Conference of the Australasian Association of Philosophy (Melbourne, August 1986), the Annual Conference of the AAP - New Zealand Division (Auckland, August 1988), and to a departmental seminar at the University of Arizona (1992). I wish to thank participants at these various venues and especially Andre Gallois (Queensland) and Keith Lehrer (Arizona) for their assistance and encouragement. I would also like to thank Alan Soble of the University of New Orleans for kindly reading and usefully commenting on an earlier draft of this paper.

3

The Right Method of Boy-Loving

Deborah Brown

I: Introduction

According to Plato,

> when a man by the right method of boy-loving ascends from these particulars and begins to descry that beauty, he is almost able to lay hold of the final secret. Such is the right approach or induction to love matters. [Speech of Socrates, *Symposium*, 211b][1]

In other words, and in what my mother would probably say is good advice, the right method of boy-loving is to get over them as quickly as possible. The fact that individual-directed erotic love has, at best, instrumental value, is regarded by many as, to use a phrase of Gregory Vlastos, "the cardinal flaw" of Plato's account of eros.[2] It is true that there is something quite disconcerting about thinking of oneself or one's lover as a rung in the ladder to the Forms. Vlastos himself sees Plato's emphasis on properties rather than individuals as the objects of love as the source of his error. But it is not really individuals which are at stake in Plato's account. The Forms, after all, *are* particulars. It is *persons* who are neglected by Plato. Being loved as a rung is not being loved as a subject of experiences, attitudes, and desires in one's own right. I shall argue here that if the *point* of erotic love is to engage in a special kind of intersubjective relationship, then the ascent up the ladder of love cannot go beyond persons. In this

---

1. Plato, *Symposium*, W.R.M. Lamb, ed. & tr., (Cambridge, MA: Harvard University Press, 1953).

2. Gregory Vlastos, 'The Individual as an Object of Love in Plato', *Platonic Studies* (Princeton: Princeton University Press, 1973), p. 31.

49

framework, Platonic puzzles about the proper objects of love simply do not arise.

The notion of *reciprocity* will be crucial to my argument. Reciprocity has often been thought to be a definitive characteristic of love but to my knowledge there has been little attempt to use it in an argument for the individual-directedness of erotic love.[3] I propose to do just that and to argue that some interesting benefits follow from it. In particular, if we let the intersubjective dimension of love take care of the matter of whether or not love is or can be individual-directed, we are free to accept, in line with Plato, that what we are attracted by in others may well be general and repeatable properties.

My strategy for dealing with these issues will be to discuss three "remedies" to the cardinal flaw in Plato's analysis which either could or have been given: (1) a nominalist solution, (2) a functionalist solution, and (3) an economic solution. I shall try to convince you that the intersubjective analysis is superior to these.

II: A Nominalist Reply

Lois has gone and got engaged to Clark, despite what her Mother told her. *Never marry a Platonist*, she said. *Think of all the Forms you'll have to fill out, for one thing. Good thing he's a clerk, Dear.* 'Clark', Mother, is his *name. Whatever...do you love him?* He's kind and surprising and faster than the speed of light. *Oh my! Do you at least get time for a cigarette? Never mind. I asked*

---

3. The exception is, of course, Thomas Nagel's 'Sexual Perversion', in *Philosophy of Sex*, A. Soble, ed., (Totowa, NJ: Littlefield Adams, 1980), pp. 76-88 in which Nagel develops the Sartrean idea that eroticism involves the awakening of another's sexual awareness through their recognition of one's own arousal which, in turn, heightens one's own arousal. I think that Nagel's adoption of the Sartrean framework and the perceptual metaphor is unfortunate for the reason that there are all sorts of unpleasant situations, from the wolf-whistle to the rape, in which the effect of the perception of another's arousal is a heightened sense of one's own sexuality. A passage which Nagel, somewhat embarrassed at the "obscure language", quotes, shows Sartre to be, as always, the most extreme: "I make myself flesh in order to impel the Other to realize *for herself* and *for me* her own flesh, and my caresses cause my flesh to be born for me in so far as it is for the Other *flesh causing her to be born as flesh.*" (Sartre's italics.) [Jean-Paul Sartre, *Being and Nothingness*, H. E. Barnes, tr. & ed., (New York: Philosophical Library, 1956), p. 391.] Some of us want to resist continually being caused to be born as flesh. This is clearly not what Nagel has in mind; it is the mutual *desire* or the interdependency of arousal which Nagel wants to capture. But more has to be said and, as I shall argue below, in arguing for love as an essentially intersubjective relationship, one has to free oneself from the Sartrean paradigm if only to avoid the paradox of the mutual desire for possession.

you whether you love him and all you've done is list his desirable properties. Of course I love *him*, Silly. *Well, dear, I'm just concerned that if he was really the object of your love then he should be the relevant cause. But it doesn't look as if he is. If your love was caused by the presence of the properties you mention, such that were they not present you would not have fallen in love, then I fail to see how their being instantiated in Clark makes a difference. Surely, Dear, any old doppelgänger of Clark would have been just as good. In fact, if what you love are the properties themselves then there is a rational constraint on you to love them, time and energy permitting, whenever and wherever you encounter them. If you suddenly discovered that two people had stolen your car, you would be equally angry with each of them. It's only rational! Why shouldn't you be as consistent with potential lovers?* Mother, I must insist! It is Clark *and only* Clark whom I love! *Now, now, Dear, you don't really want to tell me that the non-qualitative identity of Clark was somehow causally relevant, do you? Nudity is one thing, Darling, but who could love a bare particular?*[4]

Is it Kryptonite for Lois and Clark? No: they always have the option of talking with their local Franciscan and converting to nominalism. Mother's conclusion about Clark's dispensability depends, in part, on her Platonist assumptions about properties. In particular, she assumes that a property instantiated in x and in y, where x and y are distinct individuals, is one and the same thing, a universal. If what Lois loves is a universal, P, then she shouldn't mind if, *ceteris paribus*, one bearer of P is substituted for the bearer of P to whom she is currently attached. Plato's conclusion just goes one step further than Lois' mother. On his view, at some point in one's intellectual and moral development, one should be able to dispense with an interest in particular bearers altogether.

But what if there is no one *thing* in two distinct individuals which Lois *could* love because there are no universals? And what if it makes no sense to talk of *transfers* of a property from one bearer to the next? In that case, it would make no sense to talk of a property Clark has as being possessed by another individual. A nominalist could simply deny that what is loved is a repeatable property. It doesn't matter whether we think of nominalism as committed to natural classes of particulars or to resemblance relations among particulars.[5] The point is that the nominalist could say that what Lois loves are *Clark's properties* or "tropes" which are, by their nature, particular and individuated by

---

4. The latter was pointed out to me (in conversation only, I swear!) by Paul Teller.

5. I have intentionally excluded predicate nominalism from consideration here. It is not clear that predicate nominalism is committed to the existence of properties at all rather than to *ways of describing* objects. To include it would therefore make the discussion of a nominalist solution to our puzzles unnecessarily complicated.

reference to Clark. So we cannot assume that had another individual with albeit *similar* properties substituted for Clark, he would have evoked Lois' erotic love.[6]

The nominalist account of love has another possible advantage. If Clark's properties provide Lois with her reasons for loving Clark, then she might be under no rational obligation to be promiscuous. If she says that it is *Clark's properties*, the description of which makes essential reference to Clark, which attract her, then she is not rationally required to love Universe Man just because he bears tropes resembling Clark's.

But Lois is uncomfortable with the nominalist reply because she does feel under a rational obligation to treat like cases alike and worries that her loyalty to Clark is just the product of the prevailing "family-values" of State Capitalism. Why *does* she love Clark-and-only-Clark and not Universe Man as well? She can't rationally say, for each attractive property of Clark, that she just loves *this*, not *that*, member of the same natural or resemblance class, can she? That doesn't seem like a *good* reason even if it is a minimal reason for her loyalty to Clark. She knows that she can't say that she loves Clark's properties *because* they are Clark's because that would presuppose what the nominalist is trying to establish - viz., her loving Clark. Lois' loving Clark is supposed to be *explained* by her loving his properties, not the other way round.

Well, what's to be done?

III: Functional Equivalents

Ronald de Sousa has observed that lovers want, despite the close connection between money and sex, to be unlike money in one important respect - that is, *non-fungible*.[7] One five-dollar bill is as good as the next but Alcmene *cared* that it was Zeus and not her beloved Amphitryon who snuck into her bed despite her inability to tell them apart. She didn't take imitators well and her caring is evidence of Amphitryon's non-fungibility. As we have seen, on the Platonic view, her caring is inexplicable. Some philosophers, notably, Robert Nozick

---

6. Amelie Oksenberg Rorty makes the point that we might be attracted to particular instantiations of a property rather than the property itself. See 'The Historicity of Psychological Attitudes: Love is Not Love Which Alters Not When It Alteration Finds', *Midwest Studies in Philosophy* 10 (1986), p. 402.

7. Ronald de Sousa, *The Rationality of Emotion* (Cambridge, MA: MIT Press, 1987), p. 98.

and Amelie Rorty[8], diagnose the Platonic puzzle as a failure to appreciate the *historicity* of erotic love. The Platonic account is particularly weak, for example, in explaining loyalty to an individual despite changes in their original love-inducing properties.

Robert Kraut has attempted to capture both the individual-directedness and the historicity of love by developing an account of what he calls love *de re*.[9] Love can be *de dicto*, he claims, but it need not be. Jane may love$_{de\ dicto}$ whomever is the greatest defender of the jungle in which case she may love Tarzan but she may not. No one may fit the description in which case she loves no one. Suppose, however, that Tarzan uniquely fits the description. In possible world talk, Jane loves Tarzan in the actual world but in another possible world she (or her counterpart) loves Zartan who uniquely fits her love-defining description in that world and who is an individual distinct from Tarzan. But if Jane loves$_{de\ re}$ Tarzan then (i) Tarzan exists in this world, (ii) Jane's love is for Tarzan and only Tarzan in worlds where he exists and (iii) Tarzan is the object of Jane's love$_{de\ re}$ in those worlds regardless of whether or not he uniquely fits any of the definite descriptions Jane associates with the object of her love. This has the following nice features. It accommodates love for another where one is completely deluded about the other's desirable (or lack of undesirable) properties. And it explains loyalty under conditions where the desirable properties of the other alter in significant ways. For Kraut, it is the *causal relationship* between individuals which primarily defines the object of love.

The question is, however: What determines whether a particular attitude of love is of the *de re* or the *de dicto* variety? Kraut offers a functional role analysis analogous to that offered in some theories of perception. The idea is that we can distinguish between these two types of love by considering the difference between the "typical inputs and typical outputs associated with each".[10] That, in turn, depends on the truth of certain counterfactuals. Sandra worries that Walt doesn't love her as an individual rather than as a placeholder for her musicianship. Kraut claims that the question of whether Walter loves Sandra *qua* individual or *qua* ivory-tickler depends on which of the following statements is true.

S1:   Walter is disposed to occupy occurrent states of affection that are such that (among other things) their typical causes involve Sandra and only Sandra.

---

8. See Amelie Oksenberg Rorty, 'The Historicity of Psychological Attitudes', and Robert Nozick, *Anarchy, State and Utopia* (New York: Basic Books, 1974), pp. 167-68.

9. Robert Kraut, 'Love *De Re*', *Midwest Studies in Philosophy* 10 (1986), pp. 413-430.

10. *Ibid.*, p. 419.

S2:   Walter is disposed to occupy occurrent states of affection that are such
        that (among other things) their typical causes involve the presence of (not
        only Sandra but) women of noteworthy musical skill.[11]

The truth of each of these depends on what Walt *would* do if given the opportunity, not just on what actually happens. What Sandra wants is that S1 be true, not
S2. She wants *herself* alone to be the "typical input". But in terms of Walter's
functional states, what would make S1 true and not S2? Must it be false that
Walter would be amorously disposed towards any person indiscernible from
Sandra? This requirement (Kraut's "D1") is too strong for, as Kraut acknowledges, it is unreasonable to hold that in order for Walter to love Sandra it must
not be the case that he would react amorously to any doppelgänger of hers.
More generally, it cannot be a requirement of individual-directed love that it
excludes the possibility of love for each of an indiscernible pair. Thus Kraut
concludes that a weaker requirement (his "D2") is all that needs to be met for
love to be individual-directed. This is the requirement that the loving relation
"doesn't automatically transfer from (object) o to any other (object) o', however
similar to o it might be".[12]
        Something like this last claim must be true. Sometimes love moves on;
sometimes it doesn't. But it is hardly sufficient to support S1. The weaker
requirement (D2) permits Walter to react amorously to Sandra and her indiscernible friends...or not. Which way Walter will go is not specified by the theory.
However, S1 and D2 together succeed in giving a much more fine-grained
characterization of the object of Walter's love than S2 (which was probably
conceived with Warren Beatty in mind.) More than likely, however, Sandra is
still going to be miffed by these results. She is not yet the sweet irreplaceable
object of Walt's affection. She's just lucky that doppelgängers are rare and she
doesn't think that it's better to be lucky than smart. What has gone wrong?
        The problem is that it is difficult for any functionalist-causal approach to
explain individual-directed attitudes for the simple reason that the causes of a
functionally defined state are necessarily defined relative to their *type* not their
individuality. In the functionalist school, intentional states are defined, as Kraut
acknowledges, in terms of their *typical* inputs and *typical* outputs. *Sandra and
only Sandra* cannot, however, be a *typical* cause of Walter's amorous feelings.
Even if there is only one actual cause of Walter's affection, namely Sandra, the
state so defined must be of the kind which at least *could* have more tokens of the
type to which Sandra belongs. This implies that S1 may only be a more fine-
grained way of individuating the type of object to which Walter is attracted than

---

11. Robert Kraut, 'Love *De Re*', *Midwest Studies in Philosophy* 10 (1986), p. 420.

12. *Ibid.*, p. 422.

is S2. But individuation by type is still individuation by properties. If one insists that S1 individuates *Sandra* as the cause of Walter's functional state, then it is not obvious that S1 is coherent. Sandra herself cannot be a *typical* cause because Sandra is an individual, not a type. And if S1 presupposes that Walter's attitude makes singular reference to Sandra, then it is not clear what work the functionalist analysis is doing. The solution to the Platonic puzzle of love is not to treat the beloved as a token. Tokens are, after all, paradigms of fungibility.

A non-functionalist, *etiological* causal analysis of love$_{de\ re}$ is better poised to solve Plato's puzzle. Could we say, for example, that Walter loves$_{de\ re}$ Sandra because she was the *historical* (not typical) cause of his amorous condition and that the causal relationship between them is what defines his attitude of love? This may not seem to help us with the question whether love takes an individual or properties for its object since both are in the causal history of Walter's erotic state. But if love was the kind of state *to be directed only at an individual*, the way a proper name for example takes an individual and only an individual as its referent, then perhaps identifying the historical cause is all we need to do. Kraut indeed proposes something along these lines when he offers a second analogy between love and linguistic devices for making singular reference. The analogy is based on Kripkean semantics for proper names - the so-called "picture" of "rigid designation".[13] As Kraut writes: "A proper name is committed to its bearer in much the same way that a lover is historically committed to the object of his love".[14]

Strictly speaking, however, the analogy cannot work quite this well. Rigid designators have specific modal properties which lack clear analogues in matters of the heart. In Kripkean semantics, a proper name, once fixed, *necessarily* designates the same object in every possible world in which the object exists and nothing else besides. This is the case regardless of whether or not the object satisfies a critical mass of the definite descriptions which are associated with the name. Love, on the other hand, is not so stalwart. It is not *necessary* that Walter love Sandra and only Sandra in every possible world in which she exists regardless of which descriptions are true of her. He may love her in worlds where she changes her hair colour but not in worlds where she takes up axe murdering. On the one hand, love seems less detachable from the descriptions which may originally "fix" its object than a proper name is. On the other hand, even where love does survive a radical redescription of the beloved, it is difficult to maintain that it does so from metaphysical, or any other kind, of necessity.

Kraut acknowledges that love may fail, as may the reference of a name, for

---

13. See Saul Kripke, *Naming and Necessity* (Cambridge, MA: Harvard University Press, 1972).

14. Kraut, 'Love *De Re*', *Midwest Studies in Philosophy* 10 (1986), p. 424.

"pragmatic" reasons.[15] I hold to the view that if Kripke is right, the failure rate for rigid designators is bound to be much lower than that for relationships. But the main problem is that since there is no explanation on Kraut's view of why anyone falls in love$_{de\ re}$ in the first place - love, he suggests, "often" precedes and "guides" favourable evaluations of the beloved's properties[16] - it is hard to see what explanation could be offered for why it fails when those evaluations change.

All that having been said, there is something intriguing about the idea that love is the *kind* of attitude which directs one individual towards another and that love may be akin to our capacity to make singular reference.[17] But in my view, it is the actual rather than counterfactual history of an attitude which is crucial for identifying the intentional object of love. This is an idea which Robert Nozick, whose "economic" solution I discuss next, seems also to endorse.

IV: Love at the Close of Trading

When we last saw Lois she had to admit that she loved Clark for his proper-ties and wasn't willing to say that the fact that they belonged to Clark was her reason for loving him. Suppose that Universe Man is actually better endowed than Superman as by definition perhaps he should be. Should Lois "trade up" if she gets the opportunity? Things are not always so simple. She's got to reason with some degree of uncertainty about what life with Universe Man will be like. Taking them both on as lovers may sour her relationships with both of them. And it's the 90's. One always has to reason under the assumption of scarcity. Just how many superheroes are there out there, anyway? Even if Plato is right and what we love are properties, there may be independent reasons for loyalty to an individual.

This is a crude form of the "economic solution" and it is somewhat unfair to align it with the approach Nozick offers. But his strategy is basically the same: Find some reasons for loyalty to an individual independent from questions about how your lover compares with what is available on the open market. He begins with the claim that love forms a 'we' and in a 'we' the boundaries of the self

---

15. Kraut, 'Love *De Re*', *Midwest Studies in Philosophy* 10 (1986), p. 425.

16. *Ibid.*, p. 416.

17. Ronald de Sousa argues for something stronger than an analogy. He claims that emotions which are directed towards individuals presuppose the capacity for singular reference and thus, he thinks, are restricted to linguistic creatures. See *The Rationality of Emotion*, pp. 97-100.

become blurred.[18] This is an idea reminiscent of certain passages in Aristotle's *Eudemian Ethics* related to friendship, Descartes' *Passions of the Soul* and Hegel's theological writings.[19] The common idea is that, in loving, one forms a new "unity" encompassing both the self and the other/s, a unity with which the self comes to identify. It follows from this, Nozick argues, that one should be no more willing to trade up and out of a 'we' than one is willing to "destroy the personal self one identifies with in order to allow another, possibly better, but discontinuous self to replace it".[20]

Despite having the seal of approval from innumerably many Hallmark cards, the view of the self which Nozick and his illustrious predecessors advocate is quite batty. The identity of the self cannot be *constituted* by its relations to others for, as Leibniz pointed out, relations are complexes which presuppose the identity of the simples which constitute them.[21] But that aside, the relational view of the self does not support Nozick's conservatism about love. One *should* be willing to "trade up", even if one does identify with a particular 'we' provided one recognizes a better unity lies ahead. Self-development is an obvious good. The fact that this would involve discontinuity

---

18. Robert Nozick, 'Love's Bond', in R. Solomon & K. Higgins, ed., *The Philosophy of Erotic Love* (Lawrence, KS: University of Kansas Press, 1991).

19. See Book VII, 1240b, Aristotle, *Eudemian Ethics*, J. Barnes, ed., (Oxford: Oxford University Press, 1982); sections 79-83 of Rene Descartes, *Passions of the Soul*, J. Cottingham, *et. al.* & tr., *The Philosophical Writings of Descartes*, vol. 1 (Cambridge: Cambridge University Press, 1985), pp. 356-58; and Hegel's 'On Love', in F. Hegel, *On Christianity: Early Theological Writings* (New York: Harper and Bros., 1948), pp. 302-308. Another contemporary defender of this view is Robert Solomon. See, in particular, *About Love* (Maryland: Rowman & Littlefield, 1994).

20. Nozick, 'Love's Bond', p. 424.

21. In *The Principles of Nature and of Grace* VIII.1., Leibniz writes:

Les composés ou les corps sont des Multitudes; et les substances simples, les Vies, les Ames, les Esprits sont des Unités. Et il faut bien qu'il y ait des substances simples par tout, parce que sans les simples il n'y auroit point de composés; et par consequent toute la nature est pleine de vie. (G.VI.598; L.406.)

See also the letter to Arnauld (April 30, 1687). There Leibniz describes aggregates as "modes of things" (*manière d'être*) and argues that a mode presupposes the substance of which it is a mode and which is not itself a mode. Aggregates have their unity "in our mind only, a unity founded on the relations or modes of true substances". [G.W. Leibniz, *Philosophical Essays*. D. Garber & R. Ariew, ed. & tr., (Cambridge: Hackett, 1989), p. 86.]

should not deter one from "destroying the personal self". After all, there is discontinuity and destruction whenever one *enters* a 'we' but this is presumably an acceptable cost.

It is not even obvious that discontinuity *is* one of the costs. That depends on the constitution of the 'we'. For example, if the 'we' is essentially a super-collection of the properties of the lovers, then replacing one chunk of properties in the 'we' with a better set of the same properties not only preserves the structure of the 'we' but enhances it. It would only be if the 'we' were *essentially* composed of individuals that substitutions in the 'we' would signify a loss in value. But economic forces typically do not recognize the value of *this* individual rather than *that* one - they select for general properties, caring little for haecceities. In any case, Nozick offers no metaphysical analysis about the nature of the 'we' and none appear forthcoming from the analysis of the net gains of staying versus playing.

Personally, I loathe being defined as a 'we' - I want a badge which says: I DON'T KNOW WHERE HE IS - which probably explains my antipathy towards this kind of analysis. Let's take a different tack.

V: Agency, Reciprocity and Particularity

Not everybody agrees that reciprocity should or can be central in character-izing erotic love.[22] That's too bad because appealing to the element of reciproc-ity facilitates our distinguishing erotic love from close relatives in the attitude family as well as from other emotions. For example, one way to distinguish *eros* from *agape* is by noticing that agape is perfectly compatible with the absence of a desire for reciprocity. It thus appropriately describes the love that parents have for children, friends for each other, or the love for or by a Deity. *Agape* might be loosely thought of as the attitude of being concerned for the welfare of another and not only is it compatible with the absence of a desire for reciprocity, it may, on occasion, warrant the sacrifice of such a desire. Kierkegäard claims to have broken his engagement to Regina Olsen from concern for her best interests. Perhaps our clearest model of the sacrifice of *eros* for the sake of *agape*, how-ever, is the fictional character, Sydney Carlton, in Dickens' *A Tale of Two*

---

22. Notable among such sceptics would be Plato himself since, for him, the highest form of love is love of the Good but the Good is not the sort of thing which reciprocates. As I have tried to argue, however, the good aspects of Plato's theory can be captured without supposing that the object of love is a property like goodness. Goodness can still motivate love even if what you love are persons. Of course, there is a sense in which we love generosity, etc., when we love the generous person but this seems to me to be a deriva-tive kind of love and not, strictly speaking, erotic love.

Cities. In any case, there is nothing *incomplete* in *agape* which is not reciprocated. God loves you even if you don't love him, according to the Christian tradition, and if you don't, He does not lack. But Alcibiades' love is frustrated and incomplete as long as Socrates prefers *philosophical* wrestling over the *sexual* kind.

I can't think of many other emotions which seek reciprocity and are incomplete without it. One may want those one envies to envy one as well, from spite or pride, but envy that is not reciprocated is still complete. This is not to say, however, that reciprocity is not a feature of other interpersonal relations. The altruist may reasonably expect that others will be likewise altruistic. As Amelie Rorty pointed out (in conversation), the notion of citizenship may presuppose reciprocity. Being a citizen is a state which involves certain legitimate expectations of similarity of attitudes and behaviour on the part of one's fellow citizens. Even if the desire for reciprocity is not, however, unique to erotic love, it can serve the following important function with respect to erotic love: the lack of reciprocity helps to explain how love can be *unrequited.* Erotic love that is defined as unrequited entails the (frustrated) desire for reciprocity. This is compatible, however, with its still being erotic love and with there being other kinds of love which do not seek reciprocity.

Now I think that reciprocity in erotic love is connected with the possibility of individual-directed love in the following way. The first step is to acknowledge that even if erotic love is motivated by an appreciation of another's properties, that is compatible with the *point* of love being something other than to accrue whatever benefits access to the other's properties bring. Love, I believe, is closer in teleological and intentional structure to *action* than to cognitive processes like perception. What I propose is that one possible *telos* of erotic love is reciprocity. Unrequited love is therefore analogous to incomplete action. Just as one can work obsessively on an article one never finishes, shoot at targets one never hits, so one can love a person who doesn't reciprocate.

The second thing to observe is that only individuals, and individuals of a certain kind, are capable of reciprocity. Properties are not. The kind of beings which can reciprocate are, of course, persons; beings which are capable of recognizing the desires and attitudes of others and responding sexually, emotionally and in other ways in order to satisfy those desires. An important part of erotic reciprocity is that, as a reciprocator, one does not just aim to satisfy the other's desires but one must also have desires the satisfaction of which depends on the other's sexual, emotional and other responses. This does not mean that reciprocity requires that the participants have the same kind of desires. If Martha wants Ruth to be cool and aloof so that she, Martha, gets to be the pursuer and Ruth wants Martha to be the pursuer and she, Ruth, the pursued, they'll both get what they want and it won't be the same thing.[23] But it seems to me that in these cases we can still talk of reciprocity for there is a kind of interdependency of desire and satisfaction and mutual recognition of the other as a site and source of erotic interest.

Reciprocity is not, however, just the requirement of *symmetry* but rather the requirement of the *intentionality* of the recipient of one's erotic attention.[24] The third step in the argument is to show how, in order for erotic love to be completed by reciprocity, it has to be an attitude which makes *singular reference* to an individual. In order for you to reciprocate with me, you have to be aware of my desires and aware, importantly, that they make reference to *you*. Otherwise, I may be longing for you and you for me and we are both miserable. So there are two points to notice about the role of reciprocity in love. One is that it is only in an individual's capacity as a subject, rather than as an object or bearer of properties, that he or she is capable of reciprocating. The other is that love is not just directed at some individual or other but at a *particular* individual. One will not reciprocate until one recognizes *oneself* as the object of the other's desire.

I now want to say a little more about what I mean by saying that love is *complete* when it is reciprocated and *incomplete* when it is unrequited. The sense of "complete" which I intend in this context is just the ordinary sense of completeness which attaches to actions when they have attained their goal. I think analogous problems concerning the particularity of the objects of desire arise for rather ordinary actions. Consider the action of my buying a house. I may begin the process by looking for the best exemplar of a certain type of house, by being attracted to certain general properties. However, at some point, the goal of my activity will become more and more narrowly defined. I go from wanting to buy *a* house to wanting to buy *this* house. If this didn't happen I would end up no better off than the poor sod to whom Walter Burleigh uttered: "Equus tibi promittitur" (A horse is promised to you). It is not clear exactly whether a promise as such was made since no *particular* horse was ever promised and so any horse you point to is not the horse you were promised. The speaker can thus easily weasel out of their "promise". But I digress.

With regard to my buying a house, we can say that once the money is paid and the deeds transferred, my action is complete. Perhaps I shall regret having chosen this one. Perhaps I shall "trade up" towards the Form of House. Perhaps I shall start sleeping around in other houses. The point, however, is that if I do these things it is not because my original action of buying this house rationally requires me to but because I still have a lingering more general desire. To someone who tells me I *should* always trade up, it is always up to me to say that

---

23. I am grateful to Eldon Soifer for pointing this out to me.

24. I am grateful to Roger Lamb for discussion on this issue.

I got what I wanted and that I prefer a complete action to one that, in principle, may never be complete.

I shall now say, briefly, why I think that the above proposal to emphasize the role of reciprocity in erotic love as a way of understanding how love may be individual-directed avoids the pitfalls of the alternative proposals with which I began this paper. It should be clear from what was just said that the account has advantages over Nozick's account. One does not have to rely on bizarre metaphysical views of personal identity or inflate the properties of one's current lover to rationally justify not trading up. It is not irrational to prefer a completeable action to an intrinsically incompleteable one.

In contrast with the Platonic view, there is no confusion about whether properties or individuals are the appropriate objects of erotic love. Of course, all that has been claimed is that *persons* are the appropriate objects of love and if a person could be composed of several individuals (which I don't think *is* metaphysically possible), then the account would fall short of showing that erotic love is necessarily *individual*-directed. That too would be fine on my view, however, for as I have stressed, the deep issue which Plato raises is not whether love is directed at individuals but whether it is directed at persons or subjects.

This view is also distinct from nominalism in that there is no need to identify unrepeatable and non-transferable properties to secure individuals as the objects of love. One does not need to claim an allegiance to *particular* instantiations of properties to justify one's love--a move which I argued wasn't very plausible anyway.

In contrast with Kraut's analysis, there is no need to deny or downplay the role that desirable properties play in supplying reasons for loving. Even if Walter's functional state can only be described in terms of S2 - he really is a suck for a good piano player and there is nothing unique about Sandra in regard to her most desirable property - this is compatible with his *really* loving Sandra and only Sandra. In falling in love with her, he desires reciprocity and in reciprocating, she loves and is loved as a person. None of this may prevent Walter from being a complete schmuck and taking off with the next piano player he meets. But this does not, I submit, alter the fact that he could still have loved Sandra as a person. Nothing can strip Sandra of her historical role in completing Walter's love. If Walter is promiscuous, however, we need not construe his promiscuity as what he is rationally required to do by virtue of his loving Sandra. There is nothing in his desire for Sandra to reciprocate that implies that he should pursue others. Whatever new relationships he forms are just that - *new* - and not parts of his activity of loving Sandra.

There are, however, some fairly familiar objections to the account which I have been developing and I shall finish with a short discussion of each. The most extreme form of scepticism about reciprocity in love is Jean-Paul Sartre's in *Being and Nothingness*. Sartre analyzes reciprocity in erotic love as the paradoxical mutual desire for possession; paradoxical, because the other can only reciprocate through being a subject and be possessed through being an object and the two are simultaneously incompatible. What each wants, according to Sartre, is to possess the Other as a subject, a consciousness, a freedom - in other words, an intrinsically non-possessable thing. "[H]ence the lover's perpetual dissatisfaction", said Sartre, putting it mildly for once.[25] On Sartre's analysis, erotic love which seeks reciprocity is literally impossible.

The weakness in Sartre's argument is in reducing reciprocity in erotic love to the mutual struggle for possession. There is no reason to think that reciprocity has anything *essentially* to do with possessiveness. *Historically*, Sartre is, to some extent, correct in interpreting erotic love as on a continuum with slavery in involving the desire for ownership of human property, though how mutual it was is a good question. Women have been treated as *chattel*, as property, as objects, and Sartre is right to point out how dissatisfying love is for all parties concerned under such circumstances. But it is a dangerous move to propose that the struggle for possession is not merely an historical construct imposed on sexual and intimate relations between people, but a *metaphysical* property of erotic love. It is at this point that I follow Simone de Beauvoir in the departure from Sartre.[26] We should be free, therefore, to imaginatively and practically construct non-oppressive, non-possessive models for reciprocity in erotic love.

A second objection concerns whether and to what extent the above account succeeds in accommodating love which endures when "it alteration finds", as the saying goes. *Prima facie*, the emphasis on reciprocity looks promising since the fact that someone is reciprocating love is itself a reason for staying in love when all else fails. Even if Jane comes to see that her beliefs about Tarzan's prowess in the jungle are all false - he really is just a B-grade movie actor in a fake-fur loincloth - still, Tarzan is an affectionate brute and loves Jane dearly. That, in itself, is not nothing and could explain why Jane continues to love him. But the truth is that this can't tackle the really hard cases of loyalty where reciprocity is not a possible end for desire.

I am disinclined, for example, to dismiss the claims of those who insist that they "still love" their partner despite the latter's being in a permanent coma or afflicted with such mentally debilitating diseases as Alzheimer's. Yet, it is clear that such persons are or may not be capable of reciprocating. Moreover, it

---

25. Sartre, *Being and Nothingness*, H. E. Barnes, tr. & ed., (New York: Philosophical Library, 1956), p. 377.

26. See Simone de Beauvoir, *The Second Sex*, H.M. Parshley, tr. & ed., (New York: Random House, 1952) and for an excellent discussion of de Beauvoir on love, see Kathryn Pauly Morgan, 'Romantic Love, Altruism and Self-Respect: An Analysis of Beauvoir', in *The Philosophy of Erotic Love*, Solomon & Higgins, eds., pp. 391-414.

should still be possible to regard this kind of love as individual-directed. I want to make two points about such cases.

The first is that these are the hardest cases for *any* theory of erotic love to make sense of. For they are cases which are hard to justify by reference to either properties, or economic reasons, or the beloved's capacity for reciprocity. What I think such cases show, and this is my second point, is that reciprocity in erotic love is *sufficient* but not necessary for love's being an individual-directed attitude or emotion. But it is enough, for my purposes, which have been to meet the Platonic challenge about the possibility and rationality of individual-directed erotic love, to have shown one way in which love is aimed at an individual subject. It is probably also true that the class of the erotic is wider than the class of the erotic involving the desire for reciprocity. Once again, the proposal here is quite modest. Appealing to reciprocity is one way to argue for individual-directed erotic love. It would be very surprising if it was the only way.

VI: The Happy Couple Meet a Happy Ending

Meanwhile, back at the *Daily Planet*, Lois and Clark are sorting their engagement presents and planning a yard sale. Lois thinks she has an answer to her Mother's question. There is more to *love* than property; *marriage*, she can't yet speak to. But there is no doubt that it is Clark to whom her attitude is directed for it is he who, in his capacity as a person, returns her love and thus makes it complete. *Besides, Mother, as anyone waiting outside a telephone booth will tell you, he's some snappy dresser!*

- - -

This project began over lunch and a discussion about reciprocal altruism among the vampire bats, *Desmodus rotundus*, with Mohan Matthen in the *Library* pub in Edmonton, Alberta - how, is another story - and I am very grateful to Mohan for our discussions about love then and since. Amelie Rorty pointed me towards the deep end but didn't push and thus helped me sort out some of the key issues in the paper. Paul Teller and Eldon Soifer made excellent and extensive written comments on earlier drafts and I have also benefited from conversations with Tom Hurka and my Gadget. The person I owe the most thanks to and many beers besides is the editor of this collection, Roger Lamb, whose suggestions led to many points being sharpened, many abandoned and without whom this would have been a lot longer. The institutions I owe most to are the Killam Trust for funding this and other projects, the University of Alberta for hosting me for two years and York University for generous leave.

4

Union, Autonomy, and Concern

Alan Soble

When two persons prove the Pythagorean theorem together, they are
for that moment undeniably one, seeing and thinking the same things.
They are really the same that moment in a way that persons are not in
any other kind of relationship.

Allan Bloom[1]

I.

A quite ordinary (and true) thought is that when x loves y, x wishes the best
for y and acts, as far as he or she is able, to pursue the good for y. But why is x,
the lover, concerned for y's well-being? How much is x concerned for y, or to
what extent is x concerned to help y flourish, if x loves y? These are interesting
questions and, if we love at all and want to understand what we are doing,
important ones.

Some things can be said about love's benevolent concern without much
fanfare. X's loving y is not incompatible with x's not sacrificing x's life in order
to secure a much less valuable good for y, although never sacrificing anything
for y's benefit likely negates x's claim to love y. If the only thing that x's
beloved y desires is that x have all x's desires satisfied, x will satisfy all y's
desires, as soon as he satisfies his own, but x will not necessarily be benefiting y
or pursuing y's good. And x as a lover will sometimes be divided between
seeking what y wants and seeking what x thinks is best for y. Here conflict
arises between y's autonomy and x's concern. For x to abide by y's autonomous
preferences is to jeopardize y's well-being; to pursue y's well-being might
violate y's status as a person. So, if respecting a person's autonomy is a moral

---

1. *Love and Friendship* (New York: Simon and Schuster, 1993), p. 418. Bloom is
explaining Montaigne's idea of the psychological union that occurs in love.

duty owed to anyone at all, x might find himself torn between the concern x has for y as a result of loving y and the concern x has for y, or should have, as a result of more general considerations.

I focus on the relationship between autonomy and concern, but not primarily in this sense. I am interested in ways the collapse of the difference between the lovers, the loss either of their numerical (or metaphysical) independence or their autonomy, undermines the benevolent concern of love, i.e., ways in which the autonomy of y is required for x's pursuing y's good.

II.

One philosophical view of love, which I call the *unity* or *union* view, claims that the core component of love is a physical, psychological, or spiritual union between the lovers in which they form a new entity, the *we*. Unity views have long existed:

> The man said, "This is now bone of my bones and flesh of my flesh; she shall be called 'woman', for she was taken out of man". For this reason a man will leave his father and mother and be united to his wife, and they will become one flesh.[2]

In the *Symposium*, Plato put a tragicomical version of the unity view into the mouth of Aristophanes; readers of the *Symposium* often recall little about the dialogue except Aristophanes's romantic story about two halves wanting to be welded together into the whole they had once been. Diotima contended that Aristophanes's unity view was misleading: "Love is not desire either of the half or of the whole", Diotima teaches Socrates, "unless that half or whole happens to be good" (*Symp.* 205e).[3] Plato himself, for whom generic love consisted of the desire to possess the good, advanced a unity view of love, in the sense that possessing some good, for Plato, involves the inclusion, either literal or metaphorical, of that goodness into one's self.

Montaigne, inspired by his friendship with Étienne de La Boétie, proffered a unity view in his famous essay on friendship, claiming that, in love, "each gives himself so entirely to his friend that he has nothing left to share with

---

2. *Genesis 2: 23-24.* See also *Matthew 19:6* and Paul: "Do you not know that the one who joins himself to a prostitute is one body with her?--for it says, 'The two will become one flesh'" (*1 Corinthians 6: 16*).

3. *Symposium*, tr. Walter Hamilton (New York: Penguin, 1951).

another".[4] He means that in giving himself totally to his one friend, he has nothing left that he might have given to another possible friend; all such friendships are now ruled out. Montaigne seems not to realize, or to care, that if he means "so entirely" seriously (and if not, his view of friendship becomes uninteresting), he would also have nothing left for *any* third party: there would be no kindness for the stranger and, more oddly, no benevolence for one's mother or child. Montaigne does acknowledge that if the lover gives himself "so entirely" to his beloved, he has nothing left for *himself*; friendship, on his view, entails the *loss* of self. So Aristotle complains that "one or both" of the lovers in Aristophanes's tale "would certainly perish" in satisfying their "desire to grow together".[5] Aristophanes, too, worried about their perishing: the rejoined halves wouldn't stop hugging long enough to eat and would die by starvation (*Symp.* 191b).

The problem of the loss of self in union-love was attacked by Kant:

[I]f I yield myself completely to another and obtain the person of the other in return, I win myself back; I have given myself up as the property of another, but in turn I take that other as my property, and so win myself back again in winning the person whose property I have become. In this way the two persons become a unity of will. Whatever good or ill, joy or sorrow befall either of them, the other will share in it.[6]

Hence *x*, in giving himself "so entirely" to *y* and thereby having nothing left for himself, is not left bereft of goods or self after all, as long as *y* also gives himself "so entirely" to *x*; then both *x* and *y* end up having both *x* and *y*. Montaigne had, in effect, already asserted this solution; about his relationship with La Boétie, he wrote: "we kept nothing back for ourselves: nothing was his or mine" (OAR, p. 212). For genuine friends, "everything is . . . common to them both: their wills, goods, wives, children, honour and lives" (OAR, p. 214). Not only are wives and children slighted as objects of concern, but they are goods to be shared.

Hegel, in much the same spirit as Montaigne, wrote: "love is indignant if

---

4. 'On Affectionate Relationships', in *The Essays of Michel de Montaigne*, tr. M. A. Screech (London, Eng.: Penguin, 1991), p. 215 (hereafter, "OAR").

5. *Politics*, Bk. II, Chap. 4, 1262b11-15 (tr. Benjamin Jowett, *Politics and Poetics* [Cleveland, Ohio: Fine Editions Press, 1952], p. 29; R. McKeon, ed., *The Basic Works of Aristotle* [New York: Random House, 1941], p. 1149).

6. *Lectures on Ethics*, tr. Louis Infeld (New York: Harper and Row, 1963), p. 167.

part of the individual is severed and held back".[7] In our day, the theologians
Paul Tillich and Karol Wojtyla (Pope John Paul II) have contributed their own
versions of the unity view of love; the psychoanalytic philosopher Erich Fromm
argued that love, as union, was the answer to the major problem of life (aloneness); the psychiatrist Willard Gaylin made union the central theme of his book
on love; and the secular analytic philosophers J. F. M. Hunter, Mark Fisher, and
Robert Nozick have proclaimed that a union, fusion, or merging of two beings
into one lies at the heart of love.[8]

There is another view of love, one which emphasizes the role in love of the
lover's benevolent care or concern for the well-being of the beloved. Plato
pointed out the power of love to cause us to perform virtuous acts, but he
recognized the concern feature of love in only an abbreviated way: the lover's
striving for The Good is deeply motivated by a desire for his own immortality,
ontological wholeness, and happiness. Thus Platonic *eros* is self-interested,
directed at the self and its good, even if Phaedrus's contribution to the *Symposium*, as well as Diotima's teaching Socrates that one effect of love was the
desire to beget on the beautiful (*Symp.* 206b-e), indicate that *eros* is not also, or
necessarily, selfish. The thesis that love incorporates benevolent concern for the
well-being of the beloved was more pivotal for Aristotle and Christianity. What
I will henceforth call "robust concern"--x desires for y that which is good for y, x
desires this for y's own sake, and x pursues y's good for y's benefit and not for
x's (a corollary: sometimes at possible loss to x)--is more characteristic of Aristotelian *philia* and Pauline *agape* (as described in *1 Corinthians 13*) than of
Platonic *eros*. I find it plausible that robust concern is, if not a conceptual
requirement of love, a common feature of personal love or, more weakly, at
least *possible* within love.

Can the unity view of love do justice to this intuition? Can love, understood as union, include Aristotelian robust concern for the well-being of the
beloved, or must it settle for Platonic self-interested concern? The union view

---

7. 'On Love', in *On Christianity: Early Theological Writings*, tr. T. M. Knox (New
York: Harper and Bros., 1948), pp. 302-308, at p. 306 (hereafter, 'OL').

8. Tillich, *Love, Power, and Justice* (New York: Oxford University Press, 1960);
Wojtyla, *Love and Responsibility* (New York: Farrar, Straus and Giroux, 1981), hereafter
'LAR'; Fromm, *The Art of Loving* (New York: Harper Perennial Library, 1974),
'TAOL'; Gaylin, *Rediscovering Love* (New York: Viking Penguin, 1986), 'RL'; Hunter,
Thinking About Sex and Love (New York: St. Martin's, 1980), 'TASL'; Fisher, 'Reason,
Emotion, and Love', *Inquiry 20* (1977): 189-203, and *Personal Love* (London, Eng.:
Duckworth, 1990), 'REL' and 'PL', respectively; and Nozick, 'Love's Bond', in *The
Examined Life* (New York: Simon and Schuster, 1989), pp. 68-86, 'LB'. Here is Tillich,
sounding much like Aristophanes: "Love in all its forms is the drive towards the reunion
of the separated" (p. 28).

apparently has only an odd answer to the question with which we began. Why is the lover concerned for the well-being of the beloved?--*because* the lover is concerned for himself, *and* his self, when he loves, includes the beloved. Thus Aquinas reads another piece of Paul, *Ephesians 5: 28-29*, as "teaching that . . . the love a man has for himself is the motive for the love he has for the wife who is united to him".[9] The explanation must dampen our enthusiasm for love; x's benevolent concern for y is just redescribed as a species of x's natural self-interest, x's concern for himself. I will argue that contemporary unity views of love similarly fail to make room for genuine concern.

III.

Let us begin with Hegel. When a child is born, it exists in complete triadic union with its parents. The child eventually separates psychologically from them, recognizing its own consciousness as it develops into an individual person. Later, the child achieves further independence by becoming financially separate or otherwise responsible for its own affairs and continued existence. From the thesis, the unity of parents and child, we arrive at the antithesis, the separation of the child from its parents (if not its outright opposition to and rebellion against them). But this separate individual is doomed to contribute to the eternal cycle: he or she meets another separate person of roughly the same age and station and they fall in love, in virtue of which they establish their own union. This reunion, the synthesis, is expanded and completely achieved, and we have gone full circle, when out of their love a child emerges.

Love "proper", says Hegel, is "true union" (OL, p. 304). "In love, life is present as a duplicate of itself and as a single and unified self" (OL, p. 305); the two lovers become a single *we*. Of what does this unity consist? "To say that the lovers have an independence . . . means *only* that they may die" separately (OL, p. 305; italics added). Hegelian lovers are unified except in the sense that, being physical creatures, they might not die at the same time and so one might live, disunified, without the other. Hegel apparently means this literally, for he asserts that "consciousness of a separate self disappears, and *all* distinction between the lovers is annulled" (OL, p. 307; italics added). The idea, that consciousness of oneself and the other as separate selves is altogether excluded by union, makes sense within Hegel's theory; after all, in the early stages of life, where Hegel also finds union, the infant (so guess our psychologists) has no consciousness of itself and its mother as distinct entities. But the suggestion that love destroys the consciousness of separate selves is implausible about adult

---

9. *Summa Theologiae* 2a2ae, question 26, article 11, reply 2.

persons who love each other and who normally do retain consciousness of themselves as distinct persons. Of course, all human relationships involve a trivial loss of our independent existence; whenever one person becomes closer to another person, both mutually gain beliefs from the other, or abandon beliefs, and both gain and lose options for behavior. This is ubiquitous in the human condition. But Hegel's loss of consciousness of the self and other as separate, the annulment of all distinction between the lovers, means that the independence of the lovers radically drops out of the picture.

Erich Fromm's union view is a variant of Hegel's. The young child "feels one with mother" in a "symbiotic union" (TAOL, pp. 8-9). Eventually the child separates, at which point the individual person begins to experience not just invigorating independence, but also its down side: aloneness and anxiety (TAOL, pp. 7-8). The "full" solution to this despair "lies [only] in the achievement of interpersonal union, of fusion with another person, in *love*" (TAOL, p. 15). Yet Fromm, as do other union theorists, wants to reserve space within love for the metaphysical integrity of the individual, and so claims that "love makes him overcome his sense of isolation and separateness, yet it permits him to be himself. . . . In love the paradox occurs that two beings become one and yet remain two" (TAOL, p. 17). But the task of the love-as-union theorist is to explain, as Fromm does not, how or in what sense it is possible that Two become One yet remain Two, without undercutting the love they have in virtue of being One. To call it the paradox of love is to shirk this responsibility.

Mark Fisher, a contemporary philosopher trained in the analytic tradition of clarity and good sense, also offers a unity view of love surprisingly similar to Hegel's. Fisher claims that one nuclear ingredient of love is the lovers' merging into a single entity: fusion is the ideal state, it is the lovers' goal, and it is at least partially, but substantially, achievable. As love develops, according to Fisher, the lover more and more comes to see the world, everything, through the eyes of the beloved, and so comes to share his or her beliefs and desires (REL, p. 196; PL, p. 27). As this process escalates, "the lover [can] less and less . . . distinguish his desires . . . and beliefs from her[s]" (PL, p. 26). The inability to distinguish these desires and beliefs is essential to Fisher's concept of fusion; it gives body to the unified *we* created in love out of two previously distinct individuals. Persons fused in love think so much in terms of "us" rather than "I" that, as a result, the lovers even "perceive, feel and act as a single person . . . [in that] . . . neither can say who originated" the perception, feeling or act (PL, p. 28). "The boundary between our two selves becomes vague and I do not know what in our thoughts and feelings is his and what is mine" (PL, p. 103). Montaigne agrees: "In the friendship which I am talking about, souls are mingled and confounded in so universal a blending that they efface the seam which joins them together so that it cannot be found"--not even by the lovers themselves (OAR, pp. 211-12). Fisher claims that fusion in this sense is both "familiar" and "not unusual" (PL, p. 28). Further, coitus between the lovers that culminates in simultaneous orgasm is, for Fisher, at the physical level "an effective analogue of the fused self" that occurs in love at the psychological level (PL, p. 59).[10] In Fisher's account of love, we find both the high romanticism of Aristophanes's physical welding of two into one and the dialectical mysteries of Hegel's loss of consciousness of separate selves.

I think that Fisherical fusion, in which I do not know whether I or my beloved first had the idea that we should get a pizza and then head for the concert, is chimerical; even in very close relationships, lovers know quite well to whom to attribute thoughts, beliefs, and desires. Fisher is serious about this loss of a noticeable seam being a central piece of the union that is love, both in practice and as an ideal.[11] I should have thought, however, that the inability of

---

10. Rollo May thinks that the key "moment" in sex-as-union is not orgasm but "the penetration of the erection of the man into the vagina of the woman". In Eros, "the two persons, longing, as all individuals do, to overcome the separateness and isolation to which we are all heir as individuals, can participate in a relationship that, for the moment, is not made up of two isolated, individual experiences, but a genuine union. A sharing takes place which is a new *Gestalt*, a new being, a new field of magnetic force" (*Love and Will* [New York: Norton, 1969], p. 75).

Another reply to Fisher, consistent with the spirit of my later remarks, might be: "Orgasm is not the ecstasy of the mystics, but a physical event. And we should rejoice that this is the case. How would two souls united in ecstasy express affection? If we will always be bodies, always separated from each other and from God by irreducible physical being, then we will always be able to love". These are the closing lines of Peter Gardella's *Innocent Ecstasy* (New York: Oxford University Press, 1985), p. 161.

11. Not only Fisher. In the Acknowledgements of *Rediscovering Love*, Willard Gaylin writes, "It is impossible to acknowledge my wife's contribution to this book". Why impossible?--because "in all things in my life, it is difficult to know where 'she' begins and 'I' leave off". This sentiment is perfectly consistent with Gaylin's unity view of love:

"The common ingredient of all love is the merging of the self with another person or ideal, creating a fused entity." [RL, p. 100]

"The fusion of two lovers, intensified over time, breaks down the barriers of the ego, fusing the separate senses of self into a common identity." [RL, pp. 20-21]

"The concept of fusion as I will use it literally means the loss of one's identity in that of another; a confusion of ego boundaries; *the sense of unsureness as to where I end and you, the person I love, begin.*" [RL, p. 103; italics added]

Gaylin's nonacknowledgement of his wife's contribution sounds on the surface very loving and appreciative, but it is empty. Gaylin claims that he and his wife are so close
...continuing...

lovers to know whose idea it was to get the pizza could be explained better as the effect of an aging, or merely inadequate, memory; or as a result of inattentiveness to detail; or perhaps such confusions reflect merely an indifference on the part of lovers as to whose great idea it was to get the pizza. There is little reason to think that the inability to know or remember such things, when it occurs in love, is due to the love itself (or to any fusion of identities that might take place in love)--unless, perhaps, memory defects and inattentiveness are characteristically intensified by love.[12] But the important point is that the inability to know whose idea it was to get a pizza, or, better, the lovers' coming to have the same beliefs and desires in Fisherical union, excludes their having an independent perspective on the world; it cancels cognitive autonomy. As a result, as I explain later (Section VI), robust concern is excluded from love.

Robert Nozick provides another account of the nature of the union that is love, one significant feature of which is similar to the psychological synthesis of Hegel and Fisher: "intimate bonds change the boundaries of the self" (LB, p. 73) as "each [person] becomes psychologically part of the other's identity" (LB, p. 72). "The intention in love is to form a *we* and to identify with it as an extended self", Nozick claims (LB, p. 78); "in [this] *we*, the people *share* an identity and do not simply each have identities that are enlarged" (LB, p. 82). Nozick draws this picture: "we might diagram the *we* as two figures with the boundary line between them erased where they come together. (Is that the traditional heart shape?)" (LB, p. 73).

Nozick also offers a version of Fisher's thesis that the lover sees "everything" through the eyes of the beloved: "the existence of the *we* can be very palpable. ... [One can] be with a loved person who is not physically present,

---

psychologically that Gaylin cannot pick out, from all his book's brilliant thoughts, any that he can specifically attribute to her. Thus he really cannot thank her. The reason Gaylin finds it "impossible" to acknowledge his wife's contribution is not that she, as an independent thinker, contributed so much, so often, and in so many ways that he has simply lost track of her contributions. I much prefer John Stuart Mill's dedication to Harriet Taylor in *On Liberty*: "Like all that I have written for many years, [this book] belongs as much to her as to me; but the work as it stands has had [because she is dead], in a very insufficient degree, the inestimable advantage of her revision". The fact that John and Harriet are not merged identities is that which makes her criticism of drafts of the book valuable and sought after by John. It also explains why John can express genuine gratitude for the advice and help she gave him.

12. "At the height of being in love the boundary between ego and object threatens to melt away. Against all the evidence of his senses, a man who is in love declares that 'I' and 'you' are one, and is prepared to behave as if it were a fact" (Freud, *Civilization and Its Discontents*, in *The Standard Edition* [London, Eng.: The Hogarth Press, 1953-1974], *Vol. 21*, p. 66).

[by] thinking what she would say, conversing with her, noticing things as she would, for her, because she is not there to notice, saying things to others that she would say, in her tone of voice, carrying the full *we* along" (LB, pp. 72-73). But conversing with *x*, hearing *x*'s voice, seeing things as *x* would see them (like gaining beliefs or desires from *x*) are ubiquitous in the human condition, hardly restricted to love. We hear each other's voices or take on each other's perspectives even when we would prefer not to, even, much to our displeasure, when we dislike each other. This happens as much with passing strangers and acquaintances as it does among partners (or enemies) of long standing. Thus Nozick has not picked out something special to love. Nozick also asserts, with Kant, that "marriage marks a full identification with [the] *we*", and he claims, with Hegel, that "the couple's first child is [also] their union" (LB, p. 85)--two chestnuts that receive no better philosophical support in "Love's Bond" than in Kant and Hegel. Nozick believes, finally, that some kind of concern for the beloved's welfare is an essential part of union and hence of love. I address this matter below (Section V). Here I want to discuss an issue that emerges from Nozick's description of union; my comments are meant to question his attempt to make room for the independence of the lovers within the union that is love.

When I read Fisher's *Personal Love* and noticed (1) its claim that the perceptions of one person are not distinguishable by the lovers from those of the other, (2) his candid admission that the union of love, in this sense, excluded the autonomy of the lovers (PL, p. 28), and (3) his judgment that the value of love offsets the disvalue of the loss of autonomy (PL, pp. 28, 65, 98), I could not help recall the gender studies of the sociologist Lillian Rubin.[13] In certain social strata of the United States, women conceive of love similarly to Fisher and find themselves giving up autonomy for the sake of intimacy; men, by contrast, tend to attenuate or jettison intimacy for the sake of maintaining their independence. Fisher's philosophical analysis of love, then, turns out to be a description of a feminine, rather than genderless, style of love. Or it might be a description of the way men, or society more generally, desire, expect, or encourage women to love.[14]

---

13. *Intimate Strangers* (New York: Harper and Row, 1983), pp. 65-97. See also Carol Gilligan, *In A Different Voice* (Cambridge, Mass.: Harvard University Press, 1982) and Nancy Chodorow, *The Reproduction of Mothering* (Berkeley, Calif.: University of California Press, 1978).

14. For an account of love that combines a philosophy of union ("fusion of egos", p. 149; also pp. 144-45) with a critique of contemporary gender relations ("men can't love", pp. 152, 153), see Shulamith Firestone, *The Dialectic of Sex* (New York: William Morrow, 1970). Elizabeth Rapaport provides commentary in 'On the Future of Love: Rousseau and the Radical Feminists', in Soble, ed., *Philosophy of Sex*, 1st edition (Totowa, N.J.: Littlefield, Adams, 1980), pp. 369-88.

Nozick is sensitive to this gender difference, but the way he acknowledges it seems inconsistent with his account of love. Nozick supposes that a person in a love relationship "can see the *we* as a very important *aspect* of itself, or it can see itself as part of the *we*, as contained within it. It may be that men more often take the former view, women the latter" (LB, p. 73).[15] Perhaps this difference is related to the fact that in our society men have more power than women, and so, since men and women do not enter union from the same place, they do not end up, within union, in the same place: the more powerful man emphasizes his self, of which the *we* is an aspect, while the less powerful woman emphasizes the *we*, of which her self is an aspect.[16] The important issue, for my purposes, is whether these two styles--seeing the *we* as an aspect of the self; seeing the self as an aspect of the *we*--are consistent with Nozick's model of love. I think a person's seeing his or her self as only an aspect of the *we*, as a part contained within the *we*, is consistent with his model, but a person's seeing the *we* merely as an aspect of the self, and the self as not contained in the *we*, is inconsistent with it. For Nozick, "the intention in love is to form a *we* and to identify with it as an extended self"; marriage involves "full identification" with the *we*. It seems possible to say only of the first person that he or she identifies with the *we* as an extended self. If there really is going to be a Nozickian union, the genuine formation of a *we* that both parties identify with, then both must see their selves as ontologically secondary to the *we*. Consider how Nozick contrasts the two psychological styles diagrammatically: "most men might draw the circle of themselves containing the circle of the *we* as an aspect *within* it, while most women might draw the circle of themselves within the circle of the *we*" (LB, pp. 73-74). Thus, what Nozick says about a lover who might desire to abandon one beloved for another, that "the willingness to trade up, to destroy the very *we* you largely identify with, would then be a willingness to destroy your self in the form of your own extended self" (LB, p. 78), would apply only to someone who loves in the woman's style, since for her to destroy the *we* is to destroy the extended self that she identifies with, while in the men's style the *we*, only a part within the self, can be plucked out and replaced without destroying the larger self. In the men's style, there seems not to be any extended self for the person to identify with; it excludes union and hence love.

The more general question is whether substantial fusion and substantial

---

15. Nozick's distinction between the man's and the woman's style is similar to Fromm's distinction (TAOL, p. 16) between active symbiotic union (sadism) and passive symbiotic union (masochism).

16. For Hegel, love is possible "only between living beings alike in power" (OL, p. 304). This makes it difficult to understand love between men and women within a patriarchal society.

independence can coexist. If love is "the desire to form an identity with the other", "a new joint identity" (LB, p. 74) that is "a new entity" (LB, p. 70),[17] how could there be room for one's own independent identity? Nozick alleges that in both the masculine and feminine styles, "the *we* need not consume an individual self or leave it without any autonomy" (LB, p. 74). I am not convinced. The self who sees itself as contained in the *we* sees itself as ontologically secondary to the *we*, its separate identity submerged into the larger extended *we* with which it identifies. ("[H]er whole identity hangs in the balance of her love life.")[18] The self that views the *we* as only an aspect of itself, by contrast, does retain independence, precisely because the self continues to identify with itself by remaining ontologically primary over the smaller, enclosed *we*. Simone de Beauvoir, after claiming that "the supreme goal of human love . . . is identification with the loved one", describes "the woman in love": she "tries to see with his eyes. . . . [W]hen she questions herself, it is his reply she tries to hear. . . . She uses his words, mimics his gestures".[19] This is Nozick's "carrying the full *we* along". De Beauvoir's description strongly suggests that carrying the *we* involves a substantial loss of self (by, for example, using *his* words). Nozick has therefore given us reason to deny that in love "the *we* need not consume an individual self". As Fromm did, Nozick merely asserts that in union Two are One yet remain Two, without providing cause for thinking so. His heart-shaped welded circles keep coming to mind, in which Two become a big One and Two do *not* remain. In a *we*, "the autonomy of the other and complete possession too are reconciled in the formation of a joint and wondrous enlarged identity for both" (LB, p. 74). How sweet. How easy to say. Why take it seriously? Nozick's speaking of the "wondrous" *we* that reconciles autonomy and possession is no improvement on Fromm's similar recourse to calling it the "paradox" of love.

Nozickian union has another ingredient: "people who form a *we* pool . . . their autonomy. They limit or curtail their own decision-making power and rights; some decisions can no longer be made alone" (LB, p. 71). Lovers replace unilateral decisions with joint decisions, which implies, for Nozick

---

17. In a footnote (LB, p. 73), Nozick wonders whether the *we* commits him to the existence of an "added" entity in the world; he writes as if he were worried about stuffing too much furniture into the universe. My claim is that he should have been worried, instead, about ending up with too few items in the universe.

18. Firestone, *The Dialectic of Sex* (New York: William Morrow, 1970), p. 149.

19. *The Second Sex*, tr. H. M. Parshley (New York: Bantam, 1961), pp. 613-14.

himself, a diminution, not really a "pooling", of autonomy.[20] Nozick says that unilateral decision-making power is not always given up; only *some* decisions "can no longer be made alone". This is supposed to leave room for autonomy within union. But which decisions can and cannot be made alone? For Aristophanes, lovers are of like mind to begin with, having descended from the same "whole" person, so no conflicts of opinion arise. Hegel and Fisher, who write about the annulment of all distinction and the lovers' common consciousness, do not have to answer the question; on their view love obliterates autonomy altogether. Nozick has to face the question squarely. About all he says, though, is: "somehow, decisions will be made together" by the persons in love (LB, p. 71). Perhaps what he has in mind is that only important decisions are to be made jointly; these are the ones concerning which the individuals cannot act unilaterally with autonomy.[21] This means that the lovers might have to abandon independence when it counts; it is no big deal to abandon the power to decide whether to get pizza or Chinese. The answer denies there might be some important matters regarding which one lover must decide without consulting the other. A procedure of alternating decision-making power does not adequately address the problem either. In this scheme, there are no joint decisions; two separate individuals decide in rotation for both, each distinct person exercising full autonomy in the back-and-forth fashion of a tennis game.

When discussing this issue, Nozick mentions that each person "needs the other to be . . . independent and nonsubservient. . . . Only someone who continues to possess a nonsubservient autonomy can be an apt partner in a joint identity that enlarges and enhances the individual one" (LB, p. 74). Nozick glosses

---

20. Nozick's idea of "pooling" autonomy is silly. What my wife and I "pool", beyond our material resources, are our talents, our skills or expertise in different domains. And regarding decisions made in these domains, we each retain the unilateral power we had before "pooling".

21. Nozick does claim (in a murky footnote) that at least one important decision cannot be made unilaterally--whether to end the relationship:

> This curtailment of unilateral decision-making rights extends even to a decision
> to end the romantic love relationship. This decision, if any, you would think you
> could make by yourself. . . . [B]ut in a love relationship the other party "has a
> vote". (LB, p. 71)

Is this decision joint in the sense that both must decide to end it or both must decide to keep it going? No. This is not what Nozick means. Instead, "the other party has [merely] a right to have his or her say, to try to repair" the relationship; the other party has no "permanent veto", but can expect only a postponement of a decision that will eventually be made without his or her "consent". This contradicts Nozick's claim that the party-to-be-jettisoned "has a vote".

over the problem here by emphasizing the joint identity that "enlarges and enhances" the individual identities, rather than the new identity that contains the individual identities. After all, Nozick says that "in a *we*, the people *share* an identity and do not simply each have identities that are enlarged" (LB, p. 82). Further, Nozick's claim that each needs the other to be nonsubservient is misleading, since some decisions are to be joint. In these cases, each quite needs the other to be subservient to the joint will and joint good of the unified *we*; otherwise the jointness of the decision loses its point. Given Nozick's distinction between a man's and a woman's relationship to the *we*, it follows that she will be more subservient to joint decisions than he. If we rule out the unlikely possibility that *x* and *y* agree about what to do in all important situations, it is unavoidable that in many decisions one person's view prevails; and there is plenty of reason to suppose that the person who sees the *we* as an aspect of the self will be in a better position to prevail, if not dominate, than the person, a more subservient type, who sees the self as an aspect of the *we*. A decision made jointly by both partners and to which both partners remain committed seems to be the appropriate sort of decision for Nozick's union model of love; but such decisions, which would seem to come most consistently from two feminine lovers, leaves no significant autonomy.

IV.

I have argued that on a union view of love, the lovers suffer a substantial loss of independence or autonomy. Later I will say more to support this claim. Now I want to argue that a loss of independence or autonomy excludes robust concern.

Consider a plausible attempt to make room for concern in a union model of love. Karol Wojtyla argues that because two *I*s merge into a single *we* that is the fused entity of love, "we can hardly speak of selfishness in this context" (LAR, p. 84). His idea is that if the persons remain separate, then there are two distinct foci of interest or well-being, in which case selfishness is logically possible (and, given Vaticanesque human psychology, likely); but when two lovers merge into a single entity, selfishness is logically ruled out, since a single entity cannot be selfish toward itself or treat itself selfishly. Hence (we might continue the argument) love as union, in ruling out selfishness, must contain genuine concern for the beloved.

The argument, however, supports the thesis that the loss of independence in union-love is incompatible with robust concern. If a union of two people into a single entity eliminates the possibility of their being selfish towards each other, it also eliminates the possibility of their having robust concern for each other.[22] In robust concern, x wishes y well for y's own sake, not for x's, and x acts accordingly to promote specifically y's well-being, not necessarily x's own. So if the lovers merge into a single entity, that fusion destroys the logical space for both selfishness and robust concern. If, as Hegel says, in love x and y form "a single and unified self" (OL, p. 305), then in love there is only one entity acting on its own behalf. We might try to imagine a single entity or person that wished itself well for its own sake, as a single person might respect himself. This concern aimed at one's self, however, is not robust; it is only self-interest. When x and y are joined by union, x can't promote y's good for y's sake because y has no good of her own that x could promote. Similarly, were x to (try to) sacrifice x's good for the sake of y, x could only be sacrificing the xy joint good for y's sake, not x's own good, since x no longer has any good of x's own that x could sacrifice. The logical possibility of self-sacrifice is also eliminated.

"The pleasure of the lover . . . is not selfish with respect to the loved one", writes Kierkegaard, who agrees with Wojtyla--until he continues, "but in union they are both absolutely selfish, inasmuch as . . . they constitute one self".[23] Their union eliminates one selfishness, only to replace it with another. "The more securely the two I's come together to become one I" [note how Kierkegaard uses "I" to refer to the *we*], the more in loving each other the lovers love only themselves. "The beloved [is] therefore called, . . . significantly enough, the *other-self*, the *other-I*."[24]

Kierkegaard's reply to Wojtyla is that the lovers' union is really *l'egoîsme à deux*. Lovers frequently do act selfishly toward the rest of the world in fostering

---

22. It also eliminates the *agape* that, according to Wojtyla, is supposed to be at the heart of conjugal love (LAR, p. 135). For discussion, see my *The Structure of Love* (New Haven, Conn.: Yale University Press, 1990), 213-14, 364 n. 30.

23. This is spoken by the Young Man in "The Banquet", *Stages on Life's Way* (Princeton, N.J.: Princeton University Press, 1945), p. 56.

24. *Works of Love* (New York: Harper and Row, 1962), p. 68. Aquinas distinguished between love as desire and love as friendship, which are "two different ways of considering the unity between the lover and the object loved. When one has love-of-desire for a thing, one sees it as contributing in some way to one's well-being. When one has love-as-friendship for a person, one wants good things for him as one does for oneself" (*Summa Theologiae* 1a2ae, q. 28, a. 1). Aquinas then mentions that in love-as-friendship, the beloved is "another self", "an other self". But there is a difference between Kierkegaard's use of "other self" to describe the beloved in romantic (passionate, desiring) love and Aquinas's use of it in love-as-friendship. Kierkegaard means that the two lovers have joined into one, so that they are the same self; Aquinas means that the beloved remains separate, is a different (an other) and distinct self (i.e., person).

their joint interests as a single "I", so the accusation has some point.[25] A person in love often, instead, sees the world rosily and behaves kindly toward it; this is one of the benefits to the rest of the world of the (otherwise insignificant) love between (the otherwise insignificant) x and y. But such kindness toward the world is inexplicable on a unity view; this might be Kierkegaard's point, that "in union they are both absolutely selfish". The concern of love, whatever form it happens to have (robust or not), is not entirely or even predominantly a moral phenomenon; in large part it is an *amoral* concern for the beloved that the lover has in virtue of being a lover.[26] If no one is under a moral obligation to *be* a lover, then no one is under an obligation to exhibit the concern of love toward anyone. Of course, in virtue of being in a love relationship with y, x might also have special moral obligations of concern toward y that supplement his concern for her based on his love. In any event, the amoral concern of love can conflict with the concern of morality itself, e.g., with duties of beneficence the lover might have toward anyone at all. "If you loved me, you would Q", demands x's beloved, where Q is something immoral that would benefit y. In this conflict, Montaigne sides with the amoral concern of love against general moral concern (OAR, pp. 212-13). This is the right choice given Montaigne's claim that the lover gives himself so wholly to the beloved that he has nothing left to give elsewhere. But union means not only that the lover must jettison duties toward others; nothing is left in the lover even for the simple kindness toward the world that often flows from love. Everything goes to the beloved, i.e., back to the lover, through their joined good.

Kierkegaard also points out that from the fact that the lovers have merged into a single self, the "I" consumed with self-love, it does not follow that they are selfish toward each other. What they are, though, is self-interested. When two persons merge into a single entity, they are concerned for each other's interests and for the interests of their fused entity, i.e., for their own enlarged interests; but self-interest is not necessarily selfishness. Wojtyla assures us that when love is union it excludes selfishness. But what he should be doing is trying to convince us that when love is union, it contains more than self-interest.

---

25. "[S]ympathetic characters, left uncultivated, and given up to their sympathetic instincts, are as selfish as others. The difference is in the *kind* of selfishness: theirs is not solitary but sympathetic selfishness; *l'egoïsme à deux, à trois*, or *à quatre*; and they may be very amiable and delightful to those with whom they sympathize, and grossly unjust and unfeeling to the rest of the world" (J. S. Mill, 'Nature', in *Three Essays on Religion* [New York: Greenwood Press, 1969], pp. 3-65, at p. 49).

26. Phaedrus, in the *Symposium*, recognizes the difference between x's doing well for y out of love for y (Alcestis's amoral concern of love) and x's doing so uninspired by love (Achilles's moral concern). He and the gods seem to prefer love-unmotivated goodness.

As far as his concept of union is concerned, x's concern for y is at best benevolent self-interest.

J. F. M. Hunter's secular version of the unity view (TASL, pp. 75-76) is no improvement over Wojtyla's. Love, for Hunter, involves "the wish to unite one's interests with those of another person". When two people love each other, they satisfy this wish together by each person's "treat[ing] the loved one's interests as if they were [his] own". When x takes on y's interests as his own, and *vice versa*, then x's interests become y's interests, y's interests become x's interests, and as a result (as in Montaigne) their interests are identical. In this union love, x will be concerned for y, and *vice versa*; the question is whether x's concern is robust or only benevolently self-interested. Because, on Hunter's view, y's interests have become x's interests, whenever x acts to promote y's interests x is *ipso facto* promoting his own. This promotion of their joint interests is not selfishness; yet x's concern for y does not reach the level of robust concern. In a love characterized by robust concern, x views the good of y as having intrinsic value. But in a union love, x views the good of y as intrinsically valuable only in a truncated sense. Since x treats the good of y as if it were his own good, x will have the same attitude toward y's good as he has toward his own, in which case y's good is intrinsically valuable for x only in the sense in which x's own good is intrinsically valuable for x. The good of y as x's beloved becomes a solipsistic intrinsic good, protected for the reason and in the manner x protects his own good, through x's natural self-interest. This is why Montaigne says

> for just as the friendly love I feel for myself is not increased . . . by any help I give myself in my need, and just as I feel no gratitude for any good turn I do to myself: so too the union of such friends . . . leads them to lose any awareness of such services, to hate . . . all terms . . . such as good turn, duty, gratitude, request, thanks and the like. . . . . [T]hey can neither lend nor give anything to each other. (OAR, p. 214)

Montaigne rejoices that Gaylin's "nonacknowledgement" of his wife's help is accurate (see footnote 11).

V.

What is interesting about Hunter's view is that he is, in effect, trying to reconcile union and concern by positing a union *of* concern, rather than by deriving the existence of concern in love from the union that love is supposed to be (Wojtyla's strategy). Hunter already builds concern for the well-being of the beloved into the nature of the union that is love. He does not build robust concern into union (that would beg *my* question), but only a sharing of interests. But this combination of union and concern is too weak to yield robust concern.

Nozick employs the same strategy. We have already seen two ingredients of his concept of union: the lovers alienate the right to make unilateral decisions and they form a joint psychological identity. The intention in love, however, is not only "to identify with [the *we*] as an extended self", but also "to identify one's fortunes in large part with its fortunes" (LB, p. 78). Thus a third ingredient of Nozickian union is that "your own well-being is tied up with [the well-being] of someone you love" (LB, p. 70). For Nozick, too, the union of love is a union *of* concern. What he means by the metaphor "tied up" is this. "When something bad happens to one you love, . . . something bad also happens *to you*" (LB, p. 68); *x*'s "well-being is affected . . . in the same direction" as *y*'s, so that "as the other [person] fares, so (to some extent) do you" (LB, p. 69).[27] This ingredient of union is apparently the most important for Nozick, for "the extension of your own well-being . . . is what marks all the different kinds of love" (LB, p. 69). "What is common to all love is this: your own well-being is tied up with that of someone (or something) you love" (LB, p. 68). Nozick's including "or something" is noteworthy: the fact that *x*'s well-being is tied to the well-being of *x*'s beloved, where that might be an inanimate thing, shows that the concern that is for him common to all love and an ingredient of union is not

---

27. Irving Singer discusses the unity view of love in his *The Nature of Love, Vol. 3: The Modern World* (Chicago, Ill.: University of Chicago Press, 1987; see pp. 406-417); here Singer criticizes the accounts of love of two authors I do not consider, Roger Scruton and Robert Solomon. In his recent *The Pursuit of Love* (Baltimore, Md.: Johns Hopkins University Press, 1994; hereafter "POL"), Singer extends his critique of Solomon. Singer's own view of love is somewhat confusing. On the one hand, his metaphor for love, which is supposed to illustrate how his view of love is not a union view, consists of two trees whose branches and leaves are intertwined: "In that image we may see the oneness that is love. There is no suggestion of a merging. . . . No absorption or loss of identity has occurred . . ." (POL, p. 27). On the other hand, some of Singer's description of love is close to Nozick's: "what harms or benefits one of the lovers will be experienced as something that harms or benefits the other as well. It is as if each defines his being in terms of what the other is, wants, believes, and represents" (POL, p. 29). At this point in his exposition, Singer characterizes love as "a pervasive interpenetration", which is more suggestive of union than his earlier characterization of love as an "interdependence" (POL, p. 26). In any event, neither "interpenetration" nor "interdependence" seem to fit his metaphor for love: two numerically distinct trees whose leaves and branches are intertwined. Such closely juxtaposed trees fight for the same sunlight and carbon dioxide and poison each other with oxygen; these trees do not symbolize "an intimate sharing of different selves and a beneficial interdependency" (POL, p. 27), for what harms/benefits one tree benefits/harms the other.

robust. We cannot have Aristotelian robust concern for things.[28] Hence Nozick does not beg my question.

Nevertheless, Nozick's account encounters the same problem as Hunter's. From the fact that x's well-being is tied to the well-being of y, or from the fact that as y fares, so fares x, it can be concluded only that x's concern for y is benevolently self-interested. If x's and y's interests are tied so securely together that whenever y's state of being improves (or deteriorates), x's own state of being "to some extent" likewise improves (or deteriorates), then love as union could not include robust concern. The joint, i.e., joined, fortunes of x and y do not leave any logical room for x's promoting y's good for y's own sake, independently of how such acts necessarily affect x's good. Nozick attempts to inject a higher quality of concern into love when he writes, "moreover, someone who loves you helps you with care and comfort to meet vicissitudes", but he acknowledges the thinness of this concern when he continues, "not out of self-ishness although her doing so does, in part, help maintain her own well-being too" (LB, p. 71). That x helps y with care and comfort is, of course, not necessarily selfishness; but we are given (as in Wojtyla) no reason to think it is robust concern, i.e., something beyond benevolent self-interest.

When Nozick is explaining of what the joint identity of lovers consists, he relies on an analogy with the merging of two businesses: "under some conditions it will be economically advantageous for two . . . trading firms to combine into *one* firm, with all allocations now becoming internal. Here at last we come to something like the notion of a joint identity" (LB, p. 78). After merging, the two previously separate financial identities are now both subsumed under a new joint financial identity (this union reflects the feminine style, not the masculine), and each firm gives up unilateral decisions in favor of joint decisions that determine their common economic fate. Nozick's analogy confirms my argument. When merging, two firms conduct a deal that is mutually beneficial, and even if their contract with each other is not necessarily selfish, it doesn't look like robust concern. The two firms are, in Aristotle's terms, useful for each other and for that reason joined together in a merger. After merging, there is literally only one entity in the world, not two; economic decisions will have to be joint, but there is no space for anything but the one (enlarged) entity's maximizing its own well-being. What is missing from Nozick's account of love, and required for distinguishing love from a business partnership, is robust concern.

---

28. "Love for a soulless thing is not called friendship, since there is no mutual loving, and you do not wish good to it. For it would presumably be ridiculous to wish good things to wine; the most you wish is its preservation so that you can have it. To a friend, however, it is said, you must wish goods for his own sake" (Aristotle, *Nicomachean Ethics*, 1155b30; tr. Terence Irwin [Indianapolis, Ind.: Hackett, 1985], p. 21).

From this ingredient of union, that the well-being of x is tied to the well-being of y, Nozick derives one of the other components of Nozickian union, the lovers' abandoning unilateral in favor of joint decisions. Because x's and y's well-beings are tied together and so vary in tandem, "decisions that importantly affect well-being, even if in the first instance primarily your own, will no longer be made alone" (LB, p. 71). This locution is odd. It would make sense for any lovers who had or retained their own independent goods. But once x fares in tandem with how y fares, to speak of a decision as "primarily" affecting how x fares is incoherent. A decision might affect the faring of one party first in a temporal sense, but if their well-beings are joined, this fact amounts to nothing. Here Nozick apparently holds on to his view, which I have disputed, that a lover in a Nozickian union might consider the *we* to be only an aspect of his self; a self that considers itself ontologically primary to the *we* will of course have interests that are primarily its own. But if in union, as in a business merger, both x and y view their selves as contained within the *we*, asserting that important decisions "primarily" affect either party is not possible.

Nozick in effect agrees, even if not explicitly, for what he has just said is that *these* decisions, which affect "in the first instance primarily" x's well-being, are nonetheless to be made jointly, quite because y is as importantly affected as x. Why is it that x is prohibited from making a unilateral decision about what temporally first affects x's good? Why must x consult y, as if resigning himself in such a case to a joint decision? The answer is that because x's and y's well-beings fare in tandem and are joined together, whatever x does that affects x's well-being will also affect y's; y must be consulted in order that y be in a position to protect her own (even if enlarged) interests. The requirement that decisions be made jointly does not flow from selfishness, nor from robust concern, but from self-interest.

In love, I take it, x at least sometimes gives up some of his own good in order to preserve or enhance y's good. The well-beings of the lovers *not* being joined together is logically necessary for x to exhibit this sacrificial concern for y. For x to sacrifice his good for the good of y requires that their interests are disjoint enough so that x's good does not always fare as y's fares, sometimes changing in the opposite direction. Hence Nozick's union of interests that fare in tandem excludes sacrificial concern. Since robust concern entails the possibility of sacrifice, and Nozickian union excludes self-sacrifice, union is incompatible with robust concern. Suppose x were to decrease his own good in order to increase y's. Then, because their fortunes are tied together in Nozickian union, and y's good has been increased, x's good is also increased, faring as y's fares. Hence, whenever x decreases his good to increase y's, x also increases his own good. So x didn't decrease his good after all. We should have seen this paradox coming as soon as we said "suppose that x decreases his own good in order to increase y's". If y's good fares as x's fares, then as soon as x decreases his own good, y's good is automatically decreased as well. Similarly, x's benefiting himself turns out to benefit y automatically, so giving to the other is easy. Perhaps this is why Montaigne claims that the friend who is receiving is the more generous of the two: "each of them . . . is seeking the good of the other, so that the one who furnishes the means and the occasion is in fact the more generous, since he gives his friend the joy of performing for him what he most desires" (OAR, p. 214; see Hegel, OL, p. 307).

Might a drop in x's well-being, tied to a rise in y's, be compatible with a union of interests, since in many cases a self-sacrificing x is maximizing the joint xy interest? Perhaps. But an *a priori* limit is being put on the sacrifice x can carry out. In maximizing the joint xy interest, x may not suffer a loss of well-being unless that is fully compensated (or more) by a corresponding rise in y's well-being. No room exists for x's magnanimously giving up more of his good than y will receive. The self-sacrifice that is apparently compatible with union is therefore stingy. Further, by squeezing the possibility of self-sacrifice into union in this way, we would also be squeezing the possibility of selfishness into union, by admitting a separation of interests that permits the good of one person to vary apart from the good of the other. If the maximization of the joint xy interest occasionally permits or even requires self-sacrifice on x's part, it would also permit or even require selfishness on x's part. In this selfishness, x may increase his own good at y's expense only if the increase in his good outweighs the decrease in hers so that their joint interest is maximized. Indeed, the difference between self-sacrifice and selfishness disappears.[29] Both involve a drop in one person's good and a rise in the good of the other; as soon as x and y see that any such arrangement maximizes their joint interest, they would both agree to it in a joint decision. That there is a requirement to sacrifice and a requirement to be selfish, in order to maximize the joint xy interest, shows that the sacrifice and selfishness are not genuine in union (the same way they are

---

29. Perhaps this is what Charles Fried has in mind when he claims that in reciprocal love there is a "mutual sharing of interests. . . . There is . . . a new pattern or system of interests which both [persons] share and both value. . . . In this way reciprocal love represents a kind of resolution of the paradoxes of self-interest and altruism" (*An Anatomy of Values* [Cambridge, Mass.: Harvard University Press, 1970], p. 79). John Hardwig puts a medico-psychological gloss on Fried's claim: "To have you as one of my ends is . . . to see you and the realization of your goals as part of me and the realization of my goals. In healthy intimate relationships, the . . . distinction between altruistic, moral regard for the ends of others and egoistic pursuit of my own ends fails because the distinction between egoism and altruism ultimately makes no sense in this context" ('Should Women Think in Terms of Rights?' *Ethics* 94 [1984], pp. 441-455, at pp. 445-446; see also p. 448). Hardwig speaks implicitly about a conflict within an unhealthy love relationship between "altruistic, moral regard" and "egoistic pursuit". These are not the items we have been dealing with: (i) the amoral benevolent concern of love, generated by love itself, and (ii) self-interest, which need not be selfish or "egoistic".

missing from some versions of utilitarianism). This whole line of thought is preposterous, however; if x's and y's interests are joined together, then it is impossible from the very start to speak about x's sacrificing his good for a good that is just y's, or of x's selfishly promoting his own good at the expense of y's, for the same reason it is impossible to speak of a good that is "primarily" x's or y's.

Nozick does claim that "the other's well-being--something you care about-- requires [the other's] nonsubservient autonomy" (LB, p. 74). This is true because, as I have urged, robust concern requires the lovers' independence. But it is not clear how or that the claim is consistent with Nozick's view of love, and Nozick makes no attempt to justify it or derive it from the ingredients of union. Is the idea that x's doing well for y requires y to have a nonsubservient view of her own independent good? That might be true, but it cannot be what Nozick means, for that would cancel the union of well-being itself.[30] Or is the idea that for joint decisions to be made intelligently, both parties must remain objective, i.e., detached from the values, perspective, and judgments of the other? That, too, might be true, but it cannot be what Nozick means, for that severely diminishes the extent of their joint psychological identity. Or is the idea that because autonomy is a good thing, part of a person's well-being, x will promote y's autonomy? That might also be true, but it leads to the paradoxical result that two persons subservient to the joint *we* will be promoting each other's nonsubservience.

This paradox is no joke; the fact that autonomy is part of a person's good creates difficulties for the unity view. Suppose that x loves y and cares about y's well-being, and suppose that autonomy is an important good. Then x will promote y's autonomy as an important part of y's well-being. But if x's concern for y exists in virtue of a union-love, their union itself sets limits on how far x may promote the autonomy of y. For example, x is prohibited from promoting y's autonomy if doing so would lead y to make decisions unilaterally about any matter that importantly affects their joint well-being. But it seems that *any* promotion of y's autonomy by x would have the consequence that y would more often make unilateral decisions; it seems unlikely that x could promote the

---

30. According to Robert N. Bellah and his colleagues (*Habits of the Heart* [New York: Harper and Row, 1985], pp. 92-93), some Americans believe that the "consequence of passively adapting to others' needs is that one becomes less valuable, less interesting, less desirable. . . . [L]osing a sense of who one is and what one wants can make one less attractive and less interesting. To be a person worth loving, one must assert one's individuality". This is the truth captured by Nozick's claim that lovers must remain nonsubservient. But Nozick's observation is incompatible with his unity view, in that (as Bellah continues) "not losing yourself has something to do with having a sense of your own interests, . . . a set of independent preferences and the will to pursue them".

autonomy of y in general without at the same time promoting y's autonomy to make decisions unilaterally. Thus if union requires abandoning the autonomy to make unilateral decisions, x cannot be concerned for an important part of y's good, namely, y's autonomy. Or x cannot be concerned about it without threatening their love itself. So Nozick's view also entails Fisher's conclusion that autonomy and love are incompatible.

When x loves y and is concerned for y's well-being, x need not promote y's autonomy at the expense of everything else. If x is concerned for y's well-being, x will promote y's autonomy unless doing so conflicts with providing other components of y's well-being (happiness, health) that might be more important for y's overall well-being. This presupposes an independence of y's good that is incompatible with union; if love is union, x's promoting y's autonomy will be limited not by what is good overall for y, but more precisely by what is good for the joint xy well-being. This consequence is one of the least palatable implications of the unity view. The point emerges most sharply when we ask: when x loves y, and x is concerned for the well-being of y, will x promote y's autonomy even at the expense of the love relationship itself? If x's concern is robust, the answer is "perhaps"; in attempting to promote y's good and hence y's autonomy, x might have to jettison their love.

But if love is union, x cannot jettison their love for the sake of y's autonomy. Nozick claims that x will not leave his beloved y for some other potential beloved z, because x's doing so would destroy x (or x's identity) by destroying the joint xy identity (LB, p. 78). The point is not that x will not promote y's autonomy because x out of selfishness wants their love to continue. Still, x's not wanting to destroy his own identity is self-interested; x to save himself cannot let go. Further, x will not promote y's autonomy, if that would lead to the death of their love, for another reason: if the death of their love would destroy x, it would similarly destroy y. So x must not promote y's autonomy, if that would lead to the death of their love, because that would destroy y herself by destroying the joint xy identity she largely identifies with. If love is union, and hence identities are securely tied together psychologically, the weighing of goods is such that the value of y's (or x's) autonomy takes second place to the value to y of their love itself. Indeed, x logically cannot end their love if continuing it would more likely destroy y than ending it--such a case could never arise. To the contrary, I should think, at least sometimes y would be better off giving up their love; and it would be merely *ad hoc* to respond that in such devastating circumstances there is no love in the first place that could be abandoned.

VI.

I have been arguing that robust concern and union are incompatible. Deriving robust concern from union, which would demonstrate their compatibility, does not work; the derivation won't go through even when some concern is already packed into union. But there is another strategy open to a proponent of the unity view: not to derive concern from union, but union from concern. In fact, Mark Fisher argues both that the union that is love is derivable from the concern of love, and that union and concern, together, are the fine gold thread of love (PL, p. 97).

We have seen that, for Fisher, two persons who love each other form a union, or are "fused", in the sense that x comes to see the world from y's perspective and y comes to see the world from x's perspective, eventually both seeing the world from the perspective of the single cognitive entity they have become. Further, the feelings and judgments of one person are indistinguishable from those of the other, neither x nor y being able to tell in which person these states originate. Thus the fused lovers can only "seek the good of that single self" (PL, p. 70) they have become; their cognitive unity means that they think only in terms of "us and our concerns" (PL, p. 44). At least this is Fisher's ideal state, substantially even if not perfectly achievable, and something lovers seek (PL, pp. 26-28, 60).

Fisher's account of union is half his theory; the other half is the concern ingredient of his model. When x loves y, on Fisher's view, x wants for y whatever y wants; x desires for y whatever y desires; and x pursues y's good in y's own sense of that good. Fisher calls this concern "humble benevolence", because it is the object of love, y the beloved, who determines the specifics or the content of x's concern, not the lover x himself.[31] We can think of humble benevolence as a respectful sort of concern, for it says to the beloved: I assume you are clear-headed and reflective enough to know what is good for you; whatever you have decided is good for you and hence want, to that I devote myself; I will not impose on you my own ideas of what is good. Thus the humble benevolence that constitutes love excludes "paternalistic benevolence".

Fisher's humble benevolence can be robust. The reason that x desires for y whatever y desires is simply that y desires it; x wants the good for y just for y's sake, x's own good playing no role. Both "to desire her good . . . as she sees it" (PL, p. 20) and to "desire . . . the beloved's good *for her sake*" (PL, p. 19) is for the lover to recognize the independent well-being of his beloved.[32] Further,

---

31. In his early REL, Fisher declared humble benevolence by itself to be the defining feature of love: "my fundamental thought is that to love someone is to desire whatever he desires for the reason that he desires it" (REL, p. 196). In his later *Personal Love*, Fisher proposes that both fusion and humble benevolence constitute love.

32. There can be robust humble concern, in which x pursues for y her independent good for her sake, according to her own notion of that good; there can be robust paternalistic concern, in which x pursues for y her independent good for her sake in x's sense of that

...continuing...

humble benevolence, because it wants for the beloved just what the beloved decides she wants, respects the beloved's sense of her own good and thereby acknowledges the beloved's autonomy. The beloved *y* has her own values and perspective on the world that give direction to *x*'s pursuit of *y*'s good. Fisher's view of love therefore looks promising. The problem is that Fisher thinks he can get away with tacking fusion, which negates the autonomy of the beloved, onto humble benevolence, which presupposes the beloved's autonomy.

On Fisher's view, humble benevolence causally generates fusion. How so? (See PL, pp. 24-29.) In order for *x* to desire whatever *y* desires just because *y* desires it, *x* must come to value whatever it is that *y* desires; *x* must make *y*'s ends his own. "I come to see that what you desire or value is indeed desirable or valuable" (PL, p. 29). For *x* to desire *y*'s good in *y*'s sense of that good, *x* must take on *y*'s view of the world, which includes her values. More specifically, in order to view *y*'s ends as desirable, *x* must not merely be able to identify with *y*'s perspective, but must actually assimilate his own perspective to *y*'s. "I come to absorb your conception of your good" (PL, p. 26); "I will tend to absorb not only your desires but your concepts, beliefs, attitudes, conceptions, emotions and sentiments" (PL, p. 27). Thus, for Fisher, a necessary condition of *x*'s fulfilling humble benevolence toward *y* is that *x* incorporate, as his own, *y*'s values and judgments; *x* must *have* the desires of *y*. If *x*'s love for *y* is not reciprocated, *x* will assimilate his judgments to *y*'s, while *y* remains aloof, not bothering to look at the world from *x*'s earlier and own perspective; in this case, only a one-sided assimilation occurs, in which the lover, but not the beloved, has slavishly surrendered his autonomy (PL, pp. 29, 38)--*x* truly perishes into *y*. In reciprocal love, in which *y* also has humble benevolence toward *x*, *y* will take on *x*'s view of the world in tandem with *x*'s taking on *y*'s view of the world. As this mutual assimilation progresses, the lovers form a single cognitive entity; they can eventually no longer differentiate their perceptions and judgments. Their mutual humble benevolence has generated fusion.

In this derivation of union from humble benevolence, the weak link is Fisher's claim that *x* must cognitively incorporate, "absorb", *y*'s values.[33] It is far from obvious that *x*'s wanting to promote *y*'s good in *y*'s sense, purely for *y*'s sake, commits *x* to coming to agree with *y* that the values that inform *y*'s sense of her good are either decent or correct. The lover *x* need only compre-

---

good; and Aristotelian robust concern, in which *x* pursues for *y* her independent good for her sake in some objective sense of her good. Robust humble concern and robust paternalistic concern will be Aristotelian robust concern precisely when *y*'s view of *y*'s good, or *x*'s view, respectively, is the same as what is objectively good for *y*.

33. See *The Structure of Love*, pp. 268-273, and my review of *Personal Love*, in *Canadian Philosophical Reviews* 12, #1 (1992): 24-25.

hend or acknowledge *that* these are y's values. Nothing in x's wanting to promote y's good in y's sense necessitates that x must believe what y believes simply as a result of loving her and caring about her well-being. I see no prospect of establishing the strong claim that x could not desire for y what y desires unless x had her desires--not numerically the same, but desires qualitatively indistinguishable from y's. If so, the derivation of fusion from mutual humble benevolence fails.

Further, I am not convinced that when x loves y, x's concern will be only humble, that it will be directed at securing y's good only in y's sense of that good. Sometimes x will be at least divided between doing well for y in y's sense and paternalistically doing well for y in x's sense of her good, if what y wants is, in x's view, bad for y. Fisher's view entails that if x promotes y's good in x's contrary sense of that good, or even if x feels strongly pulled in the direction of wanting to do for y what x believes is better for y, that would bring into doubt, if not nullify altogether, x's love for y. (See PL, pp. 19-20, 25-27, 33-34, 35, 81.) It seems perverse that x's love for y is so easily discredited by x's sometimes acting on the thought that x knows better than y what is good for y. No such problem arises for Aristotle. Since genuine *philia* occurs only among those who are virtuous, the lovers already agree as to what is good, *simpliciter*. They agree on what is good for each other not because they are lovers or because they have fused, but because each has a firm grasp on what is objectively good. They are, like the severed halves in Aristophanes's myth (but for a quite different reason), prior to their love already of one mind. By contrast, the loves of mere mortals are frequently visited by an emotional tension caused by a conflict between humble and paternalistic benevolence. Fisher's account does not allow that this tension occurs *within* love; it is for him, instead, a symptom of the failure of love.[34]

Let us grant that humble benevolence is a central feature of love and that the derivation of Fisherical union from humble benevolence goes through. Still, Fisher's account gets caught in the paradoxes that are typical of union views of love. When x and y love each other, x desires and promotes y's good in y's sense of her good, and y desires and promotes x's good in x's sense of his good. As fusion grows, x takes on y's values and view of the world and y takes on x's values and view of the world. But if assimilation, and therefore fusion, is to be substantial, x will be taking on, as his own view of what is good for x, y's own view of what is good for x, and similarly y will be taking on, as her view, x's own view of what is good for y--these views of what is good for the other are part of each's perspective on the world they are assimilating. Thus in the devel-

---

34. "As the process of love goes into reverse I cease to want the other's good as she sees it, but may perhaps, if the reversal does not proceed too far, continue to want her good as *I* see it" (PL, pp. 33-34).

opment of fusion from humble benevolence, x will at some point be promoting y's good in y's sense of y's good, but *that* sense has changed (by y's absorbing x's view) into x's sense of y's good, in which case x will be promoting y's good in x's (own and original) sense of y's good. Through fusion, humble concern transforms itself into paternalistic concern, the kind of concern Fisher claims is absent from love.

Through repeated iterations of taking on each other's views, both x and y end up having both x's and y's views (the same way in which each of Hunter's lovers ends up having the interests of both). Modifications will be required to make the larger set held by both x and y internally consistent; but through repeated iterations, x and y should end up making the same modifications. Thus, as fusion develops, their values and views of the world mutually influence and approach each other's; two independent worldviews coalesce into a single, "indistinguishable" joint view. But if x now desires and promotes y's good in x's and y's joint sense of that good, then in virtue of this cognitive fusion x's concern is both humble and paternalistic benevolence at the same time. Or, better, it is neither; the distinction between humble and paternalistic benevolence has collapsed. In this sense, the lovers' humble benevolence has been destroyed by the very fusion it created. It is not quite right, then, for Fisher to assert that "love involves the development of a fused self through the growth of humble benevolence" (PL, pp. 30; see 98). Indeed, it is an odd result that one of the two central constituents of love disappears when the other constituent, fusion, is its deepest.

Even though the concern that remains in fusion cannot be humble or paternalistic, could it be robust? I think not. The process that conflates humble and paternalistic benevolence is the same process that replaces x's seeking y's good with x's seeking the joint good of the fused item xy. If the lovers are fused, independent judgments about their respective goods are replaced by joint judgments about their joint good. Not only have their views of their goods merged, but (as in Montaigne and Hunter) their goods themselves have merged. When consciousness of separate selves recedes, thoughts about x's and y's own goods are replaced by thoughts about *our* good, the good of the *we*. The robust concern that existed at the beginning of their love has not been maintained but has degenerated, via fusion, into the benevolent self-interest of an enlarged self. Fisher's theory now looks Hegelian: mutual robust humble concern, which exists at the beginning of love and presupposes the cognitive autonomy and independent good of the lover and beloved, leads to fusion, the deepening of their love, which in turn destroys both autonomy and robust concern.

VII.

Aristophanes cannot be right that what lovers want more than anything else is to be welded together. We undergo the difficult process, we take on the task, of separating ourselves from our parents and other powerful significant others precisely in order to become our own persons. Why would we want to forsake the fruit of that onerous and exhausting labor by establishing ourselves once again within a union. Why would we want to "pool" that hard-gained autonomy with the autonomy of someone else, thereby effectively abandoning our prize?[35] If women in our culture have more difficulty than men individuating themselves from Mother, and so achieve whatever autonomy they do achieve more painfully, why should they be so willing to throw it away? Why, then, bother to love, and why encourage others to love, especially when in union-love there is no genuine benevolent concern in the love itself? We cannot procure even that consolation for the loss of autonomy.

Montaigne is, as always, quite blunt, admitting that in a union-love genuine benevolence is absent. Further, love *qua* union has no power to transport us out of ourselves: when x gives x to y and then receives himself back from y, x has merely been wedded to himself in a narcissistic "circulation of capital". Love loses its "magnifying" effect. Love as a school of virtue is missing from the union view of love, for in union-love there are not two persons genuinely concerned for each other but only one enlarged person caring for itself. What exists is just a bigger person, a person no more and no less benevolent and giving than were the two individuals who existed before they merged together. *No less* benevolent? Even that's false, if we take Montaigne literally; the stranger, his mother, his wife, his child can all be damned for the sake of his love, i.e., for himself.

The thrust of my argument is that union and robust concern are incompatible, and hence no theory of love can combine them. If robust concern is possible in personal love (even if not, more strongly, a conceptual requirement), the unity view, as a general account of *a* (or *the*) defining feature of love, must be false. Any instance of love in which a Hunterish or Nozickian or Fisherical union is a paramount feature cannot include robust concern; such lovers will be deluding themselves if they think otherwise. We might bemoan the loss of robust concern and not find love to have much value if this is the price we have to pay for it. Or we could take the other view: robust concern is not, after all, possible in love, even though it might or should exist outside of love as the form

---

35. The union views of Hunter, Nozick, and Fisher apparently assume that before the lovers join in love, they had been separate. Not so Gaylin: "In the biological and psychological world from which I operate, there is no such creature as a 'distinct individual'" (RL, p. 22; see also p. 101). Thus, whereas Hegel (along with *Genesis, Symposium*'s Aristophanes, and Fromm) posits a life pattern of union-separation-union, for Gaylin the life pattern is union-union-union, or simply union. So Gaylin's claim that love is constituted by union follows trivially from his generality that no relationship could not be constituted by union.

taken by general moral concern; that it is not part of personal love is no cause for anguish. I find such a view of love disheartening.

- - -

My first systematic ideas on the relationship between concern and autonomy were aired at a meeting, held in Washington, D. C., December, 1990, of The Society for the Philosophy of Sex and Love, in response to a lead paper by David Annis. The earliest version of the present paper, which incorporates some of the SPSL material, was delivered on April 30, 1992, at a colloquium sponsored by the Philosophy Department of the Budapest Technical University, during my tenure there as a Fulbright Professor. For their helpful comments, I thank Margitay Tihamér, Ujvári Márta, and Fehér Márta. That draft was reworked in two ways. One variant, which includes a discussion of the analytic goal of the philosophy of love (explanation by unification) and a detailed comparison of Plato and Aristotle, has been published in Hungarian ('Egyesülés és Jóakarat', tr. Módos Magdolna, *Athenaeum* 2, #2 [1994]: 55-89). The other, briefer variant appeared in English in a multilingual Hungarian journal ('Union and Concern', *Existentia* 3-4, ##1-4 [1993-94]: 299-323). The present paper, written in 1994 and corrected in 1995 (in response to Roger Lamb's painstaking comments, for which I am grateful), is a revised and longer rendition of the *Existentia* piece. Bacsó Béla, editor of *Athenaeum*, and Ferge Gábor, editor of *Existentia*, graciously gave permission for me to include here tracts from their versions.

5

Love and Human Bondage in Maugham, Spinoza, and Freud

Barbara Hannan

"Thank God, I'm free from all that now", he thought. And yet even as he said it he was not quite sure whether he spoke sincerely. When he was under the influence of passion he had felt a singular vigor, and his mind had worked with unwonted force. He was more alive, there was an excitement in sheer being, an eager vehemence of soul, which made life now a trifle dull. For all the misery he had endured there was a compensation in that sense of rushing, overpowering existence.

W. Somerset Maugham[1]

Bondage-Love

There is a certain kind of romantic love to which I wish to call attention. You love a person who (according to your perceptions, at least) does not return your love in the same degree and who (at least on occasion) seems to use you or treat you with contempt. Your feelings are obsessive, pathological. Your deepest suspicions tell you that the object of your love is unwilling or unable to reciprocate your feelings with equal depth; still you hope desperately for reciprocation; you love with disturbing intensity.

Those who experience this type of love tend to experience it repeatedly. Some end the repeating cycle. Among these, there is never any doubt that something evil and destructive has been put away, that progress has been made. Yet there is rarely a total absence of regret. As with Maugham's hero Philip

---

1. *Of Human Bondage* (New York: Doubleday, Doran & Co., 1915), p. 403.

Carey, there is nostalgia for the intensity of the poisonous passion that has been overcome.

Let us call this form of love 'bondage-love', taking our term from the title of Maugham's novel, *Of Human Bondage*. Maugham took the title of his novel, of course, from Part IV of Spinoza's *Ethics*.[2] Bondage-love is philosophically interesting for two main reasons. First, one wants an account of just how it is possible to break out of the cycle of bondage-love. How do we learn to control ourselves in spite of intense feelings that once controlled us? This issue is especially pressing given the widespread current interest in recovery from various sorts of addictive behaviors, including obsessive love. Second, why does the former victim of bondage-love retain a feeling of nostalgia toward her previous state of unhappy slavery to her emotions?[3] Does bondage-love have value? If bondage-love is not altogether a bad thing, one wants to know precisely what is good about it.

It is necessary, first, to define bondage-love more carefully, so that bondage-love will not be confused with other conditions, such as mere unrequited love. The essential mark of bondage-love is that the lover brings deep needs and desires to the relationship, many of them unconscious, and unreasonably expects the loved one to satisfy those needs and desires. The needs and desires at issue are of such a nature that a personal relationship cannot possibly satisfy them, yet someone in the throes of bondage-love suffers from the illusion that the loved one is the answer, the solution to all her turmoil and discontent.

In some cases of bondage-love, the loved one may actually be a cruel exploiter, treating the lover with indifference except when he wants something from her, such as money or sex. In other cases, it only appears to the lover that she is being used or exploited; the loved one intends no such thing. The loved one may be an honorable person who desires a non-exploitative, loving partner-

---

2. Maugham originally planned to call the novel *Beauty from Ashes*. He acknowledged that the work was semi-autobiographical [Maugham, *The Summing-Up* (NY: Penguin Books, 1963), p. 127.] Like his character Philip Carey, Maugham struggled with a minor disability (Maugham stuttered; Philip Carey is depicted as having a clubfoot); he was raised by a clergyman uncle after his parents died in his early childhood; he studied medicine; his first career was a failure. Presumably, Maugham suffered from obsessive love affairs. Maugham was homosexual, so whoever played the 'Mildred' role in Maugham's real life was a man.

3. I will generally refer to the victim of bondage-love as 'she', and to the loved one, who is perceived as failing to return affection in the same degree, as 'he'. This may seem unfairly sexist, since men sometimes suffer from bondage-love; indeed, the Maugham character on whom this paper concentrates is male. I believe, however, that women are probably more often victims of bondage-love than are men; this may have something to do with innate female psychology, but more probably it stems from the historical oppression of women (see text).

ship but finds obsessive and unrealistic demands being made on him by his partner. Or, the loved one may enter the relationship explicitly seeking a casual liaison; his partner at first appears to be seeking the same thing; he then finds demands being made on him out of all proportion to the limited relationship he desired.

Bondage-love has been portrayed in many popular films. In *Play Misty For Me* and *Fatal Attraction*, the victim of bondage-love is a woman who seems normal enough at the beginning of the story but who turns out to be homicidal. Homicidal behavior is not a typical component of bondage-love, and Hollywood has occasionally portrayed the more typical *suicidal* form of the disorder. Think of the character played by Shirley Maclaine in *The Apartment*, who attempts suicide due to her love affair with a philandering married man. Bondage-love is usually more destructive to the lover herself than to anyone else, though in most cases it causes some degree of pain and inconvenience to the person who is the object of the obsessive love.

Bondage-love manifests itself in many different varieties; again, what identifies these various conditions as bondage-love is the psychic neediness of the lover, and her lack of realization that her partner cannot possibly meet these needs.

Here is one variety of bondage-love: so eager is the lover to devote herself to the object of her affections that she declines other social opportunities in order to stay home by the phone, waiting for him to call.[4] When he does call, she is always available; her answer is always "yes" to whatever he may suggest; she has no other projects and plans that interest her sufficiently to pull her in the direction of saying "no". When he does not call, she is despondent. The result of this situation is that the lover feels helpless and depressed. The cure for the feeling of helplessness is for the lover to exert control by saying "no" occasionally when the other party calls; to "get a life" for herself outside the relationship. But the lover's emotional condition is such that she can't bear to say "no" to her partner; she finds it nearly impossible to pursue other interests. In her mind, the loved one is her entire life. Every time he wants her, she is there with an eager "yes", telling herself that his wanting her is a sign that things are about to change; everything is about to be magically transformed.

A slightly different (and perhaps more common) manifestation of bondage-love involves the wife or girlfriend who won't allow her partner to have any "space". She insists that he call her every day from his office; she wants him to be home every day at the arranged time; she is suspicious and petulant if he goes out with friends, or has any significant relationships apart from her. She is

---

4. For a splendid example of what I am talking about, read Dorothy Parker's short story, 'A Telephone Call' [in *The Portable Dorothy Parker* (NY: Penguin Books, 1976), pp. 119-124].

jealous and insecure, showing a "clinginess" that becomes irritating and suffo-
cating to her partner.

Bondage-love on the part of women was almost surely more common in the
days prior to women's emancipation, when women were given few opportunities to exercise their talents, intelligence, and power outside the spheres of
romance and marriage. All people, females included, need and desire to exercise their minds, to develop their talents and capacities, to deploy personal
power in the world. When women were systematically prevented from doing
this in any way other than through obtaining the love of a man, many women
became neurotically obsessive about love. Men commonly despised women for
their clinginess and for their seemingly one-track minds, not realizing that such
behavior on the part of women resulted from the self-fulfilling prophecy of
telling women that their minds and bodies were suited to nothing other than the
loving service of men. I think of the harsh words of the Gauguin-like character,
Charles Strickland, in Maugham's novel, *The Moon and Sixpence*: "Because
women can do nothing except love, they've given it a ridiculous importance.
They want to persuade us that it's the whole of life. It's an insignificant part..."[5]
Literature abounds with portrayals of women who are victims of this tragedy.
Anna Karenina and Emma Bovary are just two examples.

Maugham's portrayal of obsessive love in *Of Human Bondage* is unusual in
some respects. When a person falls in love, the person loved is normally attractive, at least in the lover's eyes. In Maugham's novel, the object of Philip's
love, Mildred, is portrayed as thoroughly unattractive *in Philip's own eyes*. The
reader can't understand Philip's devotion to her. If Philip perceived her as
beautiful, or intelligent, or talented, etc., one could understand. But she is
described as appearing to Philip to be unintelligent, uneducated, insensitive, and
unkind, as well as having a scrawny body, greenish skin, bad grammar, and
affected manners. One factor that makes it difficult for victims of bondage-love
to see the true nature of their condition is the self-deception that stems from
concentrating solely on the attractive features of the loved one. ("She's so
perfect and wonderful; of course she's the answer to all my prayers.") Philip is
an unusually difficult character to understand, because he knows, from the very
beginning, that his love for Mildred is crazy; he loves her in spite of knowing
that there is nothing lovable about her. It might at first seem that Maugham
ought to have given Mildred at least one redeeming feature in Philip's eyes, in
order to make Philip's predicament more human and hence more tragic. There
is, however, a plausible psychological explanation for Philip's unusual obsession.

Psychoanalytic theory suggests that the deep, wild feelings associated with

---

5. Maugham, W. Somerset, *The Moon and Sixpence* (NY: Bantam Classics, 1995), pp.
156-157.

bondage-love often stem from childhood love for the parent of opposite sex. Where that parent has been cruel or neglectful for some reason, the child may, as an adult, feel compelled to replay the drama, trying again and again to seduce an unavailable or abusive person. Where the parent has been overly seductive, the child may become inappropriately forward in her own sexual behavior as she matures. Even where the parent's behavior has been appropriate and reasonable, Freud tells us that the "Oedipus complex" will inevitably cause psychic stress. A daughter, for example, will always perceive herself as being in competition with her mother for her father's love. She desires to take her father away from her mother and have him for herself. This desire can't possibly be fulfilled, yet trying to fulfill it is a central unconscious preoccupation of the child.[6] Bondage-love repeats the Oedipal scenario. In bondage-love, one wants something from a person, something that person can't possibly provide.[7]

Maugham's novel illustrates the Freudian aspects of bondage-love. Philip's father dies when Philip is still an infant; then Philip's mother dies when he is a small boy. At the death of his mother, Philip's life changes forever. He is raised thereafter by his narrow and judgmental aunt and uncle; he is emotionally neglected, lonely, and unhappy. If Freud is right, Philip's mother was his first and greatest love; with Philip's father dead and out of the way, there was temporarily a realization of the Oedipal dream in Philip's babyhood. Then Philip's mother died, and everything changed; all love and warmth left Philip's life. It is believable that Philip's childhood despair, bewilderment, and guilt at his mother's death might lead him, in adult life, to love the one woman who gives him nothing at all, and leaves him completely alone. Somewhere in his subconscious mind, Philip believes that if he can make Mildred love him, everything will be all right; his childhood will be rewritten, and the awful years of loneliness will be erased; he will have symbolically brought his dead mother back to life. (Mildred's scrawniness and greenish skin even suggest a corpse.)

Overcoming Bondage-Love: Spinoza's Account

How is it possible for a person in the throes of bondage-love to escape, to attain a state of self-mastery or autonomy? One turns naturally here to Spinoza.

---

6. Freud, Sigmund, *Introductory Lectures on Psycho-Analysis*, trans. by James Strachey (New York: W.W. Norton & Co., 1966), p. 256.

7. Bondage-love may come about when a person is unconsciously attempting to fulfill some impossible desire *other than* the Oedipal desire to win the parent of the opposite sex. For example, a man whose adult daughter has just left home might become involved in a bondage-love relationship with a younger woman, unconsciously attempting to bring his little girl back home. Thanks to Keith Lehrer for this point.

Part IV of the *Ethics* is concerned with the causes of "bondage" (Spinoza uses the term 'bondage' broadly, to mean slavery to any emotion or passion, not just slavery to erotic love); Part V is concerned with how bondage is overcome, and freedom achieved. Some of the same issues are touched upon by Spinoza in 'On the Improvement of the Understanding' and in 'A Short Treatise on God, Man, and His Well-Being'. Let us survey Spinoza's insights.

Let us look first at Spinoza's discussion of the "true good", since it is crucial to understanding his description of the way out of bondage.

Spinoza claims to be a relativist about good and evil; according to him, 'good' and 'bad' may be applied to the same thing in different contexts.[8] This relativism at first seems to sit uneasily with Spinoza's overall task in his writings, which is to recommend a way that people ought to live - that is, to recommend a path or course of action that is good in itself. For example, Spinoza clearly thinks it is *better* to be free (determined to action by clear and distinct ideas) than to be in bondage (determined to action by confused ideas), and the truth of this claim is not relative to one's point of view. Spinoza addresses this apparent inconsistency by telling his readers what he means by "a true good".

According to Spinoza, "men are wont to form general ideas of things natural...and such ideas they hold as types, believing that Nature...has them in view, and has set them as types before herself". Thus, people tend to form ideas of perfection in natural objects, such as the idea of a perfect human being.[9] While careful to note that "Nature does not work with an end in view"[10], Spinoza thinks that our idea of the perfect human being may be useful to us as a model, which we may emulate. "...[M]an conceives a human character much more stable than his own, and sees that there is no reason why he should not himself acquire such a character. Thus he is led to seek for means which will bring him to this pitch of perfection, and calls everything which will serve as such means a true good."[11]

---

8. Spinoza, Benedict de., 'On the Improvement of the Understanding', trans. by R.H.M. Elwes in *Chief Works* (New York: Dover Publications, Inc., 1955), p. 6; see also his *Ethics*, trans. by R.H.M. Elwes in *Chief Works*, Preface to Part IV, p. 189.

9. Spinoza, Benedict de., *Ethics*, trans. by R.H.M. Elwes, in *Chief Works* (New York: Dover Publications, Inc., 1955), Preface to Part IV, p. 188.

10. *Ibid.*

11. Spinoza, Benedict de., 'On the Improvement of the Understanding', trans. by R.H.M. Elwes in *Chief Works* (New York: Dover Publications, Inc., 1955), p. 6. Curley renders the same passage "...conceives a human nature much stronger and more enduring than his own". See 'Treatise on the Emendation of the Intellect' in *The Collected Works of*
...continuing...

Spinoza attempts to show why the knowledge of true good and true evil (knowledge of what is and is not conducive to the acquisition of a stronger and more stable character) does not easily lead to the achievement of the goal. In this context Spinoza quotes the ancient poet Ovid, who assails himself, St. Paul-like, for weakness of will: "The better path I gaze at and approve, the worse - I follow".[12] In the same place, Spinoza also mentions the words of Ecclesiastes: "He who increaseth knowledge increaseth sorrow".[13] This is a somewhat odd use of the quote from Ecclesiastes. Spinoza apparently means to imply that knowledge of the better character we might possess increases our frustration and self-dislike at our own inability to attain that character.

Why can't a person improve her character, immediately upon conceiving in her mind the idea of the better character she would like to possess? According to Spinoza, the knowledge of true good and evil cannot check any emotion in virtue merely of being true; rather, the knowledge of true good and evil must itself be transformed into a powerful emotion in order to move a person.[14] Further: other emotions besides the desire for a good character, which the person will perceive as arising from external causes, may be more vehement than the desire for a good character, and overpower that desire.[15] The goal of becoming a better person is perceived as contingent and far in the future, whereas other things one loves and desires are immediately present; it is natural for

---

Spinoza, trans. Edwin Curley (Princeton: Princeton University Press, 1985), p. 10. A similar passage is to be found in 'Short Treatise on God, Man, and His Well-Being', Second Part, Ch. IV : "And when we have conceived an Idea of a perfect man in our intellect, that [Idea] could be the cause of our seeing (when we examine ourselves) whether we have any means of arriving at such a perfection. Therefore, whatever helps us to attain that perfection, we shall call good, and whatever hinders our attaining it, we shall call evil". [Spinoza, 'Short Treatise on God, Man, and his Well-Being', in *The Collected Works of Spinoza*, trans. by Edwin Curley (Princeton: Princeton University Press, 1985), p. 103.] Elwes does not translate this latter work.

12. Curley, in a footnote to his translation of this section, notes, "These lines [from Ovid] are often quoted, or alluded to, in seventeenth-century discussions of freedom of the will. Cf. Descartes, Letter to Meland, 9 Feb. 1645; Hobbes, 'Of Liberty and Necessity', EW IV, p. 269; Locke, Essay, II, xxi. 35". *Collected Works of Spinoza*, trans. by Edwin Curley (Princeton: Princeton Univ. Press, 1985), p. 554.

13. Spinoza, *Ethics*, in *Chief Works*, tr. R.H.M. Elwes (NY: Dover, 1955), p. 200: Part IV, note to Prop. XVII.

14. *Op. cit.*, p. 198: Part IV, Prop. XIV.

15. *Op. cit.*, pp. 198-199: Part IV, Prop. XV and its Proof.

humans to be moved to action more easily by immediate temptations.[16] The result is that knowledge of true good and evil leads, in the first instance, not to improvement of character, but to conflict within the self, and to a sense of personal weakness and failure.

It is reason, clear and distinct conception, that enables one to move beyond this state of vacillation, and actually to improve one's character. According to Spinoza, an emotion ceases to be a passion once the sufferer forms a clear and distinct idea of it; and the more clearly and distinctly the emotion is understood, the more able the person is to control it.[17]

If one is to escape from bondage, then, whatever passions may be distracting one from one's pursuit of the true good must be seen in the light of reason. Spinoza is perhaps most explicit about this in the following passage:

> An emotion, which is a passion, is a confused idea (by the general Def. of the Emotions). If, therefore, we form a clear and distinct idea of a given emotion, that idea will only be distinguished from the emotion, in so far as it is referred to the mind only, by reason (II, xxi. and Note); therefore (III, iii.) the emotion will cease to be a passion.[18]

According to Spinoza, "...everyone has the power of clearly and distinctly understanding himself and his emotions, if not absolutely, at any rate in part, and consequently of bringing it about, that he should become less subject to them".[19]

From the latter two quotations taken out of context, it would appear that a person might overcome bondage-love merely by coming to a clear and distinct understanding of that passion. But in another place, Spinoza says, "An emotion can only be controlled or destroyed by another emotion contrary thereto, and with more power for controlling emotion".[20]

Spinoza's position is apparently that clear and distinct understanding of a passion is not itself sufficient to overcome that passion; a contrary emotion is also necessary.

---

16. *Op. cit.*, p. 199: Part IV, Props. XVI and XVII.

17. *Op. cit.*, p. 248: Part V, Prop. III, and its Proof and Corollary.

18. *Op. cit.*, p. 248: Part V, Prop. III, Proof. According to Spinoza, a person is passive (suffers from passions) insofar as he is determined to act by confused ideas; a person is active (performs actions) insofar as he is determined to act by clear and distinct ideas. (*Op. cit.*, p. 130, p. 135: Part III, Postulates, Prop. I and Prop. III.)

19. *Op. cit.*, p. 249: Part V, Prop. IV, Note.

20. *Op. cit.*, p. 194: Part IV, Prop. VII.

It is important here to note that Spinoza distinguishes an *emotion* from an emotion that is a *passion*. Passions are emotions that stem from obscure and confused ideas; but not all emotions are passions. There are emotions that stem from reason, from clear and distinct ideas, and those emotions are not passions.[21] Bondage is essentially the condition of being determined to act by obscure and confused ideas, i.e., being in the grip of passion. The key to overcoming bondage, achieving freedom, is to have one's actions determined by clear and distinct ideas, or reason; this is not opposed to having one's actions determined by emotions, so long as those emotions are in accord with reason (are not passions).

If a person in the grip of one passion falls victim to a new, contrary passion that extinguishes the first, the person is still in bondage. Yet another contrary emotion is needed, to extinguish the second passion. The necessary emotion, if it is to release the person from bondage, must be active and not passive, therefore in accord with reason and not confused. An example of such an emotion would be a strong desire to improve one's own character - a desire to achieve the true good.

Of course, it is not always necessary that a person's initial passion (bondage-love, for example) should be replaced by a contrary passion prior to being conquered by a reasoned emotion such as the desire to improve character. We may therefore distinguish two routes, outlined by Spinoza, leading a person out of bondage-love: (1) a more complex route, where bondage-love is first replaced by a contrary passion before the person is led out of bondage by a reasoned emotion; (2) a less complex route, where a person conquers the passion of bondage-love by means of a reasoned emotion, without the intervention of any other passion.

The first, more complex route is that taken by Philip Carey in *Of Human Bondage*, and will serve as our example. Mildred leaves Philip and has an affair with Philip's friend Griffiths. This action breaks Philip's heart; he is driven by it to suicidal despair. Maugham tells us:

> The pain he was suffering was horrible, he would sooner be dead than endure it; and the thought came to him that it would be better to finish with the whole thing: he might throw himself in the river or put his neck on a railway line; but he had no sooner set the thought into words than he rebelled against it. His reason told him that he would get over his unhappiness in time; if he tried with all his might he could forget her; and it would be grotesque to kill himself on account of a vulgar slut. He had only one life, and it was madness to fling it

---

21. *Op. cit.*, pp. 248-249: Part V, Props. III and IV, and their Proofs and Corollaries.

away. He *felt* that he would never overcome his passion, but he *knew* that after all it was only a matter of time.[22]

When Mildred returns to Philip after the Griffiths episode, Philip finds he does not love her anymore: "He was quite sure he was not at all in love with Mildred. He was surprised that the old feeling had left him so completely; he discerned in himself a faint physical repulsion from her; and he thought that if he touched her it would give him goose-flesh. He could not understand himself".[23]

Philip makes up his mind not to see Mildred anymore, and goes about his business, finishing medical school and beginning his professional life. Here is Maugham's account of Philip's reflections, months later, on his former suicidal state: "He remembered how much he had wanted to die then; his pain had been so great that he had thought quite seriously of committing suicide. It all seemed very long ago. He smiled at his past self. Now he felt nothing for Mildred but infinite pity".[24]

Philip's suicidal despair is the contrary, and more powerful, passion that destroys his obsessive love for Mildred. Spinoza tells us that the despair itself, being a passion, can only be controlled by some more powerful emotion. It is at least implied by Maugham that Philip has a strong desire to possess a more stable character, to be free of obsessive emotion. We can reasonably conclude that it is this second emotion that enables Philip to become active rather than passive. Philip makes an initial decision (not to commit suicide) which is followed by a series of other small decisions and actions, concerned with avoiding Mildred and pursuing his own career. Philip becomes ever more free, less "in bondage", during this recovery period. The ultimate result: "He was contented with life".[25]

Spinoza's account of what he means by "virtue" is relevant here. A person has virtue insofar as that person finds what is useful to her, and preserves her

---

22. Maugham, W. Somerset, *Of Human Bondage* (New York: Doubleday, Doran & Co., 1915), p. 477.

23. *Op. cit.*, p. 560.

24. *Op. cit.*, p. 569.

25. *Op. cit.*, p. 722.

own being.[26] Virtue and power are the same notion for Spinoza.[27] Spinoza believes that people are naturally inclined toward virtue; that is, everyone naturally seeks what he takes to be in his best interests.[28] Such seeking is a necessary means to the achievement of virtue; virtue is not merely the seeking of what one takes to be good, but the actual finding of what is good, and the consequent actual ability to preserve one's being.[29] It is only when we are "overcome by causes external and foreign to [our] nature" that we neglect to seek what is useful to us (neglect to seek to preserve our own being); "No one, I say, from the necessity of his own nature, or otherwise than under compulsion from external causes...kills himself...".[30] We find what actually is good by using our reason:

> ...since every man by the laws of his nature desires that which he deems good, and endeavors to remove that which he deems bad (IV, xix) and further, since that which we, in accordance with reason, deem good or bad, necessarily is good or bad (II, xli) it follows that men, in so far as they live in obedience to reason, necessarily do only such things as are necessarily good for human nature, and consequently for each individual man (IV, xxxi, Corollary)...[31]

As previously observed, it is not rare for bondage-love to lead its victims to thoughts of suicide. It may be fairly common that the moment of contemplating suicide is the moment that reason reasserts itself within the victim of bondage-love, and the emotional tide turns. Suicidal despair is indeed a powerful passion, and a very powerful passion is necessary to extinguish so deep a passion as bondage-love. Further: suicidal despair is in profound opposition to virtue, and all humans have an innate tendency to strive toward virtue. It is not surprising that at this crucial moment, a person's reasonable desires to live and be free of obsessive emotions might assert themselves, enabling the person to take the necessary first steps toward freedom.

---

26. Spinoza, *Ethics*, in *Chief Works*, tr. R.H.M. Elwes (NY: Dover, 1955), p. 202: Part IV, Prop. XX. With regard to Spinoza's definition of virtue, see also *Ethics* Part IV, Prop. XVIII, Note; Part IV, Prop. XXXVI, Proof; Part IV, Prop. LVI, Proof; Part IV, Prop. XXXV, Corollary II; Part IV, Prop. XXIV; Part V, Prop. XLI, Proof.

27. *Op. cit.*, p. 191: Part IV, Definition VIII.

28. *Op. cit.*, p. 202: Part IV, Prop. XIX.

29. *Op. cit.*, p. 202: Part IV, Prop. XX, Proof.

30. *Op. cit.*, p. 203: Part IV, Prop. XX, Note.

31. *Op. cit.*, p. 209: Part IV, Prop. XXXV, Proof.

Reading Spinoza in the light of Freudian psycho-analytic theory may throw additional light on the mechanism by which release from bondage-love is achieved. Suppose a man suffering from bondage-love possesses the reasoned desire to improve his own character, which he manifests by seeking help from a psychotherapist. Through therapy, it becomes clear to this man that adult behavior is heavily influenced by childhood experiences. He sees his own behavior in a new light; he sees that in his obsession for the perceived temptress, he has been acting out an ancient Oedipal conflict. It has great psychological plausibility, in our own post-Freudian age, that the man's emotional bondage will release its hold once he comes to understand its unconscious origins... *provided this understanding is accompanied by a strong desire to overcome the emotional bondage.*

Freud himself had no explanation for what he called "the foundation of psycho-analytic therapy", the idea that neurotic symptoms cease once their unconscious origins are brought to consciousness. He considered it to be a basic fact, not amenable to further explanation, and attributed its discovery to Breuer.[32] Freud's account of psychotherapy's efficacy is most convincing when, like Spinoza, he explicitly notes that it only works when the patient strongly wants to recover.[33]

Spinoza gives an interesting alternative account of the way to conquer bondage-love when he says that "Love is nothing else but pleasure accompanied by the idea of an external cause; Hate is nothing else but pain accompanied by the idea of an external cause".[34] Consider this in light of Spinoza's further claim that "If we remove a disturbance of the spirit, or emotion, from the thought of an external cause, and unite it to other thoughts, then will the love or hatred towards that external cause, and also the vacillations of spirit which arise from these emotions, be destroyed".[35] Necessarily, if the idea (within the affected person) of an external cause of the emotion is overturned by a more adequate etiological understanding, then the affect of love or hatred is no longer present. For love (or hatred) just is pleasure (or pain) accompanied by the idea of an *external* cause.

---

32. Freud, Sigmund, *Introductory Lectures on Psycho-Analysis*, trans. by James Strachey (New York: W.W. Norton & Co., 1966), pp. 346-347.

33. *Op. cit.*, p. 544.

34. Spinoza, *Ethics*, in *Chief Works*, tr. R.H.M. Elwes (NY: Dover, 1955), p. 140: Part III, Prop. XIII, Note. For similar or identical statements regarding the nature of love and hate, see *Ethics* Part III, Prop. XXX, Note; Part III, Definitions of the Emotions, VI and VII; Part IV, Prop. XLIV, Proof; Part V, Prop. II, Proof.

35. *Op. cit.*, p. 248: Part V, Axioms, Prop. II.

This may seem a cheap way of explaining why love or hatred is no longer present (*by definition* neither love nor hatred is present) but it seems to be Spinoza's way.[36] It's a bit like waking from a nightmare in which you have been fearful of a monster you thought was in the room (and which, accordingly, you thought was causally responsible for your fear), only to discover that the real cause is within *you*. Your fear - or at least your fear *of the monster* - necessarily dissipates when you discover that there is no monster which could be the cause of your monster-fear.

Consider the above-mentioned example of a man suffering from bondage-love, whose affect includes the thought that the woman is *the temptress*, hence the culpable cause, of his own disturbance of spirit and resultant aberrant behavior. We commonly think that such a man needs to take a good hard look at *himself*, presuming (with Spinoza) that this will go a long way toward sorting him out. If he can bring himself to think of her as not really all that fascinating, and of peculiarities in his own makeup as being integrally involved in his "disturbance of spirit", then his recovery has commenced.

The Value of Bondage-Love

Bondage-love involves the attempt to fulfill deep, unconscious desires. The emotions surrounding unconscious desires are apt to be peculiarly intense, fraught with a mysterious sense of importance. (This is surely true where the former victim of bondage-love is replaying the childhood Oedipal drama.) One who has ceased to feel such emotions may experience regretful nostalgia, because she misses both the intensity of the emotions and their deceptive aura of significance.

Perhaps more interesting than the Oedipal cases are the cases where bondage-love conceals the universal human desire to exercise one's own talents and powers. Persons whose intellectual or artistic potential has been thwarted in some systematic way are likely to become victims of bondage-love. What such persons really desire is their own meaningful work, yet, having no belief in their own ability, or no socially-acceptable means of exercising their ability, they seek obsessively to obtain or control some other person. A victim of this type of bondage-love recovers by realizing the true object of her desire, and by pursuing that object directly. (One can only pity those whose social circumstances entirely prevent them from realizing and pursuing their true desires.) In these cases, the former victim of bondage-love may remember her former state with nostalgia not merely because the emotions she felt were so intense and laden with a sense of importance, but because those emotions provided a clue as to just how

---

36. Thanks to Roger Lamb for this insight.

badly she wanted to be an active, creative person in her own right. Those misdirected, powerful feelings were a signal that an interesting self was fighting to be born.

It might appear that bondage-love is, in itself, a disordered and undesirable state; that it is valuable only instrumentally, as an opportunity to gain insight into oneself and to pass on to a state of greater wisdom and stability. This is surely how it appeared to Spinoza.

I find myself inclined to argue, however, that no state qualifies as being truly "in love" unless it is, to some degree, a state of bondage-love, and that being "in love" is an intrinsically valuable experience. Being deeply infatuated with another person requires that one confusedly see the other person as the fulfillment of unconscious desires; but the intensity of feeling (particularly sexual feeling) that can result is wonderful, and to be treasured for its own sake, as one of life's outstanding experiences.

- - -

I would like to thank Roger Lamb, Keith Lehrer, Brom Anderson, Fred Schueler and George Patsakos for helpful comments on earlier drafts.

6

Love and Autonomy

Keith Lehrer

People prefer to love others and to be autonomous. There is conflict between love and autonomy according to Sartre that leads to him to conclude that others are hell.[1] We did not, however, need Sartre to inform us of the tensions between love and autonomy. But why should there be conflict? We might wish to possess the freedom of another like a thing when we love, as Sartre suggests[2], but why should love involve that desire for possession of the freedom of the other? And why should desire to be autonomous interfere with loving another? What is there about love and autonomy that produces the strife? And is there no way that we can love and be autonomous? Is there no way that we can love and respect the autonomy of the other? To answer these questions we shall have to understand the structure of love and autonomy.

Autonomy

Let us begin with autonomy. What is autonomy? Kant thought that autonomous action required that the agent be author of the law, maxim or principle of the action[3]. This requirement places too great an emphasis on principle.

---

1. Jean-Paul Sartre, *Being and Nothingness: An Essay on Phenomenological Ontology*, trans. and intro. Hazel E. Barnes (New York: Philosophical Library, 1956): Part Three, chap. III, sect. 1. See also Part Four, chap. I, p. 522ff.

2. *Op. cit.*: Part Three, chap. III, sect. 1, 366-7.

3. Immanuel Kant, *Foundations of the Metaphysics of Morals*, first edition (1785), trans. and intro. Lewis White Beck (Indianapolis: Bobbs-Merrill, 1975): Second Section.

Action can be autonomous and unprincipled, for example, when an agent wants to act spontaneously and succeeds. Is autonomy just doing what we want then?

Autonomy is not just doing what we want. There are two reasons. One is that we may do what we want when we would prefer not to want to do what we want to do. There may be a conflict, as Frankfurt has noted, between a first order desire and a higher order preference.[4] If I am addicted to some substance, activity or person, I may find myself doing what I want to do but prefer not to want to do what I do want to do. It is not that I do not want to do what I do, I want to do what I do, but I would prefer not to want to. The ingestion or injection of some substance that I want because I am physically and/or psychologically addicted to it, but consider my addictions and the use of the substance harmful and destructive, is an example. It is not that I do not want to use the drug. I do want to use it. I want very badly to use it and may go to a great deal of effort to obtain the drug to use. It is just that I prefer not to be addicted and not to want to use the drug that I, in fact, use and want to use.

Or suppose I am addicted to exercise, to bicycling, for example. I bicycle all the time at the expense of my work and relations to other people. Perhaps it is because I am a champion bicyclist, my life is failing in many ways, I am failing in many ways, and only bicycling makes me feel like a winner rather than a failure. So I want to bicycle and I do bicycle. But I would prefer to have the strength of character to face the problems in my life and deal with those problems rather than just wanting to bicycle all the time.

Or take a third case. I am in love with a woman. She was in love with me but has rejected me. When she loved me, it was wonderful. She and her love for me had a magical effect on me. I felt valued, and valuable, desired and desirable, and these feelings filled me with further feelings of confidence and strength. She has rejected me, and I no longer feel valuable, desirable, confident and strong, but, instead, worthless, undesirable, unsure and weak. I feel awful, and I want her love back. I want to get her to love me again. I want to call her. But I know that she will not love me again and calling her will only make me feel worse. But I want to call her. So I call her because I want to call her but preferring not to want to call her. My calling her feels compelled and is not autonomous. All of these examples are ones in which I do what I want but do not act autonomously nor feel that I do. Let us refer to this as the internal problem because the actions are and feel compelled by internal states or conditions.

The second reason why I may not act autonomously, though I do what I

---

4. Harry Frankfurt, 'Freedom of the Will and the Concept of a Person', *Journal of Philosophy* 68 (January 1971): 5-20. See also Richard Jeffrey, 'Preferences Among Preferences', *Journal of Philosophy* 71 (1974): 377-391; Keith Lehrer, 'Preferences, Conditionals and Freedom' in Lehrer, *Metamind* (Oxford: Clarendon Press, 1990): Chapter 3; and Wright Neely, 'Freedom and Desire', *Philosophical Review* 83 (1974): 32-54.

want, is that my wanting what I do may be manipulated by another. One extreme example is that of responding to a posthypnotic suggestion. It is suggested to me under hypnosis that I will wash my hands when the bell rings at three o'clock. When the bell rings, I want to wash my hands and do so. I do not know why I want to do this. The question does not occur to me. There are other crueler cases in which I am brainwashed, and more extraordinary cases in which my brain is mechanically manipulated, or more familiar ones in which I respond to subtle manipulation that leads me to want to buy something of a certain brand not knowing why. Or I may simply be in a situation where the only thing that I want is to please another no matter how contrary to my own real interests this may be. In all of these cases, I may do what I want but still not act autonomously because what I want to do is manipulated by another person. Let us call this the manipulation problem.

Preference and Desire

The solution to the first problem is to require that I do something, not because I want to do, but because I prefer to satisfy the desire to do it. Desire must be distinguished from preference. Preference involves transcendence beyond the first level of desire to a higher or metamental level of evaluation and certification.[5] The importance of the second level is that it may effect freedom from the bondage of first order desire however delicious such bondage may at times be. The difference between preference and desire is like the difference between decision and motivation, particularly motivation that arises in us uninvited and even against our will. Desires, like their epistemic cousins, beliefs, arise in us more or less automatically without our bidding and sometimes in opposition to our wishes. I am content working on a philosophical paper, feeling free in philosophical fantasy and then a familiar fragrance catches my nose, a form my eyes, and I am absorbed in desire, my reflective tranquility dissolved in the immediacy of desire. The desire is there. I did not invite it or wish it, but there it is. Desire is like that. Preference results when I resolve the conflict, one way or another, between the desire for philosophy and desire for the other. Preference is transcendence above the first order motivations of desire to a higher level.

Preference for satisfying desire may solve the internal compulsion problem provided that the preference itself is autonomous, but it does not solve the external manipulation problem. Second order, third order and nth order preferences may all be externally manipulated. A preference for a desire and even a preference for that preference and so forth, however iterated, still does not guarantee

---

5. Keith Lehrer, *Metamind* (Oxford: Clarendon Press, 1990): Introduction.

that one is autonomous. One might think that if I have a preference for doing A, a preference for having that preference, a preference for having that preference, and so forth, then I am autonomous. But that is false. The whole infinite sequence of preferences for preferences might be generated by another person. Autonomy requires not just that I prefer my preference but that I be the author of that preference, that my preference be grounded in me and not in another.

The Power Preference

What does it mean for me to be the author of my preferences? It means that I have the preferences that I do with respect to A because I prefer to have those preferences. In short, there is a special preference, a kind of power preference, to have just the preference structure I do have with respect to an action A, which is essential to my autonomy. It is the preference described by *PP* as follows:

> *PP.* I prefer to have the preference structure I do have with respect to action A which I prefer to perform. (The preference structure contains a first order preference for doing A and higher order preferences so far as they exist pertaining to the preference to do A, a preference for that preference, and so forth.)

Now this preference, which I call the *power preference*, empowers me and makes me autonomous, provided that I have this preference because I prefer to have it. Thus, we must add the following condition insuring that the power preference yields autonomy:

> *PA.* I prefer to have the power preference I do have with respect to action A because I prefer to have it.

The power preference refers to itself because it is itself part of my preference structure with respect to doing A. Moreover, it is a preference that I have because I prefer to have it. If I did not prefer to have the preferences in my preference structure with respect to A, then I would not have those preferences, including, of course, this very preference itself. The power preference is self-explanatory as a result of my having it because I prefer to have it.

The self-referential feature of the preference means that the preference is not externally grounded. The truth of the statement that I have this preference is not grounded in anything external to the preference itself. The ungroundedness of some statements leads to the paradoxes of the liar

This sentence is false

and the oddity of the truth teller

This sentence is true.

But this feature of ungroundedness is precisely what is desired in the case of autonomy. That is the account of autonomy.

Extreme Love

Let us consider love. What is love?[6] Love comes in many flavors. Let us consider one form of love which is the basis of much of the world's romantic literature. I shall call it extreme love. It arises within a nexus of sexual desire and may be characterized in terms of sexual desire. Desire is exquisite in love. The desire to satisfy the sexual desires of another is one of the most delicious forms of desire. It is often thought that some trait of another is the basis of love, and so it may be, but desire is salient. Moreover, as has oft been noticed philosophically and in more intimate ways, sexual love is often aroused by the desire of one person which arouses the desire of the other and so forth into a spiral of mutual desire. Moreover, satisfying the desire of the other for pleasure is itself a pleasure as is receiving the pleasure of satisfaction. Those who desire and respond to the satisfaction of their desires with pleasure are the most seductive lovers. The takers are often wonderful givers, and the pleasure of satisfying the desires of another becomes the structure of extreme love and defines it.

Extreme love results when the lover and the loved one are united in each desiring the satisfaction of the desires of the other until the one dominant desire of each is the satisfaction of the desires of the other. This pattern of desire accounts, I think, for the magic of extreme love and the conflict with autonomy. But first the magic.

Matthew and Julia are about to become lovers. He noticed her in the lecture hall, and afterward she walked up to him at the reception and introduced herself. They knew after a short time that they were to go somewhere and become lovers, but there was the problem of getting from where they were to somewhere. As conversations drifted from here to there, Julia became animated and smiled her desire at Matthew who immediately succumbed to the power of it. The desire in her smile was delicious and filled him with desire, or had the desire in his voice evoked the desire she had smiled at him? Who knows? And what does it matter? They will find their way from where they are so that they can enjoy their desires, each enjoying his or her own desire for the other and each enjoying the desire of the other for the other, and, in a refinement of desire, each desiring the desire of the other. As they find their way from where they are to somewhere where they can make love, each will experience the miracle of the

---

6. See articles on love by Robert Kraut and by Amelie Oksenberg Rorty in *Midwest Studies in Philosophy*, X (1985): 399-412, 413-430. See also Ronald de Sousa, *The Rationality of Emotion* (1987).

pleasure of satisfying the other and the pleasure of the other at satisfying their desire. Pleasure given will be pleasure received, satisfying the desire of the other will become desired itself, and each will experience the magic of finding satisfaction in giving satisfaction and, consequently, in desiring desires in the other that one may satisfy.

The essence of extreme love is a mutual desire to satisfy the desires of the other. Desire to satisfy the desires of the other produces a natural kind of magic. Whatever happens you get what you desire with the bonus of that being desired. If you get what you desire, she will desire that you do and thus get what she desires as you, getting what you desire, also get the bonus of it being what she desires. If, on the other hand, she gets what she desires, that is what you desire, and she then gets what she desires with the bonus of it being what you desire. Your desire and her desire become entwined as a metaphor for other entwinings, and that is the magic of it.

The extension of this pattern of desire from sex to other matters is almost invisible. He gives her roses. She never liked roses, but she smells his desire for her to like roses in the roses. She desires the roses sniffing his desire in them. She makes him popcorn which he never liked, but he tastes her desire that he like the popcorn in the popcorn and he desires the popcorn. So there they are sniffing desire in roses and tasting desire in popcorn. They must be happy with sex, roses and popcorn, until the bubble bursts.

Love in Bondage

Let us leave them and look at the implications for autonomy. Though they are happy, they are in bondage. Each is driven by and dependent on the desires of another. As we noted, one can have desires that deprive one of autonomy, but in the case of love, even though one does what one desires and feels the pleasure of it, one is enslaved to the desires of the other because one desires the satisfaction of them. The intensity of the pleasure conceals the bondage. But it reveals itself readily enough. When the loved one desires something that is painful to you, though a romantic sort of masochism might carry the day or night for a while, pain will triumph over desire, and you will know that you do not desire what she desires, especially when you suffer the pain as the result of doing what she desires. She may, of course, desire that someone other than you satisfy her desires, or cease to desire the satisfaction of yours, or cease to love you in the extreme way by rejecting the roses. Desire is rife with conflict, even when another is not involved, and when your desires include the desire for the satisfaction of the desires of another, conflict will manifest itself sooner or later.

So, what do our lovers do? Suppose Julia finds Matthew's desires, or some of them, unpleasant, and, as a result, no longer desires to satisfy Matthew's desires. The magic is gone. And what is he to do? At first he may continue to desire the satisfaction of her desires, but if she does not desire the satisfaction of his desires, he will quickly enough notice that he is in bondage to her desires. Her desires dominate his desires because he desires the satisfaction of her desires while she does not desire the satisfaction of his. In this situation, he will find her manipulative, though it is his desires that empower her.

He may try to get her to desire the satisfaction of his desires again so that they can return to sniffing desire in roses and tasting desire in popcorn. So he may persevere in satisfying her desires to win back her love. But she will see that his actions are not based on his desire to satisfy her desires but on his desire for her to desire to satisfy his desires. So, in the end, he will not desire to satisfy her desires, each will be astonished that his or her wonderful giving lover has suddenly become a manipulative cad or bitch. The bubble burst. Pity.

Transcending Extreme Love

Is all this inevitable? Must the magic turn to dust? The danger is great and the way out is narrow, but let us look at what has gone wrong and, perhaps, we may defeat the pessimists and arrive at a conception of autonomous love. What went wrong? The interaction is driven by first level desire. First level desire is rife with conflict, and the conflict must emerge unless one of our lovers is masochistic. I ignore that solution to the problem. The first step is transcendence beyond the first level. We need to ask which desires to satisfy, and, more exactly, how much weight to give to those desires. The simple transcendence from desire to preference takes us in the direction of autonomy. That does not destroy the pleasures of acting on desires, even the desires to satisfy the desires of the other, but it does force the evaluation of them. The bonus of doing so is that when we prefer the satisfaction of desire, it is our preference rather than the desire of the other, even if it is a preference for satisfaction of the desire of the other, that determines what we do.

Of course, extreme love for another may enable the other to manipulate our preferences as well as our desires, and we may be bound at the level of preference. To arrive at autonomy we must prefer to do what we do, including, perhaps, satisfying the desires of a loved one, because we prefer to have that preference to do so. Although this may take some of the fun out of it, it need not deplete the pleasure of love.

Autonomous love for another should, however, not only express our own autonomy, it should respect the preferences of the other as well. The preferences of the other reflect her transcendence of first order desire and resolution of first order conflict. Her autonomous preferences, the preferences that she has because she prefers to have them, represent her transcendence to autonomy. My autonomous preference for what she autonomously prefers is or can be a form of love for her that is an expression of my autonomy that respects her expression of her autonomy. We are far from the original magic and disillusion of extreme love. Have we found the genuine article of love metamentally embedded in autonomous preference?

Autonomous Love

Let us recall what autonomy requires. A person, S, autonomously prefers A if and only if S prefers A because S prefers to have the preference structure he or she does with respect to A. Now suppose that S prefers A out of autonomous love for T. How should we analyze the notion of preference out of autonomous love? I propose the following:

AL.   S prefers A out of (mutually) autonomous love for T if and only if S autonomously prefers A because T autonomously prefers A.

Objections immediately arise. For example, someone might, it seems, prefer something out of autonomous love for another when the other does not prefer the thing in question. Tough love, as it is called in the current vernacular, arises when I prefer something for another that the other does not prefer, giving up an addiction, for example, or giving up some course of conduct that is harmful to the other, which the other does not prefer but ought to prefer. My reply to this objection is the one with which I began, namely, that love comes in many flavors, and preference out of tough love is not preference out of autonomous love, because, though it may be based on autonomous preferences of one's own, it is not based on autonomous preferences of the other. I am here concerned to articulate an ideal form of mutually autonomous love based on autonomy of the lover and the loved one.

Forms of Love

I do not deny that other forms of love are worthwhile, including tough love. I am concerned, instead, to look at the full taxonomy of love, for, in fact, I am a great admirer of love, in all the plentiful varieties in which it occurs. Here are some other forms of love that are not based on the autonomy of the other and so fall short of fully autonomous love.

D/D.   S desires A out of unilateral love for T based on what T desires if and only if S desires A because T desires A

P/D.   S prefers A out of unilateral love for T based on what T desires if and only if S prefers A because T desires A

P/P.   S prefers A out of unilateral love for T based on what T prefers if and only if S prefers A because T prefers A

AP/P.   S prefers A out of unilateral autonomous love for T based on what T prefers if and only if S autonomously prefers A because T prefers A

AP/OP. S prefers A out of unilateral autonomous love for T based on what T ought to prefer if and only if S autonomously prefers A because T ought to prefer A.

These are all forms of love. The first, D/D, the love of desire, might exist between beings which are incapable of reflection or evaluation of desires. It is a naive and very charming form of love, which when mutual becomes extreme love, but is compatible with a complete lack of autonomy. The second, P/D, the preference for what another desires, requires one component of autonomy in the lover, preference involving higher order evaluation, but allows for a complete lack of autonomy in the loved one. It is part of the love for a child by an adult. The third form of love, P/P, presupposes preference, a constituent of autonomy, in both the lover and the loved one, but it allows for the possibility that the preferences of either or both are externally manipulated. Two people who love each other in this way may be manipulated into the love by a third party, or, for that matter, by each other and their codependence. The fourth form of love, AP/P, requires the autonomy of the lover but allows for the possibility that the preferences of the loved one are manipulated. This form of love allows for the case in which the lover, who is autonomous, controls the preferences of the loved one and has a preference for what the loved one prefers because of having shaped those preferences. All of these forms of love allow for lack of autonomy on the part of either the lover or the loved one with all the potentialities for manipulation of the nonautonomous person or persons involved in the relationship. These are, therefore, all forms of love that may be purchased at the cost of autonomy.

Unilateral autonomous love for what the loved one ought to prefer, the fifth form of love, AP/OP, has a more complicated relationship to autonomy and is the sort of love advocates of tough love might recommend. It does not require that the lover prefer what the loved one desires or prefers, indeed, the unilateral autonomous lover may prefer the opposite of what the loved one prefers or desires because the loved one ought to prefer it instead of what he or she does. There is no doubt that this is an important form of love and, in some cases, fully appropriate.

The conflict between unilateral autonomous love for what the other ought to prefer and mutual autonomous love for what the other autonomously prefers is one of the most profound conflicts in human relations. This form of unilateral love gives us a kind of moral paradigm, but it falls short of the paradigm of love. Morality and love may clash, of course, but it is love that concerns me here. Autonomous love seems to me to be the highest form of love between autonomous beings, however immoral the lovers might be in what they prefer. Perhaps that is why it is comparatively easy to identify with characters in fiction who love autonomously but live wantonly. We identify with their love as we condemn their preferences. The attempt to reduce morality to love or love to morality is a philosophical mistake. It is comparable in defect to the attempt to reduce morality to reason. One may love and reason immorally and autonomously.

Autonomous love is, in contrast to the other forms of love, a form of love based on mutual autonomy as is clear by consideration of our definition of it.

AL. S prefers A out of (mutually) autonomous love for T if and only if S autonomously prefers A because T autonomously prefers A.

Autonomous love is expressed by the autonomous preferences of the lovers for the other's autonomous preferences. It is based on the autonomy of the lovers. It thus avoids the pessimistic claim that love is bondage and manipulation standing in opposition to freedom and autonomy.

Objections and Qualifications

There are, however, objections other than moral ones to autonomous love. One is that the notion of autonomous love is contradictory. Suppose that S prefers A autonomously--something implied by S preferring A out of autonomous love for T. Then S has the preference structure S has with respect to A because S prefers to have that preference structure including the preference for A itself. So S prefers A because S prefers to prefer A. If, at the same time, S prefers A out of autonomous love for T, then S prefers A because T prefers A. Thus, S must prefer A because S prefers to prefer A in order to be autonomous; and yet S must prefer A because T prefers A in order to love T.

This objection can be met, but it is basic and important for an understanding of love which avoids the bondage dilemma implicit in the idea that if I love another than I am a prisoner of the preferences of the other. I can, in fact, prefer what the other prefers because the other prefers what they do without becoming a prisoner of the preferences of the other. Everything depends on why and how I prefer what the other prefers. It all depends on whether I prefer what the other prefers primarily because the other prefers what she does which is, in fact, bondage, or because I prefer what the other prefers primarily because I prefer to prefer what I do and only secondarily prefer to prefer what the other prefers.

Consider the following two statements:

I prefer A because T prefers A
I prefer A because I prefer to prefer A.

The objection is that these two are inconsistent, and my reply is that they are not. I prefer what T prefers because I prefer to prefer to have that preference. That is what combines love with autonomy successfully.

Consider the following analogy. I am asked to review a book for a journal that Stew edits, and I decide to do this to assist Stew. Consider the following two statements:

I prefer to read the book because I prefer to review it.
I prefer to read the book because I prefer to assist Stew.

These statements are not inconsistent. I prefer to review the book because I prefer to assist Stew. I prefer what Stew prefers because I prefer to prefer what Stew prefers. Though my preference appears to be determined by the preference of another, in fact, my preference is determined by my preference for it.

Scope and Knots of Love

The scope of my autonomous love for another can be either broad or narrow in scope. The limiting case of narrow scope is the case in which I autonomously prefer the preference of another for a single and rather limited action. The limiting case of broad scope is where I prefer the preferences of the other over all actions that the other prefers because she prefers them. The term 'love' is vague, however, and there is no answer to the general question of how broad the scope of love must be before one really loves another. Relationships that last expand and contract the scope of autonomous love to meet the needs and enhance the pleasures of the lovers.

There are love knots that conflict with autonomous love. Suppose that another prefers that I prefer what she prefers not because I prefer to prefer what she prefers but just because she prefers what she does. In that case, she is preferring that I love her nonautonomously. I think that the preference for such love is common, but it cannot be fulfilled by autonomous preference on my part. A preference of another to be loved nonautonomously can be fulfilled but not out of autonomous love. The preference that another prefer what I prefer, not because she prefers to prefer what I prefer but just because I prefer it, is a preference for her to love me in bondage. If she complies, then she is enslaved to my preferences in the way that a person is enslaved to the desires of another in the case of extreme love.

Advantages of Autonomous Love

Suppose, however, that I autonomously love another and prefer her preferences because I prefer to prefer them. I may act in the same way as someone who loves in bondage, for as soon as I determine what the loved one prefers I will prefer it as well. Have I thereby lost my autonomy? If not, what is the difference between autonomously loving another in wide scope and loving another in bondage? The difference may not be visible in the actions that occur at a given point in time. But autonomy is not visible in action. A person who does what she wants without acting autonomously may do the same thing as a person who acts autonomously, that is, acts from autonomous preference. The difference lies in why you prefer what you do, in the influence of higher order evaluation and metamental certification. You cannot read off internal etiology from behavior. If you take metamental ascent and autonomy seriously, you must give up behaviorism.

There are, nonetheless, some diachronic implications of the distinction between autonomous preferences and other motives. Desire changes slowly in response to reasoning and evaluation. If I have intense desires concerning another, for example, that the other should have some specific desires and beliefs concerning me, to be with me because I am wonderful for her, for example, those desires will probably not be altered quickly by evaluation and reasoning. For example, reasoning leading me to the conclusion that the other will not come to have the desires and beliefs I desire her to have will probably not extinguish the desire. Desire is often like that. Full of inertia. I am left desiring that the one I love will love me in the way that I wish even when evaluation and reasoning convince me that what I desire is hopeless. I am left with the misery of an intense desire I am convinced will not be satisfied. The intensity of desire may cause me to try to get her to love me in the way I desire though I know this is hopeless. The typical masochistic dysfunction of the unrequited love of bondage lies along this path.

Autonomous love based on autonomous preference lacks the dysfunctional character. For, evaluation is a component of preference. If the evaluation changes, so does the preference. Thus, autonomous love based on preference is not subject to the bondage of extreme love resulting from the unresponsiveness of desire to higher level evaluation. Of course, we must not convert autonomous love into a libertarian utopia. Having loved another autonomously may itself create desire for the continuation of the love relationship even when it is evaluated as hopeless. I may cease to prefer to satisfy the desires of the other but at the same time continue to desire to satisfy the desires of the other. Preference not to satisfy the desires of another does not bring about that result immediately, but it has an effect if action is driven by preference. In any event, there is a difference between preferring something out of autonomous love for another and preferring it out of bondage to the other's desires. The person who prefers out of autonomous love to satisfy the preferences of the loved one prefers to do so because of a preference for having that preference. The preference is, therefore, not manipulated by another and leaves you with autonomy provided preference is the spring of action.

Autonomous Love and Trust

It is possible to love another and to love the autonomy of another. To love the autonomy of the other is to prefer that the other prefer what they do, including the loving preferences for your preferences, because they prefer to have those preferences. The preference to be loved autonomously is a preference that accepts the autonomy of the other in love. The natural difficulty in loving autonomously arises from the insecurity one may feel when the love one receives is autonomous love. One knows that the very preference that the person has for what one prefers, even concerning what matters most to you, is the result of the other autonomously preferring to have that preference and may disappear with the disappearance of the autonomous preference of the other. One may feel that one has no control over whether one is loved and suffer the resulting vulnerability.

Reciprocal autonomous love must be based on trust in the preferences of the other and, for that matter, on trust in one's own preferences. Autonomous love is a love founded on trust rather than on control. Trust in the preferences of oneself or another should be founded on the acceptance of the trustworthiness of oneself and the other. If you accept that the other is trustworthy in what he or she prefers, then you should accept that she is also reasonable in what she prefers. The same applies to oneself. If I accept that I am trustworthy in what I prefer, then I accept that I am reasonable in what I prefer. Trust in oneself and the other in love implies that one accepts both are trustworthy in what they prefer and, hence, reasonable in what they prefer including the preferences of love. Trust and reason combine to offer us their stability in place of control. Autonomy, trust and reason are the bedfellows of autonomous love and secure it against the fickle flux of fortune.

Preference and Passion

Have we taken the passion out of love? No. One can have a preference for passion. A preference for passion is, of course, not the same thing as passion nor does it automatically bring it about. Passion like desire arises without our bidding and sometimes against our will. We may, however, have a preference for a passionate life, and though that preference will not guarantee passion, it is the positive evaluation of passion and thus an ally of it. There is a practical conflict between passion and preference which may be resolved creatively. Passion is weakened by reflection and driven by impulse. The positive evaluation of passion must certify at least a temporary silencing of the voice of higher order evaluation to allow one to be driven by first level impulse, for that is the pleasure of passion. Allowing oneself to be driven by passion can, however, be an autonomous preference.

If I and the person I love autonomously share a preference for passion, we may love autonomously and passionately. If one prefers passion and the other does not, the less passionate lover may find a preference, an autonomous preference, for the preference for passion in the other, or, on the contrary, prefer not to prefer the other's preference for passion. That is a limitation in the scope of autonomous love. Some of one's preferences may not be preferred by the other, but it is important to remember that one may be autonomously loved with broad scope even when not all one's preferences are preferred by the other.

Degrees of Preference and Egalitarian Love

I conclude with a deeper look at preference. Preference comes in degrees and, consequently, preference is not an all or nothing attitude. I may give some preference, some weight or degree of preference, to my preferences and to yours. How much preference for the preferences of the other is enough for love? I cannot find any decisive answer to this question, but each giving more weight to the preferences of the other than to one's own may become unstable. If we reciprocate, we find that each prefers what the other prefers which, if we begin with opposite preferences, leads to confusion and cycling back and forth between the preferences of the one person and those of the other.

If, on the other hand, one gives equal weight to the preferences of another and to oneself, that seems to me to represent a kind of love for the other, equal, at any rate, to the love one has for oneself. This form of egalitarian autonomous love will yield many ties among preferences in cases of conflict. It may, however, be better to flip a coin than cycle back and forth, though the latter may have some charm that the former lacks. Egalitarian autonomous lovers will find that indifference between choices often replaces initial conflict between alternatives.

Negotiation in egalitarian love will tend to favor the preferences of the lover with more intense preferences, however, and that may necessitate the adjustment of the weights of love to keep the less intense lover from being regularly co-opted. Love, it seems to me, requires adjustment of weights to produce negotiation conducive to the happiness of both lovers. The weights may differ in different domains to acknowledge privacy and independence. Thus, no fixed scheme, even the egalitarian one, seems essential to the love relationship. The lovers must discover how much weight to assign to the preferences of the one they love in diverse domains just as they must find how wide the scope of the weights may be. Putting degrees of preference into the configuration of love allows for infinite variation and possibilities in the love relationship and the theory of it. The construction of that theory is an act of love left for the future.

- - -

An earlier version of this paper was presented to the Russellian Society of the University of Sydney and published in their proceedings and was also published in *Conceptus* in German. I am very indebted to Roger Lamb for critical discussion and editorial improvement of the present version.

7

Love and Solipsism

Rae Langton

1. Solipsism

The meditator peers through a window. He sees people in their hats and coats, and wonders if they may be machines. We pity the solipsist. Poor lad, how is he to defeat the goliath of scepticism, armed only with the slings and stones of an all too finite intellect? We admire his willingness to follow the argument wherever it might lead. But we can spare a thought for the people below, should the meditator leave his stove-heated room unconvinced by his counter-sceptical ruminations.

Suppose I were in fact the only person, in a world that looked just like our own. I would interact with things, but I would treat them as people. I would laugh at the worries expressed in that old book, attributed (falsely) to Descartes. I would laugh at the idea that the beings beneath the window, with their coats and hats, were mere machines. Solipsism would be true, and I would not believe it. I would reject solipsism, but my world would be, in a way, solipsistic. Imagine now the reverse. Suppose the world were crowded with people, but my attitude were solipsistic. I would interact with people, treating them as things. Solipsism would be false, and I would believe it true. I would accept solipsism, and my world would be, in a different way, solipsistic. If both worlds are solipsistic, then (in different senses) I am not socially interacting with people in either. Where I am alone, I am not interacting with people at all, but with things. Where I am surrounded by people, there is nothing social about my interactions, if I act as if I am alone.

Suppose Lois would love to meet Superman. She wins a competition, whose lucky winner will meet Superman. She puts on a funny helmet, she puts on a funny glove, and she meets Virtual Superman. She returns to work. 'So disappointing!' she says to her colleague. 'Too bad!' replies Clark. Has she met Superman? Yes and no, but mainly (I think) no. To meet Superman--to meet him properly--he has to *be* Superman (not Virtual Superman), and she has to *treat* him as Superman (not as Clark). That provides a kind of analogue with solipsism. To avoid the solipsistic worlds, some of the beings with whom one interacts must *be* people (not things); and one must *treat* them as people (not as things). 'Treat' is here being used as a shorthand for a group of epistemic and practical attitudes which deserve more analysis (correction: *far* more analysis) than I give them here. The solipsist who fails to treat existing people as people adopts an attitude which has both epistemic and practical aspects. It manifests itself in a certain practical orientation, certain ways of acting, towards the beings around him; and if belief is a disposition, then there will be a conceptual connection between his person-denying behaviour, and his person-denying beliefs. Thus described my attitudinal solipsist is an uncomfortably vague and blurry figure. Is he the metaphysical solipsist, who believes he *is* the only person? Is he the epistemic solipsist, who believes he is the only *knowable* person? Is he the moral solipsist, who believes he is the only person who *matters?* Perhaps each of these in turn. I shall be more interested in the connections here than the divisions.

There can also be small, local solipsisms.

Sometimes there is a small, local version of the second world I described, the world of the attitudinal solipsist. Sometimes a person will, in a particular context, *treat some people as things*. What it is to treat a person as a thing depends on what a person is, and what a thing is, and this means that opinions about solipsism will be linked to opinions about persons and things. If a thing is a mere cog in the vast machine of nature, then one treats a person as a thing by treating her as if she were a mere cog in the vast machine of nature. If a thing is a mere body, then one treats a person as a thing by treating her as if she were a mere body. If a thing is a potential possession, then one treats a person as a thing by treating her as if she were something that could be possessed. If a thing is an item whose value is merely instrumental, then one treats a person as a thing by treating her as if she were an item whose value is merely instrumental. Philosophers often condemn this reduction of persons to things, this local solipsism. How they condemn it depends on the particularities of the case, and on their opinions about persons and things. Philosophers might say that such an attitude fails to treat the other person as an end in herself. Or they might say that it violates the autonomy of the other person. Or they might say that it objectifies the other person. They say that something goes wrong morally, and also (perhaps) epistemically, when people are treated as less than human.

Sometimes there is a small, local version of the first world I described, a solipsistic world that is peopled by phantoms. Sometimes a solitary person will *treat some things as people.* A young child sings gently to her doll, sleep my little one sleep. A farmer raises his eyes to streaming thunderclouds, and whispers thank you. A mother pleads before a painting of a woman in blue. A teenager writhes in solitary sexual ecstasy, murmurs to her pillow, oh my darling. But a pillow is nobody's darling. There is no lady in blue to hear any plea. There is no one to thank for the rain. A doll cannot sleep, or wake. Each person in these examples is alone. There are differences between them, of course: some believe they direct their actions towards someone, and others simply make believe. But the examples illustrate the way that human beings, adults and children alike, have a striking capacity to glean real joy and comfort from merely imagined relations with merely imagined people.

These local solipsisms tend to be thought praiseworthy at best, and at worst harmless--though Kant is something of an exception. Like moralists of past times (and some present) he has something hostile to say about the sexual example. He says that sexual desire is 'unnatural' when a person 'is aroused to it, not by its real object, but by his imagination of this object, and so in a way contrary to the purpose of the desire, since he himself creates its object'. But the charge of unnaturalness betrays a hostility that is ill-founded by Kantian lights, as he himself seems uneasily to acknowledge. The important question, for Kant, should not be about the naturalness of an action, but about the implications it has for people.[1]

Sexual solipsisms are among the most local of all, and they can come in either variety: a sexual solipsist can be someone whose sexual partner is a thing, which he in some sense treats as a human being; or a human being, which he in some sense treats as a thing. The first sexual solipsist may treat a thing as a human being in some ways, and not in others: he may attribute to a thing some human properties, and not others. The first solipsist takes as sexual partner a thing, which he treats as a human being, but he may do so in ways that fall short of treating it as a *person*. Perhaps the thing is a piece of paper, perhaps it is a doll, perhaps it is the electronically created virtual being imagined by Jeanette Winterson:

> If you like, you may live in a computer-created world all day and all night. You will be able to try out a Virtual life with a Virtual lover. You can go into your Virtual house and do Virtual housework, add a baby or two, even find out if you'd rather be gay. Or single. Or straight. Why hesitate when you could simulate?
> And sex? Certainly. Teledildonics is the word. You will be able to plug in your telepresence to the billion-bundle network of fibre optics criss-crossing the

---

1. In this paper I draw on Kant's *Doctrine of Virtue* (1797) in the translation by Mary Gregor (Harper and Row, 1964), Vol. VI in the Academy edition; and on his *Lectures on Ethics* (1775-1780) in the translation by Louis Infield (London: Methuen, 1930), from the notes made by Brauer, Kutzner and Mrongovius, edited by Paul Mentzer. These two works are abbreviated *DV* and *LE* respectively. The passage quoted in this paragraph is at *DV* 87-88. The signs of unease: 'it is not so easy to produce the rational proof that the unnatural...use of one's sexual power is a violation of duty to oneself' (*DV* 88). Kant then goes on to say that such a use is incompatible with reverence for humanity in one's own person.

world and join your partner in Virtuality. Your real selves will be wearing body suits made up of thousands of tiny tactile detectors per square inch. Courtesy of the fibre optic network these will receive and transmit touch. The Virtual epidermis will be as sensitive as your own outer layer of skin.

For myself, unreconstructed as I am, I'd rather hold you in my arms....Luddite? No, I don't want to smash the machines but neither do I want the machines to smash me.[2]

Here we have it all: a housework machine, a baby machine, a love machine. What more could one want? The fantastical imaginings of philosophers-- experience machines, brains in vats--may be closer to reality than they have been in the past. Perhaps such imaginings are about to make a transition from thought experiments to experiments in living. Like Winterson's unnamed narrator, we can live in hope that we shall not be smashed.

These solipsisms--global, local and sexual--are also the topic of this essay's companion piece, 'Sexual Solipsism'.[3] There I discuss in more detail the solipsism of treating things as people, the animation of things, in which some human qualities are projected, seriously or otherwise, on to things that lack them. And there is a focus on the sexual version of this solipsism, hinted at in Kant's description of a sexual desire that is aroused 'not by its real object', and hinted at in Winterson's description of virtual sex. This solipsism is a theme of some feminist thinking about pornography: it is sometimes said that in pornography, things are treated as women. Catherine MacKinnon, for example, says that the use of pornography is 'sex between people and things, human beings and pieces of paper, real men and unreal women'.[4] But the opposite solipsism is a more common theme of feminist thinking about pornography, which is that in pornography women are treated as things, women are objectified. And one question pursued in this essay's companion piece concerns the connection, if any, between these apparently different, even contradictory, feminist ideas about sexual solipsism in pornography.

Both essays focus on a solipsism in sexual love, and what Kant had to say about it. Kant said, with apparently extravagant pessimism, that 'sexual love makes of the loved person an object of appetite', and that thereby a 'person becomes a thing and can be treated and used as such' (*LE* 163). Each essay explores a different interpretation of what Kant might mean. But both essays

---

2. Jeanette Winterson, *Written on the Body* (London: Jonathan Cape, 1992) pp. 97-8. Winterson here imagines two real lovers having sex across the network, but the telepresence could be entirely fictional.

3. 'Sexual Solipsism', *Philosophical Topics* vol. 23, no. 2 (Fall 1995), pp. 181-219.

4. Catherine MacKinnon, *Only Words* (Cambridge, MA: Harvard University Press, 1993) p. 109.

also focus on a possible *escape* from solipsism, and what Kant had to say about it. And that is my topic now.

2. Escape

My world is solipsistic if I am alone, interacting with things, but treating them as people. My world is also solipsistic if I interact with people, treating them as things. How one is to escape these worlds is a matter of philosophical debate. One pursues the path of virtue, perhaps. One finds a reply to the sceptic. In practice however, an effective remedy for (and proof against?) both worlds is to be found in love and friendship. One cannot believe of a friend that he does not exist, cannot be known, does not matter. If he is a friend, then evidently he does exist, he is known, and he does matter. It is true that some of the functions of a friend may, with luck, be performed by beings that are not people: a doll, a teddy bear, a fictional construct of some religious practice. A hymn may tell us what a friend we have in Jesus, all our sins and griefs to bear. But the need for a hymn points to the slenderness of the friendship. We do not need songs to tell us who our real friends are. There are limits on the extent to which the functions of a friend may be performed by beings that are not people --limits that are placed by nature. An imaginary friend is a friend in the way that fool's gold is gold. Fool's gold may be *believed* to be gold. But there are limits on the extent to which the functions of a friend may be *believed* to be performed by beings that are not people--limits that are placed by reason. There are limits on the extent to which people can treat things as people when it comes to treating things as friends. An imaginary friend is not believed to be a friend, without the assistance of self-deception--or so I suspect. If so, an imaginary friend is even less like a friend, than fool's gold is like gold.[5]

The idea that friendship provides escape from solipsism is to be found, I think, in Kant. He says that friendship provides release from the 'prison' of the self. The man without a friend is the man who is all alone, who 'must shut himself up in himself', who must remain 'completely alone with his thoughts as in a prison' (*DV* 144). Kant says that each person has a duty to seek out friendship, and escape from the prison. Each of us has a duty 'not to isolate ourselves' (*DV* 145). It is a duty both to ourselves and to others, and Kant suggests that it is partly implied by our own self-love. We must love ourselves, but according to Kant, 'self-love cannot be divorced from our need of being loved by others (i.e. of receiving help from them when we are in need)'. In loving ourselves we desire that others will love us, and that they will desire to make our ends theirs. This imposes a duty on us to love others as we love ourselves,

---

5. Thanks to Roger Lamb for comments helping to clarify this.

and to make their ends ours (*DV* 53, 118) There is a suggestion here that we cannot exercise even the self-regarding virtues unless we are part of a moral community of people, among whom there are some who love us, and are loved by us in return. In friendship the reciprocity characteristic of moral relations in general is present with a unique intensity: friendship is 'the maximum reciprocity of love' (*LE* 202); it is an 'intimate union of love and respect', an ideal of 'emotional and practical concern' for another's welfare (*DV* 140).

Friendship is a matter of doing, and feeling, and also knowing: it has aspects that are both practical and epistemic. Friends do things together, act in ways that bring joy to each other; but this is possible only if each (partly) knows the mind of the other. In friendship one must exercise an active power of sympathy, a capacity that is no sentimental susceptibility to joy or sadness, but a communion that is practical in its orientation, providing a way to 'participate actively in the fate of others' (*DV* 126). Friendship is a duty to know another person, and to allow oneself to be known. The need to 'unburden our heart' is a basic human need, and in order that

> this release may be achieved, each of us needs a friend, one in whom we can confide unreservedly, to whom we can disclose completely all our dispositions and judgments, from whom we can and need hide nothing, to whom we can communicate our whole self. (*LE* 205-6)

In friendship at its best, there will be a 'complete confidence of two persons in revealing their secret thoughts and feelings to each other' (*DV* 143).

In allowing oneself to be known by another, one is able better to know oneself, and thereby to fulfil the first of the duties to oneself. Kant describes the Socratic injunction to 'know thyself' as the first command, despite the fact that one can never fully fathom the 'depths and abyss of one's heart' (*DV* 107). Kant's chief interest in the matter of self-knowledge is in knowledge of one's own motives and character. And he suggests that friends can help one to obey the Socratic injunction by providing scope for communication and correction. The process of putting thoughts into communicative words enables us better to learn what we think and feel and desire. Kant might well have said of the communication of friends what he in fact said of prayer, namely that it is

> necessary *for our own sakes*....To grasp and comprehend his concepts a person must clothe them in words. (*LE* 98-9, emphasis added)

One's own thoughts are but dimly grasped and comprehended unless one has the opportunity to clothe them in words, and communicate them to another. Even Descartes' attempt to grasp the possibility of solipsism is clothed in words and addressed to a reader. Besides communication there is also correction. When we 'clothe our concepts in words' in the process of unburdening our heart to a friend, our judgments about ourselves and our motives are as fallible and in need of correction as our judgments about anything else, and more vulnerable to self-deception. Kant says that 'self-revelation' in friendship is 'a human necessity for the correction of our judgments'.

> To have a friend whom we know to be frank and loving, neither false nor spiteful, is to have one who will help us to correct our judgment when it is mistaken. (*LE* 206)

To have a friend is to have someone who enables you to escape from the prison of the self: someone whom you can know, someone to whom you can make yourself known, someone who will help you better to know yourself, someone who will help you to be good, someone who will bring you happiness.

A friend thus brings a vast number of benefits, prudential, moral, and epistemic. But none of these self-regarding benefits can be the point of the friendship. The point always involves reciprocity: mutual knowledge, mutual sharing of activity, mutual love and respect. Christine Korsgaard draws attention to the metaphors of self-surrender and retrieval in Kant's discussion of reciprocity in friendship. Kant says,

> If I am to love [my friend] as I love myself, I must be sure that he will love me as he loves himself, in which case he restores to me that with which I part and I come back to myself again....Assume that I choose only friendship, and that I care only for my friend's happiness in the hope that he cares for mine. Our love is mutual; there is complete restoration. I, from generosity, look after his happiness and he similarly looks after mine; I do not throw away my happiness, but surrender it to his keeping, and he in turn surrenders his into my hands. (*LE* 202-3)

This is an ideal of friendship, which is never to be encountered in this perfect form, according to Kant, for 'in practical life such things do not occur'. But ordinary friendships aspire to this ideal, and approximate it to a greater or lesser degree. There is an element of risk. I care for my friend's happiness in the hope that he cares for mine. I trust my friend to keep my confidence, and expect him to place a similar trust in me. This is hope and trust, and not a bargain.

If friendship can provide an effective escape from solipsism, can love --erotic love--provide the same? Kant sometimes sees erotic love and friendship as alike in their power to unlock the prison of the self, their power to create a communion, an 'intimate union of love and respect'. Kant sometimes seems to say that erotic love, like friendship, can be moral love.

> Love, whether it is for one's spouse or for a friend...wants to communicate itself completely, and it expects of its respondent a similar sharing of heart, unweakened by distrustful reticence.

> Whether it is for one's spouse or for a friend, love presupposes the same mutual respect for the other's character.[6]

Kant writes this in a letter to Maria von Herbert, a young woman who believes she has been abandoned by a 'friend'. The status of the 'friendship' is at first unclear, but Kant says in his reply that, for the purpose of his moral advice, 'it makes no significant difference', since the same mutual honesty and mutual respect is characteristic of love, 'whether it is for one's spouse or for a friend'. If Kant is right in his letter to Maria, then love can be a particular kind of friendship, with the network of benefits, virtues, and duties that this implies. Korsgaard points out that Kant uses the very same metaphors of self-surrender and retrieval in describing the reciprocity of sexual love. Of friendship, Kant writes, if I love my friend 'as I love myself', and he loves me 'as he loves himself', 'he restores to me that with which I part and I come back to myself again' (*LE* 202). Of sexual love, Kant writes, 'if I yield myself completely to another and obtain the person of the other in return, I win myself back' (*LE* 167). The friendship does not leave everything as it was, so Christine Korsgaard suggests: one is restored to oneself, but one is also transformed.[7]

If love and friendship are alike, then love, like friendship, will be a matter of doing, and feeling, and knowing. Lovers, like friends, will show 'emotional and practical concern' for another's welfare, they will do things together, act in ways that bring joy to each other. Each will want to know the other, and to allow himself, herself to be known. Each will exercise an active power of sympathy towards one another, a communion that is practical in its orientation, that provides a way to 'participate actively in the fate of others' (*DV* 126). If Kant is right, then love, like friendship, will also provide that scope for communication and correction which enables one better to know oneself. It involves the same trust--the 'complete confidence of two persons in revealing

---

6. Kant's letter to Maria von Herbert of Spring 1792. See *Kant: Philosophical Correspondence*, tr. Arnulf Zweig (Chicago: University of Chicago Press, 1967). I have adapted the translation. The letter appears in the Academy edition of Kant's works in Vol. XI, p. 331. In the text the point about mutual respect comes before the point about communication. This passage is also discussed in 'Sexual Solipsism', and in my paper 'Duty and Desolation', *Philosophy* 67 1992, pp. 481-505, whose subject is the correspondence between Kant and Maria von Herbert.

7. My understanding of Kant's views about friendship owes a great debt to Christine Korsgaard's work in 'Creating the Kingdom of Ends: Responsibility and Reciprocity in Personal Relations', *Philosophical Perspectives 6 Ethics*, 1992, pp. 305-332. Korsgaard sees in this aspect of Kant a possibility of answering that feminist critique of Kant which alleges that he makes the self independent of personal relations (p. 328, n15). As will be evident to the reader, I am sympathetic to Korsgaard's defense of Kant on this issue.

their secret thoughts and feelings to each other' (*DV* 143). If Kant is right in his letter to Herbert, then a lover can also be a

> friend...in whom we can confide unreservedly, and to whom we can disclose completely all our dispositions and judgments, from whom we can and need hide nothing, to whom we can communicate our whole self. (*LE* 205-6)

3. Desire

Kant goes too far (by his own lights, as we shall see) if he says that it 'makes no difference' whether the relationship he considers is one of love or friendship. Sexual love brings with it an entirely new constellation of emotions, among which is a sheer delight in the body of another person which sets it apart from friendship. We can find little acknowledgement of this dimension of love in Kant's own writings. But there are vivid descriptions of it by countless novelists and poets, one of whom contributed to a very old book for which Kant had at least some respect.[8] The Biblical poem describes a dialogue of call and response between two lovers, and a few lines are enough to capture the difference in the mood.

> 'Thou hast ravished my heart, my spouse,
> how fair is thy love!
> Thy lips, O my spouse, drop as the honeycomb,
> honey and milk are under thy tongue.
> A garden inclosed is my spouse,
> an orchard of pomegranates with pleasant fruits,
> camphire with spikenard, spikenard and saffron,
> calamus and cinnamon, myrrh and aloe,
> a fountain of gardens,
> a well of living waters.'

> 'Awake, O north wind, and come thou south;
> blow upon my garden,
> that the spices thereof may flow out.
> Let my beloved come into his garden,
> and eat his pleasant fruits.
> Drink, yea, drink abundantly,
> O beloved.'[9]

---

8. Kant often refers favourably to the Bible; some (random) examples from the works considered here are at *DV* 63, 95, 113, 130; *LE* 10, 100, 108, 114. But I don't mean to suggest he would approve of this particular biblical poem.

9. *The Song of Solomon*, Ch.4: 9-16, Ch. 5: 1 (from the King James version of the Bible). The Song is supposed to have been written by King Solomon in 1014 B.C, but

...*continuing*...

A gulf of three thousand years divides this poem from ourselves, and yet there is no mistaking the phenomenon it depicts. Readers who suspect a certain metaphorical intent may be pleased to learn that the poem's more recent editors suspect one too. Then again, they may not. Cautious subtitles, in my edition, inform the reader of the true and hidden meaning of these verses: 'Christ setteth forth the graces of the church', and 'the church prayeth to be made fit for his presence'. The news is theologically intriguing but hardly necessary--unless one needs an excuse for erotica in church. This garden of earthly delights, this oasis in the desert, stands for a union that is more familiar, and at least somewhat less mysterious. The captive heart, the driving hunger for which ordinary hunger and thirst provide faint metaphors, the delight in the body, all of these set sexual love well apart from any theological simulacrum, and set it apart from the 'intimate union' of friendship of which Kant spoke.

These features of love make Kant suspicious. Although his letter to Maria expressed a cautious optimism about sexual love, seeing it as a relation of communication and respect, such moments of optimism are rare. There is also the pessimism I alluded to earlier. Kant tends to think that any virtues to be found in sexual love exist in spite of, not because of, sexual desire. Perhaps this is not entirely surprising. We can anticipate that a rationalistic Kant will be wary of love's delusions, its blind and reckless passions. And so he is. A lover is a wishful thinker, who is quite blind to faults in the beloved. Kant warns against the perils of romantic love.[10] But Kant's concerns are at once more basic, and more complicated, than this.

The sexual impulse, he says,

> ...is *an appetite for another human being*...Human love is good will, affection, promoting the happiness of others and finding joy in their happiness. But it is clear that when a person loves another purely from sexual desire, none of these factors enter into the love. Far from there being any concern for the happiness of the loved one, the lover, in order to satisfy his desire and still his appetite, may even plunge the loved one into the depths of misery. Sexual love makes of

---

later critics have dated it to the 3rd or 4th century B.C. See the *Oxford Companion to English Literature*, ed. Margaret Drabble (Oxford: Oxford University Press, 1985). The passage has been compressed, and I am responsible for the (doubtless inauthentic) arrangement in lines. I attribute the last two lines quoted to the woman, but that is open to interpretation.

10. The wishful thinking of lovers is discussed in *DV* 94; Kant warns against the perils of romantic love in a letter to Elizabeth Motherby, February 11th 1793, citing Maria von Herbert as a cautionary example. The letter is discussed in 'Duty and Desolation'.

the loved person an object of appetite; as soon as that appetite has been stilled, the person is cast aside as one casts away a lemon which has been sucked dry. (*LE* 163)

A bleaker view of sexual love is hard to imagine. Sexual love is not really 'human' love at all--except in the sense that one might be prepared to describe the appetite of a cannibal as a love of human beings. Sexual love makes of the beloved an 'object of appetite'. The beloved is consumed by it, sucked dry, reduced to an empty rind, and cast by the wayside. The lover is, in the end, alone, the appetite stilled, a sour taste in the mouth.

Sexual love is said to make of the loved person an 'object of appetite': but what does that mean? Given the moral character of Kant's evident dismay, he appears to mean that in sexual love, or in merely sexual love, one treats people as things. Sexual love is not a remedy for solipsism at all, but forces solipsism upon us. Looking at passages like these, it can be hard to see how Kant imagines that sexual love is even compatible with the moral relations of friendship. That is why I said he goes too far *by his own lights*, if he suggests it 'makes no significant difference' whether a relationship is one of friendship or erotic love. His harsh words are modified, to be sure, by an attempt to allow their compatibility:

Sexual love can, of course, be combined with human love and so carry with it the characteristics of the latter, but taken by itself and for itself, it is nothing more than appetite. (*LE* 163)

In a comparable passage he allows that, while sexual passion 'really has nothing in common with moral love', it can nevertheless 'enter into close union with it *under the limiting conditions of practical reason*' (*DV* 90). This uneasy grafting of antagonistic attitudes falls short of the love described in his letter, whose core is affection and respect--but it does show Kant thinks there are solutions to any problems posed by the character of sexual desire. And perhaps it is no surprise that his solution has a familiar and prosaic face: 'the limiting conditions of practical reason' turn out to be those of marriage (*LE* 167).

While there may be room to doubt this particular verdict, there is no room to doubt that Kant is acutely suspicious of sexual desire, or at any rate, of its common pathologies. It is worth asking why. And in what follows, I look at three ways to understand Kant's idea that a person might be made an *object* of appetite. The first is innocent, and gives no cause for moral alarm. The second (suggested by Barbara Herman) *would* give some cause for moral alarm, and so too would the third suggested by Korsgaard), but for a different reason. In the final section of the paper I take up Korsgaard's interpretation, which describes an attitude that has, I think, been accurately mapped by Proust. It is an attitude which appears, at first, to have something in common with friendship, but it becomes in the end the solipsism of someone alone, shut up in himself, as in a prison.

4. Three ways to read 'object'

Kant's reference to an 'object of appetite' is not very clear. Although the concept of an object is in many ways central to his moral philosophy, there are different ways to understand it. If sexual love makes of the loved person an 'object' in the sense of making her thing-like, less than human, then it will be incompatible with Kant's moral principles. But 'object' is not always a pejorative, not always a red flag to be waved before some moralizing bull. It has a role in talk about *intentional* attitudes, which is morally neutral: it refers to what Kant elsewhere calls an accusative of thought--an intentional object. When, in the biblical poem, the woman thinks of her lover, he is the object of her thoughts: her thoughts are directed towards him. She thinks that his eyes are like jewels, that his mouth is most sweet, that he is altogether lovely. She thinks about him and says to herself: 'his desire is *toward me*'.[11] He is the object of her thoughts, her thoughts are toward him; she is the object of his desire, his desire is toward her. In this usage, one is never an 'object' *simpliciter*, but 'an object of __', where the blank is a place-holder for some intentional attitude: one can be an object of someone's thought, or respect, or knowledge, or devotion, or loathing--or desire. One can evidently be made an object of someone's intentional attitude without thereby being made an object in some pernicious sense. To make a person an object in this merely intentional sense is not to adopt a solipsism. On the contrary, one escapes epistemic solipsism only by making another person the object of one's knowledge; one escapes moral solipsism only by making another person the object of one's respect and love.[12] We therefore have a *duty* to make persons into objects, in these ways. Why then Kant's moral dismay at the prospect that sexual love 'makes of the

---

11. *Song* 5: 12, his eyes are 'fitly set', i.e. 'set as a precious stone in the foil of a ring' according to the analytical notes on the Hebrew in my edition; 5: 16; 7: 10, emphasis added.

12. This is something I also discuss in 'Sexual Solipsism'. It seems to me that the intentional sense and a morally pernicious sense of 'object' may be conflated by some phenomenologists, such as Sartre, when they say that consciousness inevitably makes an 'object' of the other, and that a tendency to oppressive social relations is thus located in the structure of consciousness itself. Perhaps there is another version of this in Luce Irigaray, who seems to locate oppressive social relations (partly) in the *grammatical* category of a direct object, and would therefore like to avoid it, hence her title, *I love to you* (London: Routledge, 1995).

loved person an object' of some intentional attitude? As a moral claim, it looks like a punning *non sequitur*--unless there is something special and pathological about making someone an object of the particular intentional attitude (or attitudes) in question, of sexual desire.

Kant's claim that sexual love can make people into objects finds a modern incarnation in feminist claims that sexual relations, in conditions of oppression, objectify women. This reminds us of a second way to read the notion of an object. Perhaps when Kant says that sexual love makes a person into an object, he means that it objectifies a person, reduces a person to a thing. What this means exactly is also open to debate: but in the Kantian context it will have some of the dimensions I described before. To be a thing, or an object, is to be a determined cog in the machine of nature; or it is to be merely a body; or it is to be something that can be possessed; or it is to be something whose value is merely instrumental. To make a person an object is to reduce her to a thing, in any of these ways. Barbara Herman has drawn attention to the common ground between Kant's views and those of such feminists as Andrea Dworkin and Catherine MacKinnon, and these aspects of the notion of an object have surely all had a role to play in feminist analysis of oppression.[13] Herman shows us the following passages from Kant.

> Taken by itself [sexual love] is a degradation of human nature; for as soon as a person becomes an object of appetite for another, all motives of moral relationship cease to function, because as an object of appetite for another a person becomes a thing and can be treated and used as such by every one.

> Because sexuality is not an inclination which one human being has for another as such, but is an inclination for the sex of the other, it is a principle of the degradation of human nature....That [the woman] is a human being is of no concern to the man; only her sex is the object of his desires. Human nature is thus subordinated. Hence it comes that all men and women do their best to make not their human nature but their sex more alluring and direct their activities and lusts entirely towards sex. Human nature is thereby sacrificed to sex. (*LE* 163-4)

Here we have a clear expression of Kant's idea: sexual love does not merely make the beloved the object of some intentional attitude, but in sexual love 'a

---

13. Barbara Herman, 'Could It Be Worth Thinking about Kant on Sex and Marriage?', in *A Mind Of One's Own: Feminist Essays on Reason and Objectivity*, ed. Louise M. Antony and Charlotte Witt (Boulder: Westview Press, 1993). I do not do justice to Herman's interesting paper here. Herman finds in Kant's argument for the apparently conservative solution about marriage a potential feminist argument for legal institutions to provide solutions to problems in 'private' sexual relations: one possible legal solution being anti-pornography legislation.

person becomes a *thing*', where the concept of a thing is explicitly contrasted to that of a person or a human being. Herman compares these Kantian thoughts to the following, from the writings of Andrea Dworkin.

> There is a deep recognition in culture and in experience that intercourse is both the normal use of a woman...and a violative abuse, her privacy irredeemably compromised, her selfhood changed in a way that is irrevocable.

> It is especially in the acceptance of the object status that her humanity is hurt; it is a metaphysical acceptance of lower status in sex and in society; an implicit acceptance of less freedom, less privacy, less integrity...a political collaboration with his dominance...[In intercourse] he confirms for himself and for her what she is; that she is something, not someone; certainly not someone equal.[14]

Herman points out the common thread in these bleak writings: that sexual relations, or at least heterosexual relations, somehow turn women into objects--that they are, as Herman puts it, 'not compatible with the standing of the partners as equal human beings'. Kant does seem to acknowledge that sexual relations pose a special problem for women, but he is not much concerned with the objectification of women in particular. The human nature of men and women alike is, he says, 'sacrificed to sex'. While the burden of objectification has doubtless fallen chiefly on women, there is something right, I think, in Kant's gender-neutral talk, something right in the suggestion that any human being can objectify another, given the appropriate context and the power. So without ignoring the fact of gender, we can try here to explore the issue in the way that Kant presents it: as a question about what it might be for one human being to make another an object. And the literature we consider is not, in any case, one from which easy conclusions about gender can be drawn.[15]

   The problem with sexual desire, on Herman's understanding of Kant, is that it is directed towards a person not *qua* person, but *qua* thing. Kant says that when a man desires a woman, the fact 'that she is a human being is of no concern to the man; only her sex is the object of his desires' (*LE* 164). She is a human being, a rational creature, with desires and plans of her own, an active capacity for sympathy and friendship, a capacity for grasping the moral law and

---

14. Andrea Dworkin, *Intercourse* (New York: Free Press, 1987), pp. 122-3, 140-1.

15. The narrator of Winterson's beautiful novel is not only nameless, but of a gender that is left unknown to the reader, while the author herself is lesbian. Albertine in Proust's novel is a woman, but an ambiguity is introduced when one knows that the novel is largely autobiographical, that the author is homosexual, and that the relationship with Albertine is partly based on a relationship with a man. In contrast to the relatively gender-neutral discussion of solipsism in this essay, its companion, 'Sexual Solipsism', explores feminist aspects of the theme.

conforming her actions to it: but none of that, says Kant, is relevant to the man who desires her. Only her sex, only her eroticized body, is the object of his desires. And he presumably supposes that the same is true, *mutatis mutandis*, when a woman desires a man.

If Herman's interpretation is right, there is obviously truth in what Kant says. Love is indeed 'written on the body', to borrow Winterson's phrase, and the biblical poem provides as good an example as any. The poet is entranced by the body of the woman he loves. She is fair as the moon, clear as the sun, terrible as an army with banners. The joints of her thighs are as jewels, her belly as wheat set about with lilies, her breasts as clusters of the vine. And, in the poem, she returns the compliments. She says that her beloved is the chiefest of ten thousand, his eyes are as the eyes of doves, his lips as lilies, his belly as bright ivory.[16] Imagine if she were to say instead that her beloved is the most rational of ten thousand, that his intellect is as the morning sun, and as a precious jewel his capacity for autonomous choice. Thud. The song would not, let's face it, be the same. The biblical love song does not speak of autonomy, freedom, capacity for rational choice, moral agency. What love song would? Each lover talks instead about the unique beauty of the body of the beloved.

It could be that Kant is imagining a prospect that is more reductive than this, when he says 'only her sex is the object of his desires'. He may be thinking, more pessimistically, that sexual desire is entirely impersonal, even genital in its interest--that it is of the kind expressed today in some pornography, and in some novels, where a woman is described by the narrator as a sexual 'automaton', whose body is gratifyingly 'anonymous', 'marvellously impersonal', a kind of sexual experience machine.[17]

But whether the body is viewed as an object of unique aesthetic delight, or as an anonymous instrument, it is still, on Herman's interpretation of Kant, a body that is the object of sexual desire. So what? one might ask. Any philosopher who has qualms about this must be both a puritan, and a metaphysical fantasist, who imagines that bodies have nothing to do with people, that bodies

---

16. These descriptions are from *Song*, chapters 5, 6 and 7.

17. Henry Miller, *Tropic of Capricorn* (New York: Grove Press 1961) pp. 181, 82. See Kate Millett's excellent discussion of Miller's inanities in *Sexual Politics* (Garden City, NY: Doubleday, 1970). Especially interesting is the comparison of Miller with D.H. Lawrence. Note that when Kant says 'only her sex is desired', what he says is ambiguous in various ways, some of which I do not discuss. He may mean, as I have suggested, following Herman, that only her (sexed) body is desired; or he may mean that she is desired only *qua* member of a particular gender, not in so far as she is a person, and to that extent there is the suggestion that any other woman would do just as well. This is noted by Korsgaard, who acknowledges the passage that Herman cites, and says it spoils the interest of Kant's point. ('Creating the Kingdom', p. 327 n11)

are irrelevant to real people, that a person is a pure, transcendent being, a *noumenal* being let us say, who exists beyond the messy world of bodies. This, one might conclude, must surely be the philosophical source of Kant's old-fashioned angst. Not at all, or at any rate, not exactly. It must be admitted that Kant has a heavy puritanical streak. No-one who reads Kant's work on sexuality could seriously deny it, and to that extent the work of Korsgaard and Herman (and myself) is bound to be at least partly reconstructive. However, the puritanical streak is not the essence, and his view about bodies has something to recommend it.

On Kant's view human beings are partly *constituted* by our bodies:

> ...our life is entirely conditioned by our body, so that we cannot conceive of a life not mediated by the body and we cannot make use of our freedom except through the body. It is therefore obvious that the body constitutes a part of ourselves (*LE* 147-8)

Kant's moral concerns about sexual desire do not flow from a Platonic hostility or blindness to human embodiment, but from an acute awareness of it. Since a human being is partly constituted by her body, the surrender of one's body is a surrender of one's own person. Puritan or no, Kant is not, at least here, a metaphysical fantasist.

There is a third way to read the notion of an object. A different interpretation of Kant's claim that sexual desire makes a person into an object of appetite has been suggested by Korsgaard. What is wrong with sexual desire is that it is directed towards a person *qua* person: that from the outset it takes, not a body, but a person as its intentional object. There is some plausibility in what she suggests. Consider what Kant says:

> Amongst our inclinations there is one which is directed towards other human beings. *They themselves*, and not their work and services, are its objects of enjoyment...There is an inclination which we may call an appetite for enjoying another human being. We refer to sexual impulse. Man can, of course, use another human being as an instrument for his service; he can use his hands, his feet, and even all his powers; he can use him for his own purposes with the other's consent. But there is no way in which a human being can be made an object of indulgence for another except through sexual impulse...it is an appetite for another human being. (*LE* 162-3, emphasis added)

> Sexual inclination is...not merely a pleasure of the senses...It is rather pleasure from the use of another person...[it has] nothing in common with moral love. (*DV* 90)

Sexual desire is directed not towards a body, but towards a person in his or her entirety. 'They themselves', and not their services, or their body, are its objects of enjoyment. Korsgaard suggests that what troubles Kant is the idea that sexual love demands that the beloved put not simply her body but her entire self at the lover's disposal. 'Viewed through the eyes of sexual desire another person is seen as something wantable, desirable, and, therefore, inevitably, possessable. To yield to that desire, to the extent it is really that desire you yield to, is to allow yourself to be possessed.'[18] Kant says that 'a person cannot be a property': to allow oneself to be possessed would be to allow oneself to become a thing (*LE* 165).

Of these three ways to read the notion of object in Kant's remark, the last two give grounds for moral suspicion. We have two moral interpretations of Kant's claim that sexual love 'makes of the loved person an object of appetite'. On Herman's reading, sexual love can make of the loved person an object, by viewing her as a mere body: *something*, not someone (to borrow Dworkin's phrase), and something to be used and possessed. On Korsgaard's reading, sexual love does not make of the loved person a mere body. It is directed towards a person in her entirety, viewing her therefore as *someone*, not something, but nevertheless someone to be used and possessed. Must we choose between these two readings? And what plausibility does either of them have as a story about the reality of sexual life, or some aspect of that reality?

Perhaps we could bring the two readings together by distinguishing opaque and transparent versions of Kant's claim. Kant thinks that the extensional object of sexual desire is in fact a person, and on this (transparent) reading Korsgaard is right; but the desire is for that person *qua body,* and on this (opaque) reading Herman is right. Sexual desire is a hunger for a (person's) body. When Kant says, in the passage crucial to Korsgaard's interpretation, that '*human beings.... themselves,* and not their work and services' are the objects of sexual desire, what he says is ambiguous between the opaque and the transparent readings-- and compatible with Herman's interpretation if we take the opaque. The earlier point about bodily constitution is relevant here. Perhaps the idea is that sexual desire takes just a body as its intentional object (as Herman suggests), but since the body partly *constitutes* the person, one cannot surrender one's body without in fact surrendering one's self. Kant says that

> The body is part of the self; in its togetherness with the self it constitutes the person....But the person who surrenders [only for the satisfaction of sexual desire] is used as a thing; the desire is still directed only towards sex and not towards the person as a human being. But it is obvious that to surrender part of oneself is to surrender the whole, because a human being is a unity. (*LE* 166)

On this interpretation, Korsgaard would be partly right: she would be right to say that, on Kant's view, sexual love demands that the beloved put not simply her body but her entire self at the lover's disposal. But Korsgaard would be partly wrong. Sexual love demands that the beloved put her entire self at the

---

18. 'Creating the Kingdom', p. 310.

lover's disposal, not because the lover desires the person *qua person* (as Korsgaard suggested)--but rather because of the *essentially embodied* nature of the person desired. The demand stems not from the (intentional) content of the desire, but from the (extensional) nature of the one desired. On this compromise interpretation, Herman is right, and Korsgaard partly right, partly wrong. However, since Korsgaard, like Herman, is actually aiming to describe the *intentional* content of sexual desire, on Kant's view--that it is a desire for a person *qua person*--the attempted compromise fails to do her justice.[19]

A different path to compromise might be to say that Kant holds both views about the intentional content of sexual desire, and that they apply to different kinds of sexual desire, both morally suspect. Perhaps he did not distinguish them very clearly. Perhaps sexual desire can sometimes be a desire for a person *qua* body, a *reductive* desire; and perhaps it can be a desire for a person *qua* person, but what we can call an *invasive* desire. I am not sure whether this is what Kant means: to take this path is admittedly to retreat from the universalizing aspect of Kant's remarks, the appearance he gives of wanting to describe the inevitable character of sexual desire. But his remarks are plausible, as descriptions of some (possibly common) pathologies. It is true that sexual love can sometimes focus on the body of a person, in a way that is reductive; and it is true that sexual love can sometimes focus on a person as a whole, in a way that is invasive. Each of these two ideas is worth pursuing in its own terms. I find the seeds of each of the two ideas in Herman and Korsgaard, respectively, but I shall develop them in ways that they may or may not endorse. I address the first idea, the reductive desire discussed by Herman, in the companion piece to this essay.[20] In what follows I address the second. My aim is very limited. It is to consider what such an invasive desire might look like, and whether Kant's moral dismay would be well-founded, if the desire did, indeed, look like this.

5. Invasive Desire

The 'appetite for a human being' which Kant describes might be, as Korsgaard suggests, a desire which takes as its intentional object a person in his

---

19. Thanks to Roger Lamb for helping me to get a little clearer on this possible compromise.

20. 'Sexual Solipsism'.

or her entirety. As she says, it is likely to be 'more of a problem about sexual love than about casual sexual encounters'.[21]

Proust describes a desire that seems to have just this character. His hero, Marcel, has been watching Albertine, of whom he as yet knows nothing, and with whom he is in love, and he reflects on his desire.

> For an instant...I caught her smiling, sidelong glance, aimed from the centre of that inhuman world...an inaccessible, unknown world...If she had seen me, what could I have represented to her? From the depths of what universe did she discern me? It would have been as difficult for me to say as it would be, when certain features of a neighbouring planet appear to us thanks to the telescope, to conclude from those that human beings live there, that they can see us, and to guess what ideas the sight of us can have aroused in them.
>
> If we thought that the eyes of such a girl were merely two glittering sequins of mica, we would not thirst to know her and to unite her life to ours. But we sense that what shines in those reflecting discs is not due solely to their material composition; it is, unknown to us, the dark shadows of the ideas that being cherishes about the people and places she knows. It is she, with her desires, her sympathies, her revulsions, her obscure and incessant will. I knew that I should never possess [her] if I did not possess also what was in her eyes. And it was consequently her whole life that filled me with desire; a painful desire because I felt it was impossible to fulfil, but exhilarating, like the burning thirst of a parched land--a thirst for a life which my soul, because it had never until now received one drop of it, would absorb all the more greedily, in long draughts. (I 851-2/793-5)[22]

The biblical poet saw his beloved as a fountain of gardens, a well of living waters. One lover called out to the other, 'Drink, yea drink abundantly, o

---

21. What I am taking from Korsgaard is the idea that sexual desire may take as its object a person in his or her entirety. The Proustian interpretation I give this, however, goes beyond what Korsgaard says, and may be in some conflict with it. She takes the idea to involve a kind of *aesthetic* appreciation of a person, an idea which I do not take up here, despite its manifest interest. See Korsgaard's 'Creating the Kingdom', p. 310, 327 n12. The quotation is from n13.

22. *Remembrance of Things Past*, translated by C. K. Scott Moncrieff and Terence Kilmartin (London: Chatto and Windus, 1981); *A la recherche du temps perdu* (Gallimard, 1954). References are to the page numbers in the translation, followed by the page numbers in the Gallimard edition. The translations given are usually very close to Montcrieff/Kilmartin, although they have occasionally been adapted somewhat by me, and in this particular passage the translation is substantially mine. The Proust I describe is doubtless crude and oversimplified, but it would take a longer work to do him justice. Thanks to Richard Holton for generously lending me his volumes of Proust despite my unkindness to the hero; and for perceptive comments on earlier drafts which have helped to improve this essay.

beloved'. We have here the same familiar metaphors of thirst and its quenching, but they take on a different and sinister cast in the meditations of Marcel. He is gripped by 'a thirst for a *life*' which he wants to 'absorb...greedily, in long draughts'. Marcel's desire has a predatory, almost cannibalistic, quality: and perhaps it is this possible quality of desire that appalled Kant, and led him to speak of it as an appetite for another human being. Marcel's desire for Albertine is not simply a desire for her 'material composition' (quaint phrase), not simply a desire to gaze into her glittering eyes, not simply a desire to unite his body with hers, but a desire to annexe her whole being: a desire to 'unite her life' to his (or to 'ours' as he in fact says, with a conspiratorial use of the plural). It is a desire to know those dark shadows of her inner life, 'her desires, her sympathies, her revulsions, her obscure and incessant will'.

Marcel's desire, thus described, is a thirst for knowledge, and in particular, a thirst for knowledge of the mind of another human being. But thus described, is it not a desire to break out of the 'prison' of the self of which Kant spoke? Is it not a desire for an 'intimate union' in which Albertine will satisfy him by 'revealing [her] secret thoughts and feelings' (*LE* 202, *DV* 143)? Kant said that a certain kind of lover ignores the humanity of the one he desires: the fact that the one he desires is a human being is 'of no concern' (*LE* 163). That would be a false description of Marcel. The fact that she is a human being is precisely his concern: 'it is she, with her desires, her sympathies, her revulsions, her obscure and incessant will'. What Marcel desires is that she will reveal the dark shadows of her inner life, that she will (in a heavier Kantian idiom) 'disclose completely all [her] dispositions and judgments', that she will 'hide nothing', that she will 'communicate [her] whole self' (*LE* 206). This does not seem to be a desire that reduces persons to things. This desire for knowledge of another person, this desire for revelation of a self, is distinctively associated with friendship, according to Kant. Should we not say, then, that Marcel's desire is a desire to *escape* from solipsism? Should we not say that Marcel desires Albertine not only as a lover but as a friend?

To say this would be to ignore the predatory character of Marcel's desire. The arrangement he anticipates is, as Kant would say, 'one-sided'.[23] Recall that Kant contrasted the 'appetite for another human being' with that 'human love' which is 'good will, affection, promoting the happiness of others and finding joy in their happiness' (*LE* 163). It seems right to contrast Marcel's love with the love that Kant described as 'human'. Marcel seeks an intimate union of some kind, but it is nothing so prosaic as an 'intimate union of love and respect'. There is none of the reciprocity Kant attributes to friendship. Instead there is the driving desire for Albertine, which is at the same time a

---

23. Kant describes various kinds of sexual relationship as 'one-sided' in his chapter on the topic, *LE* 162-8.

desire to know her, and at the same time a desire to possess her. 'I knew I should never possess her if I did not possess also what was in her eyes'. Knowledge of her thoughts, desires, and sympathies is described as a possession of what was in her eyes: a possession of what it is that makes her a human being, what it is that makes her eyes something more than glittering sequins of mica. If he can possess this, he can possess her. The desire to know and the desire to possess are indistinguishable, for Marcel. He describes 'perfect knowledge' as 'the complete *absorption* of a person' (I 859/802, emphasis added). This is not communication but consumption. To know someone is to invade an alien territory, and annexe it. To know someone is to absorb and assimilate, and the activities of eating and drinking provide the metaphors.

> Whenever the image of women who are so different from us penetrates our minds....we know no rest until we have converted these aliens into something compatible with ourselves, the mind being in this respect endowed with the same kind of reaction and activity as our physical organism, which cannot abide the infusion of any foreign body into its veins without at once striving to digest and assimilate it. (I 859/802)

Marcel's desire is not a reductive desire to enjoy a person's body, as one might enjoy a fruit in the garden. It is a desire to swallow up a human life. And although it is inspired by an apparent yearning to escape the prison of the self, Marcel's desire is in one way quite as solipsistic as a reductive sexual desire which ignores the person altogether. It is interesting to observe the moral and epistemic dimensions to Marcel's attitude, how they interact with one another, how they change over time. While in one way Marcel does not, at this stage, ignore the humanity of the one he desires, in another way he does. There is a yearning to escape from epistemic solipsism--a yearning for knowledge of another mind, another human being with unknown but knowable desires, sympathies--and in this sense he does not ignore the humanity of the one he desires. In his desire to escape epistemic solipsism, he treats a person *as a person* . But in another sense he *does* ignore the humanity of the one he desires: for there is at the very same time a moral solipsism, which treats a person *as a thing*. In treating Albertine as something to be possessed and controlled, Marcel treats her as a thing. In the Kantian idiom, Marcel fails to treat Albertine as an end in herself. Kant wrote (to Maria) that 'love presupposes' a certain 'respect for the other's character', and there is none of that here. Marcel treats Albertine as a knowable human being, who is to be known--and possessed, and controlled. The desire to escape the epistemic solipsism coincides with a desire to create a moral solipsism--or rather, *is* that desire, if the desire to know *is* a desire to possess.

Marcel aims to convert the 'alien' into something compatible with himself, he aims to 'digest and assimilate' her: but because he thinks of knowledge in terms of possession and control, he tries to make her conform to a rigidly script-ed role that he brings to their encounters.

> I carried in my mind...the mental phantom--ever ready to become incarnate--of the woman who was going to fall in love with me, to take up her cues in the amorous comedy which I had had all written out in my mind from my earliest boyhood, and in which every attractive girl seemed to me to be equally desirous of playing, provided that she had also some of the physical qualifications required. In this play, whoever the new star might be whom I invited to create or to revive the leading part, the plot, the incidents, the lines themselves preserved an unalterable form. (I 951/890)

Marcel's desire, the desire to know and possess, is not to be fulfilled, and the frustration is foreshadowed in that first description: 'It was...her whole life that filled me with desire; a painful desire because I felt it was *impossible to fulfil*'.

Why is the desire impossible to fulfil? Marcel's answer, in the end, is that it is because knowledge of another person cannot be had. His answer is the answer of epistemic solipsism. We can imagine a different answer. Marcel's desire is impossible to fulfil, not because knowledge of another person cannot be had, but because something else cannot be had: knowledge of another person *that is possession* of that person. The goal of possession is not identical to the goal of knowledge, as Marcel thinks, but inimical to it. For Marcel to treat Albertine as a potential possession, a puppet whose actions are controlled and scripted, is for him to doom himself to *ignorance* of her. To aim for possession and control is to thwart the knowledge that was his goal in the first place. Marcel ends as an epistemic solipsist, because he began as a moral solipsist, and one of a certain kind: the kind described by Korsgaard, who desires a person *as a person*, but as a person *to be possessed*. This moral solipsism can lead to epistemic solipsism in more ways than one. To possess and control someone is *not* to know them: so to the extent that Marcel succeeds in possessing and controlling, to the extent that he *succeeds* in making Albertine play his scripted role, to that extent he fails to know her. That is one way in which the moral solipsism might lead to the epistemic. However, if one *believes* that to possess and control someone is to know them, then one believes that failure to possess is failure to know: so to the extent that Marcel *fails* to possess and control, and believes that he fails to possess and control, he believes that he fails to know. That is another way in which the moral solipsism might lead to the epistemic. Hope of knowledge is blocked by the attempt to control and possess, *whether the attempt succeeds or fails*. Perhaps that is why Marcel's projects of posses-sion are, as Martha Nussbaum says, doomed before they begin.[24]

---

24. Martha Nussbaum, 'Love's Knowledge', in *Love's Knowledge: Essays on Philoso-*
...*continuing*...

If there is this connection between the moral solipsism and the epistemic, then we can note that moral virtues and epistemic virtues may be interdependent. On Kant's view, as we saw earlier, the morally good life depends on some epistemic virtues. He mentions in particular the need for an active 'power' of 'sympathy'. Some knowledge of other minds is a condition of many moral actions, since it is a condition of sharing others' goals. And there seems to be a dependence in the other direction too. The epistemically good life, so far as it relates to knowledge of people, partly depends on some moral virtues. The person Kant describes will not reveal his 'secret thoughts and feelings' when he is 'hemmed in and cautioned by fear': he will allow himself to be known only when there is 'complete confidence', the kind best achieved in friendship, that intimate union of love and respect (*DV* 143, 140). Albertine will not 'reveal her secret thoughts and feelings' when she is 'hemmed in and cautioned' by Marcel's demands. Some moral attitudes are a condition of some knowledge of other minds. So there is a kind of reciprocal dependence of the epistemic and moral virtues.

Believing his desire impossible to fulfil, Marcel abandons his 'thirst' for another life. The character of his love changes accordingly. Abandoning the thirst for another life, he turns inward. Proust gives us one of the most claustrophobic portraits in literature of what it can be like to be the solitary described by Kant: the one who has 'shut himself up in himself', who remains 'completely alone with his thoughts as in a prison' (*DV* 144). Love is not a relation between two human beings, but at most 'a rather interesting relation with oneself', as Nussbaum aptly comments.[25] Communication is irrelevant to such love.

> I knew now that I was in love with Albertine, but alas! I didn't trouble to let her know it...the declaration of my passion to the one I loved no longer seemed to be

---

phy and Literature, (Oxford: Oxford University Press, 1990) p. 271. I have learned much from Nussbaum's essays on Proust, especially the final part of her discussion of Marcel in 'Love's Knowledge'. I discuss in a more Kantian idiom many themes discussed by her, including that of solipsism. We are both interested in the connection between the moral and epistemic aspects of Marcel's solipsistic attitude. Her conclusions about the commonality between prayer, love, philosophy and literature I find depressing and (fortunately) implausible. If love were like prayer, we would be back in the prison of solipsism, in a world peopled by phantoms. For a different kind of discussion of the relation between love and the rejection of scepticism, see Bas van Fraassen, 'The Peculiar Effects of Love and Desire', *Perspectives on Self-Deception*, eds. Brian McLaughlin and Amélie Rorty (Berkeley: University of California Press, 1988).

25. 'Love's Knowledge', p. 272.

one of the vital and necessary stages of love. And love itself seemed no longer an external reality, but only a subjective pleasure. (I 987/925)

Or else love is not a relation, but a monadic property of the individual:

I realised in the end that...my love was not so much a love for her as a love in myself...not having the slightest real link with [her], not having the slightest support outside itself. (III 568/557)

When we are in love with a woman we simply project on to her a state of our own soul. (I 891/833)

It is only a clumsy and erroneous form of perception which places everything in the object, when really everything is in the mind...love places in a person who is loved what exists only in the person who loves. (III 950-1/912)

A love story is not a story about two people, but one. The individual is 'irremediably alone', and must find the courage to free himself from 'the *lie* which seeks to make us believe that we are *not* irremediably alone' (I 969/908, emphasis added).

The individual lover must perform a kind of sense-datum reduction of any apparent relationship with another existing human being.

Courage was needed...it meant above all to abandon one's dearest illusions, to stop believing in the objectivity of what one had oneself elaborated, and instead of soothing oneself for the hundredth time with the words, 'She was very sweet', to read through that, 'It gave me pleasure to kiss her'. (III 933/896)

Here we have an application of a venerable philosophical principle. Let us retreat from ontological commitment. Let us retreat to sense-datum constructions. We can do it for electrons and photons....nothing but blips and flashes. We can do it for apples and desks and cats....nothing but rather different blips and flashes. It's not always easy, admittedly, to follow the principle wherever it leads. Cats, for example, seem hungry from time to time; yet as a puzzled philosopher said, a bundle of sense data is as incapable of hunger as a triangle is of playing football. Still, perhaps success will come with persistence. Whoever wishes to become a philosopher must, after all, learn not to be frightened of absurdities.[26] And now, if we can do it for science, if we can do it for everyday life, why not do it for the ones we love? Do not say, 'she was kind'. Say

---

26. The point about the cat, and the point about absurdities, are both from Bertrand Russell, *The Problems of Philosophy*, first published in the Home University Library, 1912, reprinted (Oxford: Oxford University Press, 1974), pp. 11, 9. Russell goes on to say that 'the difficulty in the case of the cat is nothing compared to the difficulty in the case of human beings' (p. 11).

instead, 'it gave me pleasure to kiss her'. Do not say, 'she was cruel'. Say instead, 'I was filled with grief'.

Solipsism provides the excuse for leaving the character of Albertine a hollow shell: she is not much more, for the reader, because she is not much more for the lover, the narrator, and (let me be naive) the author.

> A novelist might...be expressing...another truth if....he *refrained from giving any character to the beloved*...Our curiosity about the woman we love overleaps the bounds of that woman's character, at which, even if we could stop, we probably never would...Our intuitive radiography pierces them, and the images which it brings back, far from being those of a particular face, present rather the joyless universality of a skeleton. (I 955/895, emphasis added)

The driving thirst for a life, that 'intuitive radiography' which seeks to invade the depths of her being, defeats itself. A person cannot be consumed or possessed. But the attempt to consume or possess blinds the lover to the knowledge which was his goal in the first place. The initial 'thirst for another life' did have something in common with the human love of which Kant spoke: a desire to reach beyond the self, a desire whose satisfaction could perhaps be found in that 'intimate union of love and respect' which is friendship, and which involves those mundane virtues of which Kant wrote, trust and sympathy, communication, and respect.

But that is not how Marcel has proceeded. His love has followed a different pattern. First there was the dim awareness of another life. She exists. Then: If she exists, I can know her. I want to know her. Then: If I can know her, I can possess her, since knowing is possessing. I want to possess her. Discovery: I cannot possess her. Marcel performs a gruesome *modus tollens*. I cannot possess her. Therefore I cannot know her. Therefore she does not exist. And Marcel contents himself with this conclusion, instead of treating it as the *reductio* of his strategy: the *reductio* of his equation of knowledge and possession.

The inference pattern applied to Albertine is likewise applied to friends.

> The sign of the unreality of others is shown in the impossibility of their satisfying us...friendship is a simulation, since...the artist who gives up an hour of work for an hour's chat with a friend knows that he sacrifices a reality for something that doesn't exist (friends being friends only in that sweet folly which we lend to ourselves throughout the course of life, but which we know deep down to be the delusion of a fool who chats with chairs and tables, believing them to be alive). (III 909/875)

Albertine fails to satisfy him; so she does not exist. His friends fail to satisfy him; so they do not exist. And Marcel extends his inference to every other human being.

> It is the misfortune of beings to be nothing more for us than useful showcases for the collections of one's own mind. (III 568/558,)

Chairs, tables, display cases--not people, but things. Marcel lives in a world that is crowded with people, but his beliefs are solipsistic. He interacts with people, treating them as things. Solipsism is false, but he believes it true. Is Marcel the metaphysical solipsist, who believes he is the only person? Is he the epistemic solipsist, who believes he is the only knowable person? Is he the moral solipsist, who believes he is the only person who matters? He is (at least sometimes) each of these.

What we have here is a complex web of solipsisms, a web that shifts over time. Marcel becomes an epistemic solipsist, I suggested, because he was a moral solipsist in the first place: one whose attitude to other human beings was predatory, one who matched Korsgaard's description, one who desired a human being as a person ('she, with her desires and sympathies...'), but as a person to be possessed. Given the moral solipsism which governed his relations with others from the start, the project of knowing others was itself understood in terms of possession and control. That strategy undermined the possibility of knowledge that was its goal, in the ways we looked at before. But once the epistemic solipsism is in place, the shift to metaphysical solipsism becomes apparently easy. From the fact that he cannot come to know another person, Marcel infers that he is irremediably alone. His friends have no more life than a chair, or a table. The only mind is his own.

However, other beings have their *uses*. Other beings are *useful showcases* for the collectables of one's mind. Albertine herself, despite her inability to satisfy his 'thirst for a life', nevertheless has her uses. She begins as unknown person, a human territory, ripe for invasion; and she ends up as a thing to be used.

> These painful dilemmas which love is constantly putting our way teach us and *reveal to us, layer after layer, the material of which we are made*...By making me waste my time, by causing me grief, Albertine had perhaps been more useful to me, even from a literary point of view, than a secretary who would have sorted my papers. (III 947/909)

> ...the important thing is not the worth of the woman but the profundity of the state; the emotions which a perfectly ordinary girl arouses in us *can enable us to bring to the surface of our consciousness some of the innermost parts of our being*, more personal, more remote, more quintessential than any. (I 891-2/833, emphasis added)

Albertine is more useful to Marcel than a secretary, since she helps him to know the one thing he can know about, the one thing worth knowing about, the one human being that really exists: his own dear self, in its innermost parts, the material of which he himself is made.

Here we have a final strand in the messy knot of solipsisms. We end as we began, with a moral solipsism again--but there is a twist. This time there is a moral solipsism apparently vindicated by the metaphysical solipsism which preceded it. If I am the only person, then of course I am the only person who matters. And there is another twist. This time there is a moral solipsism that is not the solipsism Korsgaard described, which desires a person *qua* person (but as a person to be possessed). Albertine is no longer desired as a person *qua* person: as a human being with discoverable desires, sympathies and will. She is desired as a useful tool. Desire, if it exists, is no longer invasive in character but, if anything, reductive. Albertine, like any other being, has the status of a table, a chair, a showcase. This moral solipsism is reductive--but not quite in the way that Herman describes either, in her interpretation of Kant. Marcel's attitude is not quite--not *even*--the attitude of one who reductively desires someone as a body that is a pleasure-giving sexual automaton. Albertine is reduced not merely to her own physical properties, but to Marcel's own psychological properties: Albertine is a showcase, not for *her mind*, not even for *her body*, but for *his mind*.

And a showcase can be very useful indeed, if one's mind is a splendid treasure trove. Albertine unwittingly helps him to mine the treasure. Marcel does not know Albertine, he does not possess her in the way he desires, she--as an independent human being--is no longer an item in his ontology. But she none the less helps him obey the Socratic injunction: know thyself. She does not help as a friend helps: she cannot provide the opportunity for communication and correction of his judgments. She cannot do that, because that takes human interaction, and Marcel does not allow her to be human. That takes faith in the perception of another person, and a trust which is quite foreign to Marcel. Albertine helps in a different way: and it is by providing him with new experiences. She produces in him experiences he would never otherwise have encountered--not (primarily) sexual experiences, but experiences of grief and pain. That is how she helps reveal to him the material of which he is made.

It all sounds oddly familiar. My awareness of my own self is much truer and more certain than my awareness of Albertine. If I were to judge that she exists from the fact that I experience profound emotion, clearly this same fact would entail much more evidently that I myself also exist. If I were to suppose that, beneath the hat and coat, there exists another thinking being, that would prove only that *I* exist, as a thinking being--not that she is more than an automaton. Every consideration which contributes to my experience of Albertine cannot but establish even more effectively the nature of my own mind. The more I seem to learn about anything else, the more I learn about me. The more I seem to learn about any*one* else, the more I learn about me. My mind is better known than anything else. Nothing else, no-one else, is to be known. Marcel is a Cartesian solipsist who has abandoned his stove heated room for something that he calls love, but he is still alone with his thoughts, as in a prison.[27]

This last strand of the web, this last reductive moral solipsism, is born from the metaphysical solipsism, or so I have suggested. It is plausible to think that metaphysical solipsism might lead to a reductive moral solipsism--that if I am the only person, I am *a fortiori* the only person who matters. There are no other persons, but only things to be used. This kind of link between the reductive moral solipsism and the metaphysical solipsism is explicit in Marcel's own thinking, as we can see in the passage above, now quoted in more detail.

> I had guessed long ago...and had verified since, that when we are in love with a woman we simply project on to her a state of our own soul; consequently the important thing is not the worth of the woman but the profundity of the state; the emotions which a perfectly ordinary girl arouses in us can enable us to bring to the surface of our consciousness some of the innermost parts of our being, more personal, more remote, more quintessential than any. (I 891-2/833)

Love is an experience that happens to be caused by some being, let us say a 'woman'. It has 'not the slightest real link with that person': it does not quench one's thirst for knowledge of another life, it is not a love 'for her' but rather a love 'in me'. Any property that we mistakenly attribute to her is really 'a state of our own soul'. 'Consequently', says Marcel, 'the important thing is not the worth of the woman but the profundity of the state'. *Consequently*. Albertine is not a person, who is kind or cruel: she is that unknown something which causes him pleasure or anguish. One might entertain futile hypotheses about 'dark shadows' of a human reality behind this appearance, shadows of the ideas she cherishes about people and places she knows, shadows of desire, sympathy, revulsion, obscure and incessant will. But any such reality is unknowable. Consequently, it is irrelevant to practical life. Albertine exists merely as a screen on which emotions can be conveniently projected.[28] Consequently, the important thing is not the worth of the woman. Consequently, her worth is simply instrumental. If Albertine has no more inner life than a piece of furniture, a chair, a table, a display case, then she can have only the value of a

---

27. *Cf.* Descartes' Second Meditation, in *The Philosophical Writings of Descartes* vol. II, tr. John Cottingham, Robert Stoothoff, Dugald Murdoch (Cambridge: Cambridge University Press, 1984), p. 22. At this stage the meditator is certain only of his own existence, and considers hypothetically: if he were take his sense experience to indicate the existence of other things (which he at this stage does not), that would entail much more evidently his own existence. And so on.

28. This treating a person as a kind of canvas for projective thoughts is discussed in 'Sexual Solipsism', and compared with the projective aspect of the solipsism in pornography use.

tool. Then indeed she proves useful, as an engine for producing those feelings of love and grief that are so interesting to the literary narcissist. She proves more useful than any secretary in her capacity of an experience machine.

Kant thinks that relations with others can help one to obey the Socratic injunction: know thyself. He thinks that friends can help us obey it, and lovers too, in so far as love and friendship are thought to share a common moral core-- when, and to the extent that, they are relationships of reciprocity. Proust at least partly agrees. He thinks that love can help one to obey it--that despite its scope for self-deception, love can help 'reveal to us, layer after layer, the material of which we are made'. What role does the lover play, though? The human need for communication, the need to 'clothe our concepts in words', can be met by a friend or a lover 'to whom we can communicate our whole self'. But Marcel's lover cannot have this role. The need to clothe one's concepts in words, the need to communicate one's whole self, is not met in love, but in solitary writing. Love provides knowledge of oneself, not through a process of communication, reciprocal interpretation, and correction, but rather by providing an experimental test. As Nussbaum says, the role of the lover is almost incidental.[29] Proust draws a chemical analogy. The moment of self-knowledge here is provoked by Marcel's discovery of Albertine's departure, and he instantly learns that he loves her.

> Our intelligence, however lucid, cannot perceive the elements that compose it and remain unsuspected so long as, from the volatile state in which they general- ly exist, a phenomenon capable of isolating them has not subjected them to the first stages of solidification. I had been mistaken in thinking that I could see clearly into my own heart. But this knowledge, which the shrewdest perceptions of the mind would not have given me, had now been brought to me, hard, glitter- ing, strange, like a crystallised salt, by the abrupt reaction of pain. (III 426/420)

She has helped him learn something. Notice the minimal role she plays in his great discovery.

On Marcel's way of thinking, love happens to be occasioned by some being: some pleasure-causing, anguish-causing being. Love brings suffering, and suffering is a catalyst that brings self-knowledge. And that is how a lover can help one know oneself. This is, to put it mildly, a different conception of what it is to be helped by someone else to learn about oneself. Suppose I do not know the answer to some question about myself: suppose I do not know, for example, *whether I am brave*. There are two ways a friend could help me find out. He could help me reflect intelligently on the character of my past actions,

---

29. Nussbaum discusses this moment of 'discovery' in great detail in 'Fictions of the Soul', and 'Love's Knowledge'. She describes the minimal role played by Albertine in Marcel's quest for self-knowledge on p. 271 of 'Love's Knowledge'.

argue with me, alert me to revealing details I may otherwise miss; or he could push me off a smallish cliff. With the former method, he offers communication, interpretation, correction; with the latter, he gives me an experiment. In both ways I am helped by someone else to learn about myself: but with the former method, it must be some*one* else; with the latter, it could as easily be some*thing* else (a gust of wind, a loose shoe-lace) that provides the test of courage.

Solipsistic love provides no communication, but only the experiment: a nasty fall, and then not even a shoulder to cry on. The role of the other is better played by an absent ex-lover than by a lover or friend. Ordinary love, on the other hand, might well provide both routes to self-knowledge. Perhaps love can be a bit like falling off a cliff. Perhaps it does provide a new experimental setting. Perhaps unexpected aspects of one's self do come to light, and we discover new layers of the material of which we are made. In addition, though, there is something else. Any apparent self-discovery generated by the experiment has the chance to be tested and revised in the fires of communication and mutual interpretation:[30] that is, if a lover can also be a friend 'whom we know to be frank and loving', one who will 'help us to correct our judgment', one from whom 'we can and need hide nothing' (*LE* 206); if a lover can be one who cares for my happiness, as I care for his.

In any case, the assumption here is wrong. *Self*-discovery is hardly the point. Why look back to the prison? Why look back to the prison, when the gate is open to a garden, an orchard of fruits where things are growing (calamus and cinnamon, myrrh and aloe), where there are cool breezes, the sound of water --and someone seems to be calling? There are risks, perhaps. There might be no time to record a remembrance of things past, a remembrance of years in solitary confinement. There might be no time for that, because time has a well-known habit. Time does tend to fly, when you're having fun.

---

30. For an interesting discussion of the role of interpretation in friendship, although not (to me) wholly convincing, see Dean Cocking and Jeanette Kennett, 'Friendship and the Self', ms. 1995. It is argued there that reciprocal interpretation, and a reciprocal willingness to be interpreted, are essential features of friendship.

8

Love and Its Place in Moral Discourse

Philip Pettit

When people develop a relationship as partners in love, one aspect of what happens is that each becomes aware not just of loving, but of being loved, and not just of loving and being loved, but of this being itself a matter registered by both of them. In short, the fact that the partners are in love becomes a matter of shared awareness.

But this awareness of love is not awareness of a natural phenomenon that wears its nature on its face. What it is to be in love is something available only in terms of the discourse of love that the local culture and society provide. The symptoms of love, the expectations that lovers should have of one another, the demands that other people may require lovers to meet: these are all matters that are codified, at least in outline, in the local discourse of love. They are matters of conventional--conventional though not necessarily arbitrary--construction.

The culturally articulated character of the loving relationship means, in a phrase, that being in love is as much an institutional fact as a natural fact. There is an institution of love, as there is an institution of kinship and friendship and mateship.

One feature of the institution of love in our society is that we are allowed to explain and justify our treatment of a certain person, both to ourselves and to one another, by reference to the fact of loving that person. It is quite intelligible under received norms that a lover should favour a beloved, for example, displaying a partiality of attitude; or that a lover should be utterly self-sacrificing towards the beloved. And not only is that intelligible, the norms also ensure that such behaviour on the part of a lover is, at least in most contexts, justifiable: it is behaviour, at the least, which others are not in an effective position to fault. Thus, partiality on the part of lovers is cast as loyalty, self-sacrifice as devotion, and each is presented as a comprehensible and commendable phenomenon.

I want to focus in this essay on two questions which this aspect of the institution of love raises. The first question is whether the dual role of love, as both an explainer and justifier, means that love is cast as a sort of virtuous motivation, on a par with other virtuous motives that both explain and justify certain behaviour: motives like kindness or fairness, for example. I shall argue that the explanatory-justificatory role of love does not mean this: that love is not virtuous in the way in which kindness and fairness may be. The second question I raise, then, is whether the dual role of love means that love is at least something desirable by our common lights: whether it is a universal value. Here I shall argue for a positive answer. To state the lesson of the paper in a rather flat way, love is not a virtue; but it is a value.

1. Is Love a Virtue?

There is no difficulty about how we can invoke something's being a fair way of behaving both to explain and to justify a person's doing it. The fact that an option is fair will serve to justify the choice of it, to the extent that fairness is a value. And the fact that someone believes that the option is fair will serve to explain the choice, to the extent that we think the person is fair and we expect fair people to be moved by that sort of belief.

Things are a little more complicated, but not excessively so, in other cases. The fact that an option is kind will justify its choice, since kindness is a value by our shared lights. So far the case is like that of fairness. But it will not be the fact that someone believes that the option is kind which explains the choice in the case of someone we take to be kind. For we expect kind people to be moved, at least in most cases, not by the belief that this or that option is kind --that is too reflexive for comfort--but rather by the belief it has those features that happen--and the agent need not be aware of this--to ensure that it is kind. We justify the choice by the fact that it is kind. We explain it by the fact that we think the agent is kind and that we expect kind agents to be moved, not necessarily or typically by the belief that an option is kind, but by the belief that it has such features as serve in the context--so it happens--to make it a kind choice.

A comment, in passing. The more complicated story that is exemplified by kindness may also be the more general one. In fact, it may be that this story is the appropriate one for many cases of people's being moved by fairness. An agent could be moved by fairness, and could act in a way that was justified by its fairness, without actually having a word for fairness. And in such a case it would have to be the more complicated story that applied.

In both the simple and the complicated cases, we find a straightforward structure. That a certain value is realised by an option justifies the choice. And that the agent has a certain corresponding belief explains the choice: the agent believes that the value is realised in the option chosen, or believes of certain properties which happen to realise the value that they--however the agent sees them--are realised in that option. No doubt further qualifications may be needed but this account of the structure displayed by kindness and fairness seems to be on the right track. We can think of it as a structure associated with virtue.

The dual role of love as an explainer-justifier would be immediately intelligible if love displayed the same structure as we find in the case of fairness and kindness. If it did display that structure, then we might well think of love as a virtue on a par with fairness and kindness. Love is sufficiently like kindness and fairness in other respects to be regarded as a virtue of the same kind, so far as it displays the same explaining-justifying structure.

But love does not display the same structure. The fact that I love someone may serve to justify my treating her in a certain, say, partial or self-sacrificing way. But it is doubtful whether I could claim to be properly a lover, if it was my recognition of the fact of loving her--or my recognition of a realiser of that fact--which explained my action: if all that needed to be said in explaining how I behaved was that I saw I loved her or saw I bore a relation to her which, as it happens, means that I loved her.

This may seem too quick. Perhaps I am moved in love, as I am moved in kindness, by a recognition that the acts I choose have features, whether or not I see them in this way, that make them loving acts. Perhaps love and kindness show their similarity at the level of acts: kindness involves a sensitivity to features that make acts kind, love a sensitivity to features that make acts loving.

But a little reflection reveals a fatal weakness in this suggestion. Someone may be sensitive to features that make acts loving in relation to someone, not because of being truly in love, but rather because of being committed to behaving in a loving way: not because of a lover's commitment, as we might put it, but rather because of a commitment to love. It cannot be sufficient for love, therefore, that a person displays the sensitivity in question. Love must explain the actions of a lover in a different manner.

The characteristic explanation of a lover's behaviour towards a beloved is not the recognition of the fact of loving her, nor the recognition of the presence of any related features, but rather the fact of loving itself. Thus my loving someone will be naturally invoked to explain my keeping note of her birthday, my giving readily of my time to help her, and perhaps my sharing all that I have with her. The idea is that loving the person makes those responses easy and even compelling: that it leads me to identify with her, as we say, and to make her good my good, her bad my bad.

Suppose that my behaviour was not to be explained in this characteristic way but rather in the manner of a virtue like fairness or kindness. Suppose, for example, that I tried to keep note of the person's birthday, that I gave freely of my time to help her, and so on, because of registering in each case that this was someone I loved: because of registering this and not, as we would say, because I loved her. In that case, I might be praised for my moral determination to honour the relationship but I could not be said, without qualification, to be acting out of love. To act out of love, as we might put it, is to be moved by love and not by the recognition of being in love.

Consider the person who acts out of friendship. As Michael Stocker[1] has made us all aware, the friend who comes to see me in hospital because of seeing herself as a friend, and because of wanting to do the right thing as a friend, is not acting out of friendship. She is behaving as a good moral agent, doing the right thing because it is the right thing. But she is not doing enough--in a way, she is doing too much--to count as someone who is manifesting friendship.

When I do the loving thing by someone, but only because of my recognition that this is someone I love, then it can equally be said that I am not manifesting love. I am going through the motions of love, for sure, but not out of the motives that would mark me off as a lover. I am displaying a commitment to love rather than a lover's commitment.

While the commitment to love does have the same structure as that displayed by virtues like kindness and fairness, the lover's commitment does not. Someone committed to love will take account of the fact of being a would-be lover--or of some related fact--and this will explain what they do in the way in which the fair person's taking account of the fairness of an option will explain what the fair person does; the justifier of the choice--that the agent loves the person benefited--will figure in the same manner in its explanation. A lover in the proper sense will have no need for such reflective thoughts in order to be motivated to pursue the beloved's good. And this, despite the fact that the lover's behaviour may be justified by the fact that they love the person favoured.

In holding that the lover's commitment is distinct from the commitment to love, I do not mean to dismiss the latter as unimportant. Aristotelian continence is a substitute for virtue in the sense that it involves behaving as the virtuous agent would behave, but out of something other than the normal mental set of the virtuous person.[2] Continence is something less than virtue, in this sense, but something that can serve as an important standby for virtue: something that can take the place of virtue, for example, on the bad day that comes to most of us. As continence stands to virtue, so a commitment to love stands to a lover's commitment. It is something less than a lover's commitment but it is an attitude that may stand a lover in good stead, if his or her love ever fails, as fail it is sometimes bound to do.

We need to discuss one further issue before moving on to the second question I raised. I said that the characteristic or canonical way in which love figures in the explanation of loving behaviour need not involve the agent in delibera-

---

1. Stocker, Michael, 'The Schizophrenia of Modern Ethical Theories', *Journal of Philosophy*, Vol 73 (1976), pp. 453-66.

2. *Cf.* Pettit, Philip and Michael Smith, 'Practical Unreason', *Mind*, Vol 102, pp. 53-80.

tively reflecting, however implicitly, on facts like the fact of loving the person in question. But what sort of reason do we imagine having an influence on the lover's mind? After all, it is not as if loving someone produces behaviour in a blind, reason-free gush of passion or in an unthinking exercise of habit.

Reasons vary in a number of dimensions. They may be agent-neutral, in the sense that the content of the reason--say, 'this will increase human happiness', 'this will benefit Australia'--is intelligible without knowing who is the agent for whom it is a reason. Or they may be agent-relative, in the sense that there is no understanding what exactly is the moving consideration, there is no understanding what it involves, without knowing who is the agent in question. Examples of agent-relative reasons would be: 'this will increase my happiness', 'this will increase my family's happiness', 'this will benefit my country'.[3]

If a reason is agent-neutral, then it may be purely universal, in the sense that it does not mention any person, place or other individual. Or, mentioning such a person or place or whatever, it may be particular in nature. 'This will increase human happiness' is universal or, if the reference to the human species particularises it, 'This will increase happiness' is certainly universal. 'This will benefit Australia' or 'This will benefit the least densely populated of the advanced countries', on the other hand, is a purely particular reason.

The reference to Australia as the least densely populated of the advanced countries is non-rigid, in the sense that as we envisage changed scenarios the expression may refer to different countries. The reference to Australia by name is rigid, on the other hand, in the sense that the expression locks onto that very country, no matter what possibilities are countenanced. Either way of referring to a particular entity will make an agent-neutral reason particular rather than universal. But the rigid way of referring to Australia means that the reason essentially involves that country, whereas the non-rigid way of referring to it does not. The one sort of particular reason is rigidly particularised or individualised, as we may put it--rigidly individualised in favour of Australia--the other is not.

If a reason is agent-relative, then of necessity it is a particular rather than a universal reason: it will explicitly or implicitly refer back to the agent; indeed it will refer rigidly to that agent, since the reference will be via an indexical like 'I' or 'me' or 'my' or whatever. But agent-relative reasons often refer also to other entities or persons; they will do so, for example, when they are reasons of patriotism or loyalty or friendship or love. And so there is a distinction to be

---

3. On these matters, see: Parfit, Derek, 'Prudence, Morality and the Prisoner's Dilemma', *Proceedings of the British Academy*, Vol 65 (1979); Nagel, Thomas, 'The Limits of Objectivity', in *Tanner Lectures on Human Values*, Vol 1 (1980), ed. S. M. McMurrin, (Cambridge: Cambridge University Press), pp. 75-139; Sen, Amartya, 'Rights and Agency', in *Philosophy and Public Affairs*, Vol 11 (1982), pp. 3-39.

drawn among such agent-relative reasons that parallels the distinction between non-rigidly particularised and rigidly particularised agent-neutral reasons: a distinction that parallels the distinction between the sort of agent-neutral reason that refers to the least densely populated of the developed countries and the sort that refers to Australia.[4]

'There is a friend of mine in need' is of the first, non-rigidly particularised kind. The identity of the person it would lead the agent to benefit is not essentially involved in the consideration, since the consideration may apply in this scenario to one individual, in that scenario to another. 'This, my friend, is in need' is of the second, rigidly individualised variety. There is no way of knowing exactly what the content of the consideration is--no way of understanding it fully--without grasping who the particular friend is. The reference to that friend is rigid in virtue of involving the demonstrative 'This' and the reason is rigidly particularised in favour of that person.

The considerations that move a loving person when they act out of love towards someone may be agent-neutral or agent-relative: the lover may be moved by a thought that refers to the beloved by name, for example, so that the consideration is agent-neutral; or the thought which moves the lover may identify the beloved by reference back to the lover, as in 'my beloved' or whatever. But it seems clear that in either case the consideration must be rigidly individualised in favour of the beloved. Moreover, this individualisation of the reason, be the reason agent-neutral or agent-relative, must be relevant to the reason's capturing the attention, and stoking the motivation, of the agent. The reason that moves the lover must essentially involve the identity of the beloved in the very thought that motivates the lover's response.

Why so? Well, consider the situation where the identity of the beloved is not involved essentially in the thought which moves the agent. Consider the situation where the lover or would-be lover favours the beloved on the neutral ground that this will testify to the value of love, or on the neutral ground that this will help the most attractive person in the area, or on the agent-relative ground that it will help someone that they happen to love. In each of these cases, the favour that the beloved enjoys is enjoyed as the result of an accident. The beloved is not favoured for their own sake, as we might put it, but only because of happening to be the one in a position to gain from the lover's project of testifying to the value of love, or of helping the most attractive person around, or of helping anyone they happen to love: only because of happening to fall under the trajectory marked out by the lover's beneficent but more or less impersonal schemes.

I conclude, then, that when love is manifested in the canonical way, when

---

4. Pettit, Philip, 'The Paradox of Loyalty', *American Philosophical Quarterly*, Vol 25 (1988), pp. 163-71.

an agent displays a commitment to a beloved by acting out of love, then the reason that moves the agent has to be rigidly individualised in favour of the beloved. It has to be a reason in which the beloved figures as an essential component, whether by courtesy of a name or demonstrative or whatever. And it has to be a reason that moves the lover, at least in part, by virtue of involving the beloved in that way.[5]

The need for a rigidly individualised reason connects with the fact that to act out of a commitment to love--to act out of a recognition of the consideration that justifies the action: that this is someone I love--is not to act out of a lover's commitment: a commitment to the beloved. For justification always abstracts away from particularity and when I say that I love someone in justifying what I did, the identity of the particular individual in question is not relevant; all that is essential to the justification is that it is an act of love. To act out of a recognition of that justifying consideration, then, would not be to act on the basis of a reason that is rigidly individualised in favour of the beloved. It would be to fail to register the sort of thing that is part and parcel of thinking as a lover.

2. Is Love a Value?

In the last section we focussed on the explanatory role of love, and in particular on the fact that it figures in explanation in a manner that does not pair off nicely with how it figures in justification. In acting as a lover, the fact that I love someone may justify what I do; but it is not my recognition of that fact which explains, but rather my recognition of a rigidly individualised fact: my recognition that Mary needs help, that Mary would like those flowers, or whatever.

We change the focus now to the justifying role of love. The fact that I can justify my behaviour, other things being equal, by claiming to have acted out of love seems to say something important about love. But what exactly does it say? In particular, does it mean that we should all recognise love as a value--a universal value--and that I justify my behaviour by showing that it instantiates or promotes that value: by showing that it relates to that value in a suitably respectful way, as the deontologist will have it; or in a suitably maximising

---

5. The point here is different, it should be noticed, from the point made by John Perry in 'The Problem of the Essential Indexical' [*Nous*, Vol 13 (1979), pp. 3-21]. He shows that there has to be an indexical, and therefore particular, element somewhere in the beliefs that lead any agent to act. I argue that there must be a particular element in the motivating belief, as we might call it, of the loving agent--that is, roughly, in the belief which identifies the agent's goal or ground in acting--and not just in beliefs bearing on a means or opportunity for realising that goal or satisfying that ground.

fashion, as the consequentialist will require?[6] Or can the justifying role of love be made intelligible in some other, less straightforward way?

I favour the straightforward way of making the justifying role of love intelligible. I think of love as a value that we should all recognise, though I say nothing here on whether the appropriate claim of the value is to be understood in the deontological or consequentialist manner: that issue is orthogonal to my concerns.

But there is an alternative view of how love comes to play a justifying role and I need to consider this and provide an argument against it.[7] The alternative view is that love is not a universal value, not something that we all have reason to favour, but rather that it offers a universal schema for framing the particular value that this lover places on this beloved, that lover places on that beloved, and so on. None of us has to value love, just because we invoke it to justify certain behaviour. Each of us values or cherishes those whom we love--you cherish Fred, I cherish Mary--but that does not mean that there is something we should value in common.

How then does the appeal to love justify? How do I justify to you the way I behave towards Mary by pointing out that I love her, when it is not given that you have to value love and not given, of course, that you have to value Mary? The answer, on this approach, is that I justify my behaviour to you, not by showing that it stems from anything that we should value in common, but rather by showing that it stems from a valuing that is of a kind with a valuing that you would approve in your own case: it stems from a valuing of Mary that is of a kind, say, with your valuing of Fred.

This approach builds on an important insight. The insight is that I may justify what I do by your lights, not just through showing that it is grounded in a value that you also should countenance, but through showing that it is grounded in a value that is isomorphic to a value that you do or would approve in your own case. You cannot complain if you are shown that my action is grounded in a value that you ought to recognise. But equally you cannot complain if you are shown that my action is grounded in a value that stands to me as something that you recognise as a value--an actual or potential value--stands to you. As the approach has it, you cannot complain if you are shown that my act of favouring Mary is grounded in the value that I qua lover invest in Mary, when you yourself qua lover invest a similar value in Fred: or, if there is no Fred about, when you would approve in your own case of being a lover and of investing other people with such value.

---

6. Pettit, Philip, 'Consequentialism', in Peter Singer, ed., *A Companion to Ethics*, Oxford: Blackwell, pp. 230-40.

7. I am greatly indebted to conversations with Frank Jackson and Michael Smith on related matters.

The difference between the standard account of the justificatory appeal to love and this alternative account comes out in different ways in which the lover may respond to the demand that they universalise the justifying consideration offered in a remark such as 'This is someone I love'. I mentioned earlier that justification always abstracts away from particularity and it is interesting to see the different ways in which the two approaches achieve such abstraction: the different ways in which they try to show that the justifier in a remark like 'This is someone I love' is implicitly universal and does not hold just for the agent in question.

If you follow the standard line, then you will say that the justifier is universalisable, because you recognise that for any X and any Y, if they are lovers, then it is a good and valuable thing that one should favour the other: it is valuable that X should favour Y, and Y favour X. If you cleave to the alternative approach, you will say that the justifier is universalisable, because you recognise that for any X and any Y, if they are lovers, then the good of each is a value for the other: It is valuable so far as X is concerned that Y should enjoy favour, valuable so far as Y is concerned that X should enjoy favour; for short it is X-valuable that Y be favoured, Y-valuable that X be favoured.

The standard approach, as I have been describing it, sees a commitment to the universal value of love as implicit in the way lovers invoke their love to justify their actions. The alternative approach sees a commitment to a universal schema that is displayed by particular lovings, not to any universal value, in this practice of justification. So how does the standard approach fare in competition with the alternative? Is love itself a value or does it represent just a schema for valuing?

What may certainly be granted to those attracted by the alternative approach is that it could have been the case that love had the role of a valuing schema, not a common value. There is a possible world, as we might put it, where this is so. In that world, each person finds that they become attached to one or more others in a fashion that they cannot justify by reference to any commonly compelling value: any value in becoming so attached. Called upon to justify this attachment, and the way in which it leads them to behave, they are each at first, as we might imagine, in a situation of some embarrassment. They each recognise that there is nothing about the people to whom they are attached that merits the favour they give them, by any common lights; it is just a brute fact about them, as it were, that the attachment has occurred. But the embarrassment lifts as each recognises that they are not unusual in becoming attached in this way to particular others; it transpires that this sort of attachment occurs all over the place. Each now recognises that without justifying their favour on any common basis, they can at least justify it on the basis of its conforming to a common pattern.

There is no pretence on anyone's part in this world that other lovers share a common commitment with them. Imagine a situation where X can favour X's beloved only at a cost to how Y favours Y's, and vice versa. There is no suggestion that, love's justifications notwithstanding, this is anything less than outright war. It is a situation where, for all the justifications that love supplies, each is justified in doing all they can to undermine the other's efforts and further their particular end: the benefiting of those that they own as theirs, the favouring of those with whom they happen to have formed a liaison. The pairs which consist of mutual lovers are like self-help gangs of two. Their members work to one another's special benefit but need not share any value in common with the members of other such gangs. If they manage to provide cross-gang justifications of how they each favour the other in their gang, the justification has an *ad hominem* aspect: each is justified by the lights of every other because no other is in a position to throw stones; no other is entirely uncontaminated by gang-membership.

The actual world, as projected in the discourse of love, may give love the role only of a schema for valuing; it may resemble the possible world just discussed. But I doubt it. It is part of the discourse of love that being in love, and living up to the expectations of love, is a good thing. In the possible world imagined, people are stuck within their own perspectives, so far as their actual valuings go. They value their own favourites, but do not value the love that binds them, as it binds others, to those they favour. In the actual world, people transcend those perspectives and recognise that love is something of value, regardless of who the lover and the beloved are.

That this is so comes out in the fact, precisely, that we distinguish in the actual world between the situation where someone is a favourite--a favourite in the sense in which a teacher's pet is a favourite--and the situation where someone is acknowledged as a beloved. Teachers might justify among themselves the special treatment they give their favourites by pointing out that the pattern of having favourites is a common one and that no other teacher can throw stones. But this sort of justification is quite different from that which lovers offer when they present their treatment of another as a manifestation of the love which they bear them. The teachers certainly silence complaints about their behaviour; they excuse it, as we might say, but do not justify it. The lovers invite a positive celebration of what they feel and do.

Love is a value, if this is right, not just a schema for valuing. Love justifies, because love is and ought to be a common object of value, not because loving is a common way of valuing. The considerations I have raised may not definitively close the issue between the two sides of the debate. But they do seem to favour the standard side quite strongly.

One last query. Might love serve to justify in both of these ways at once? Might it represent both a common value and a common schema for valuing? I do not think so. There is quite a tension between the justification advanced when someone claims to be acting on the basis of a value that others ought to share and the justification put forward when they claim to be acting out of a mode of valuing that others are not in a position to fault: the justification that looks more like an excuse than a justification proper. It is hard to imagine that people might be proposing such mutually uncongenial forms of justification at one and the same time, and in one and the same utterance. The mind-sets of the justifications are just too different. The discourse of love is complex but I doubt if the complexity runs to such an extreme.[8]

- - -

This paper does not cover all of the ground in my paper, 'The Paradox of Loyalty' [*American Philosophical Quarterly*, Vol 25 (1988), pp. 163-71] but, where it does, it supercedes the earlier piece; it does this mainly through introducing further, important distinctions that I had neglected before.

8. I owe an enormous debt of gratitude to Roger Lamb for his painstaking and penetrating comments on an earlier draft.

9

Jealousy and Desire

Daniel M. Farrell

Recall the worst experience of jealousy you have ever had, and ask yourself exactly what it is you were feeling on that occasion and what, if anything, your susceptibility to this emotion revealed about you. Was your emotion basically just an intense experience of indescribable anguish, revealing nothing more than the fact that, like most of us, you feel psychic pain when certain things do not go the way you want them to go? Or is it possible to describe a bit more perspicuously exactly what this experience involved and exactly what it did or did not reveal about you as a person? Was the anguish essentially a matter of fear, for example, mixed with anger, as some writers would say, or was it more a matter of grief, as Freud claimed, with an admixture of pain and anger because of the "narcissistic wound" that was involved?[1] And *was* there a "wound" of some sort, or is this really a bit too dramatic, even for an emotion most of us are none too anxious to experience if it is at all possible to avoid it? And, again, whatever the answer to these questions, what does your having been capable of being "pained" (if not in fact wounded) in this way reveal about you, at least as you were then? Did it, as we just imagined, simply show that it hurts to lose (or think you have lost) something or someone you dearly wanted not to lose? Or is it possible that it revealed something rather more unattractive about you--that, for example, you are, or were, in some important sense still at an essentially *infantile* stage of psychological development? Or that you are, or were, clearly a person who thought of at least some one other person as a "thing" that "belonged" to you, like property, not to be tampered with by others, at least without your permission?

---

1. For the first view, see the discussion and references in G. White and P. Mullen, *Jealousy: Theory, Research, and Clinical Strategies* (NY: Guilford Press, 1989), pp. 23-24; for the second, see Sigmund Freud, 'Some Neurotic Mechanisms in Jealousy, Paranoia, and Homosexuality', *The Standard Edition of the Complete Psychological Works of Sigmund Freud*, ed. James Strachey (London: The Hogarth Press, 1955), p. 232.

There are two general questions behind the various specific questions that have just been raised: what *is* jealousy, at bottom, and what, if anything, does the fact that one experiences this emotion in a given set of circumstances show about one as a person? Some time ago I suggested the following answer to the first of these questions, an answer I believe is still fundamentally sound: *jealousy is an essentially three-party emotion in which one person--the jealous person--is in some way bothered by the fact that, as he believes, someone else whom he wants to favor him in some way, and who he believes has thus favored him for a time, currently favors (or is likely to begin to favor) someone else in that way instead.*[2] There are, of course, some terms of art here--particularly the terms 'bothered' and 'favored'--that need explication, and there are things left implicit that need to be made explicit before this analysis will be able to be evaluated by the reader, much less responsibly accepted or rejected. Before pursuing these matters, though, I want to illustrate the basic thrust of the analysis with what I hope will be some relatively uncontroversial examples. Then we can return to the rough points in the analysis just sketched and briefly refine them, before taking up what will be our central concern in the remainder of the paper--namely, the task of answering the question of what, if anything, the occurrence of jealousy tells us about the jealous person.

I

When most people think about jealousy, they think about what I prefer to

---

2. 'Jealousy', *The Philosophical Review*, Volume 89, Number 4 (October, 1980), pp. 527-559. Note that there need not actually *be* a third party, on my view--the jealous person merely needs to *believe* there is. Note also that my present view differs from my earlier view in suggesting that we are dealing with jealousy, rather than some other, possibly quite similar emotion, only if the allegedly jealous person believes she *has* been "favored" in the relevant way (see below) at some point in the past. Someone who *wants* to be favored, on my current view, but who has thus far not (so far as she knows) *been* so favored, can be quite agitated but not strictly speaking *jealous* of attentions or favors directed to some third party. (For an alternative, admittedly not implausible view, see my 'Jealousy', *op. cit.*, pp. 529-530.) Finally, note that in certain cases--e.g., the case of a frustrated desire for sexual exclusivity, in which one continues to enjoy the second party's sexual favors but not *exclusively*--it is not strictly correct to say that one is bothered by the fact that the second party is now favoring someone else in the relevant (i.e., the originally desired) way *instead*; for, of course, neither one's rival nor oneself is getting sexual exclusivity under these circumstances, and yet it seems plausible to say one might nonetheless be *jealous* in such a case because of the sexual favors one's rival is now receiving. This creates a complication for my view that I cannot discuss here, except to say that this is not a complication that is relevant to the principal new questions the present paper attempts to raise and address.

call "romantic jealousy" (a form of jealousy, by the way, that differs from what we might call "sexual jealousy" only by virtue of being a general sub-category of jealousy that includes the latter as a special case): someone, A, believing that someone else, B, is attached or attracted to them romantically, and wanting B to continue to remain so attached, comes to believe (or at least suspect) that B has begun to become attached (or attracted) to some other person, C, instead, and experiences, because of this belief (or suspicion), one or more of a fairly large number of possible (essentially negative) feelings: panic, for example, or anger, or despair, and so on. A classic example, of course, is Othello, in Shakespeare's play, and his counterpart, Otello, in Verdi's opera: he wants, and initially believes he has, Desdemona's love and affection directed exclusively towards himself; he comes to believe that Desdemona is giving her love (and more) to Iago instead; and he is, to say the least, pained by his belief that this transfer of love and affection has occurred. Whatever we think about it, and about him for falling into it, we call what Othello (Otello) is experiencing "jealousy", and we use this case as a kind of paradigm of at least one species of this seemingly very powerful emotion. Indeed, we not only *call* the relevant emotion "jealousy" in cases like this; we take it to be capable of explaining a great deal of what the sufferer subsequently does: "He killed her in a jealous rage", we say, meaning not merely that he was jealous when he killed her but that his being jealous somehow explains what he subsequently did.

It would be a mistake, though, to think that this paradigm of one *species* of jealousy is an instance of something like the "primary application" of the term. To see this, we need only note that cases fitting our analysis occur in all sorts of other (non-romantic and non-sexual) contexts as well, and are readily called cases of "jealousy" when they occur. In the arts, for example, some performers want not only to be excellent at what they do, but to be *thought* to be excellent as well. What's more, some of the latter might want to be thought to be both excellent, in their own right, and distinctly *better* than other performers in their area of expertise. A leading operatic baritone, for example, might want not only to excel, but to be thought to excel by the relevant public, and to be thought to excel far beyond the capacities of any of his contemporaries (and, indeed, far beyond the capacities of any baritone who has ever lived). Imagine, then, a singer who has this latter desire and who for a while plausibly believes that his public believes him to be exactly what he wants them to believe him to be-- namely, the best baritone in the world. Then imagine that another, younger singer appears who gradually begins to inspire even more praise than his senior colleague--who begins, in short, to be thought to be supplanting the latter as "the best baritone in the world". Surely it would not be odd to learn that the older man, seeing that he was beginning to be supplanted, was acting as though he were jealous because of the attention (and adulation) his younger contemporary was beginning to receive. And, indeed, it would not be odd for him to *be* jealous of his younger colleague: to be "bothered", that is to say, by the fact that, despite his own desire to be "favored" by the public in the relevant way, his rival is apparently coming to be thus favored by them instead. The point is not that a singer with the relevant desires would *have* to be jealous in the circumstances we have imagined. On the contrary; it is interesting and, as we shall see below, important that this need not occur: the older singer might simply accept the fact that the younger singer is better than he, and is rightly thought to be better by the public, and might subsequently reflect, if he reflects on the matter at all, only on the renown he enjoyed when *he* was considered the best baritone in the world. Rather, the point is that we can easily understand the older singer being jealous because of the attention and regard the younger singer is starting to receive, and that we can understand this because we can imagine him experiencing various sorts of negative feelings because of the recognition he wants from the public but sees that the other singer is beginning to receive.

Let us call these latter cases instances of "professional jealousy". I suspect the reader will have no difficulty imagining even more convincing examples of this form of jealousy for himself. Notice, though, that in addition to professional jealousy, we can imagine other kinds of jealousy, in addition to romantic or sexual jealousy, as well: so-called "sibling rivalry", for example, while sometimes *simply* an instance of rivalry or competition between siblings, is actually quite often both that *and* what we might call "sibling jealousy"; it would be the latter, for instance, if, as typically happens, what the siblings were competing for was the attention or affection of one or both of their parents, and if concomitant with this competition either of them was experiencing negative feelings because of her (conscious or unconscious) belief that she was not getting the attention or affection she desired.[3]

Finally, and more generally, we should note that what we have been calling "sibling jealousy" is itself simply a special case of a larger class of possible jealousies that are themselves instances of neither "professional" nor "romantic" jealousy--namely, cases where one person is bothered by the fact that some other person is no longer "favoring" him in some way in which he wants to be favored, but in which there is no professional or romantic connection between the jealous party and the party whose "favor" he desires. I want to continue to be the person with whom you discuss your romantic and professional problems, for example, but I am starting to see that you would rather talk with some other friend instead, and I am pained by the fact that, at least as I believe, this is so.

---

3. Actually, as I explain in Section II below, these feelings would have to have a specific intentional object, conscious or unconscious, before we could confidently call them instances of sibling jealousy: the psychological "pain" or "botherment" the child was experiencing would, as in the cases imagined above, have to be directed at the fact that she was (apparently) not being favored in the way in which she wanted to be favored, rather than at some contingent consequence of the fact that this was so.

There are, in short, any number of different kinds of situation that fit the analysis sketched earlier, and that are, in fact, situations in which it is natural to say that a person is experiencing the emotion we call "jealousy". This is an important point to note, as we shall see below, because of the common tendency to identify jealousy with what I have called "romantic jealousy". I shall show that at least some of the features of romantic jealousy that are commonly thought to be rather puzzling, or otherwise troublesome, philosophically, are also features of these other forms of jealousy, *mutatis mutandis*, and hence ought, *prima facie*, at any rate, to strike us as puzzling or otherwise troublesome in these sister cases as well. What's more, the fact that in these other cases these analogous features do *not* typically strike us as puzzling, or otherwise problematical, is itself of considerable interest, as I shall try to show. For it then turns out, if I am right, that while romantic (or specifically sexual) jealousy *is* uniquely puzzling or problematical in certain ways, this is not (simply) because it is *jealousy* but, rather, because it involves beliefs, say, or desires, or feelings, which strike us as odd when they have a romantic (or sexual) content but not when they have a non-romantic or non-sexual content. Of course, at first blush this might seem unsurprising; after all, it is a commonplace that desires may strike us as odd or peculiar when they are desires for one thing--sex under certain circumstances, for example--but not when they are desires for something else (something else under those same circumstances, that is to say). However, things are not this simple when it comes to the types of beliefs, desires, and feelings I have alleged are a necessary part of jealousy in any of its various forms; or so, at any rate, I shall try to show below.

II

Nothing that has been said thus far constitutes an *argument* for the claim that the analysis of jealousy sketched above is sound. Nor do I propose to present a sustained argument for this claim in what follows, since, as already indicated, I have attempted to do this elsewhere. I do want to propose a challenge, though, to anyone who is inclined to think that this analysis is deficient, either because it excludes some cases he is inclined to think are real cases of jealousy or because it includes, as instances of jealousy, cases he believes are not genuine instances of this emotion; and then I want to make a few brief comments about two ways in which it might seem easy to meet this challenge but in which I think it is in fact not likely to be met. The challenge, of course, is this: present a case where either (a) we have a clear case of jealousy, yet one or more of the individually necessary conditions embodied in the preceding analysis is not met; or (b) all of the individually necessary conditions embodied in the preceding analysis are met, but we do not in fact have a case of jealousy. It is my contention that no case of either sort can be found, every apparent example of such a case failing, because either: while one or more of the individually necessary conditions embodied in the preceding analysis is admittedly *not met* in the example, the case so described is, after all, not a case of jealousy; *or* because while we *admittedly* do not have a case of jealousy in the example, neither do we, after all, have a case where *all* of the individually necessary conditions are met.

Against this, there are, as I have said, two different *kinds* of counterexample that will undoubtedly have occurred to the attentive reader. The first of these is a reaction to the fact that on my view jealousy is an essentially *three-party* emotion: the jealous person is "pained" or "bothered" by the fact that (as she believes) another person has chosen (or appears to be likely to choose) to "favor" some other person over her, in some way in which she wants to be favored instead. But now consider, in response to this, the following example of a not uncommon kind of case: seeing that I have managed to achieve some goal you and I were both attempting to achieve, you say (not necessarily in a particularly unfriendly way), "Wow! I'm *so* jealous! I never thought you'd do it first!" (I have managed to lose twenty pounds, let us suppose, which is something you also want to do but have not yet managed to accomplish.) Here there is no third party whom I am apparently "favoring" in some way in which you want to be favored by me; there are simply you and I and my having managed to accomplish something, before you, that you wanted to achieve as well (or, in some cases, in my stead). And yet it seems perfectly appropriate for you to speak exactly as we have just imagined you speaking--claiming to be jealous because of what I have managed to achieve--and in fact people speak this way all the time.

What I want to say about cases of this sort is that, our ordinary ways of speaking notwithstanding, what one is actually experiencing in such cases is not jealousy at all but *envy*. To see this, we need first to imagine some simple paradigms of what everyone would agree are clear cases of envy--cases in which I envy you your wealth, for example, or your good looks, or the knack you have for making friends so much more easily than I--and then attempt to identify, as we did in the case of jealousy, what appears to be essential to such cases being (clear) cases of envy. I shall not attempt to do this here, except to say that I think it can be done and that the result is that we find that envy, unlike jealousy, is an essentially *two-party* emotion, in which one person is "bothered", in any of a number of possible ways, not by another person's *choices* but, rather, by what some other person either literally or figuratively *has*--or, rather, to speak more accurately, in which one person is bothered not by another's *choices*, *vis-a-vis* some third party, but by the fact that the second party *has* something that she (the first party) wants but does not have. (Notice that I am not suggesting that envy does not occur in three-party contexts, but that it does not need a three-party context in order to occur. When envy does occur in a three-party context, moreover, it has a quite different intentional object than jealousy would have, and would have to have, on my view, in an exactly similar context. To see this, imagine that in addition to being jealous because my lover appears to be falling in love with someone else, I also find myself envying her new lover for his having been able to win the affections of my lover as he did. The object of my emotional "pain", insofar as I am jealous, is my lover's choice of the other person over me; the object of my "pain" insofar as I am also envious, on the other hand, is her new lover and the fact of his having been able to win her attentions as he did.)[4]

So much for at least one kind of case in which it might appear that we have an instance of jealousy without its being the case that we have the elements required by my analysis of what is involved when someone experiences this emotion. In a moment I shall consider a class of cases in which we seem *not* to have instances of jealousy but in which it is thought we do have the elements my view suggests are sufficient for the occurrence of this emotion. First, though, I need to comment briefly on two seemingly obscure elements in the view I am defending here, the first of which might well appear to make my view seem, at best, incomplete.

To begin, notice that in the case of both jealousy and envy, as I have analyzed them, I have spoken of the agent (or sufferer's) being "bothered" or "pained" by her belief that something or other connected with her desires is or is not the case. Clearly, this might seem objectionable--not merely because of the extraordinary obscurity of these terms, but also because, at least in the case of jealousy, many readers may be inclined to believe that with enough work we ought to be able to say exactly what the painful affective component of this emotion really involves--that is, exactly whether the affective component in jealousy is anger, fear, grief, etc., or some combination of these and any number of other familiar affective states, or whether the affective component of this emotion is in fact a distinct feeling in its own right, perhaps related to these other, more familiar feelings, but quite distinct nonetheless.

The idea that there is some unique phenomenological experience which is "the experience of jealousy", or, more plausibly, "the unique affective component" in this emotion, is widespread, not merely among lay-persons but in the work of those with a professional interest in this emotion as well. Nonetheless, I think this idea is deeply and importantly mistaken, and while limits of space forbid a full discussion of this matter here, it is important to see that both ordi-

---

4. For a fuller discussion of this last point, see 'Jealousy', *op. cit.*, pp. 530-534. I should note here, by the way, once again, that what is necessary for jealousy, on my view, is not the actual *existence* of the "third party" my view requires, but simply the belief, on the part of one individual, that another individual is favoring some third individual in the relevant way. This third party may well be a figment of the first party's imagination; the point is simply that, for jealousy, there has to be a belief that she or he exists.

nary experience and thoughtful literary representations of this emotion suggest a very different idea: namely, that, given both a belief and a desire of the sorts identified in our analysis, plus the "intentional focus" discussed at the end of the present section, any of a large number of familiar "feelings" can constitute the affective component of jealousy. Othello's affective state, before he murders Desdemona, is represented by Shakespeare, and later by Verdi, as essentially one of anger, mixed occasionally with something very much like grief; and yet, given our knowledge of what he believes and desires, we say, quite confidently, that he is *jealous*, rather than, say, simply very angry at what he believes is Desdemona's inconstancy and occasionally very sad or "grieved", as well, at the thought that their love-affair has ended. Nor would we change this judgment if we learned that Othello's anger was merely feigned and that what he was really experiencing, phenomenologically, was basically just a diffuse but very intense feeling of agitation at the thought of Desdemona wanting Iago over him. For this, too, given our knowledge of what he currently believes and desires, would count as experiencing jealousy, as I think is obvious from other, less dramatic experiences we have all had with this emotion, either in our own persons or in that of various family members and friends: the presence of one or more of any number of different affective states is consistent with one's emotion being "jealousy", provided these states are induced by a contemplation of what one believes is a transfer, to someone else, of a certain kind of interpersonal "favoring" that one wants for oneself and that one in fact believes one has enjoyed, at least for a while, until now.[5]

At this point we come to the second element in my analysis that needs elaboration. According to that analysis, someone who is occurrently jealous is someone who wants to be "favored" by another in some way--over all others or over some special (perhaps unitary) set of others--but who believes that, while she *has* been so favored, at least for a time, up until now, also (now) believes that she either is currently no longer so favored or, at any rate, is *in danger* of no longer being so favored in the near future.[6] And the question is: what does all this talk of one person wanting to be "favored" by another really mean?

Consider, first, by way of answer, some of the things we know from experience, as well as from our earlier examples, jealous people sometimes want but believe or fear they are no longer getting (or are in danger of soon losing):

---

5. Note, again, that it is controversial to assume, as I am doing here, that jealousy requires that one believe one *has* (already) been "favored" by the second party in the way in which one wants to be favored and now believes one is not favored. However, while this assumption raises an important and admittedly debatable issue, this is not an issue that needs to be resolved here, given my present purposes.

6. Again, see notes 2 and 5 above in this connection.

sexual exclusivity; professional regard in relation to other professionals in a given field; attention or affection from a parent or a loved one; preference as the one (or one of the ones) to whom another will choose to speak about their deepest thoughts and feelings; and so on. Superficially, this is quite a mixed bag. And, as we shall discuss at greater length below, even upon reflection we can be astounded by the type and variety of things people sometimes want from others, where their desire for these things is such as to dispose them to experience great psychological discomfort when it appears that that desire is in danger of not being satisfied. Still, it is clear that there is a fairly obvious common thread behind these and all the other desires frustration of which could lead to jealousy, and it is the presence of this common thread that leads me to use the term 'favored' as a way of glossing what it is that a person might want in a case where we would say that she was jealous if she became "pained" or "bothered" about the fact that, as she believed, she had had what she wanted for a time but was now in danger of either losing or having lost it. For in all such cases, it seems to me, the jealous person wants to be treated or wanted or regarded by another in a certain way, rather than wanting simply to have or possess some *thing* (or even some person, if persons can indeed be "possessed" or "had" in the relevant, object-like way). It is professional *regard* that we want, in professional jealousy, for example, but feel we are not getting (or are about to lose), though it is, of course, not *simply* regard: we want, rather, to be regarded or esteemed in certain ways in relation to one or more (perhaps all) others in a given field, and it is when we suspect we have lost or are about to lose that regard, or "favor", that we are liable to feel the pain or botherment we call "jealousy". And similarly for romantic and sexual jealousy, as well as for what I have called "interpersonal" (but non-professional and non-romantic) jealousy: we want to be "favored" by the relevant other(s) with some special esteem, affection, or regard, or, in some instances of sexual jealousy, with a treatment of others that leaves us the sole recipients of sexual attention or interaction or desire (see Section IV below for more on this last kind of case). Hence the word 'favored' in our analysis, which is meant simply as a place-holder for these various ways in which one might want to be treated or regarded by another, such that, were one to think one had had, but then lost, that treatment or regard, one might well be pained or bothered in the way we call "being jealous".

We can now turn, in concluding this review of a view whose truth I propose to take for granted in the sections that follow, to the second type of counterexample mentioned above, in which it is alleged that the elements of that analysis are all present but in which it would not appear to be appropriate to say of the agent in question that she is jealous. Discussion of this *type* of counterexample will enable me not only to attempt to deflect another likely objection to my view, but also to refine my earlier statement of that view.

Imagine a case, then, like Shakespeare's or Verdi's famous cases, in which we would initially be inclined to say of someone that he is clearly quite jealous, and in which we would be inclined to say this precisely because the elements of the analysis I have been defending all appear to be met and to be met quite straightforwardly: our protagonist wants very much to be favored in some way (romantically or sexually, let us suppose) by some particular person, and has for at least some time rightly believed that he *is* so favored; recently, though, he has for a number of reasons begun to believe that he is no longer favored in the way in which he desires to be favored (with sexual exclusivity, say, or exclusive romantic love); and, finally, because of his belief that this is so, he is currently directing a great deal of anger both at his lover and at her new lover as well. Suppose, though, in addition, that in this particular case we get an opportunity to talk to our protagonist about exactly what he is angry about, and, when we do so, we discover that he is angry because, given his beliefs about his lover's current and likely future affections, he further believes he will now have to find another lover, with all the time, expense, and psychic energy that this will require. Suppose, in fact, he is outraged about what he sees as the recent developments in his relationship with his current lover, but that what he is outraged about is not the fact that she has apparently chosen (or begun to choose) another man over him but, rather, the fact that, if this is true, it means (as *he* sees things) that he has in effect wasted a lot of time, effort, and money on this person--time, effort, and money that he will now have to expend all over again in securing a replacement.

Having learned all this about him, or, more precisely, having learned what I am supposing we have learned about the cause (and the object) of his anger, would we still be inclined to say of this man that he is *jealous*? It seems to me we would not. We would say, rather, that he is *angry* because of the inconveniences he expects to suffer because of what he believes to be his lover's recent (or incipient) transfer of affections. And if this is the only thing he is angry about, and essentially the only thing he is feeling in connection with his lover's choice, we would appear to have no grounds for saying he is jealous.

But now it seems we have a case of exactly the sort promised by our critic-- namely, a case in which all the elements of my view appear to be present, but in which it would be implausible to say that the individual in question is jealous. And since any number of cases like this could easily be imagined, it seems we have discovered not just one admittedly rather odd case, but a whole class of cases in which the analysis suggested earlier gives us the wrong result.

This last claim is true, though, only if the analysis suggested earlier leads to the conclusion that the protagonist in these cases is jealous, despite the fact that the object of his concern is as we have described it, in the preceding case, and as we would have to describe it, in other, similar cases, in order to get the desired result. Is this so? It seems to me it is not, though admittedly our earlier statement of the analysis may not have made this sufficiently clear. What needs to be the case, on our view, for jealousy to be present, is that the party in position "A" is somehow bothered by the fact that, as he believes, he is not favored in some way in which he wants to be favored (and believes he has been favored, at least for a time). Is the protagonist of our story above bothered by the fact that he is not favored as he has been favored and presumably wants to continue to be favored? In one sense he is: he is bothered by this fact because of what it implies about what he will have to do given certain other desires he has (for example, to find a "replacement", as quickly and efficiently as possible, if and when he loses his current lover). If, however, we take our analysis to imply that one is jealous only if, *inter alia*, one is bothered not (or not merely) by the likely *consequences* of not being favored as one wants to be favored but, rather, by the *very fact* that one is no longer so favored, then the sorts of cases we are imagining are not only *not* a threat to that analysis, they in fact help us to see its strength. For, thus interpreted, our analysis explains *why* the sorts of cases we have just been discussing do not appear to be cases where the protagonist is jealous.

Now, nothing in the analysis we have proposed precludes interpreting it in this latter (stronger) way, and in fact it seems to me that reflection on cases of the sort we have just been considering suggests we *ought* to interpret it in this way. What's more, while I shall not attempt to show this here, I think further reflection on cases which do not have the complexity, or at least the oddity, of the sorts of cases we have just been considering would show that the stronger interpretation of our analysis is actually the one that is suggested by these simpler or more realistic cases as well: even in ordinary cases, that is to say, it is botherment at the very fact that one is not favored as one wants to be favored, and believes one has been favored, that constitutes being jealous in light of one's appreciation of this fact, and not just botherment at some expected consequence (or known concomitant) of this fact. Hence, rather than seeing cases of the sort we have been discussing as *counterexamples* to the view I have proposed, I am inclined to see them, as I argued a moment ago, as *consistent* with that view and, indeed, as indicative of one of its strengths.

III

Suppose the foregoing analysis is basically sound. Apart from its value in enabling us to understand exactly what jealousy *is*, this analysis also suggests what I believe is a fruitful approach to certain other questions about jealousy in which philosophers and others have recently shown an interest. Suppose one believes, for example, as many writers appear to do, that jealousy is importantly (and non-trivially) connected with some form of personal insecurity. Then, if our analysis is correct, one should be able to support this view by showing how being "pained" or "bothered" by the belief that one is not favored in some way in which one wants to be favored, and believes one has for a time been favored, is indicative of the relevant sort of insecurity. Or, rather, one should be able to show this *or* be able to show how the *desire* to be thus favored is indicative of the relevant sort of insecurity, independently of whether or not the individual in question is "pained" or "bothered" in the relevant way when (as she believes) that desire is frustrated; for on the view defended above, both the desire and the "pain" or "botherment" are necessary for (occurrent) jealousy, and hence the presence of either could in theory be the basis of the alleged connection between jealousy and personal insecurity. If one is sceptical about this alleged connection, on the other hand, one ought to be able to show why it is *rational* for one to be sceptical, by showing why it is implausible to suppose that being pained or bothered in the relevant way is indicative of personal insecurity *and* why it is implausible, as well, to suppose that *wanting* to be favored in that way is indicative of personal insecurity. And similarly for any number of other things one might be inclined to say about jealousy or the (occurrently) jealous person: for any given claim, one ought to be able to show how the presence of the relevant desire, or the occurrence of the "pain" or "botherment" necessary for jealousy, supports or otherwise renders plausible that particular claim.

Elsewhere, I have explored this line of thought in connection with certain very common claims about what jealousy shows about the jealous person: that such a person is necessarily insecure, as a person, in various identifiable ways; that such a person necessarily holds the (pretty clearly false) view that love and affection are "limited commodities" of a certain sort, or that the "game" of getting and giving love is in some deep and important sense a zero-sum game; or that, in sexual jealousy, at any rate, the jealous person is necessarily a person who thinks of the party in the "B" position as an *object* rather than as a person.[7] I now believe, however, that my treatment of these issues, while sound as far as it went, left a number of related and possibly deeper issues untouched. For behind the particular issues just described, it seems to me, there are other, larger issues that also deserve our attention, partly because of their intrinsic interest and partly because they are connected with more general issues in the theory of action, the theory of rationality, and the philosophy of mind. In what follows, then, I want to indicate what I think these larger issues are, how they are related to the more general areas of philosophy just mentioned, and why I continue to think that the best way to deal with these issues is to start from the assumption that the analysis sketched above is sound.

IV

It will be useful to begin with the claim that jealousy shows an important kind of personal insecurity, since a brief discussion of this claim will take us

---

7. 'Jealousy', *op. cit.*, pp. 546-558.

naturally to one of the larger issues I now believe lies in the background here. Obviously, there is one sense in which jealousy does appear to reveal a kind of insecurity, at least if our analysis is correct: if to be jealous is to believe or at least suspect that one is not favored in some way in which one wants to be favored, then to be jealous is to be insecure, or *unsure*, about one's hold on another's admiration, affection, and so forth, for oneself. However, quite apart from the fact that in some cases one is quite clearly *not* unsure about whether or not one is still favored in the relevant way--cases in which one would say one *knows* one is no longer loved or admired, say, above all others--this cannot be the sense of 'insecurity' the advocates of the insecurity thesis have in mind. For what they want to explain is why some people are prone to jealousy while others are not. And this is not something that can be done simply by pointing out that jealousy necessarily involves beliefs or suspicions of a certain sort--of a sort that can be linked with the type of "insecurity" just described, that is to say. To be sure, a tendency to adopt the relevant sorts of beliefs *prematurely*, or in the absence of adequate evidence, might be linked with an interesting form of personal insecurity. However, the mere fact that a person believes, on the basis of good evidence, that she is not favored in some way, tells us *nothing* about her, in and of itself, other than that she is capable of inferring plausible conclusions from appropriate evidence.

What the advocates of the insecurity thesis need to be alleging--as our analysis in fact shows--is, rather, that there is something in either the jealous person's affective *response* to the relevant belief, or in the *desire* that accompanies and partly accounts for that response, that bespeaks the insecurity that is allegedly necessarily involved in jealousy. Once we realize this, though, it is not immediately clear why we should suppose the insecurity theorist is right. For what he has to be saying is *either* that the relevant response, or the relevant desire, *itself* reveals the insecurity he has in mind, *or* that, while not itself entailing this form of insecurity, this response, or desire, is invariably *linked*, causally, with independently identifiable insecurity of the appropriate sort. And why should we suppose that any of this is true? Why, for example, should our singer's desire to be considered the best operatic baritone in the world be thought to be sufficient, in itself, to show that he is in some important sense deeply and interestingly insecure as a person? Or why should the fact that he is terribly pained, if indeed he is, at the thought that he is no longer considered the best baritone in the world, be thought to be sufficient, in itself, to show that he is personally insecure? Why not suppose, instead, so far as the desire is concerned, that he simply has a gargantuan ego, and, so far as the subsequent pain is concerned, that some people with large egos suffer greatly when they do not get certain things they very badly want? To be sure, it might be conceded that the fact of personal insecurity is not *entailed* by the presence of the relevant desire, nor by the occurrence of the pain or botherment that sometimes follows frustration of such a desire, but maintained, nonetheless, that only those who are deeply and interestingly insecure, as persons, tend to *have* such desires or to be significantly bothered when those desires are frustrated. And this may be right. Curiously, though, there has been remarkably little empirical research on this question, and what research has been done is at best inconclusive, so far as the resolution of this issue is concerned.[8]

It would be a mistake, however, to suppose that, apart from further empirical research, no case whatsoever can be made for "the insecurity thesis", as we have called it, or for some *version* of this thesis, at any rate, *given* the approach that accepting our analysis suggests we take in attempting to resolve the insecurity issue.[9] To see why this is so, recall that on our view the "affective" side of jealousy can be quite variable, ranging, as we have seen, from a vague displeasure or mild uneasiness, to intense anger, extreme fear (or even panic), terrible rage, and so on. Now, suppose we ask what significance there might be, if any, in the fact that the affective side of jealousy takes the form of something like *fear*, say, or *panic*, in some people, while taking the form of *anger* or *rage* in others. One very plausible answer would go as follows. People who react to the loss of favored "status" (or the *perceived* loss of such status) with extreme anxiety or fear, much less with a sense of panic, are obviously people who are very heavily invested, emotionally, in the "state" or "condition" of being favored in the relevant way. What, then, we might ask, is the best or *prima facie* most plausible explanation of such an extraordinary investment--what, that is to say, is a plausible explanation of a desire to be "favored" which is so intense that its (perceived) frustration leads to anxiety, fear, or even panic of the sort we are imagining? One very tempting answer is that this desire is very likely *itself* motivated by a need to find in the relevant "status" an indication of self-worth that the individual in question would otherwise not feel--that she clearly does *not* feel, one might want to say, when, believing she is no longer thus favored, she reacts with the extreme anxiety, fear, or panic we are imagining.

It might be objected that this sketch of an account of how insecurity might be connected in an interesting way with jealousy is entirely conjectural: no *evidence* has been adduced to show that what this sketch suggests is in fact true. And this would be a completely legitimate objection, if the point of the sketch was to prove that insecurity is connected with certain instances of jealousy in the suggested way. The point, though, was not to prove (here) that jealousy is connected with certain instances of insecurity in this way, but merely to show

---

8. G. White and P. Mullen, *Jealousy: Theory, Research, and Clinical Strategies* (NY: Guilford Press, 1989), pp. 96-99.

9. The remarks that follow are heavily indebted to observations communicated to me by Roger Lamb, who seems to me to have thought more clearly and more carefully about these matters than anyone I know. It will be obvious, I hope, that much more needs to be, and can be, said about these matters than I have been able to say here.

how, on the analysis defended earlier, one might plausibly *predict* that jealousy might be connected with insecurity, thus showing, at the same time, how research might most usefully be conducted to confirm or disconfirm the relevant line of thought.

It might also be objected that nothing we have said so far shows that those who experience jealousy as a species of *anger* or *rage* are significantly different, so far as the probability of insecurity is concerned, from those who experience this emotion as a species of anxiety or fear: after all, those for whom the affective side of jealousy consists of the former emotions, at least in their more intense forms, can plausibly be said to be just as heavily "invested", emotionally, in the attainment of the relevant ("favored") state or condition, as those for whom the affective side of jealousy consists of intense anxiety or fear. This objection, though, overlooks the fact that desires whose frustration leads to anger or rage, supposing these latter feelings really are what they seem, and are not simply a disguise for what is really fear or panic, are far less plausible candidates for the insecurity explanation sketched above for the desires we imagined leading to panic or fear. In the case of the latter, it seemed plausible to suppose, pending empirical inquiry, that such a desire would very likely be motivated by a need to find a "prop", in the esteem, affection, or admiration of others, for an antecedently insecure sense of self-worth. In the case of the former sorts of desires, by contrast--those whose frustration tends to lead to anger or even rage--it seems much less plausible to say, even conjecturally, that they are likely motivated by a need for affirmation of one's worth *via* the desired form of favoring. Anger, if not rage (which makes one suspicious that some form of fear *is* involved, albeit unconsciously), seems more like what one would feel in the face of an insult, or at the loss of a valued form of pleasure, while anxiety and fear, not to mention panic, seem more like what one would feel in the face of a serious threat to one's continued existence as a worthwhile being.

All of this, of course, is almost ludicrously conjectural. Two important points nonetheless emerge from these reflections. First, we see how *useful* our analysis can be in exploring the sorts of claims that concern us here--claims about what jealousy allegedly does or does not *show* about the jealous person. Secondly, we see the first inklings of a point I shall press and explore much more vigorously below: while, as we shall see, there is nothing *inherently* odd or objectionable about the *kinds* of desires jealousy presupposes on our view, there *are* cases where the particular shape or intensity of these desires suggests that something is in some important sense "wrong" with the person who has them. In saying this, though, I anticipate points that will be much clearer below.

Suppose, for now, we leave for a moment the question of whether the sorts of desires and reactions that interest us are somehow connected with personal insecurity, specifically, and ask, instead, whether there appears to be anything at all *odd* or *curious* about such desires and the affective responses to which their frustration sometimes leads. It is certainly rare for someone to want to be thought to be the best operatic baritone in the world, and in that sense someone with such a desire, and the desire itself, might be said to be "unusual". But really superb operatic voices are themselves rare and hence are themselves "unusual" in this same sense. Our question, obviously, is not whether desires of the relevant sort are "unusual" in this sense but, rather, whether in the case of a person for whom such a desire at least makes sense--i.e., who might stand at least a remote chance of having such a desire satisfied--there is nonetheless something odd or otherwise curious about his actually *having* such a desire, rather than not having it, or about his being disposed to react in a way we would call "being jealous" in the event his desire is frustrated. Our question, in other words, is whether there is anything especially *puzzling* about having such a desire, rather than not having it, and whether, in addition, there is anything especially puzzling about being disposed to be significantly pained or bothered in the event one's desire is frustrated.

Now, in the case of professional jealousy, and in the case of non-professional, non-romantic interpersonal jealousy of the sort described at the end of Section I above, it seems to me most people would say there is nothing especially odd or curious about either the desire or the affective reaction that needs to be present for these forms of jealousy to occur. To be sure, with even a touch of imagination one could describe ways of being favored which are such that a desire to be favored in any of *these* ways *would* strike us as an "odd" or "curious" desire, even in a professional or a non-professional, non-romantic context; and there are certainly actual examples of affective *reactions* to the frustration of the relevant sorts of desires that would strike us as rather extreme and hence as "odd" or "curious" precisely *because* they are so extreme. By and large, though, it seems to me we take the fairly regular occurrence of the relevant sorts of desires as something to be expected in these contexts, and, what's more, while we find the occasional rather strong affective response somewhat baffling, we are for the most part not at all puzzled by the fact that some of the people who desire to be favored in the relevant ways are upset in the ways they are sometimes upset when their desires are frustrated.

What about the desires and reactions that are necessary for romantic and, specifically, sexual jealousy, on our view? Offhand, these may seem no more "odd" or puzzling than the desires and reactions just discussed. Sexual jealousy, after all, is something with which most of us are probably far better acquainted, both as sufferers and as observers, than we are with any or all of the other forms of jealousy thus far described. Absent further commentary, therefore, we may be tempted to assume that romantic and sexual jealousy, however unpleasant, and, indeed, disturbing, in certain instances, are no more odd or puzzling, at least in principle, than these other forms of jealousy we have identified.

Upon reflection, though, it is not at all clear that this is right. To be sure, the desire to be favored, either sexually, with some form of exclusivity, or romantically, in any of a variety of familiar ways, appears to most of us, I suspect, to be no more puzzling, in its own right, than the analogous desires we have alleged are involved in professional and non-professional, non-romantic jealousy. Indeed, if we allow ourselves a bit of armchair speculation about the likely biological bases of the dispositions that typically constitute these desires-- those involved in sexual jealousy, at any rate, and possibly, by extension, in romantic jealousy as well--it will not seem at all surprising that we, like many other animals, are naturally disposed to look for a certain kind and degree of exclusivity in our sexual and pre-sexual relationships. After all, if the relevant sort of exclusivity has a sufficiently high selection-value, as in fact it frequently does, the dispositions underlying it are precisely the sorts of dispositions we might expect to find selected over time.

It is when we reflect on the nature, and particularly on the intensity, of the "affect" characteristic of sexual jealousy, it seems to me, as well as on the nature and intensity of the affect involved in romantic jealousy generally, that things begin to look rather different. For here we find not just the *occasional* "odd" or puzzling case, where someone seems to care about the relevant "favoring" beyond anything we would ever have expected from an otherwise normal person; rather, we find that a relatively intense affective reaction, bespeaking a relatively intense or serious desire, is more or less the norm. It is true that the affective side of romantic and sexual jealousy, like the affective aspect of the other forms of jealousy we have been discussing, is quite variable from person to person and from case to case. If, however, we were to try to quantify the degree or intensity of the "pain" or "botherment" that is typically present when these various forms of jealousy are instantiated, we would surely expect to find that the median "pain-score" for sexual jealousy is, for most individuals, far higher than that for these other forms of jealousy.[10]

Suppose I am right about this. Isn't this exactly what we should expect, given that we are supposing that a desire to be favored in the relevant ways is not especially odd or puzzling and that the dispositions which constitute such a desire may well be, at least in part, biologically based? Why should the intensity characteristic of the affective side of romantic and sexual jealousy be thought to be an odd or puzzling feature of these forms of jealousy, in other words, given that we are supposing that the desires which underlie these affective responses are perfectly natural desires (or, at any rate, are desires that are in themselves neither odd nor especially puzzling)?

The answer, it seems to me, is that the intensity typical of the affective side of romantic and sexual jealousy is in fact far beyond what one would reasonably

---

10. Many studies, and a great deal of anecdotal evidence, suggest that the behavior that issues from sexual jealousy tends to be much more extreme--e.g., far more violent--than the behavior that typically issues from our other forms of jealousy.

expect, given our experience with other forms of jealousy, *even* on the assumption that the desires that are connected with the affective response in such cases are themselves, at least in general (biological) terms, perfectly understandable desires. To see this, we might begin by noting that both in ordinary life and in literary and dramatic representations of sexual (and romantic) jealousy, we find that there is almost nothing a sufficiently agitated person is incapable (or is deemed incapable, in the case of literature) of feeling, saying, or doing, in the relevant sorts of cases. We find, that is to say, that, unlike the typical case of professional or non-professional, non-romantic interpersonal jealousy, a typical case of sexual or romantic jealousy can easily be imagined to reach, fairly quickly, a level of affective intensity which is such that we can readily imagine someone in that state feeling, saying, and doing any number of extraordinary and quite awful things.[11]

Suppose one is willing to grant what I am alleging here--that our experience, both actual and literary, with sexual (and, to some extent, romantic) jealousy is such as to distinguish it, quite strikingly, from other forms of jealousy, so far as its typical level of affective intensity is concerned. A natural question that then arises is this: why should this particular form of jealousy produce such incredibly intense affective reactions, given that it is in fact no different, structurally, from the other forms of jealousy we have distinguished?

One obvious answer, already mooted, is that sexual jealousy (and perhaps also romantic jealousy generally) tends to have these curiously intense affective consequences simply because the relevant *desires*, at least in the case of sexual jealousy, are so much more intense, or important to us, than the analogous desires that must be present in the other forms of jealousy. But this, while certainly plausible as far as it goes, simply replaces one puzzle with another. For the question then becomes why the desires that sexual (and perhaps also romantic) jealousy involves tend to *be* so much more intense and important to us than those other desires that are involved in the other forms of jealousy. Why, for example, do people who care about sexual exclusivity tend to care *so much* about it, while those who care about or desire other (non-sexual and non-romantic) forms of "favoring" do not, by and large, tend to care nearly so much?

It might be thought that here we can plausibly resort, once again, to speculations about the biological bases of this form of jealousy: "That's just the way we're wired", someone might say, "and when we know more about the details of hominid evolution, we'll know more about why we're wired that way rather than in some other way". Surely, though, this sort of response is much less

---

11. As I have indicated above, I am aware that the other forms of jealousy occasionally instance themselves in equally dramatic ways. My point is simply that for these other forms of jealousy this is the exception, not the rule, whereas in the case of sexual (and romantic) jealousy, it is more or less the rule.

satisfactory in the present context than it was in the earlier context, when we speculated that the desire for sexual exclusivity might at least in part be genetically determined (specifically genetically determined, that is to say). After all, it is one thing to suppose that biology plays some role or other in these matters and quite another to introduce speculative biological considerations to answer a very specific question: namely, why some arguably quite large numbers of people care so much about the sort of special "favoring" that sexual and romantic jealousy presuppose, while caring so much less about the other, analogous forms of "favoring" that the other forms of jealousy presuppose.

At this point, of course, a very different sort of answer is likely to be proposed: biology to one side, the etiology of desires (and reactive dispositions) of the sort we are now considering is quite obviously a matter--and clearly a quite complicated matter--of cultural determination. With that said, this view might continue, there is nothing more that *can* be said, in the absence of the appropriate sort of empirical research, though neither is there any puzzle about the fact we are taking as a given: namely, that people who care about sexual exclusivity (and perhaps also people who care about various other types of romantic exclusivity or "favoring") tend to care much more intensely about it than do people who care about other (non-sexual and non-romantic) forms of "favoring". The fact is that people care about what they have come to care about, as a causal result of their own peculiar genetic make-up and subsequent socialization, and that's all there is to it. There are no special puzzles, here anymore than anywhere else in nature, on this view; there is just an incredibly large number of things about which we must admit we know relatively little.

But surely this answer is too glib. Perhaps it is true that all human desires can ultimately be explained, at least in principle, along the lines just sketched. In the meantime, though, we are left with the fact, if indeed it is a fact, that among these desires is the rather curious subset we have been discussing: the set of those desires for sexual or romantic "favorings" that, if thwarted, are likely to lead to enormous personal suffering, both for the person who has the desire and, quite possibly, for others as well. Anyone who, like me, is puzzled by the fact that so many people seem to care so much about the objects of those desires, is not likely to stop being puzzled simply by being reminded of the fact that the relevant desires can ultimately be explained, at least in principle, by an ideally successful natural social science. Indeed, it is at least in part the puzzlement of those of us who are puzzled by such desires, I take it, that fuels the search for the promised explanation.

But, now, what *exactly* is so puzzling about these desires, according to someone like me? I have granted that the general structure of desires of this sort is not at all surprising: that some people want to be "favored" by others in various ways, I have suggested, is, for most of us, a perfectly understandable fact about us. Why, then, should this particular subset of such desires--the ones that are directed at sexual or romantic "favorings" and that typically involve so much more intensity than the others--strike us as being any more odd or curious than the latter?

The answer, of course, is simply that it is precisely the fact that these sexual or romantic desires are so much more intense, and typically lead to such volatile behavior when frustrated, that leads some of us, at any rate, to find them odd or puzzling. For, in connection with such desires, one wants to ask: why should desires of this particular type be so much more intense or serious than the others, and why are so many people disposed to feel and act so strangely when desires of this sort are frustrated?[12]

V

I am afraid I have no general answer to this question.[13] What's more, if I did have an answer, I suspect it would point not to some one general cause of the phenomena that interest us but to some number of possible causes, different ones more or less operative in the life-histories of different individuals. And this, of course, so far as it goes, sounds exactly like the answer I rejected a moment ago as "too glib". I also believe, though, that knowing the causes of any given individual's propensity to have the relevant sorts of desires, and to be disposed to react to frustration of those desires in the relevant sorts of ways, would not entirely dissipate the feeling many of us have that there is something odd or curious about the intensity of such desires and about the affective and behavioral dispositions that so often accompany them. For, as I shall now try to show, a good part of what puzzles us about these desires, and the correlative dispositions, has to do not with our uncertainty about their etiology but, rather, with something else about them, something we have so far ignored.

We can begin by returning to the fact that many writers, along with a large number of ordinary observers, are tempted to think that jealousy, in any form, suggests an interesting, non-trivial form of personal insecurity: something about the jealous person's affective reaction, we are told, or about his desire to be

---

12. Here, our earlier remarks about insecurity-based desires are surely relevant, though limits of space prevent me from pursuing this connection just now. The idea, as Roger Lamb has convinced me in correspondence, is that desires to be favored that are based on deep personal insecurity will be particularly *urgent* desires, and hence their frustration will very likely be followed by especially intense affective reactions.

13. See note 12 above, however, in this connection. It is conceivable that working out the line of thought suggested there (about the urgency of insecurity-based desires and the likely effect of this on the intensity of their affective consequences when such desires are frustrated) would yield at least *one* very compelling *general* explanation of the sort we currently lack.

favored in the way(s) in which he wants to be favored, reveals a lack of confidence, as we might say, in his own worth or value as a person. I argued above that, applied to jealousy *tout court*, this is an implausible thesis: the occurrence of the relevant desires and reactions certainly does not *entail* an interesting (non-trivial) form of personal insecurity, and what evidence we have suggests there is no general *causal* link between them either. What's more, even if applied only to sexual jealousy, or to sexual and romantic jealousy, it seems to me the thesis is still too strong: Othello is not shown to be interestingly insecure, as a person, simply by virtue of the fact that he desires to be uniquely favored by Desdemona, nor is he shown to be thus insecure simply because, in addition, his desire is such as to lead, if frustrated, to the reaction with which we are familiar from Shakespeare's play. This having been said, though, it also needs to be said that there *is* something odd--something almost suspicious-- about the *depth* of Othello's devastation when, as he believes, he learns with certainty of Desdemona's faithlessness. There is, in particular, the sense that this man is in some sense curiously incomplete, as a person, if, as it appears, he can hardly *bear* the thought of her being faithless to him and is, indeed, driven to murder her as he reflects on the very possibility of her infidelity. And similarly for many other, less dramatic but equally puzzling cases: one moves quite naturally, it seems to me, from an appreciation of the jealous person's affective state, and what that state is capable of impelling him to do, to the suspicion that there is something wrong with a person who would suffer that much, and be impelled in exactly *those* directions, by the relevant loss--specifically, that there is something missing, something that, in its presence, would keep all this from happening exactly as it has happened, or appears likely to happen.

Suppose this is right--suppose, that is, most observers would agree that, at least in these extreme kinds of case, a person who is disposed to react in these ways to the apparent frustration of the relevant sorts of desires is, quite apart from what he may subsequently feel, seriously disturbed or "damaged" in some way, as a person. (In another time, we would have said, simply, that he is quite clearly "ill".) Obviously, these ways of describing our intuitive reaction to such cases are themselves too intuitive, or figurative, to accomplish much more than simply serving as convenient indicators of the general direction our puzzlement about such cases typically takes. But now notice that when we are inclined to think and speak of another person in this way, because of what we know or think we know about him, there are two directions in which we can proceed if we want to attempt to say, more perspicuously, what we are getting at with these terms. On the one hand, we might attempt to show that in fact this person, along with others like him, *is*, quite literally, *ill*--i.e., that such individuals suffer from some debilitating and clinically describable physical or psychological condition that explains their behavior in straightforward scientific terms. This, of course, is what, in his own way, the "insecurity" theorist is trying to do, though perhaps it is a bit strong to think of personal insecurity, except in extreme cases, as a psychological *illness*. On the other hand, though, we might move in a very different direction, as we attempt to make out, in a clearer and more perspicuous way, what we mean when we say of someone like the person who currently interests us that he appears to be somehow "incomplete" or "damaged", as a person, in light of what we know about his desires and dispositions in the sorts of circumstances we have in mind. For we might admit straightaway that we are not so much making a rough clinical *diagnosis* in speaking in this way but, rather, simply expressing our acceptance of certain substantive *norms* for what we believe are appropriate desires, dispositions, and feelings in circumstances of the relevant sort. In speaking of the relevant individual as "incomplete", in other words, or in saying of him that his condition suggests there is "something wrong with him", we may simply, and quite consciously, be saying that we believe that something about him is not as it should be, given acceptable norms for the sorts of things about him to which we are attending.

Suppose one is tempted to proceed in this second direction. One problem one must then face, of course, is that of articulating the relevant norms: what are "appropriate" or "permissible" desires, for example, *vis-a-vis* another person's choices in regard to oneself, and what are "inappropriate" or "impermissible" desires in this regard? What are "appropriate" or "permissible" feelings, in response to frustration of one's desires, and what are "inappropriate" or "impermissible" feelings? And so on. Another problem is that of explaining the alleged *force* of these norms: are they to be thought of as moral norms, for example, or are they social norms of some other, non-moral sort (like norms of etiquette, say, or good gamesmanship)? Or are they perhaps norms of rationality, so that, in violating them, one convicts oneself of having irrational or, perhaps better, unreasonable desires, beliefs, or feelings? Obviously, these and a number of other very pressing problems would have to be faced by anyone who, like myself, wants to allege that what is most striking about the desires and affective and behavioral dispositions of people of the sort we have been imagining--people capable of remarkably intense feelings of sexual and romantic jealousy--is that these desires, etc., are in some clear and important sense *inappropriate*.

The biggest problem the proponent of this approach must face, however, is not the problem of articulating the (admittedly very important) details his normative view requires; rather, the biggest problem he must face is that of explaining why we should take his view seriously--of explaining, that is to say, not merely how we *can* look at the relevant phenomena in terms of the norms he proposes, but of how in some sense we *must* look at those phenomena in these terms if we are really to understand them. Suppose, for example, a proponent of this sort of view is inclined to say that the force of the relevant norms is that of some species of rationality: it's just irrational, he says, to desire certain things, or to desire them with a certain degree of intensity; it is equally irrational to feel certain things in response to certain antecedent occurrences, or to feel them with a certain degree of intensity; and so on. One can of course *say* this about certain desires and certain feelings, and for some desires and some feelings, given the right context, one can say it, *prima facie*, at any rate, with a certain initial plausibility. But the proponent of the relevant sort of view must, as we have just seen, be prepared to do much more than this. He must be prepared to show that continuing to say this sort of thing is something a reasonable observer will be inclined to do, even after a great deal of reflection; he must be also prepared to show that talk of this sort is something in which we *have* to engage, if we are to understand the phenomena in question; and he must be prepared to answer the objections of those who disagree with either or both of these first two points. And these, as the history of such enterprises shows, are not tasks that are easy to accomplish. Indeed, so far as the particular sort of ("rationality") analysis just mooted is concerned, the predominant contemporary view, at least in Anglo-American philosophy, is that such an analysis is doomed to failure. For in this tradition the dominant contemporary view about rationality is essentially Hume's view, which holds that things like feelings and desires are not the *sorts* of things that can meaningfully be termed "rational" or "irrational".[14]

Why, one might ask, given the dismal history of analyses of the requisite sort, would one be inclined to continue the enterprise of attempting to find a set of norms that will make sense of our feeling that there is indeed something wrong with the sorts of people we have been discussing, and to find, as well, an account of such norms that is philosophically defensible? The answer, I hope, is obvious, from our remarks in Section IV above: nothing short of such an account, and such a set of norms, will explain the relevant intuitions in an adequate way--in a way that will be adequate, that is to say, to the views of those of us who feel that a purely *causal* account of the relevant phenomena will leave a considerable part of what is most interesting about these phenomena unexplained. The point of the second half of the present paper, in which I have been unable to do anything more than underline the need for such an alternative

---

14. Hume, *A Treatise of Human Nature*, ed. L.A. Selby-Bigge, Second Edition P.H. Nidditch (Oxford: Oxford University Press, 1978), Book II, Part III, Section III (pp. 413-418). Hume does allow, of course, that passions can be "contrary to reason" in either of two ways--by being "founded on the supposition of the existence of objects which really do not exist", or by being such as to lead us to "choose means insufficient for [our ends]" (*ibid.*).--but these are clearly "extended" uses of what Hume in fact sees as the central and proper use(s) of the notion of contrariety to reason or "irrationality", as we would say. Contemporary versions of the doctrine attributed to Hume in the text above are myriad, but I think the best (and surely the most sophisticated) recent statement is Allan Gibbard's in *Wise Norms, Apt Feelings: A Normative Theory of Judgment* (Cambridge: Harvard University Press, 1990). For an interesting contemporary defense of an alternative (non-Humean) view, see Charles Taylor, *Sources of the Self: The Making of the Modern Identity* (Cambridge: Harvard University Press, 1989).

account, has been to try to encourage other writers to take the need for such an account much more seriously than they have recently been inclined to do.[15]

15.   I am indebted to Roger Lamb for an enormously helpful set of comments on an earlier draft of this paper, and to Linda Farrell for editorial help without which the paper would be twice as long as it is.

10

Love Undigitized

Ronald de Sousa

> You shall love your crooked neighbour
> With your crooked heart.
>   W. H. Auden

Introduction: Digital Love

In a remarkable and little known paper, Karen Rotkin[1] described how
Freudian theory might have gone in a world dominated by women. Instead of
women being held to an ideal of mature *genitality*, requiring them to achieve
vaginal orgasms (thus making satisfaction more convenient for men), the challenge would be for men to make the difficult ascent to a mature form of sexuality, and the epitome of their success would be a capacity to experience *digital
orgasms*, that is, orgasms obtained in the course of stimulating a clitoris with a
finger.

I have always found this fantasy compelling. But Rotkin's sense of digitality is related only in a roundabout way to the sense of the word intended in my
title. What I want to explore here is an idea that may at first seem even more far-
fetched than Rotkin's: namely that love is "digital" as opposed to "analog", in
the sense in which a system of signs or mode of reproduction is digital or analog.[2] (Here as often in talk of sex or love, the pun on 'reproduction' is not quite

---

1. Rotkin, K., 'The Phallacy of our Sexual Norm', in *Beyond Sex Role Stereotypes:
Readings Towards a Philosophy of Androgyny*, Kaplan, A.G. and J.P. Bean, eds. (New
York: Little, 1976).

2. *Analog* and *digital* are terms that describe not anything in the real world but systems
of discrete representation and reproduction. An analog representation strives to match

...continuing...

irrelevant.) Rotkin's form of "digitality" is in fact designed to draw attention to a special case of the kind of digitality I am concerned with. For her fantasy would have no edge, were it not for the fact that psychoanalysis lays down a rigid set of normative definitions about what counts as a proper, mature, successful, in short a *real* orgasm. The concrete experience of different individuals might offer a continuous range of possibilities, in which the experience characterized as "vaginal orgasm" might (or might not, allowing for the possibility that it is entirely fictional) find its place as one specific point along a continuum. But the language of normative definition parodied by Rotkin's notion of digital orgasm privileges that specific point. It makes it into a paradigm, a kind of Platonic Form to which all others are to be compared and in terms of which all are to be judged, as matching or failing to match it.

This process of labeling regions on a continuum according to their fit with a limited number of discrete paradigms is of the essence of the "digital". Though digitality in this sense now seems associated most vividly with computers, it is actually among Plato's greatest inventions. For it was he who suggested that we should reinterpret the resemblance relation which links things of one kind as a three-term relation, involving the parallel "participation" of the two original objects in a third. Plato, however, didn't notice the principal benefit of this idea: if we regard resemblance as a three-term relation, then successive copies of an original can be made without loss of accuracy. Since no copying process is absolutely perfect, the resemblance between any two copies is not a transitive relation. *A* may be indistinguishable from *B*, and *B* from *C*, but *C* might be noticeably different from *A*. Degradation is swift and inevitable. In digital copying, by contrast, when you are making a copy *C* of an item *A*, what you are *really* doing is making a copy of a *third* object *B*, a paradigm of which *A* is itself merely a copy. Every copy, however distant, is only really two steps away from the original. In the first step, you find the paradigm *B* of which *A* is a copy. In the second, you copy *B*. So copies may be made indefinitely without substantial degradation.

But digitality has a drawback. The number of possible representations is limited to the number of original paradigms, for any putative representation is either assigned to an existing paradigm, or else is no representation at all. To add paradigms is not impossible, but it amounts to adopting another system of representation, and there may be costs associated with that. Thus it would certainly be technically possible to accommodate those refined audiophiles who

---

every variation in continuous quantities; its accuracy is necessarily a matter of degree. A digital one exists only in the context of a system which provides a limited number of discrete paradigms into which every actual value must fit. In terms of the relevant system, a digital representation can therefore be perfect.

claim that no CD music disk can match old-fashioned analog recordings: all that would be needed is to raise the sampling rate sufficiently to decrease any harmonic distortion below the threshold of any possible human ear. But the price of the switch is prohibitive.

One more characteristic of digital systems should be noted. Since resemblance admits of degrees, and copying can be more or less accurate, there can be better or worse copies. From there a fallacious slide leads too easily to the idea that better *copies* are *better*, without qualification. This quasi-corollary does not figure in the purely technical uses of digital representation, for their whole point is that all representations fitting a given paradigm are equivalent. But it is central to Plato's identification of metaphysics with ethics, and it is, as we shall see, a natural assumption in the typology of love.

My hypothesis, then, is that the categories within which we "naturally" try to fence in love, as well as sex, gender, and emotions in general, are the result of a process of digitization. This invites speculation about what function such digitization might serve: in what sense does our emotional life need to be pre-adapted to the rigours of multiple copying?

In a moment, I will return to this question, and ask also how digitization of this kind actually takes place. But first I want to list some puzzles and paradoxes to which the paradigms of love apparently give rise.

Paradoxes and Paradigms

The very notion of a *union* of *individuals* has struck many as paradoxical.[3] But there are less metaphysical, more specific puzzles that often baffle us in practice. Here are some of them:

1. Jealousy

Most people take seriously the dictum that *Real love makes you feel jealous*. One also commonly hears it said that *Real love makes you unconditionally want the other's good*. But jealousy not infrequently involves the need or wish to harm the loved one. So these commonplaces conflict.

2. The Priority of Pain

Closely related to this is the idea that pain is a more reliable test of love than pleasure. Again this thought, paradoxical in the light of the commonplace

---

3. Solomon, R. C., *About Love: Reinventing Romance For Our Times* (New York: Rowman and Littlefield, 1994), pp. 64 *ff.*

that erotic love is concerned with intense pleasure, is enshrined in some familiar lines of poetry:

> Fantastick Fancies fondly move,
>   And in frail Joys believe,
> Taking false Pleasure for true Love;
>   But Pain can ne're deceive.
>   (John Wilmot, Earl of Rochester: 'The Mistress'.)

3. Sex and Love

The relation of sex to love is also subject to paradox. "Making love" is frequently said to be best done as an "expression" of love; but there's a fine line between expressing love, and doing something motivated by love. The latter sounds too much like making desire into a means: just as any motive but truth for agreeing with someone is epistemically irrelevant, so in sex any motive but desire is erotically irrelevant--love included. If you make love to me out of love, then I can never really be sure that you desire me.[4]

4. Freedom and Rules

Love, like poetry, requires rules for the freedom of its expression to flourish. Insofar as these rules are like the constitutive rules of a game, there is nothing paradoxical in that.[5] But there is something paradoxical in the *feeling* that great love, not only erotic but also divine, both liberates and binds at the same time. Witness John Donne *Holy Sonnet XIV*:

> Take me to You, imprison me, for I,
> Except Y'enthrall me, never shall be free
> Nor ever chaste, except You ravish me.

The final paradox, which I believe partly explains all those just listed, directly encapsulates the digitization of love. At first sight, what one individual might find to love and hate in another should vary indefinitely in indefinitely many dimensions. It should form a continuous theoretical space of possibilities. Why, then, is love thought of as being a highly specific location in that space,

---

4. See Vannoy, R., *Sex Without Love* (Buffalo, NY: Prometheus, 1980). Love is, no doubt, as good a *reason* as any for faking an orgasm. The related epistemic point is made in Plato, *Phaedrus* 233a: "it ought to be better to listen to [a non-lover] rather than a lover, for a lover commends anything you say or do even when it is amiss...."

5. *Cf.* Hart, H.L., *The Concept of Law* (Oxford: Clarendon Press, 1961), p. 9.

into which we aptly describe people as *falling*, as into a vortex or black hole? Why is it so generally taken for granted that love, rather than being as endlessly variable as the individuals that experience it, is confined to a small number of highly specific types or patterns of connection and feeling? The answer, I suggest, lies in the phenomenon of *'essence anxiety'*. It is, we might say, the emotional variant of Meno's paradox. I'll make it the last on my list, and call it

5. The Paradox of Recognition

How can you tell if it's real love?
--You'll know it when you feel it.
But how, Meno, could you ever recognize it, if you don't already know it?
(Plato, *Meno*).

The problem of recognition leads one to a search for criteria of "real love", reliable tests that can be directly applied to relieve essence anxiety. Essentialism in the definition of human identity--whether in terms of gender, or race--has recently come under sustained attack in various quarters.[6] But no sceptical cloud, it seems, casts a shadow on the search for the essence of love.

Solomon's latest book about love[7] provides a good illustration. It defends a conception of love as unpredictable, essentially dynamic, involving indefinable individuals who together forge a new self. It proclaims that "pluralism [in love is] not only possible but necessary" (p. 18), and warns against a number of popular misconceptions including the idea that love is a *feeling* and that it is "essentially bound up with the beautiful" (76). These are all claims calculated to forestall the charge of burdening us with rigid categories.

Yet within a few pages Solomon has already laid down the following conditions for calling anything "love". Whatever is properly so called, according to Solomon, must conform to the following criteria (italics in the original); real love must be:

(i) *"exclusive* love of a *particular* person"[8] (39);

---

6. *E.g.* on gender: Richards, J. R., *The Sceptical Feminist* (Harmondsworth: Penguin, 1982), and Spelman, E., *Inessential Woman* (Boston: Beacon Press, 1988); on race, Appiah, K. A., *In My Father's House: Africa in the Philosophy of Culture* (New York: Oxford University Press, 1992).

7. Solomon, R. C., *About Love: Reinventing Romance for Our Times* (New York: Rowman and Littlefield, 1994).

8. This requirement appears to be mitigated on p. 185, where Solomon writes: "Loving is a passion that, at the lower-frequency end of the spectrum, can be generously shared,

...continuing...

- (ii)   "necessarily *reciprocal*" (41);
- (iii)   "to want to be *indispensable* to the person who is already indispensable to you" (42);
- (iv)   "sexual in origin and motivation" (43);
- (v)   "spontaneous and voluntary" (43);
- (vi)   "between equals" (43).

Solomon says these six necessary conditions are "not even close" to amounting to a definition (47). There is also "[13-year-old] Becky's theorem":

- (vii)   the target of love is "*not a friend!*" (48);

and some more serious positive conditions:

- (viii) "idealization lies right at the heart of love" (89);
- (ix)   love involves fantasy and imagination (though preferably not the fantasy of making love to someone else) (161).

Finally, Solomon's most important positive characterization is that love is a "central ingredient in personal self-identity" (62): in other words, love is

- (x)   "getting excited about the transformation of oneself" (149, 194 *ff*; see also R. Nozick's *The Examined Life*, p. 82).

Perhaps it is somewhat unfair to pick out of Solomon's book these indications of what I am calling essence anxiety. For he repeatedly stresses the transformative character of love, its unique effect upon every unique pair of unique individual lovers. This would seem to imply that one couldn't specify in advance what form the relationship should take, that new paradigms of love and lovers might constantly be in the process of creation. But that too can be seen as an essentialist *demand* made of love. Despite Solomon's disclaimers, therefore, it is difficult to avoid the sense that his characterizations carry a heavy normative burden. The vehicle of that burden is digitization, which it is time to explain in more detail.

What is Digitality? The Analogy of Language

I have already characterized digitality as having its conceptual ancestry in

---

but at its height it is--like the most desperate being "in love"--reserved pretty much for one lover and one lover alone".

Plato's theory of forms. I want now to look at it from a somewhat more concrete point of view, by setting up a comparison between our emotional repertoire, and particularly our repertoire of forms of love, and our acquisition of language.

Consider two possible pictures that one might have of how language is acquired. The two might be labelled the Empiricist and the Innatist. (The former is inspired by Skinner[9], and Quine[10]; the latter by Chomsky[11], and Fodor[12].

On the empiricist picture, language learning is the product of a myriad individual experiences, few if any of which are identical to any experiences of other learners of the same language. What I mean by a given word, or how I use a certain phrase, is not determined by a "rule" laid down for all alike by an Académie, by a teacher, or by a standard dictionary, but is the subtle precipitate of all those experiences of hearing or reading the word in a certain range of contexts, in each of which their occurrence contrasted with other words or phrases that might possibly have been used there instead. The exact identity of these distributive and contrastive sets, moreover, is probably unique to every speaker; hence each of us speaks a subtly different unique *idiolect*.[13] Peter Reich[14] has highlighted this uniqueness of idiolects by asking students in a large number of successive classes to report on what they would include in the extension of the word 'vehicle' (cars, motorcycles, roller skates, mother kangaroos, etc . . . .) Repeating for a number of other common words, he claims never to have found any two students whose usage patterns for a small set of words were identical.

Our emotional repertoire, like our language, is formed by a myriad individual events in an individual life. So one might expect an infinite variety of individual emotional possibilities, arising from an infinite variety of stories and situations in which each individual's capacity to feel has been honed. On this picture, the names of love, hate, jealousy, anger, or any other emotion designate areas within a multidimensional continuum, much as colour names roughly

9. Skinner, B. F., *Verbal Behavior* (New York: Appleton-Century-Crofts, 1957).

10. Quine, W. V. O., *Word and Object* (Cambridge, MA: MIT Press, 1960).

11. Chomsky, N., *Aspects of the Theory of Syntax* (Cambridge, MA: M.I.T. Press, 1965); and *Language and Mind* (extended edition) (New York: Harcourt-Brace-Jovanovich, 1972).

12. Fodor, J., *The Language of Thought* (New York: Thomas Crowell, 1975).

13. The language of "contrastive and distributive sets" is that of Paul Ziff in his *Semantic Analysis* (Ithaca: Cornell University Press, 1964), pp. 146 *ff*.

14. Personal communication.

mark out areas within a continuous spectrum of hues without having much influence on our capacity to discriminate between hues anywhere in the spectrum.

If we think of the acquisition of either linguistic or emotional repertoires on this model, what is remarkable is how we manage to learn a sufficiently robust common core of language to be able to communicate. This is not to deny that misunderstandings are rife in both domains.[15] But insofar as understanding is indeed possible, the empiricist hypothesis seems to fall short of explaining the relatively high degree of structure in linguistic space. The innatist hypothesis is intended to come to the rescue by providing a biological explanation.

On this view, the important constancies of language are innate, and common to all the members of the human species as such. Experience is obviously not irrelevant to the acquisition of language, but it serves mainly as a trigger for the slotting of empirical information into something like preexisting grammatical and semantical pigeon-holes.

On the analogous hypothesis for the acquisition of emotions, love, like the other emotions, has a biologically determined functionality. Therefore all the phenomena of love are tailored by biology to fit specific categories. There is no such thing as being a little bit of a husband, wife, parent, or sibling. These are all well defined roles that obey specific rules determined by the requirements of biological organisms as such.

We might call this, accepting the serendipitous connotation, the 'Catastrophe theory of love'. Digitization by itself provides the needed convenience of categories that we count as discrete (as in the case of colour); the element of "catastrophe" is provided by the tendency of our actual emotions to coalesce in certain regions of the space of possible emotions. Feelings polarize or escalate, converging on the salient regions picked out by their names. Attraction quickly becomes passion, irritation becomes hate, suspicion jealousy, and so forth. So it seems that to some extent what I have called 'digitization' is not merely a matter of cutting up a continuum, but of the continuum having a profile in which some points are actually more crowded while others are deserted.

Digitization: Sources and Uses

Biology abounds in mechanisms that make for the relative hardening of differentiated types. Speciation is a classic example. The differentiation of species probably also begins with some small difference, gradually widening

---

15. On emotional misunderstandings, see the wonderful "Short Dictionary of Misunderstood Words" in Kundera, M., *The Unbearable Lightness of Being* (New York: Harper and Row, 1984), pp. 89-104.

over a period of time during which two subgroups are isolated from one another. Soon, the very fact that some difference has arisen will create selection for further differentiation. There are two reasons for this: first, selection may penalize interbreeding, second, it will favour those members of the subgroup who carve for themselves a new ecological niche, one in which there is no competition with members of the other subgroup.[16]

Sex, conveniently enough, provides excellent examples. The many levels of sexual dimorphism are all essentially governed by principles of economics or game theory, which find a natural application in the processes of evolutionary change. At one level, for example, extreme dimorphism in gametes (the numerically abundant but nutritionally indigent sperm contrasting with a select few nutritionally rich ova) can be imagined as inevitably developing from small variations in size and self-sufficiency among originally undifferentiated gametes. Once any degree of difference has set in, selection will favour gametes that gamble on increasingly extreme strategies.

At yet another level of analysis, the ratio between the sexes is the result of an evolutionary stable strategy.[17] The mere fact of a predominance of one sex over the other will give a selective advantage to the other in the next generation. (Think of the few as having more partners among whom to spread their genes in the next generation; the many, on the other hand, have fewer.)

Yet biological mechanisms are not the only ones that can establish or reinforce "digitization". Other obvious mechanisms are purely social: teaching, institutions, conventions, are all potential sources of more or less stable digitized reproducible cultural units, or "memes".[18]

Whatever we know, we must categorize. From the continuum of our experience, we need to extract a finite and relatively fixed number of categories, in terms of which we recognize (or re-cognize) different occurrences of the same thing, or different tokens of the same type. Linguistic communication would not survive were it not for the constant "rectification of names" afforded by some sort of reversion to types. This is obviously compatible with linguistic drift, but the drift is slow enough to allow for periodic fixes to be taken on the state of a given language in dictionaries and grammars. Much the same mechanisms operate at the level of culture. Thus, a rather diverse set of biological facts has been subjected to a kind of cultural digitization process, which has regi-

---

16. Dawkins, R., *The Blind Watchmaker* (New York: W.W. Norton, 1987).

17. Maynard-Smith, J., 'Game theory and the Evolution of Behaviour', *The Behavioral and Brain Sciences* 7 (1984), pp. 95-126.

18. Dawkins, R., *The Selfish Gene* (Oxford: Oxford University Press, 1976); and *The Extended Phenotype: The Gene as Unit of Selection* (Oxford: Oxford University Press, 1982).

mented these facts into the simple dichotomy of paradigms known as "sexual dimorphism." For as Kathryn Morgan[19] has argued, sexual dimorphism itself is made up of several elements (including gametes, chromosomes, anatomy, hormones) some of which are more inherently discrete than others. But the most crucial factor in the determination of dimorphism in behaviour is the hormonal, which is also the least inherently discrete, even if hormonal levels result (in part) from purely discrete genetic factors. So our insistence on seeing maleness and femaleness as a *dichotomy* may in part be the result of an ideological construction.

Again, language affords the best analogy. Language, Talleyrand is supposed to have said, "was given to our species that we might disguise our thought".[20] The example of slang or specialized vocabularies, and perhaps also the evolution of dialects suggests that much the same mechanisms are at work here as in the biological process of speciation. But in the case of cultural "memes", unlike genes, it is not so much the need for holding separate strategies that maintains a certain constancy of types, but the need for a reasonable degree of *reproductive accuracy*. Reproduction is of the essence of the meme, as of the gene. Perhaps the most startling fact about genes is that beyond being a certain kind of chemical in a certain sort of configuration, they constitute a system of digital representation. That reproduction should be governed by such a digital system is a *sine qua non* of evolution.[21] In biology, however, the rigidity of this digital code remains hidden; the clusters of resemblance which are species are mainly statistical. When we look at individual members of species, the underlying variety of nature remains reflected in the apparently inexhaustible variety of phenotypes.

Note, however, that there is in memes no analog to the difference between phenotypes and genotypes; or rather, we might say, a meme is all phenotype. So the meme's type must be interpreted in terms of a sufficiently clear system of representation, in which type constancy is maintained by some form of social pressure, experienced as having normative force. Otherwise, given the degradation that must inevitably follow successive analog copying, no meme is likely to last long enough to acquire a name. Biological regularities, by contrast, may endure as statistical patterns without taking on any normative flavour.[22]

---

19. Morgan, K. P., 'Sexuality as a Metaphysical Property', in *Philosophy and Women* (Belmont, CA: Wadsworth, 1979).

20. As quoted in Nyberg, D., *The Varnished Truth: Truth Telling and Deceiving in Ordinary Life* (Chicago: University of Chicago Press, 1993).

21. Dawkins, R., *The Blind Watchmaker* (New York: W.W. Norton, 1987), pp. 112 *ff*.

22. One example: according to Helen Fisher, the quasi-universal pattern of typical

...continuing...

For anything that owes its existence both to biology and culture, therefore, the process of digitization is a natural one, aided by converging factors. The combination of culture and genetic evolution may itself reinforce this, in what Lumsden and Wilson[23] have baptized "gene culture coevolution". The sort of mechanism in question here involves a cyclical positive feedback. Lumsden and Wilson offer as an example the case of sibling incest, in which the social taboos reinforce genetic predispositions selected for by the degenerative consequence of sibling incest.[24]

This particular case is interesting in the present context, since sibling incest, at least after early childhood, is one of the categories which a liberated sexuality, as opposed to an enlightened reproductive policy, ought to ignore. But actually the Lumsden and Wilson story is not altogether credible. For insofar as incest *avoidance* (the genetic obstacle to incest) is effective, there is no need for an incest *taboo*; conversely, insofar as an incest taboo is in force, the carriers of the incest avoidance gene will do no better than those who are genetically predisposed to incest. Sometimes, the existence of a social taboo will weaken, not reinforce, a selective pressure in the same direction.[25] So we can imagine at least some scenarios in which the existence of social taboos that supposedly "reinforce" epigenetic rules will have an exactly opposite effect. This will happen when the taboo is sufficiently effective to make those who lack the avoidance gene imperceptible to natural selection.

What then is the lesson of this case? I want to retain two thoughts: first, it is at least possible that biological and social conditioning both had a hand in the erection of what are, from the point of view of our conception of love, merely irrational prejudices. There is no rational basis for either the taboo or the emotional ground of incest avoidance among adult siblings. Secondly, the ideal

---

decay in marriages is 4 years: "Perhaps ... our ancestors only needed to form pair-bonds long enough to rear their young through infancy". [*Anatomy of Love: The Mysteries of Mating, Marriage, and Why We Stray* (Fawcett Columbine. New York: Ballantine, 1994), p. 153.] But this remains a purely statistical truth. For there to be anything intrinsically digital about that period, there would have to be, say, an entirely different concept of divorce that pertained to the 4 year period, as opposed to any other period.

23. Lumsden, C. J. and Wilson, Edward O., *Promethean Fire: Reflections on the Origin of Mind* (Cambridge, MA: Harvard University Press, 1983).

24. *Ibid.*, pp. 119 *ff.*

25. The classic case of this is that of social castes, which are actually likely to foster just the diversity within groups that they are intended to prevent. Dobzhansky remarks: "It may chagrin some people to learn that increasing equality of opportunity enhances, not reduces, genetic differences between socioeconomic classes". [Dobzhansky, T., *Genetic Diversity and Human Equality* (New York: McGraw Hill, Colophon, 1973), p. 29.]

of liberated sex and love requires the complete abandonment of the category in the context of love (though not necessarily in the context of reproduction, at least until our control over the genetic details of our progeny is more extensive than it is now). But both culture and biology have conspired to impose it.

Individuality, Categorization, and the Lesson of Queer Theory

To speak of the "imposition" of such categories raises the question of their prescriptive force. The mere existence of a category would not seem, at first sight, to carry any particular prescriptive force. (That we have a category of rapist doesn't enjoin anyone to be one.) But what seems to happen is that emotional and sexual categories are automatically *signed*: there are few purely neutral categories in matters of sex and love. Consider, for example, what is likely to happen when a couple is said to have "broken up". There is always a default assumption, usually that it is *a sad thing*; but in the nature of the case some of the people who have just parted must think it was a good idea. Similarly with words and phrases like 'lover', 'mistress', 'husband', 'wife', 'incest', 'sunset romance', etc.: people may feel differently about them, but almost everyone will make some default assumption about whether their referents are good or bad. Would one make the same assumptions about culinary categories? *Protein*; *vegetables*; *carbohydrate*; *liquid*; *wine*; *soup* . . . . Might they not all be said to be good or bad on the particular occasion, without having to defeat a default assumption?

Many have suffered because their singular desires failed to fit the norms implicit in erotic, sexual, or emotional categories. Their choice has been to live or die outside the boundaries of society, or else to constitute themselves as members of some specific oppressed group. Of these, some have more success than others in resisting the political forces arrayed against them. Pedophiles, for example, have had little success; gays have had a good deal more, and practitioners of S/M have fared somewhere in between. But the first strategy of any such group has generally been to neutralize the prescriptive onus of the category in which society had classed them.

I will come in a moment to the significance of the struggle by gays and lesbians to win recognition of their category as a morally neutral one. But we can see already that if I am right in my surmise that most such categories are "signed", the likelihood of the categories being successfully neutralized is slight. The mere fact that digitization has taken place yields a presumption of prescriptive force, either negative or positive, attaching to the resulting categories. Hence, no doubt, the "gay pride" movement, in which the aim is not merely to neutralize the category but actually to glorify it.

What I first want to turn to, however, is the question of what reason there might be for resisting the impetus of digitization. What calls for resistance, I shall argue, is the claim of the *individual* as such.

If there is any consensus on the nature of love it is that love is essentially of the individual.[26] Thus the phrase *individual love* is something of the pleonasm in this context. I shall use it, however, to bring to mind two sets of connotations: first, that every episode of love is both itself particular in space-time and unique in kind; second, that both those features are derived from the particularity and uniqueness of the individuals whom it relates. Loving someone because of the social role they play, or for the sake of family alliance, or money, or vanity, or power, or even sex, is generally disparaged as "not real love", precisely because it is assumed that such love is focused on a role, not on the individual that fills it.

Still, the work done by the concept *individual* in the phrase 'individual love' remains problematic. Many categories are involved in anyone's definition of "true love"; *roles* and *individual* are themselves among them. These two concepts, it seems, must inevitably be in tension, except that insofar as one pursues as a goal the ideal of individuality, *being an individual can itself turn into a role*.[27] So it is not entirely clear what the abolition of categories would amount to in matters of sex, gender, or love: a call for the abolition of traditional categories, like many another revolutionary cry, sometimes merely disguises an allegiance to the equally tyrannical hegemony of new ones. The claim that heterosexual categories are not natural ones, for example, may be merely a plea for the inclusion among natural categories of ones relating to lesbian or gay practices.[28] But as Cheshire Calhoun has argued,

> With the exception of early liberal feminists' recommendation of androgyny and possibly contemporary French feminists' deconstruction of 'woman', the feminist project has not been the elimination of the category 'woman'. Instead, the project has been one of reconstructing that category.[29]

---

26. The Platonic tradition--or at least one interpretation of it, in which the object of love is essentially a Form--seems to be an exception: but Nussbaum has persuasively argued that even Plato can be seen as falling in with the consensus, providing we see Alcibiades rather than Diotima as the culminating figure in the *Symposium*. [*Cf.* Nussbaum, M., 'Love and the Individual: Romantic Rightness and Platonic Aspiration', in Nussbaum, M., *Love's Knowledge* (Oxford, NY, Toronto: Oxford University Press, 1990), pp. 314-334); and this volume, pp. 1-22.]

27. Case in point, a 50's *New Yorker* cartoon by Rowland Wilson, in which two women are looking askance at a third whose garb marks her as a beatnik; one of the two exclaims: "Thank goodness I'm not an individual!"

28. See Rich, A., 'Compulsory Heterosexuality and Lesbian Existence', *Signs* 5 (1980), pp. 631-660.

29. Calhoun, C., 'Separating Lesbian Theory from Feminist Theory', *Ethics* 104 (April 1994), p. 565.

Nevertheless, some categories are more genuinely liberating than others, because they are essentially negative, and represent themselves as resisting the dominant stereotypes, including the very concepts of *man* and *woman*, masculine and feminine. Calhoun quotes Wittig: "Lesbianism is the only concept I know of which is beyond the categories of sex (woman and man), because the designated subject (lesbian) is not a woman".[30] And she argues, quoting Judith Butler, that the meaning of 'woman' and 'man' has been determined by heterosexist ideology:

> ..."intelligible" genders are those which in some sense institute and maintain relations of coherence and continuity among sex, gender, sexual practice, and desire.[31]

The breaking of those "relations of coherence" is crucial to the project of liberation from categories or stereotypes. To be sure, however, there is no simple means to this end. Only individuals of flesh and blood--particulars in time and space--can boast that their properties are literally infinite, and that they cannot ever be contained by any number of categories. Yet in practice our self-knowledge and our self-descriptions must be articulated in terms of categories. We can approach individuality only *negatively* and *asymptotically*.

The *negative* approach consists in picking categories that are defined in terms of the explicit rejection of stereotypes. Such is the approach advocated by Calhoun: ". . . to be gay or lesbian is to be a kind of person who violates heterosexual law, in part but not solely by having same-sex desires",[32] calling attention through lesbian feminist history to "the constructedness, parochialism, and, ultimately, the arbitrariness of our cultural denial of the possibility of romantic love and family life within same-sex couples".[33] The destruction or "deconstructing" of the concept of 'woman' just alluded to is a good example of this negative approach.

The *asymptotic* approach may at first seem slightly paradoxal, in that it aims at the escape from the tyranny of categories by dint of their multiplication. In terms of lesbian theory, this approach has sometimes given rise to criticism, to the effect that they merely replace old rigidities and conventions and preju-

---

30. *Ibid.*, p. 563.

31. Judith Butler in *Gender Trouble: Feminism and the Subversion of Identity* (New York: Routledge, 1990), p. 17--as quoted by Calhoun, *op. cit.*, p. 566.

32. Calhoun, C., 'Denaturalizing and Desexualizing Lesbian and Gay Identity', *Virginia Law Review* 79 (1993), p. 1870.

33. *Ibid.*, p. 1875.

dices with new ones,[34] or merely take over the oppressive forms of patriarchy.[35] But the multiplication of categories can have a liberating effect, insofar as sheer complexity might loosen the grip of a system of public control and public oppression which presupposes simplistic classifications.[36]

Is there a more direct approach to the elimination of oppressive categories? The likely place to look is in the analogy of aesthetic response.

In the aesthetic realm, we have been escaping from paradigms as we have been getting further and further away from Plato's conception of art. Once we give up the conception of art as mimesis, then the issue of copying becomes irrelevant. And digitality is only useful, as I pointed out, in the context of a practical need for multiple copying. In modern (and post-modern) art, that is irrelevant. What art presents us with is rather a world in which works are created to fill unexplored locations in an infinite space of possibilities.

Why should not human feelings and relationships seek similarly to fill empty locations in that infinite space? Why should they be pigeon-holed into essences?[37] *Prima facie*, given the variety of sources of aesthetic response and the particularity of their genesis in individual people, there must be distinguishable emotional responses appropriate to any of the indefinite number of different objects that might confront a human being. For the sources of variation include

---

34. Witness this complaint on behalf of bisexuality: "Bisexuality seems to be in disfavour everywhere . . . . The dominant culture views it by the same heterosexist norms which condemn lesbianism as a perversion, and woman-centred heterosexuality as nonexistent or grotesque. The women's liberation movement views it as either non-existent (where do I fit into the current 'lesbian-heterosexual split'?); destructive (dabbling in women from the security of heterosexuality); or as frivolous". [Gregory, D., 'From Where I Stand: A Case for Feminist Bisexuality', in *Sex and Love* (London: Women's Press, 1983), pp. 141-156. See p. 142.]

35. See Samois, *What Color is Your Handkerchief? A Lesbian S/M Sexuality Reader* (Berkeley: Samois, 1979), and the attacks on it in Linden, R. R., *Against Sadomasochism: A Radical Feminist Analysis* (East Palo Alto: Frog in the Well, 1982).

36. The political worth of this strategy is another matter, since the bureaucratic backlash that could be generated here might instead reduce categories even further, forcing a procrustean simplification of the available repertoire of behaviour or relations. This is precisely what seems to be going on in the United States today, where the dominant party's "contract with America" (or should it be "on America"?) proposes to abolish welfare support for unmarried mothers in order to promote healthy family life.

37. Sue Campbell has made a subtle and persuasive argument for thinking of emotions in terms of a far more comprehensive, in fact a potentially infinite, repertoire, on the model of potential aesthetic response. [*Cf.* Campbell, S., *Emotion and Expression*, unpublished doctoral dissertation (Toronto: University of Toronto, 1992), and Campbell, S., 'Being Dismissed: The Politics of Emotional Expression', *Hypatia* 9(3), pp. 46-65.]

the possible permutations of subjective states of preparation coupled with the potentially infinite number of objective situations.

The claim is sometimes made for literature that its true value is that it is about the individual rather than about general ideas.[38] This can't really be true, since novels and stories still have to be told in words and sentences. Any sentence (except one that explicitly refers to an actual individual) might in principle be true of more than one particular person or situation. All that novels can provide is a significant increment of our repertoire of categories. Only a real individual can logically resist categorization: that is the one advantage that reality retains over fiction. Any entity that is not individual flesh and blood existing in time, is unique only contingently, and theoretically susceptible of being completely specified by some set of descriptions. Only the concrete particular can literally transcend all the categories into which it might be fitted.

The need for knowledge is inescapable, as power to manipulate the world. But aesthetic apprehension of the particular can alone put us in touch with real individuals in space and time. If love is really *of* the individual, therefore, it (and perhaps the plastic as opposed to the literary arts as well)[39] matters precisely because it provides our only escape from solipsism on the one hand and the generality of knowledge on the other.

Viewed in this perspective, then, the question is this: are we to treat our loves as aesthetic or as functional? In the first case, their meaning is predominantly private; in the second, predominantly public. Are they to be *individual* realities or *social* realities?

These questions are unlikely to have answers constant for all time. Hence the *historicity* of love: in different times and places, the possibility of individual love may be more or less tolerated. Love, we might say, is always individual *in matter*, but social *in form*. Which prevails or dominates depends on the state of equilibrium between the social and the private. It would be an interesting research project to ask whether some correlation can be found between those different conceptions of love and prevailing views of art as individual expression or as celebration of communal values.

Conclusion

Particular loves link particular persons. There is no essence of love. My

---

38. *Cf.* Nussbaum, M., *Love's Knowledge* (Oxford, NY, Toronto: Oxford University Press, 1990), p. 37.

39. All those, in fact, which Nelson Goodman classifies as *autographic*. See his *Languages of Art* (Indianapolis: Hackett, 1976), pp. 113-116.

question in this paper has been: why is this fact so surprisingly difficult to accept?

Biology probably plays some role in favouring certain evolutionarily stable strategies which act as attractors in what would otherwise be an undifferentiated space of possibilities.[40] But it is hardly plausible to think of love as confined to a set of biologically fixed types. "Essence anxiety" intervenes to dictate that we should accept all sorts of characterizations, however contradictory, rather than give up on the quest for an essence of love. This fact lies behind the paradoxes I listed.

1. Jealousy

Sometimes one wants the best for someone, and sometimes the worst. Sometimes one wants them to be happy; sometimes one merely wants an exclusive franchise on the right to cause their happiness. Some of this is troubling and sad; but none of it is paradoxical, once one ceases to pretend that these various impulses are severally and together criterial for a single emotion called "real love". A side benefit of giving up the quest for essence, is that the bad could safely be evaluated as bad, instead of enjoying the protection of the label 'True Love'.

2. The Priority of Pain

If one looks for a test of love, the myth of the ordeal comes readily to mind. The knight will gain the princess, or the princess the knight, only if they can endure this or that trial. This makes sense, in terms of the engagement of the will: for whether and how much the will is engaged really can be a hard question to answer. But it in no way follows that pain is less *deceptive* than pleasure. To think otherwise begs the question of what there is to be deceived about. If our natures are such that when rubbed together they spark pleasure, that could be just what you and I can have together. It is a different and interesting question, how much worth having it is. And the question of whether it can be "real love" is a different one again, but unless one is governed by essence anxiety, this one is of no interest whatever.

3. Sex and Love

Among the anxieties of sex and love, *essence anxiety* is a close second to *performance anxiety*. The idea of being offered eros in the name of agape may

---

40. Maynard-Smith, J., 'Game Theory and the Evolution of Behaviour', *The Behavioral and Brain Sciences* 7 (1984), pp. 95-126.

well be distressing, but it can only present itself in this form if one has already agreed to the hegemony of that vocabulary. Sex is only slightly more likely to be pure than love. But to care about purity presupposes a commitment to the myth of essence.

4. Freedom and Rules

If being free is following one's will, then again here is no paradox. For love that does not engage the will is indeed a contradiction in terms. But it wouldn't occur to anyone to wonder about this, unless *t'* ey started with a list of conditions that true love has to meet. To look at suc*ı* a list is necessarily to wonder at how rarely the will could possibly converge on all of them at once. Without such a list, however, there is no problem to wonder about.

5. Recognition

This is, I have suggested, just the direct expression of the anxiety of essence. That absent, there are plenty of other issues to worry about in a relation of love: where it is going, what are its sources of happiness and misery, what is it about my loved one that excites, disappoints, stimulates, or bores me. But to worry about nomenclature is doubly irrational: first, insofar as names are merely names; second, because the purposes behind the nomenclature may be irrelevant or antithetical to the interests of individual love. Lucretius had a suggestive explanation of magnetism in terms of the "hooks and eyes" formed by the atoms of iron and magnet.[41] The image has passed into the French language, which speaks of people whose affinities bring them together as having "hooked atoms", *des atomes crochus,* as if the uniquely shaped atoms of our individual natures enabled us to lock in specific ways into another's complementary nooks and crannies. That image seems to me to approach love at a level more apt than the question of whether we should be called 'lovers', 'companions', 'spouses', 'friends'--or 'perverts'. These terms may have a social utility; but their use is irrational if we allow their prescriptive weight to carry over from biological or social utility to the reality of private love.

Love, like music, lives in the unique curves, in the fractal intricacies of our particular selves. It is first cast according to ancient templates, no doubt, and later cut to standard shapes according to social need. But just as some music lovers regard the best analog recordings as superior to any digital transcriptions, so lovers *tout court* should perhaps pursue *an ideal of love that eschews the ideal.*

---

41. Lucretius, *On the Nature of Things,* trans. R. E. Latham (Harmondsworth: Penguin, 1951), Book VI, 1085-1089.

I have suggested that our emotions, for reasons that hark back both to our biological and to our social natures, are constantly pulling us back toward *types*. To resist this, our main aid is the gift of aesthetic attention which aims at the apprehension of particulars in their uniqueness. To list the conditions that a love must fulfil in order to earn its licence as Real Love, is precisely to miss the unrepeated pattern that might be generated by the several "hooked atoms" of two particular people. Cora Diamond has prescribed a recipe for preserving the "adventure" of reading: a "live sense of moral life as containing more possibilities, more wonderful, more interesting, more attaching, possibilities than can readily be seen".[42] This surely is also a good equipment list for the adventure of love. Our imagination and our fantasies thrive on types. What we need in love, however, is to approach the mystery of individuality which transcends all types. We can do no more than *approach* this, of course; for this ambition is impeded both at the inarticulate level where we are plausibly driven by buried imperatives from biology and from childhood, and at the level where what we relish are literary snippets, derivative ways of seeing and thinking about our own experience. On the other hand, despite all the quirks of our inimitable idiolects, borrowed phrases are all we have to speak of what is most intimate. It is out of that second-hand vocabulary that we must make sense of our unique experience. Yet we must at least try to break the molds of rhetoric which tie us to the roles and scenarios that our mythology assigns to lovers: *wife, mistress, husband, lover; exclusiveness, reciprocity*, and even, in its several meanings, *sex*.

Champions of law and order have always instinctively known that lovers are their enemies. Lovers are natural outlaws, natural anarchists. Those advocates of love are not radical enough who are willing to settle into roles as well defined and confining as those they have rejected. To attend to the infinite possibilities of the aesthetic; to multiply possible descriptions and categorizations; to invent categories to suit just this or that pair of individuals, or group of individuals (for that it must be a *pair* is also, after all, a piece of bio-social tyranny): such is the challenge of individual love. It is up to each to discover just what might suit, just what new shapes might spring from linking up their crooked atoms, that they might love their lovers, each with a love unlike any other, with their crooked heart.

---

42. Diamond, C., *The Realistic Spirit: Wittgenstein, Philosophy, and the Mind* (Cambridge, MA: MIT Press, Bradford, 1991), p. 316.

11

Is Love an Emotion?

O. H. Green

1. Introduction

The answer almost always given to the question, 'Is love an emotion?', is 'Yes'. Certainly love is bound up with hopes and fears, joys and sorrows. Given the close relation in which love stands to emotions, this answer is, perhaps, natural. Still, it presents problems, especially this: emotions have belief-based intentionality and rationality; love, at least often, does not. For this reason and others, I will argue that the answer is 'No'. Love, I think, is not an emotion but a complex conative state, a set of desires. This answer enables us to understand the intentional and rational features of love, and much else besides --including the range of love-related emotions.

Answering the question, 'Is love an emotion?', can be complicated in several ways. For one thing, all sorts of things--virtues like generosity, moods like euphoria, doxastic shifts like surprise--are sometimes called 'emotions'. The question as I understand it, however, is not primarily one about ordinary usage; it is a theoretical question about the principal properties of love and such acknowledged emotions as anger, fear, pride, and remorse--properties that euphoria, generosity, and surprise do not share.

There are also important differences between the main theories of emotions --the Component Theory, the Evaluative Theory, and the Belief-Desire Theory.[1]

---

1. These theories can be distinguished on the basis of the account which they provide of emotional intentionality and rationality and of the relationship of emotions to non-intentional phenomena. Component Theories take the intentionality and rationality of emotions to be derived from beliefs to which they are causally or constitutively related and take non-intentional phenomena to be constitutive of emotions. For Evaluative Theorists, emotions are evaluative beliefs or judgments and are intrinsically intentional and rational. According to the Belief-Desire Theory, emotions are intrinsically intentional and rational because they consist in structures of beliefs and desires. On both the

...continuing...

Nevertheless, it is a common feature of these theories that the intentionality and rationality of emotions depend, at least in part, on beliefs, given a suitable understanding of the extension of 'belief'.[2]

A further thing which can complicate answering the question is that love is a polymorphous phenomenon. There are various forms of love--romantic love, parental love, love of friends, love of country, and even love of fried chicken. I think that ultimately an account of love should exhibit these as forms of the same basic phenomenon; but for now, I will concentrate for the most part on romantic love. Romantic love itself admits of variation, but I take it to be familiar enough. It is not some arcane phenomenon out of the Age of Chivalry but something which often obtains in our lives in the relations of men and women, and of lovers of the same sex.

2. Love is not an Emotion

It is, as I said, a common contention of the several theories of emotions that the intentionality and rationality of emotions are based on belief. It is held, that is, that emotions have an intentional content or take an intentional object because of the causal or constitutive relation in which they stand to belief. If Hannibal fears that the elephants won't make it through the pass, he must believe (without certainty) that the elephants won't make it through the pass. If Magellan is proud that he has circumnavigated the globe, he must believe (with certainty) that he has circumnavigated the globe.

Also, the beliefs upon which emotional intentionality is based are commonly held to underlie the rationality of emotions. For one thing, the rational justification of emotions depends on the desirability of what is believed.[3] If it is undesirable that the elephants not make it or if having circumnavigated the globe is desirable, then Hannibal's fear or Magellan's pride is so far rationally justified.

Love is often based on beliefs about the properties of one who is loved which are taken to be attractive or desirable. Cleopatra, for example, may love Antony because she believes that he is exciting and handsome. If love is construed as an emotion, it is because of these beliefs about Antony that he is the one she loves, and they contribute to the rationality of her love for him.

Evaluative and Belief-Desire Theories, non-intentional phenomena may be caused by emotions but are not constitutive of them. [See Green, O. H., *The Emotions* (Dordrecht: Kluwer, 1992), pp. xi-xiv.]

2. See Green, O. H., *The Emotions* (Dordrecht: Kluwer, 1992), pp. 32-33.

3. See Green, O. H., 'Emotional Rationality' (forthcoming).

Often too, love is not like that; it is simply not based on beliefs about the attractions of one who is loved. Common enough is the case of the girl in a song by Jerome Kern and P. G. Wodehouse. She sings: 'I love him because he's...I don't know...because he's just my Bill'. That he's just her Bill, I take it, is not the expression of a love-supporting belief but just another way of saying that she loves him. Of course, the girl presumably must have some beliefs about Bill--about who he is, at least. Perhaps she believes he's the boy next door. Beliefs like this, however, do not justify her love for Bill. It's hard to see what could be special about living next door; one has such identificatory beliefs about thousands of people. The fact is, the girl evidently has no beliefs which provide reasons for her loving Bill and connect Bill with her love as its object. If love is construed as an emotion, her love seems to lack intentionality and rationality.

It is not just that sometimes love is simply not belief-based. We have an idealized conception of romantic love according to which love is supposed to be *exclusive* and *constant*. Love is supposed to be for one person to the exclusion of others, even those believed to have the same desirable properties; and love is supposed to be constant, even when the loved one is no longer believed to have the attractive properties.

To the extent that *A*'s love for *B* is exclusive, *A* will have no reasons for loving *B* rather than *C*, who is believed by *A* to have the same desirable properties; nor will such beliefs provide any basis for thinking that *A* loves *B* rather than *C*. To the extent that *A*'s love for *B* is constant and persists after *A* ceases to believe that *B* has certain attractive properties, *A*'s love will be without both reasons and object so far as those beliefs about *B*'s desirable properties are concerned.

Love, of course, is not always exclusive or constant, but where it conforms to the ideal in these respects, it lacks the basis in belief for intentionality and rationality which emotions have. And, of course, there are cases like that of the girl in the song who just loves her Bill. The standard response is that love is an *anomalous emotion*. To say this is simply to shelve the problem which understanding love as an emotion presents.

In his treatment of love Alan Soble does take on this problem.[4] Soble claims that love is not an anomalous emotion; other emotions, like love, may lack belief-based intentionality and rationality. This seems only to spread the problem of understanding the intentional and rational features of love to cover emotions as well. Soble, however, thinks there is no problem.

To determine whether this is so, consider the plight of Daniel in the lions' den. At least before the lions lay down and went to sleep, Daniel was presumably afraid of the lions. Suppose, however, that he did not believe that the lions

---

4. Soble, Alan, *The Structure of Love* (New Haven: Yale University Press, 1990), pp. 117-19.

would devour him and, indeed, that he had no thoughts at all about the lions being dangerous. How, then, could Daniel be afraid of the lions? That he was surrounded by big hungry lions is not to the point; cognitively he might as well have been out to lunch. There would be no belief to forge the intentional link necessary for Daniel to be afraid of the lions.

Soble suggests that any such worries might be assuaged if Daniel said that he had an 'inner experience' of a kind that he would always call fear and that the experience was directed toward the lions. This hardly helps. There is no inner experience which is necessary for or characteristic of fear. A sinking feeling in the stomach, for example, may or may not accompany fear; and it may come not only with fear but with a dip on a roller coaster ride. For an inner experience to be an experience of fear, it must be caused by fear.

In any case, an inner experience hardly accounts for Daniel's fear having its intentional object. Sinking feelings and the like are often, though incorrectly, taken to lack intentionality. If, more accurately, they are regarded as vaguely proprioceptive, they turn out to be about the state of one's insides. Either way, inner experiences are of no help in understanding how Daniel is afraid of the lions.

In the absence of a basis in belief, Soble thinks that a fear like Daniel's should be irrational. It is hard to see how: what is there to be irrational? Rationality and irrationality require representation. If Daniel's fear of the lions is irrational, it must be so in view of some belief (or other representation) he has concerning the lions. An inner experience, which is at any rate not about the lions, will not suffice instead. There is simply nothing left to be irrational.

John Deigh also argues that emotions need not have belief-based intentionality, so that love may not be an anomalous emotion. He holds that there are primitive emotions which 'occur as an immediate reaction to some sensory experience and therefore independently of any belief or other propositional thought'; fear of snakes is given as an example. 'Accordingly', Deigh claims, 'love, even though its intentionality is not based on belief, could be a primitive emotion'.[5]

There are human reactions of the kind Deigh has in mind, including, perhaps, fear of snakes. It is an important feature of these reactions that they occur even in very young children and that they occur universally. No beliefs about snakes acquired by learning are necessary for this putative fear. One does not need to believe that snakes bite or otherwise do harm. What explains the primitive reaction to snakes is that they are a threat to us; the reaction seems to be the product of our evolutionary history, rather than a function of our beliefs.

I find it doubtful that romantic love, or anything amounting to more than

---

5. Deigh, personal correspondence, 1994; also, see Deigh, John, 'Cognitivism in the Theory of Emotions', *Ethics* 104 (1994), 824-54.

simple sexual attraction, could be understood along these lines; still, what Deigh has to say about primitive emotions wants looking into. Suppose a little child sees a snake and draws back in agitation. Given this stimulus-response pattern we tend to ascribe fear to the child. In doing so, we take what Dan Dennett calls 'the intentional stance', interpreting the child's behavior in terms of intentional attitudes.[6] On considering what the content of her attitudes might be, however, it becomes clear that she could hardly have thoughts about so much as there being a snake. We are thus forced back to 'the design stance', again in Dennett's terminology, viewing the child's behavior as automatic or stimulus-bound; no intentional attitudes are involved at this level of understanding. The point, then, is this: in the absence of beliefs or other propositional thoughts, it makes as much sense to ascribe fear of snakes to the child as it does to ascribe fear of overheating to the thermostat of an air conditioner.

Deigh attempts to find room for intentional fear without propositional attitudes--in the child, not in the thermostat! The child perceives something 'scary', he supposes. In this way problems with doxastic sophistication and propositional content specification do not get in the way.[7] To say that the child sees something scary, however, is only to say that what she sees is apt to elicit fear. We are left without any basis for supposing that it is fear that is elicited.

The primitive reaction of the child to a snake and similar cases do not provide instances in which there is an intentional emotion without beliefs or other propositional attitudes. Nonetheless, Deigh suggests that rational assess-ment is possible in the case of these reactions; 'primitive fear' of a snake may be 'groundless'--after all, garter snakes as well as rattlesnakes may elicit fear.[8] Where fears are groundless, what is feared is not really dangerous, but Deigh must deny that in his case any misrepresentation is involved. No representation that is accurate or inaccurate is involved on his view. Thus, if the reaction is to be 'groundless', this must mean that it is deficient viewed from the design stance, or that it would be so, interpreted from the intentional stance. Without any serious ascription of belief, however, the reaction cannot be taken to be literally groundless.

There is indeed a problem about the intentionality and rationality of an emotion like fear where there is allegedly no basis in belief. The same thing goes for love when love is understood as an emotion. The problem has different solutions in the two cases. Without beliefs about the lions being dangerous, Daniel is not afraid of them; nor could a child fear a snake without any belief

---

6. Dennett, Daniel, *Brainstorms* (Montgomery, Vermont: Bradford, 1978), and *The Intentional Stance* (Cambridge, Massachusetts: MIT Press, 1989).

7. Deigh, John, 'Cognitivism in the Theory of Emotions', *Ethics* 104 (1994), p. 842.

8. *Ibid.*, p. 837.

about its being dangerous. Even without beliefs about his attractions, the girl in the song still loves her Bill. Emotions require belief as a basis for their intentionality; love does not. Where beliefs do not provide a basis for love's intentionality, love is not an emotion.

There are still many cases in which love is based on beliefs about the attractions of one who is loved, of course; and in these cases, at least, it might be held that love is an emotion. This contention, however, cannot be sustained. In general, if A believes that p, there will be no emotion unless A cares whether p--unless A desires that p or that not-p. Not only are both the belief and the desire required, the belief and desire must be about the same state of affairs-- whether it is, or is to be, the case that p. If, for example, A is glad that p, A believes that p and A desires that p; and if A is sorry that p, A believes that p and A desires that not-p. Suppose that A believes that B is beautiful and A wants to be with B. There is so far no emotion which A has in virtue of his belief and desire. Of course, A might have other desires concerning what he believes, or beliefs concerning what he desires. A might believe that B is beautiful and desire that B be beautiful. In that case A is glad that B is beautiful. Or A might believe that he is not with B and desire that he be with B. In that case A is sorry that he is not with B. In each case there is an emotion--gladness or sorrow--but, though perhaps related to love, the emotion clearly is not love.

Where love is not based on beliefs about the attractions of one who is loved, it could not be an emotion; and where such beliefs are present, if there is an emotion based on the beliefs, it is not love. The conclusion I draw is that love is not an emotion.

This conclusion may be resisted on theoretical grounds. If love does not fit the mold cast by the main theories of emotions, this appears to create a theoretical crisis. Love, it will be said, is surely an emotion if anything is. Peripheral cases like depression or euphoria may perhaps be excluded from the domain of a theory of emotions, if reasons are found to do so; but a paradigm case like love is one which any adequate theory simply must accommodate.

This theoretical crisis may not be all that serious, for the demand that love must be accommodated by a theory of emotions is open to question. For one thing, love is closely allied with friendship, which is not commonly considered an emotion; and as love resembles friendship, it differs from acknowledged emotions. The most salient similarity between love and friendship is that they are both relationships; the attitude of friendship or love is one which friends or lovers have for each other. Anger or fear or joy is not a relationship; there is no expectation of reciprocity. Another thing is this. The theoretical aim in understanding emotions is to provide a coherent account of as many states regarded as emotions as possible. Whether a given state which is supposed to be an emotion falls within the theoretical domain depends ultimately on its likeness or unlikeness to the range of states accommodated by the theory. If love is substantially unlike emotions explained by an otherwise plausible theory, it may be entirely reasonable to exclude it from the range of emotions, especially if a credible alternative account of love is available.

3. Love is a Set of Desires

If love is not an emotion, what is it? Love, I suggested, is like friendship; both are relationships. In order to understand love or friendship, we must consider the attitude of friend toward friend or lover toward lover. The attitude, of course, may be found without the relationship, where it is not reciprocated; but the reciprocation of the attitude is what makes up the relationship of love or friendship.

It is in this vein that Aristotle, in Books VIII and IX of the *Nicomachean Ethics*, considers *philia*, which is translated both as 'friendship' and as 'love' or 'liking'. Aristotle examines not only the beliefs which occasion friendship but the desires which love or liking involves. Friendship is based on the belief that the friend is virtuous or pleasant or useful. On the conative side, in love or liking we wish our friend well for his or her sake, at least in the case of friendship based on virtue. We also have the desire for association with the friend. Aristotle says, 'Nothing is so characteristic of friends as their fondness for each other's society'.[9] Further, it is at least implicit that we desire that one who is loved or liked reciprocate. Mutual goodwill and spending time together are held to be necessary for friendship, and that our affection cannot be returned is given as a reason why there can be no friendship with inanimate objects.

Gabrielle Taylor gives an account of love (or friendship) which runs along the same lines as Aristotle's. According to Taylor, beliefs related to love are those which support desires which love typically involves. About these desires she says, 'If [A] loves [B] we have on the one hand [A's] wants to benefit and cherish [B], on the other his wants to be with [B], to communicate with [B], to have [B] take an interest in him, to be benefited and cherished by [B]'.[10]

To my mind, these accounts of love (and friendship) suggest an understanding of love in terms of desires. In several ways, however, they stop short of providing such an understanding. Love is not unequivocally identified with desires: whether desires constitute or are caused by love, and whether desires are essential for or typical of love, are matters left unclear. Also, on both accounts love is still considered an emotion or classified with emotions.

In framing a conative theory of love along the lines suggested by these

---

9. Thomson, J. A. K., *The Ethics of Aristotle* (London: George Allen and Unwin, 1953), p. 224; 1557b19.

10. Taylor, Gabrielle, 'Love', *Proceedings of the Aristotelian Society* (1975-76), pp. 153-4.

accounts, I want to come down squarely on these issues. Love is identical with a set of desires: desires are constitutive of love, not just caused by love; and desires are essential to, not just typical of, love. And, of course, though related to emotions, love is not an emotion.

In considering the desires which constitute love--particularly romantic love--my aim is programmatic. I want to show that the intentional, rational, and other features of love can be adequately explained if love is understood as a complex conative state, as they cannot if love is taken to be an emotion. I will say only enough about the kinds of desires which constitute romantic love to render their inclusion plausible.

As a basic specification of the kinds of desires constituting romantic love, I propose the following.

A loves *B* if and only if:

1. *A* desires to share an association with *B* which typically includes a sexual dimension;

2. *A* desires that *B* fare well for his or her own sake; and

3. *A* desires that *B* reciprocate the desires for association and welfare.

I think that it is intuitively clear that such desires are necessary for romantic love. If *A* is indifferent or averse to being with *B*, to *B*'s happiness, or to *B*'s caring for *A*, *A* can hardly love *B*. And if *A* wants to be with *B*, for *B* to be happy, and for *B* to care about *A*, it is hard to see what more is needed for *A* to love *B*. If the set of desires is not only necessary and sufficient for love, but explains the intentional, rational, and other prominent properties of love, it is reasonable to take the set of desires to constitute love.

Some comments on this fundamentally Aristotelian specification of the kinds of desires constituting love are needed. First, the account given by Aristotle in the *Ethics* is, of course, not tailored to fit romantic love as we conceive it. Still, we have only to add that the association desired has a sexual dimension to make it complete. That the basic Aristotelian account does not capture the essence of romantic love is, in fact, an advantage. It is open as regards the features of particular varieties of love or friendship. This allows us to grasp what is common to the structure of love's varieties, at the same time permitting additions and subtractions to account for the differences.

Next, in Aristotle's discussion of love and friendship, the desire for the good of the friend or loved one enjoys special prominence. To take this desire to be primary is, I think, inaccurate. The desires which constitute love are rationally structured--something I shall have more to say about later. For now, let me suggest that in the rational structure of love it is the desire for association with one who is loved which comes first. The attractions a loved one is believed to have are those which render him or her suitable for the desired association and so rationalize that desire; they do not directly provide reasons for desiring any benefit or reciprocity. One who desires association has reason to desire benefit and reciprocity as well, since the association cannot flourish without mutual benefit or exist without reciprocation. And when, with frustration, the desire for association is abandoned, one ceases to be rationally motivated to desire benefit and reciprocity.

Also, in the Aristotelian account the desire to benefit is qualified: in the higher sort of friendship or love, which is based on virtue, the good of the friend or loved one is desired for his or her sake. The intuition which motivates the qualification is that love is no tit-for-tat relationship. Aristotle's reason for holding that only in friendships of virtue do friends wish one another well for their own sake is that those who are not virtuous desire only their own advantage. This is probably false, but the point remains that love is not a matter of simple exploitation. But nor is it a matter of abstract benevolence. Aristotle clearly holds friendship of virtue to be an advantage for the virtuous man. That the good of one who is loved is desired for his or her sake, then, does not mean, at least in the case of romantic love, that the relationship does not depend on mutual benefit.

The basic desire for association motivates and sets parameters for the desire for the good of one who is loved. It is the goods of association which are primarily desired; *A* wants conversation, sex, and other shared activities to be good for *B*. The goods desired for *B* also may transcend those of association; *A* may want *B*'s career to flourish, for example. Goods of the former kind obviously promote association; so, too, do those of the latter, for we desire to associate with those who wish us well. On the other hand, *A* will not desire what is inimical to association; to the extent that the advancement of his career gets in the way of their association, for instance, it will generally be something *A* does not desire for *B*. Also, should association be precluded by a failure of *B* to reciprocate, *A* will no longer have reason to desire *B*'s good, at least not beyond the level of general altruism.

Finally, the satisfaction of desires constituting love may be blocked. *B* may be happily married or bound by a vow of celibacy, for example, and *A* may know this. Though the satisfaction of desires for association and reciprocity may be precluded in this way, if *A* still loves *B*, *A* will have corresponding wishes. A wish is a disposition to desire, where there is an absence of feasibility of satisfying the desire. Thus, strictly speaking, we should say that love is constituted by a set of desires or wishes.

4. The Intentionality of Love

The conative account enables us to understand the intentionality of love even in the absence of a basis in belief, as the view that love is an emotion does

not. The girl in the song loves her Bill even if she does not believe he is handsome. The essential thing is that she still wants to be with him, wants him to
care about her, and so on. Even if she did believe that Bill is handsome, if she
did not have such desires (or wishes), she would not love him.

Taking love to be a complex conative state accounts for the intentionality of
love which is exclusive or constant, as well as impetuous love. Where A loves B
to the exclusion of others who are believed by A to have the same attractive
properties, it is because of love-related desires which A has for B but not for
others; and when A's love for B is constant, enduring after A ceases to believe
that B has certain desirable properties, this is because A still has the love-related
desires for B.

Further, on the view that love is an emotion, where beliefs do appear to
explain love's intentionality, it is unclear how they could do so; for the same
beliefs provide reasons for love. Consider gladness. A is glad that p. The
relevance of reasons for A to be glad depends on what A is glad about. If A is
glad that p, of course A believes that p. That A believes that p is hardly a reason;
the justification of A's gladness turns on the desirability of its being the case that
p. The belief that it is desirable that p is not the belief on which the intentionality of A's gladness is based. A is not glad that it is desirable that p. In general,
beliefs which provide reasons for emotions are not the beliefs on which their
intentionality depends; reason-providing beliefs concern the desirability of what
is believed in having an emotion and what the emotion is about.

On the conative model, the intentionality of love depends, not on beliefs
about the attractions of one who is loved, but on desires for association, benefit,
and reciprocity. The beliefs provide reasons for love's desires, beginning with
the desire for association.

Desires are propositional attitudes. The satisfaction of a desire requires that
a state of affairs obtain, and what is desired is that that state of affairs obtain.
This might seem to pose a problem for an explanation of love's intentionality in
terms of desires. The object of love is non-propositionally specified; 'A loves
that p' is syntactically deviant. This problem, I think, is readily resolved. That
what is desired is that some state of affairs obtain does not mean that the content
of desires must be propositionally specified; content and content specification
must be distinguished. Pragmatic considerations often result in the content of a
propositional attitude being non-propositionally specified. Constituting A's
love for B are desires having various propositionally specifiable contents--that A
be with B, that B fare well, and so on--having in common only the reference to
B. The desires are about B, so it is B that A loves.

If the intentionality of love is a function of that of constitutive desires, there
is another potentially more worrisome problem: desires bear semantic assessment in terms of satisfaction and frustration; love, it seems, does not. The
resolution of this problem, I think, lies in the fact that love, of its conative
nature, eludes semantic assessment. Love is not simply satisfied; the satisfac-

tion conditions of desires constituting love are various and open-ended. *A* wants to be with *B*. *A* also wants *B* to care about her. The one desire might be satisfied but not the other, so that love would not be altogether satisfied. Moreover, even if love's desires are satisfied for the time being, they are not fully satisfied, since *A* wants to go on being with *B* and wants *B* to continue caring for her. The variety and scope of what is desired in love also stand in the way of love's frustration. Still, love may face frustration when a loved one turns away, perhaps, certainly when a loved one dies. Even then, however, if love is strong, it may survive, since we may yet hope or wish for what it seems at least we cannot have. If love is strong and lasting, it tends to elude semantic assessment in terms of frustration; if love is not strong or lasting, we may question whether it is really love. Semantic assessment, then, is not easily applied to love, and this is because of what is desired and how much it is desired.[11]

5. The Rationality of Love

Antony loves Cleopatra because he believes she is beautiful. On the view that love is an emotion, such beliefs provide reasons for loving. This is indeed part, though only part, of the story of the rationality of love. Still, there are problems. For one thing, the reason-providing beliefs may be absent without our being able to say *tout court* that love is irrational. The love of the girl in the song is not absurd but something we can quite understand; and where love proves constant, though the loved one is no longer believed to have the attractions, this is also understandable.

Another thing is this. If love is considered an emotion, even where beliefs about the attractions of one who is loved are present, there is a problem understanding how the beliefs provide reasons for love. Antony's belief that Cleopatra is beautiful is quite as compatible with various emotions, or with no emotion at all, as with love. Octavia also believes that Cleopatra is beautiful, and she is envious. Cleopatra's mother believes that Cleopatra is beautiful, and she is proud. Further, if Antony were gay, Cleopatra's beauty would leave him cold.

The rationality of love is much easier to understand on the conative model.

---

11. It is worth noting that problems about propositional content and semantic assessment arise not only for a conative account of love but for a view of love as an emotion as well. Though he may love her because he believes she's exciting, he doesn't love that she's exciting; and if she is exciting, that doesn't mean that his love is true. What we call 'true love' is great love or love that lasts; this has little to do with whether or not a loved one has attractions she is believed to have. The variety of beliefs with a common referent upon which love may be based makes possible a solution to the propositional content problem parallel to that afforded by the conative account, but the semantic assessment problem appears intractable.

The intentionality of love depends, not on beliefs about the attractions of one who is loved, but on desires for association, benefit, and reciprocity. Beliefs about the attractions of another are in effect beliefs about his or her suitability for association. Given human nature and our individual proclivities, we find it desirable to associate with someone who has certain properties; believing another to have such properties, we have reason to associate with him or her. An ensuing desire for association provides reason in turn to desire the good of the other and his or her reciprocation, since without mutual benefit and reciprocal desire, the association cannot form and flourish. It is in this way that the desires which constitute love are rationally structured.

Antony's belief that Cleopatra is beautiful is a reason for him to love her, since he finds romantic association with a beautiful woman desirable. In general, for beliefs about B's attributes to be reasons for A to love B, the attributes must render B suitable for association with A. Aside from supporting an associative desire, the beliefs provide no reasons for love.

Cleopatra's beliefs that Antony is exciting and good looking rationally support her desire to share a life of adventure and intimacy with him. The love of the girl in the song lacks such rational support. More generally, wherever love is constant or exclusive it tends to go beyond such reasons for loving. This does not mean that in these cases love is altogether irrational. There is still the desirability of sharing a life with someone, and this at least provides a reason for loving. As Aristotle observes, 'Man is a social animal, and the need for company is in his blood'.[12] Without friends or loved ones our life is lonely; with them we have at least the comfort of companionship.

The distinction between heart and head is nowhere more poignantly drawn than in respect of love, and the rational reconstruction of love may seem to place it on the wrong side of that distinction. Love does indeed enjoy relative immunity from rational criticism. There are several reasons for this: that association with someone is not supposed to be desirable does not mean it is undesirable; what attributes render him or her suitable for association is to a considerable extent a personal matter; some undesirable attributes may be offset by others which are desirable; and association itself is something we value. Still the point is not that love is always based on reasons but that love admits of rational assessment. This is something that the conative account makes understandable.

6. Actions, Emotions, and Love

Love is bound up with emotions and is also numbered among the springs of

---

12. Thomson, J. A. K., *The Ethics of Aristotle* (London: George Allen and Unwin, 1953), p. 250; 1169b18.

action. This much is clear. What needs explanation is how love relates to emotions and actions.

For a lover, separation from her loved one is an occasion for sadness, his attentions are a source of pleasure, and a threat to him is a cause for concern. Love, of course, is usually taken to be an emotion. This is hardly helpful as an explanation of the connection between love and emotions. Love-related emotions are various, and each emotion has a determinate hedonic character. In joy and hope we are pleased or tend to be pleased; we are pained or tend to be pained in sorrow or fear. The contribution of love to the hedonic character of experience is variable. Such, I take it, is the complaint in these lines of Jonathan Swift.

> Love, why do we one passion call
> When 'tis a compound of them all?
> Where hot and cold, where sharp and sweet
> In all their equipages meet;
> Where Pleasures mix'd with Pains appear,
> Sorrow with Joy, and Hope with Fear.

Swift says love is a compound of emotions with mixed hedonic character. This is not right either. In love one is not always experiencing joy and sorrow, hope and fear. Rather love disposes one to feel the range of love-related emotions. This is the point made when love is called a 'sentiment' by Alexander Shand, from whom the quote from Swift is drawn.[13] Still, we want to know how love disposes one to feel the range of emotions, and this Shand does not tell us.

The explanation might be supposed to lie with beliefs about the attractions of the beloved, but this does not work out. Let's get back to Cleopatra. She believes that Antony is tall, dark, and handsome. Now, Antony is away for a time on a business trip to Rome. So what is Cleopatra supposed to feel? Nothing, so far as these beliefs are concerned. The case is different if she wants to be with him, whether or not she believes he is tall, dark, and handsome. Given her desire, of course she will miss him when he is away.

In general, it is the set of desires which make up love that explains the disposition of the lover to have love-related emotions. Cleopatra not only misses Antony when they are apart since she wants to be with him, she worries that something might happen to him because she cares about him, and she is thrilled when upon his return he brings her roses because she wants him to care about her.

Love is also a motive for action. We expect the lover to seek to be with his beloved, to woo and to cherish her. Beliefs about her attractions simply do not

---

13. Shand, Alexander, *Foundations of Character* (London: Macmillan, 1905), p. 56.

explain this. Antony believes Cleopatra is beautiful. So what is he supposed to do? Nothing, so far as this belief is concerned.

John Rawls endorses Shand's contention that love is a sentiment and stresses the disposition to actions, as well as emotions. He writes:

> If A cares for B, then failing a special explanation A is afraid for B when B is in danger and tries to come to B's assistance.... Love is a sentiment, a hierarchy of dispositions to experience and manifest these primary emotions and to act in the appropriate way. [14]

The problem is still that we are not told what we want to know. Of course Antony's love disposes him to pursue Cleopatra, but why? Once more, it is not just because he thinks she's beautiful. Antony knows many beautiful women in Egypt and in Rome, but he doesn't pursue them all. On the other hand, if he wants to be with her, then, whether or not he thinks she's beautiful, his behavior is something we can understand.

It is the conative structure of love which accounts for its motivational force. Desires move us to action, and love is a set of desires. Antony wants to be with Cleopatra, so of course he pursues her; he also brings her roses because he wants her to be happy and to return his affection.

The intensity of love is manifest in love-related actions and emotions. This too is explained, not by reference to the beliefs which may occasion love, but in terms of the desires which constitute it. If Antony is willing to go to great lengths to be with Cleopatra, this is because he wants so much to be with her; his beliefs about her beauty may not get him out the door. If Cleopatra would do anything to make Antony happy, this is not because of her beliefs about his good looks, but due to her great desire that he be happy.

7. Varieties of Love

There are different varieties of love. This is sometimes seen as an obstacle to analyzing love. It need not be so. If love is understood in terms of its constituent desires, the varieties of love differ with respect to what is desired.

Traditionally, eros and agape are distinguished as different varieties of love. Ignoring for the moment the fact that eros is taken to be sexual love, while agape is not, the two are supposed to differ in that agape is not based on beliefs about the attractions of one who is loved, while eros at least often is based on such beliefs. On this account, agape is held to be a purer sort of love than eros, capable of withstanding the threats to constancy and exclusivity which beset eros with its basis in beliefs about the attributes of one who is loved.

There are difficulties with this distinction. If love is considered an emotion,

14. Rawls, John, *A Theory of Justice* (Oxford: Oxford University Press, 1971), p. 487.

clearly there are not two kinds of love at all; for agape, in lacking the basis in belief required for emotional intentionality and rationality, is obviously not an emotion at all. The distinction is also in difficulty if love is understood as a complex conative state. Save insofar as attribute-based reasons for love relate to what is desired in love, they do not bear on the distinction between different varieties of love; and love, of whatever sort, need not be backed by such reasons.

To the extent that love proves constant or exclusive, it does indeed go beyond reasons for loving provided by attractions the loved one is supposed to have; it is, in this respect, agapic. This, however, is not something that works in reverse. There is no special reason to think that agape, or love without attribute-based reasons, will be constant or exclusive. If parental love, unlike romantic love, is especially constant, this is not because it is agapic, even if it is so, at least up to a point; it is because, relative to romantic love, it gives more and asks less--that is, because of what is desired and how much it is desired. Note, too, that, since we typically love all our children, parental love does not even tend to be exclusive.

Romantic love, I suggested, incorporates a desire for association which typically has a sexual dimension. This, of course, is a loose characterization; the association desired in romantic love is in fact rich and various. As Aristotle says of love between man and woman, at least of the best kind, they come together, not for sexual union alone, but 'to provide whatever is necessary to a fully lived life'.[15]

Still, it is the sexual dimension of romantic love which most obviously distinguishes it from friendship, and from parental love as well. In the variety of friendship considered best, Aristotle describes the desired association as involving 'conversation and exchanging ideas. For that is what is meant when human being speak of "living together"--it does not mean grazing together like a herd of cattle'.[16] Aristotle also describes cases in which friends come together to share pleasant pursuits or to do business. Friendships of these kinds, of course, need not be exhaustive or distinct.

Love, as we see in the cases of romantic or parental love, and of friendship as well, is a relationship. As for the attitude, it is what is desired in the manner of association which primarily determines the variety of love. The benefits desired for a friend or lover are primarily those of association; the wider the scope of association desired, the broader the range of benefits desired. In a friendship of pleasure, for example, what is desired is that the friend enjoy the pursuits which are shared; in love turned toward mutual flourishing, what is

---

15. Thomson, J. A. K., *The Ethics of Aristotle* (London: George Allen and Unwin, 1953), p. 226; 1161b20.

16. *Ibid.*, p. 226; 1170b12-13.

desired for the loved one may be virtually all the good things in life. The reciprocation desired in love or friendship is the reciprocation of the desires for association and benefit.

There are also conative states which involve one or more of the desires which are constitutive of love. They lack a desire for reciprocity at least, and there is no corresponding relationship. They are at most truncated forms of love.

Consider the love of the patriot or the sports fan. He loves his country or his team. Each wishes the object of his love well; the patriot wants his country to prosper, and the sports fan wants his team to win. There is also a desire for association of a sort; the sports fan wants to be in the stands for the game, and the patriot wants to participate in the life of his country. The desired association, however, is definitely one-sided. Reciprocity is out of the question; the patriot or the fan does not even wish that his affections be returned.

Consider also love of wine or fried chicken. Not only does the oenophile or fried chicken fancier not desire that her affection be returned, she can hardly wish the object of her affection well. All that we find is a desire for the enjoyment of eating or drinking, which is a unilateral kind of association at best. In fact, we naturally hesitate to talk about love in these cases; what we have is better described as liking.

Finally, love and hate are usually taken to be opposed emotions. They are indeed opposed but not in that way. Like love, hate is not an emotion. It may or may not be based on beliefs about the defects of one who is hated; its intentionality and rationality do not require a basis in belief. Relative to love, hate is a truncated conative state. It incorporates no desire for association (nor yet for disassociation, at least not necessarily) and certainly no desire for reciprocity. All that is necessary for hate is a malevolent desire. Love and hate are opposed in that love involves a desire for the good of one who is loved, while hate involves desiring evil for one who is hated.

8. Conclusion

Unlike emotions, love does not have belief-based intentionality and rationality. The conclusion to be drawn is not that love is an anomalous emotion but that it is not an emotion. Rather, love is a complex conative state, a set of desires. The conative account, unlike the view that love is an emotion, makes possible a plausible explanation of love's intentionality and rationality and of love's emotional and motivational force and its varieties, as well.[17]

---

17. I am grateful to John Deigh and Roger Lamb for helpful comments on an earlier version of this paper.

12

Love and Intentionality: Roxane's Choice

Sue Campbell

ROXANE
I never loved but one man in my life,
And I have lost him -- twice...

CYRANO
No...
That is not in the story!

Edmond Rostand, *Cyrano de Bergerac*, Act V

I. Emotion and Object

In *The Rationality of Emotion*, Ronald de Sousa asks the intriguing question: Could you be in love and not know with whom?[1] If this were possible, the *character* of your feeling, as well as its object, would be thrown into question. We do not normally allow that a person can knowingly be in love without their knowing whom they love, for we believe that their finding a certain person cherishable both causes their love and supplies it with an object. There are two points here. The first is that many emotions, and love certainly, are essentially object-directed. I am not in love prior to having found someone to love. The second point is that I take it to be a common view that it is the way in which we appraise a certain object or situation that gives an emotion its character. According to Alison Jaggar, for example, in a summary of contemporary theories of emotion, "[we] define or identify emotions not by the quality of the physiological sensations that may be associated with them, but rather by their

---

1. Ronald de Sousa, *The Rationality of Emotion*, (Cambridge, MA: MIT Press, 1987), p. 110.

intentional aspect, the associated judgement".[2] To state, however, that our love depends on how we view a person--our attitudes, perceptions and beliefs about that person--or that our fear depends on our appraising a situation as dangerous, might make it seem that the emotions are completely formed through our appraisals of objects, people, and situations, and independently of our acts of expression. Many philosophers are, in fact, committed to this thesis and I shall argue that it is false.

In order to examine the role of expression in the *formation* of emotion, I take up, in section II, de Sousa's question for a case of love gone badly wrong: predictably, Roxane's love in *Cyrano de Bergerac*.[3] The case should be viewed philosophically as it is theatrically: the drama of a failed effort to individuate the appropriate object of an emotion. My analysis is meant to go some distance towards persuading the reader that acts of expression help form feelings. On my reading of the play, Roxane's love develops through her expressive actions. After performing a certain number of such actions, Roxane cannot easily withdraw her claim that she loves. However, Roxane's expressive actions do not fulfill the role of establishing an appropriate object for Roxane's love. Consequently, her love is ill-formed. Diagnosing the failure of Roxane's love makes it possible to show the role that expression plays in forming emotion, particularly the role that expressive action plays in establishing an object.

The alternative to my account is, of course, that Roxane's actions do not play a role in determining whom she loves. On this alternative, when Roxane expresses her love, she is expressing or revealing what is already true to say of her prior to her actions. It is true to say of her that she loves someone in particular although she herself may be mistaken about who this is. She may even express her love to the wrong person. That Roxane's actions play no role in determining whom she loves is the alternative to which I take many contemporary accounts of emotion and object, those, for example of Amelie Rorty and Ronald de Sousa, to be committed.[4] I shall briefly outline my dissatisfaction with this alternative. My analysis of *Cyrano* is meant to be a challenge to it.

The object-directedness of emotions has played a particular crucial role in contemporary attempts to explain the importance of feeling in motivating behaviour. Emotions have been attached to behaviour through cognitivist theo-

2. Alison Jaggar, 'Love and Knowledge: Emotion in Feminist Epistemology', in Marilyn Pearsell and Ann Garry (eds.), *Women, Knowledge and Reality: Explorations in Feminist Philosophy* (Boston: Unwin Hyman, 1989), pp.129-154, p.133.

3. Edmond Rostand, *Cyrano de Bergerac* (New York: Bantam Books, 1959). Translated by Brian Hooker.

4. De Sousa, *op. cit.*, p.115. Amelie Rorty, 'Explaining Emotions', in A. Rorty (ed.), *Explaining Emotions* (Berkeley: University of California Press, 1980), pp.103-127. See especially pp. 106-08.

ries or perceptual models of how emotions come to have objects and thereby give us information about world:

> In various ways, emotions provide us with information about ourselves and the world. Objects represent the variety of types of such information and their different relations to thought and behaviour.[5]

If emotions, by virtue of involving appraisals of some sort, give us information about the world, information like Roxane loves Christian for his beauty, they can then make intelligible our behaviour. Roxane marries Christian because she loves him for his beauty.

Arguing that belief or perception or appraisal establishes the information content of an emotion so that the emotion then has a rationalizing connection to behaviour involves the view that the real object of an emotion is established by the appraisal, prior to and independent of behaviour. Thus cognitive/perceptual models have the following negative commitments about the role of expression in object-acquisition: 1) the expression of an emotion does not play a determining role in the establishing of the object of that emotion but presupposes that the object has been fully established by the causal history of the emotion, where this history is the appraisal or series of appraisals that give that emotion its character; 2) if the object of an emotion has not been successfully established, this failure is to be explained by mistaken beliefs or misperceptions at some point in the causal history of that emotion. Cognitive/perceptual models separate what they take to be the cause of an emotion from what they take to be the expression of that emotion in behaviour, giving priority to the former in establishing the intentional core of an emotion, and hence its appropriate description. The separation of cause from consequent behaviour is clear in this passage from Rorty: "When we focus on their consequences on behavior, most emotions can also be described as motives.... But when we speak of a *psychological state* as an

---

5. De Sousa, *ibid.*, p. 107. Rorty takes cognitive appraisals to supply the intentional content of emotions; de Sousa models emotions on perceptions. Another prominent cognitive theory is Robert Gordon, *The Structure of Emotion: An Investigation in Cognitive Psychology* (Cambridge: Cambridge University Press, 1987). Other theorists who now use a perceptual model include Robert Kraut, 'Love De Re', *Midwest Studies in Philosophy* 10 (1986), pp. 413-20, and Stanley Clarke, 'The Emotions: Rationality Without Cognitivism', *Dialogue* XXV (1986), pp. 663-74. Perceptual models are a response to problems with cognitivist approaches. Relevantly to my topic, they seem to offer a non-derivative account of object-acquisition. If a belief both causes an emotion and gives it its object or information content, the emotion, usually a feeling, appears to have an object only derivatively. On a perceptual model, although an emotion is similarly caused by an appraisal of some sort, the emotion is something like a perceptual gestalt, and thus, it is argued, takes an object directly. I reject both sorts of account for the reasons given within. An approach closer to my own is Helen Fay Nissenbaum in *Emotion and Focus* (Center for the Study of Language and Information, 1985).

emotion...we focus on the ways we are affected by our appraisals, evaluative perceptions or descriptions" (emphasis mine).[6]

My deep concern about cognitive/perceptual models is that, in the end, they frustrate their own good intentions. The choice of working within a cognitive/perceptual model is encouraged by: 1) the possibilities of securing a place for emotions in theory of behaviour by making them securely intentional; and, 2) the further possibility of arguing that emotional behaviour can be understood as well-organized through an examination of the emotion's causal history. The first motivation is related to the concern, noted by Jaggar, above, that the option to a cognitive/perceptual model is a view of emotions as simply physiological disturbances. The second motivation, my interest here, responds to those cases where emotional responses seem confused, anomalous or irrational. The cognitive/perceptual model offers the resource of examining an emoter's cognitive history. Proponents of the view suggest that through an investigation of this history, we can sometimes redescribe the intentional component of a particular emotional state and thereby see the emotional response as more intelligible than previously. These theories, however, leave actual *emotional behaviour* unnecessary to the formation of emotion, often destabilizing the individuating description of the very behaviour for which they mean to account.

The following kind of case, adapted from Rorty and simplified, typifies the problem.[7] We wish to explain the following situation: Jonah resents Ester, his boss, as evidenced by his behaviour towards her. His behaviour is not rationalized, however, by any of his beliefs about his boss. We search further back in his cognitive history, in what Rorty refers to as his intentional set, and note that his appraisal of his mother as hostile or domineering allows us to postulate Jonah's mother as the real object of his resentment. We conclude our explanation by pointing out the perhaps accidental ways that Ester reminds Jonah of his mother.

The difficulty is not just that we have failed to explain Jonah's behaviour, i.e. the behaviour we have picked out as needing explaining. On a cognitive/

---

6. Rorty, 'Explaining Emotions', p. 105. Similarly, de Sousa, *The Rationality of Emotion*, p. 120, says the behaviour expressive of emotion, "...[does] not relate directly to the perceptual model".

7. Rorty, *op. cit.*, p. 106. Rorty's presentation is more complex. Her interest is partly in the conservation of emotion and she presents the case as one where Jonah's changing his evidently false beliefs about Ester, beliefs, which, if true, would have rationalized the resentment, does not significantly alter the nature of his response towards Ester. As well, Rorty and others use the term 'target' to refer to a non-propositional object of an emotion, separating emotions that take targets (like love, envy or anger) from emotions that take propositional objects (like hope). I have chosen to use a very simplified terminology in this paper. Further, I do not address the question of how far the kind of account I offer can be extended to emotions that do not take targets.

perceptual model, the difficulty is deeper. In allowing the emotion to get its intentional description solely from the appraisal, we lose the individuating description of the very behaviour that we mean to render intelligible by our account. If there is nothing in Jonah's intentional set that rationalizes resentment towards Ester, it is difficult to see how we can maintain 'resentment towards Ester' as the description of his behaviour. If the response is that the behaviour we are trying to explain is evidently resentful, we then need an account of expressive behaviour that gives it, on such an occasion, some role in the intentional, and hence individuating description of the emotional episode to be explained.[8]

The importance of expression to our determining the description of an emotion can be emphasized by considering the following response on behalf of the cognitivist: that what wants explaining is only Jonah's apparent resentment of Ester. That is, we do not require the individuating description "Jonah resents Ester" in order to pick out the episode in question. We require only "Jonah apparently resents Ester". We leave intact, here, an individuating description of the behaviour we want to explain while opening up the option that it is Jonah's resentment of someone else that best explains his behaviour towards Ester, behaviour which does not play a role in defining the emotion.

If Jonah is only play acting resentment, I see nothing wrong with the above description. However, the motivation for the redescription suggests we should read it to mean that Jonah resents, but only apparently resents Ester. Arguing for this redescription of Jonah's situation simply furthers our obligation to attend to Jonah's expressive behaviour. Resentment is essentially object-directed, Jonah really resents someone, and we must address the question of what makes it appropriate to postulate Jonah's mother as the object of his resentment. The cognitivist suggests that Jonah's appraisals of his mother as domineering when conjoined with the absence of resentment-guiding appraisals of Ester should lead us to postulate Jonah's mother as the real object of his resentment. However, I argue that this suggestion requires a prior settling of whether Jonah, in fact, resents *his mother*. That Jonah has reasons to resent his mother, that he finds her domineering, for example, will not necessarily license a redescription of Jonah's psychological state as one of 'resentment of his mother' even if these very same reasons are part of the full explanation of why he is acting resentfully towards Ester. For there is the possibility that Jonah fears his mother and consequently resents women who remind him of his mother but who have less power over his life. To determine whether Jonah resents his mother, we must

---

8. Cases similar to Rorty's are presented in de Sousa, *op. cit.*, p. 115, and in Tormey [Alan Tormey, *The Concept of Expression* (Princeton: Princeton University Press, 1971), p. 20.] These cases are, like Rorty's, meant to raise questions about how to describe a confused emotional episode, and I wish to stress that the resolution of these cases on a cognitive/perceptual model involves redescription of the emotional state.

again have recourse to his expressive behaviour. To postulate Jonah's mother as the object of his resentment does require that we allow his expressive behaviour a role in the individuating description of his psychological state.[9]

That we will have to establish that Jonah's expressive life warrants our postulating that Jonah resents his mother already moves us beyond the resources of what a cognitive/perceptual model has to offer for identifying emotional states, but we may for completeness sake, consider what our response to this case should be on establishing to our satisfaction that Jonah does resent his mother. Will that allow us to conclude that Jonah's mother and not Ester is the real object of his resentment? Once again, I think not. Given that Jonah comes to believe he was in some sense confused in his response to Ester, it is natural that he would think he owes Ester an apology and we may ask what the appropriate content of such an apology would be. Should Jonah say, "I'm sorry I acted resentfully towards you: it was resentment but it wasn't you I resented, it was really my mother"? Or, should he say, "I'm sorry I acted resentfully towards you: you didn't really do anything to deserve that"? I grant that we will allow a certain amount of acting out in people's emotional lives, but only a certain amount. When we disallow an explanation of acting out it will be on behavioral grounds. At some point Jonah's behaviour will have so thoroughly implicated Ester as the object of his resentment that his resenting her without adequate reason to is what he will need to apologize for.

Denying that expressive behaviour has a role in establishing the object of an emotion seems especially tempting to the cognitive theorist in cases of emotional confusion. My analysis of Jonah suggests, on the contrary, that, on such occasions, we must allow expressive behaviour to play a determining role in the description of the emotional state we are trying to understand. I shall present Roxane's dilemma--by the end of the play she can neither deny that she loved nor, perhaps, specify an appropriate object for her love--as one in which the actions she undertakes are integral to our description and to Roxane's own description of her love.

I now then offer Roxane's dilemma with the following note: 1) I do not deny the importance of the causal history of an emotion--rather, I place the importance of this history within an account of expression; 2) My case against cognitive/perceptual models is a negative one. We sometimes, and for some emotions, need as thorough an understanding of the expressive dimension of

---

9. Many of our emotional responses are associational, and a full explanation of any particular response may require a thorough understanding of the etiology of the response. In order to accommodate this we do not need to redescribe a present response and I would suggest the very ubiquity of this feature of our emotional lives is an argument against a generous policy of redescription. We need some way to limit the category of cases we want to allow as acting out.

emotional experience as we do of the cognitive dimension in order to adjudicate puzzles about the object of an emotion.

II. Roxane's Choice

My analysis of *Cyrano* will offer the following thesis: The complete individuation of an emotion includes a specification of its object and, in some cases, it is the actions of the subject of the emotion that establish who or what that object is. A spirited story of love that does not successfully establish an object, although it seems, at times, to have one, is *Cyrano de Bergerac*. Cyrano, hidden, writes and speaks as Christian, and the two men win Roxane, the woman that each loves, together. Christian is beautiful and brave, but, in love, ineloquent. Cyrano is brave and eloquent, but grotesque. When Roxane, in the throes of infatuation for Christian, cries out: "He is beautiful and brilliant--and I love him" (Act III), she is foretelling the increasing complexity of a situation where she comes to love for qualities that are not instantiated by a single individual, but by two different men. There is no doubt that each man loves Roxane uniquely. Whether Roxane loves one of them uniquely is the problem of the play, and the playwright seems to answer no. By the end of *Cyrano de Bergerac*, Cyrano and Christian are both dead, the closure to a misbegotten love. I take the ending of the play to be confirmation of our intuitions that Roxane's love has not been successfully object-directed and, therefore, cannot be completely formed. The play offers several options as to whom Roxane might love. She might love Christian, Cyrano, both men, or neither. Roxane, herself, concludes

> I never loved but one man in my life,
> And I have lost him -- twice... (Act V)

I will try to make some sense of her diagnosis.

One possible explanation of the failure of Roxane's love is that, as a matter of fact, the qualities for which Roxane *comes* to love are necessary to *the sustenance* of her love, and these qualities are separately instantiated in two different people. Although it is common to say that what Roxane really loves is Cyrano's wit and Christian's beauty, or even more problematically, Cyrano's soul in Christian's body, the play specifically excludes the possibility that the difficulties in individuating the object of Roxane's love rest finally with the different qualities for which she loves being instantiated in two different real objects.

Christian cannot display wit to Roxane, but has wit in his encounter with Cyrano (Act II). His inability to make love in words is not meant to reflect on either his character or the quality of his love for Roxane. In particular, and implausibly, there is no conceptual connection between what Christian feels and his mode of expression. Cyrano can express Christian's love. ("And am I to ruin yours/Because I happen to be born with power/To say what you--perhaps--feel?") (Act IV). And Christian is a man of fine and lovable character--this, Cyrano has been careful to verify. In fact, that "good, brave, noble Christian" (Act V) has a soul very much like Cyrano's own. Cyrano is grotesque, but Roxane comes to realize that physical beauty is unnecessary to sustain her love. She decides she loves a soul. This dramatic merging of the qualities of the two men strains plausibility and Roxane's love for a soul, seems to me, less dramatically persuasive than Cyrano's very particularized love for Roxane ("I know--/ All small forgotten things that once meant you") (Act III), but it is a necessary conceit of the play. Otherwise, the romantic deception would be an act of cruelty by the two men who purportedly love Roxane. The difference between the qualities of the two men is so drastically and deliberately undercut, that by the end of Act IV, the qualities relevant to Roxane's love are instantiated pretty well by either man.

The play offers three opportunities to analyze what goes wrong with Roxane's love. I consider below the three crucial scenes: the balcony scene of "Roxane's Kiss" (Act III), a scene at the battlefield where Christian will die (Act IV), and a scene at the monastery where Cyrano will die (Act V). What goes wrong, however, is complex, and involves both appraisal and expressive action. The conventions of romantic love that govern the treatment of love in *Cyrano* require that Roxane's love should have a single object. There are times when her appraisals seem to pick out a single object, at the beginning of the play Christian, at the end Cyrano, even though many of her appraisals of Christian are inaccurate. But Roxane's love develops through object-directed action which fixes both Christian and Cyrano as objects of her love. Or so I shall now argue.

Cyrano is a heroic comedy in the grand manner, but its treatment of love is relatively subtle. Though no one character articulates, in speech or action, a view of love adequate to the complexities of the dramatic situation, Cyrano comes closest to doing so. He envisions a situation where he and Christian must win Roxane together, for neither has completely those qualities for which Roxane will come to love; nevertheless, he supposes that Roxane, in loving, will come to love a person, and that person will be Christian.[10]

> I know --
> Afraid that when you have her all alone,

---

10. See Kraut, 'Love De Re', *Midwest Studies in Philosophy* 10 (1986), pp. 413-20, for a defence of the Platonic option I do not consider: that the object of romantic love could be a quality or set of qualities. I would argue that the object of an emotion is restricted as to type by what could count as behaviour expressive of that emotion. One cannot make love to a quality. As this argument can be made on grounds of what would be minimally necessary to distinguish an emotion like love from other sorts of attitudes, I take it to be support for the general approach of this paper.

> You lose all. Have no fear. It is yourself
> She loves -- give her yourself put into words --
> My words, upon your lips! (Act II)

Cyrano assumes that the qualities for which Roxane loves will cause her love, that in loving, she will love a person, and must assume as well that what sustains her love will not necessarily be the same as what caused it. Cyrano concludes from this, however, that though both men may be required to win her, one can keep her. But this will depend on whether Roxane's expressive acts are successful in fully forming her emotion by establishing an object for it. Cyrano counts too much on his own agency in structuring the possibilities for Roxane's love and takes too little account of the importance of Roxane's agency.

Cyrano, who is naturally eloquent, also stands for sincerity and integrity of expression, an underlying theme of the play. In a speech to Roxane in his own voice, but shadowed in the shrubbery and disguised to her as Christian, he pleads against the demand for an eloquence that strains sincerity in the expression of love:

> Look once at the high stars that shine in heaven
> And put off artificiality!....
> ROXANE: But...Poetry?
> CYRANO: Love hates that game of words!
> It is a crime to fence with life -- I tell you --
> There comes one moment, once -- and God help those
> Who pass that moment by! -- When Beauty stands
> Looking into the soul with grave, sweet eyes.
> That sicken at pretty words! (Act III)

The lesson of the speech is that those who fail at appropriate expression fail at love. Ironically, as this crucial Act called "Roxane's Kiss" progresses, Cyrano insists that Christian perform the direct expressive act that the moment calls for. ("Climb up, animal!") (Act III). And Roxane, who, throughout the play, demands expressive eloquence, performs conventional acts of expression that begin to give a character to her emotion that she cannot repudiate.

I propose to treat "Roxane's Kiss" as Roxane's first unsuccessful attempt at forming an emotion traceable to a failure at performing expressive acts that individuate a single appropriate object. To understand Roxane's failure at giving form to her feelings, I will give Roxane a certain preliminary authority, not about *whom* she loves, but about *when* she loves. Like Ryle, I will take her avowals as the best and most direct evidence that she has come to love. I characterize this authority as preliminary because it is defeasible. We can be mistaken in all sorts of ways about our emotions, and at this point, I wish to leave open the possibility that Roxane might not only be mistaken about whom she loves, but also about when or even whether she loves.

In "Roxane's Kiss", Cyrano speaks to Roxane from the dark, pretending that he is Christian, and Roxane, while assuming that the speaker is Christian, is tremendously moved by the speech and the voice and claims she has come truly to love for the first time:

> Yes, I do tremble...and I weep...
> And I love you...and I am yours...and you
> Have made me thus   (Act III)

She kisses and marries Christian before the scene is out.

In Roxane's speech, and in the actions that follow, she undertakes or undergoes at least six distinguishable actions or behaviours, which I will list below. I use the doubled term 'response/feeling' as a way of indicating that there is no clear separation between these features in the formation of Roxane's love. As will become clear, on my view, an emotion like love develops gradually through the very sorts of actions that Roxane undertakes.

1. Roxane *undergoes* a significant *response* (trembling and weeping);
2. she *affirms* that the *cause* of her *response/feeling* is *apparent* to her (the speaker);
3. she *identifies* the *cause* of her *response/feeling* (the speaker);
4. she *identifies* the *object* of her *feeling* (the speaker);
5. she *identifies* her *feeling* (love);
6. She *engages* in *actions expressive of love* (she avows her love, kisses, and marries).

I would like to point out that 4 and 5 take place coincidently in Roxane's avowal of her love. She discriminates her feeling and its object through the action of her avowal. That is, on my reading, it is through an action expressive of love that she performs acts of identification which are central to determining the intentional component of her emotional state.

Roxane has made a serious mistake at 2. The identity of the cause of her response is only partially apparent to her. She correctly identifies the cause of her response as the speaker, but she believes that the speaker is Christian when it is really Cyrano. It is Cyrano's speech and voice that have (in large part) caused her response, trembling and weeping, which do not themselves require an object. But the further actions of Roxane's that are expressive of love do require an object, and in undertaking these actions, Roxane begins to determine whom she loves. She avows her love to the speaker, Cyrano, but kisses and marries the man whom she believes to be the speaker, namely, Christian. Roxane has identified an object for her love, but she has failed to establish one uniquely. She has begun to fix the object through actions that pick out two men, not one. Cyrano's words cue the audience to the object confusion that is the outcome to the scene: "...Kissing my words/ My words, upon your lips!" (Act III)

The difficulty, at this point, is to say how Roxane's actions or expressions of love can be loving in the sense of being formative of her love without falling into locutions that suggest they are loving because they are revealing of her love. As John Dewey pointed out, the very phrase "expression of emotion" carries the--to Dewey--misleading implication that an emotion is formed prior to its expression.[11] We then take the expression as evidence of the existence of the already formed emotion. We are especially inclined, I think, to do so in cases where the expressive action is an avowal which we may tempted to interpret as a self-description. However, in agreeing that when Roxane expresses her love she is doing what gives us good evidence that she loves, we are not committed, outside of prejudice, to the view that she is revealing a prior state. Rather, she may be engaged in publicly interpretable behaviours that give us reason to attribute a psychological description to her--that she loves--precisely because they are formative of her love.[12] My aim will be to establish that this approach offers a better understanding of Roxane's situation than can be gotten from a cognitive/perceptual analysis.

My preliminary obligation is to show that Roxane has behaved in such a way that her behaviour, itself, can be clearly interpreted as emotionally expressive behaviour. Roxane's behaviour has consisted of trembling, weeping, avowing love, kissing and marrying. All are conventional, albeit somewhat clichéd, ways of expressing love. On the assumption that Roxane is sincere, these behaviours have their expressive character in virtue of being embedded in well-defined social practices that are partly constitutive of romantic love.[13] Cyrano, himself, elaborates the significance of the kiss:

> And what is a kiss, when all is done?
> A promise given under seal -- a vow
> Taken before the shrine of memory --
> A signature acknowledged -- ...   (Act III)

Many of the passions are expressed in performances directed towards their objects--a kiss is such a performance. In kissing Christian, and by doing so in

---

11. John Dewey, 'A Theory of Emotion', in *John Dewey: The Early Work, 1882-1898*, Vol. 2 (Carbondale: Southern Illinois University Press, 1967) pp. 152-88, p. 152.

12. The contrast with 'public' in this paper is 'epistemically private'. Roxane may, of course, perform many publicly interpretable actions in socially private spaces.

13. Some theorists (see p. 135 in Jaggar, *op. cit.* fn. 2, this paper) suggest that romantic love is to be wholly understood in terms of conventional social practices, which we engage in much as actors playing roles. I do not accept this strong a social constructivist account of love although I do go on to refer to it in the text as a controlled social practice. I mean by this that there are strong constraints on what will count as non-deviant love in a society, many having to do with whom one can love. These constraints inform our practice.

this particular situation and sincerely, Roxane is engaged in an action that is socially designated as expressive of love, and this is because it brings into being a certain state of affairs. She has thereby committed herself to Christian. Avowing love is also such an action, and this she has done to Cyrano. In offering this analysis of Roxane's expressive acts, I echo J. L. Austin's analysis of performative utterances: linguistic acts that, in felicitous circumstances, help bring about certain states of affairs. As a reminder, in Austin's account, if the circumstances are infelicitous, the act does not come off.[14] I will discuss at a later point whether Roxane can claim that her expressive actions were not felicitously performed.

Roxane does not simply kiss, marry, and avow love. These are general types of action, but their instances take particular objects. Therefore, a full description of an action socially expressive of love is 'Roxane kissed Christian' or 'Roxane avowed love to Cyrano'. These action-descriptions do not only specify a feeling, but also the object of the feeling. Because of the nature of love as a controlled social practice, this object is limited to type. Cyrano's assumption that Roxane will come to love Christian somewhat independently of how her emotion is caused depends on recognizing the importance of expression in fixing an object, and believing that the expressive conventions of romantic love will lead to the decisive establishment of a unique object. However, it is Roxane's actions that establish or fail to establish who that object is.

To generalize, what type of expressive behaviour forms or individuates an emotion like love may be partly established by the place of that behaviour in practices conventionally associated with the emotion. However, a description of these practices does not, of course, fully individuate the specific behaviours, many of which are actions requiring objects. Some of these actions will have, as their object, an item with properties causally relevant in instigating the process of our response. Performing these actions fixes their objects. So a full account of the expressive behaviour that helps form an emotion may involve a considerable number of actions: acts of identification, as well as performances that are culturally standard, or even required, for expressing particular feelings. Roxane has not failed to perform actions expressive of love, but she appears to have failed to perform actions that individuate a unique object. This leads to confusion as to whom she loves.

It may be objected at this point that although Roxane's avowal was delivered to Cyrano, she did not avow love to Cyrano in any way that would

---

14. J. L. Austin, 'Performative Utterances', in J. O. Urmson and G. J. Warnock (eds.), *Philosophical Papers*, 2nd edition (Oxford: Oxford University Press, 1970). See, especially pp. 237-241 for a description of the ways in which performatives may be infelicitous.

implicate him as an object of that love. Even if the performance of an avowal is partly creative of love, it needn't be spoken to the person one is coming to love. Roxane's initial avowal of love in Act II is, in fact, an avowal of love for Christian delivered to Cyrano as a witness and audience. I can surely avow my love for X to Y, and, moreover, can do this even in cases where I mistake the identity of Y. So perhaps Roxane avows her love for Christian to Cyrano, mistakenly believing that Cyrano is Christian. But, to say this is to *assume* that it is Christian, not Cyrano, that she loves, and that is precisely what is in question throughout the play. That she avowed her love by saying *to Cyrano* "I love you", when conjoined with the fact that she avowed her love to the very man whose *eloquence* has played a major role in causing her love ("And you have made me thus"), casts reasonable doubt on the assumption that it is her love for Christian that is being expressed. He, after all, was neither eloquent, nor addressed in her avowal of love. Cyrano was both. Christian's beauty, however, has also played a causal role in Roxane's developing love, and she kisses and marries him. The play does not offer merely a simple case of mistaken identity, which might, by itself, have no consequences whatsoever.

I wish particularly to stress the point that Roxane's mistaken beliefs or perceptions are, by themselves, an inadequate explanation of the confusion which begins to develop.[15] By the time "Roxane's Kiss" takes place, Roxane already has mistaken beliefs: that the writer of certain letters she has received is Christian (it is Cyrano), and that Christian is eloquent. These mistakes lead to no loving actions taken towards Cyrano, but rather to loving actions that individuate Christian. Up until "Roxane's Kiss", Roxane's appraisals and actions have both supported the same object for her love, Christian, even though some of her appraisals of Christian have been inaccurate. We can imagine that Roxane might have gone through her life happily loving Christian for qualities that he does not straightforwardly have, but which she believes that he has. This sort of situation, we suspect, occurs all the time. "Roxane's Kiss" offers only a slight variation on misperceptions already in place. Roxane now believes that the speaker is Christian (it is Cyrano), and still believes that Christian is eloquent. But Roxane's avowal to the speaker begins to implicate Cyrano as an object of her love. To display its lesson about the importance of expression, "Roxane's Kiss" adds action to a situation already characterized by misperception. Insofar as misperceptions are important to the emotional

---

15. In describing this situation as confused, I do not mean that Roxane, at this point, feels confusion as to whom she loves. I mean there really is confusion as to whom she loves, for the audience and, increasingly, from this point, for Christian, Cyrano, and finally Roxane.

confusion, it is because these misperceptions lead to actions taken towards two persons.[16]

Act IV of *Cyrano de Bergerac* offers Roxane a second chance at fixing a single object for her love, and removes it by Christian's death. Tremendously moved by the letters that she believes Christian has written her every day from the front, she again is urged to action and travels to the front to tell Christian that now she believes she *truly* loves him, for she would continue to love him even if he were ugly. Roxane's avowed change from an immature to a mature love gives her the renewed possibility of locating a unique object and the audience the permission to accept the result.

It is, of course, Cyrano who has, again, written the letters. The dismissal of beauty as a feature necessary to sustaining Roxane's love appears to open the possibility that Roxane could come to individuate Cyrano as the sole appropriate object of her love, and Christian and Cyrano, recognizing this development, decide to tell Roxane of their deception. Before they can do so, however, Roxane is again moved to act. She avows her love anew ("It is yourself/I love now: your own self"), and pledges it for an eternity ("Oh, my Christian, oh my king,--/.../It is the heart of me that kneels to you,/And will remain forever at your feet--"). Christian interprets the avowal as an expression of love *for Cyrano*, thinking that Roxane does not yet know that this is whom she loves. But Roxane's pledge is clearly a pledge of love *for Christian* to Christian. Before discovery of the true identity of the author of the letters, Christian dies, Cyrano's last letter to Roxane by his heart. Roxane: "On his letter--blood...and tears". The tears are Cyrano's but the blood is Christian's. The scene repeats and intensifies the drama of failed unique individuation. Roxane takes no further action that could be interpreted as expressive of loving Cyrano, but goes into seclusion further fixing Christian as the object of her love.

Fifteen years after Christian's death, and on the day Cyrano is mortally wounded, Roxane discovers that the cause of her feelings has not been fully apparent to her. Her options for saying what was true of her love, before and after discovery, reveal possibilities for further understanding the object-directedness of her love. Let us designate t (before discovery) as a time after Roxane has kissed and married Christian but before Christian dies, and t' (after discovery) as a time after Roxane discovers that Cyrano loves her and that Cyrano and Christian have deceived her, but before Cyrano dies. I will offer my analysis through an investigation of Roxane's response to her discovery.

---

16. A cognitivist might point out that in avowing love to the speaker, Roxane has appraised him as cherishable and this is a crucial misperception responsible for the resulting situation. I would respond that this likely appraisal does not cause her avowal but takes place through it. That expressive behaviour is often our only ground for attributing an emotive appraisal seems even more reason to think that a model which discounts the importance of expressive behaviour is inadequate.

In trying to clarify for herself the nature of her love, Roxane attempts to understand the sense in which her loving has been object-directed. At t', Roxane has a maximum of four options of what to say about her love at t. She now understands, as well as she can, the causal account of her coming to love. She now knows, as well, that Cyrano loves her. She has the option of saying that at t she loved only Cyrano, that at t she loved both men, that at t she loved only Christian, or that at t she did not love. None of these options is entirely satisfactory. All need to be assessed with reference to the actions Roxane has taken.

Roxane's first inclination, on evidence of her speech to Cyrano at t' (below), is to deny her love for Christian, and conclude that the soul she has loved has always been Cyrano. She tries explicitly to retell the causal story of her love so that she can finally individuate a single appropriate object for it:

> R. I understand everything now: The letters--
>   That was you
> C. No!
> R. And the dear, foolish words--
>   That was you...
> C. No!
> R. And the voice... in the dark...
>   That was... you!
> C. No!
> R. And... the Soul!--
>   That was all you.

Put somewhat fancifully, Roxane might be thought of as here calling on the resources of the cognitive/perceptual model to attempt a redescription of the intentional component of her love. As Jonah might realize that his appraisals of a powerful woman as hostile, however these appraisals have been expressed, have supported resentment only towards his mother, Roxane might argue that her appraisals of a soul as eloquent, however these appraisals have been expressed, have supported only her love of Cyrano. Jonah's mother is the real object of his resentment; Cyrano is the real object of Roxane's love. But Jonah's and Roxane's actions preclude such redescriptions. The majority of Roxane's actions have fixed Christian and not Cyrano as the object of her love, and she has pledged her love, eternally, to Christian just moments before his death. Cyrano interrupts Roxane's retelling to remind her that actions have consequences that cannot be undone:

> Cyrano (holds the letter out to her): The blood
>   Was his.

It seems implausible that Roxane loves only Cyrano at t--she has mistaken too much of the cause of her feelings, and consequently Christian has been the object of much of her socially significant expressive action.

If Roxane cannot retell her love to make it true that she loved only Cyrano at t, might she then, at least, claim that she did love Cyrano at t and loved Christian as well? The momentum of her retelling races back towards the moment when she first avowed her love to Cyrano, and I have argued that she begins to fix Cyrano as a object through this avowal. But I suggest that Roxane has not yet done enough to make it clearly the case that she loves Cyrano at t. In particular, although we might interpret her avowal as, at the same time, an appraisal of the speaker as cherishable, Roxane does not yet know who the speaker is. Cyrano has not yet, therefore, been made the object of the sort of practice of loving action that Roxane has undertaken towards Christian.[17]

We are left with two options: that at t, Roxane loved only Christian, or that at t, Roxane did not love. Roxane's speech to Cyrano indicates her reluctance to affirm that it was only Christian that she loved at t. She recognizes that the eloquent words that have caused much of her response have been Cyrano's words in Cyrano's voice. Further, Cyrano has, at t, been the object of some of her loving action. It is not clear that she loved only Christian at t. Can Roxane claim then that at t, she did not yet love? This would involve denying she loved Christian at t, without attempting to replace him with Cyrano in her retrospective account.

I believe that Roxane could take the option of denying that she loved Christian at t but, realizing the importance of her own acts of expression towards Cyrano, does not take this option. Roxane's expressive actions towards Christian have been sincere and conventionally appropriate for love. However, these actions have been undertaken in circumstances of Roxane's being deliberately deceived about whose eloquence is motivating her to act. Deception might vitiate the force of her actions. I am suggesting that Roxane could, as an option to appealing to a cognitive/perceptual model, appeal to something like Austin's analysis of performative utterances, extending this analysis to expressive actions. She could claim that her expressive acts were not felicitously performed and, therefore, did not bring about a states of affairs in which she loved Christian at t. The deceptive circumstances, however, have grounded action taken towards both men. In denying that her actions have established her love for Christian, Roxane would risk the implication that her avowal to Cyrano has similarly lacked the performative force of initiating Cyrano as an object of love. In annulling the meaning of her response towards Christian, she would have little ground for now pleading her love to Cyrano in Act V.

In summary, Roxane's expressive actions are relevant to her t' understand-

---

17. The importance of an object of love as the object of a loving practice can be stressed by thinking of what might have happened if Roxane had continued to mistake Cyrano for Christian. Repeated situations like the balcony scene of Act III would have further fixed Cyrano as an object.

ing of t in the following ways. Her actions have implicated Cyrano as an object of her love and established Christian so decisively that she cannot redescribe her love to make it persuasive that she loved the man whose qualities have, in the main, caused her to engage in loving. She may, I believe, deny having loved at t. The grounds she could use to do so would leave expressive actions central to the formation of love, but set conditions for felicitous expressive actions. As her expressive actions have initiated Cyrano as an object of love, however, Roxane does not wish to claim that her avowal in Act III has been infelicitous. She therefore cannot claim that her expressive actions towards Christian have misfired. Thus, although Roxane is reluctant to affirm that she loved only Christian at t, the best she might be able to do is to say that she loved Christian at t, and maybe loved Cyrano just a little bit as well.

What Roxane can say at t' of her love at t' is, I think, more clear. The longer the period in which Roxane engages in loving action, the less it will be possible for her to claim her expression had misfired, even given the deception that Christian and Cyrano have practiced. By Act V, at t', Roxane has nearly twenty years of her life at stake in loving action. Roxane, for love, has kissed, cried, married, gone to war, and worn widow's weeds for 15 years. She has declared and redeclared her love, and in doing so, has performed every type of identification and engaged in every social performance necessary to individuate the object of an emotion. Fortunately, the discovery at t' both gives Roxane reason to affirm the felicity of her expressive actions and places Cyrano as the potential object of an ongoing practice of loving action. The process of individuation that forms her loving is complete at t', and Roxane is able to give a description of her love. She has loved Christian through engaging in a temporally extended social practice. She has come clearly to love Cyrano when she finally identifies him as the appropriate object of yet further actions expressive of love. ("You shall not die! I love you! --) By t' and with Roxane's final avowal, Roxane loves both men. It is Roxane's understanding that her appraisals have supported actions taken towards two men in a single process of loving that allows the play to reach resolution:

> I never loved but one man in my life,
> And I have lost him -- twice...

Roxane's description of the object of her love is, at the same time, a description of what she has done in loving, and of the consequences of those actions. Roxane's love has fixed two men as the single object of a temporally extended practice. But the actions through which Roxane has come to love--the kiss, the pledge, the various avowals--each conventionally guarantees faithfulness towards a unique individual. Roxane's love is not possible and Cyrano now dies.

In "Roxane's Choice", I have offered an example of a situation in which the object of an emotion is established, completing the formation of that emotion, partly through the expression of culturally significant actions which themselves require an object. What makes a particular object appropriate is: 1) our identification of that object as having qualities that caused our initial significant response; and, 2) our taking *that* object to be the appropriate object of further response. In this identification and in our subsequent actions, the object becomes established or formed as the object of that emotion. In other words, the causal history of our emotion and the object of that emotion are related through the need to take action involving a causally relevant item, and in the taking of that action. This is to offer a sketch for the relation between the cause and object of an emotion that acknowledges the importance of the cause, but gives it its importance within an account of expression. I conclude that on some occasions, we must allow expressive action a role in determining the intentional component of an emotional state.[18]

---

18. For help with the present version of this paper, I am grateful to Ronald de Sousa, Rockney Jacobsen, the Dalhousie Philosophy Colloquium, and especially Roger Lamb for his many helpful suggestions. Much of the work was done while on a Killam Postdoctoral Fellowship at Dalhousie University.

13

Love's Truths

Graeme Marshall

> *Cleo.* I dream'd there was an Emperor Antony:
> O! such another sleep that I might see
> But such another man...
> His face was as the heavens..
> His legs bestrid the ocean; his rear'd arm
> Crested the world; .. For his bounty,
> There was no winter in't, an autumn 'twas
> That grew the more by reaping; his delights
> Were dolphin-like, they show'd his back above
> The element they liv'd in; in his livery
> Walk'd crowns and crownets, realms and islands were
> As plates dropp'd from his pocket...
> Think you there was, or might be, such a man
> As this I dream'd of?
> *Dol.* Gentle madam, no.[1]

I

Dolabella is surely right: leaving aside whatever questions there might be about fictional entities, Cleopatra's dream Antony is not Antony and does not even possibly exist. Yet Cleopatra was not wrong; how she saw Antony was not unjustified and ungrounded. The exaggeration which is one of love's glories is the exaggeration of something and is certainly not unintelligible to us. There is a truthfulness in her seeing which a theory of interpretation for lovers will enable us to uncover. Such a theory begins with beauty and some necessary stage-setting. In Part II, I draw on the application to aesthetic perception of Wittgenstein's remarks about aspects and seeing-as in order to account for the

---

1. *Antony and Cleopatra*, Act V, Sc.II, William Shakespeare.

perceptions of lovers. In Part III I shall be concerned with what is desired in love and the effects of it on the perception of the beloved. In Part IV I shall address the truths love reveals and how they might be known.

The overall argument is, first, that erotic love, for that is the only kind of love I am here concerned with, sees its object as beautiful. From Plato and beyond this has been taken as obvious and it gets its clearest articulation in the *Phaedrus* and *Symposium*. There seems to be no adequate substitution for beauty here. It won't do, for example, merely to say that the lover finds something sensuously salient in the beloved since that need have no connection with the high positive evaluation that love entails and could be in any case almost anything.

Though Plato might not agree, the love of the beautiful is to be distinguished from the love of the good and there is point to the distinction. The second involves commitment, loyalty, and depth whereas in connection with the first it is more natural to speak of intensity and the disposition to enjoy. And while the beautiful is not exclusively physical it is necessarily so, which is not the case with the good. Love of the beautiful and love of the good also involve time differently: although both occur in time, the depths the good may call forth emphasize the future; beauty focuses on now: that is the timelessness of it. Of course, the erotic love which is occasioned by the perception of beauty is not confined to its celebration in a present but is borne along by a succession of them.

Erotic love is not the whole of love though it is an interesting question how much a part of the different kinds of love it is. I take it that it is standardly between people, with narcissism as a limiting case. Losing oneself in oneself is losing oneself indeed. Erotic love is not lust because it does not predate its object, though the distinction may begin to vanish under closer examination. Its object remains, however, entirely non-fungible[2] which may not be the case with lust.

Secondly, while the beautiful other is the formal object of love, the question is whether the concept of beauty so identified can be used at the quotidian level to characterize what the lover perceives in the beloved. It is the task of a theory of interpretation to show that it can, presenting the beloved as, for example, soft, elegant, sensual, gentle, noble, stunning, charming, full of grace, strong, powerful, handsome, athletic, sensitive, gorgeous. This is not to say that one loves under a description; one loves and finds the descriptions.

Essential to both the identification and interpretation is our delight as lovers in the beauty which flashes or dawns upon us. It is confronting, it

---

2. Ronald de Sousa discusses fungibility in his *The Rationality of Emotion* (MIT Press, 1987).

demands attention, and, as Kant says,[3] has no interest as its determining ground. Objects of delight engender at first only the desire to carry on attending to them. Essential to the erotic delight in beauty, however, is the further and consequent desire to possess and be possessed by the other which is at least sexual though perhaps only in the widest sense. The beauty perceived becomes eroticised and the question of possession is raised. This entails the recognition of the possibility of reciprocity. Here is beauty with which one can interact, that can enhance one while remaining totally other. The desire to possess and be possessed is the desire that the lover and the beloved together be so filled with the love the lover feels that each for a time is made to feel complete. This reciprocity, intimacy, together with the expectations and trust laid down by the maternal care that has enabled one to develop at all, explains the typical exclusiveness of erotic love and the possibility for jealousy it sustains. John Bayley well said that love stands both for the frightful difficulty of knowing other people and for the possibility of that knowledge.[4] That is true of unrequited love as well.

Thirdly, what love sees stands to what is to be seen as what is seen to be beautiful stands to the object so seen. While what the lover both sees and desires in the beloved may not be experientially distinguishable, and are, indeed, internally related and mutually reinforcing, what is seen is not mediated by the desire. Cleopatra did not see Antony as she did because she first desired him. Love's perceptions, though they may be false and be discovered by the lover to have always been false, are not made so by uncovering a bit of wishful thinking born of some antecedent desire for the beloved, otherwise no sense could be made of the desire in question. This is not to dismiss the possibility of self-deception in the lover; it is only to resist the claim that it is necessarily there in the lover's love itself. Martha Nussbaum rightly says 'We deceive ourselves about love--about who; and how; and when; and whether'.[5] But I think that she would agree that that is due to other things true of us, our needs for instance, not to the nature of love itself. She says that knowledge of love is itself a love story, which returns us to Cleopatra and what she sees and desires.

We must observe, however, that the perception of the other as beautiful by itself is necessary but not causally sufficient for erotic love else we should be thrown into much greater confusion than we are. There is as well what we might call the susceptibility condition which is very complex and is made up of many factors, physiological, psychological, historical, prudential, from the constitutional through the episodic to the reflective. These make for our similar-

---

3. *Critique of Judgement*, Pt. I, Bk. II, Sec. 41.

4. *The Characters of Love* (London: Constable, 1960), p. 149.

5. 'Love's Knowledge', *Perspectives on Self-Deception*, ed. McLaughlin and Rorty (University of California Press, 1988), p. 487.

ities rather than our differences. They are the *kind* of background conditions we take for granted in our understanding of each other without that entailing uniformity. We are as familiar with the thought that different people are differently susceptible to presentations of erotic beauty as we are with the rich variation in motivation for human behaviours. Although some theories of interpretation have attempted to reduce that richness to a handful of drives, the variety keeps on coming back in. The same is true of the susceptibility condition. There is the danger here, and we cannot avoid it, that the more we rely on the susceptibility condition to account for love in any particular case the less of a role we give to the perception of beauty or the more that perception itself becomes open to the same, now plainly reductive, explanation. That reduction must be resisted in the cause of good interpretation.

A final introductory point. It follows from what I have so far said that unless for the lover the beloved is both beautiful and desired, either it is not erotic love in question or the love is in some way perverse, under the influence of such Freudian strategies as displacement, denial, condensation, perhaps. Love without desire sounds like the poet who has his finger stuck under the pedestal on which he has placed his lady[6] and desire occasioned by something other than beauty smacks more of power than love. Perhaps it is lust, that 'expense of spirit in a waste of shame', though we should no doubt heed Fiona Pitt-Kethley's remonstration in one of her poems: 'Come off it Shakespeare, lust's a lot of fun'.

II

It was Virgil Aldrich[7] who first applied Wittgenstein's[8] theory of aspects to our perception of aesthetic objects. Wollheim[9] and Scruton had the same idea a bit later and the subject has now become much discussed in the literature. Aspects are not properties of things because they are not instantiated in them. They are the things themselves perceived in a certain way. But they are not simply the things themselves since it is by reference to the first-order properties of the things themselves that questions about the appropriateness of perceiving them in the way one does are settled. 'My seeing an aspect raises the question of the appropriateness of what I see *in* the object *to* the object in which I see

---

6. I think it was Craig Raine who said something like this once.

7. 'Picture Space', *Philosophical Review* LXVII (July 1958).

8. *Philosophical Investigations* IIxi (Oxford: Blackwell, 1963).

9. *Art And Its Objects* (London: Harper and Rowe, 1968).

it.'[10] This is fine distinction. Seeing something under an aspect ought to make nonsense of the dichotomy between the object seen and how it is seen. Yet there is familiar room for that distinction. It is not just the difference between hot and cool judgements--being struck in an engaged way with his beauty as distinct from coolly sitting back thinking isn't he marvellous; it is rather after the recital, being able to ask Cleopatra's question: was there or might there be such a man? It is a matter of realizing that there are other aspects under which the beloved can be seen. But then what identificatory sense can be made of the reference to the beloved simpliciter? It is not that there is something which stands behind the aspects; rather the aspects invite comparison. Davidson would perhaps not object to this: empirical reality exists in what interpreters interpret to each other.[11] Cleopatra's wondering is her recognition of Antony seen otherwise.

Perceiving an aspect of a thing may vary with respect to several parameters especially relevant to the perception of aesthetic objects. First, it may be more or less under the control of the will as some of Wittgenstein's cases show. The Maltese cross may suddenly change from being a black cross on a white ground to being a white cross on a black ground whether one wants it to or not, though one can also learn to produce the change. By contrast seeing a triangle as hanging from its apex or standing on its base requires something more deliberate. Second, perceiving an aspect may incorporate more or less explicit beliefs. To perceive a face as sad may involve as little thought and belief as any other case of perception--one may simply be struck by it as Wittgenstein says. By contrast, Iris Murdoch's familiar example,[12] a mother may perceive her daughter-in-law as not noisy but gay, not vulgar but refreshingly different. Here beliefs, interpretations perhaps, mediate the perception. Third, perceiving an aspect may be more or less affective in character. Taking another's behaviour as reserved is rather different from taking it as charming. There may be no affect in the first case whereas there almost certainly is in the second, though there are visual impressions at least in both. And fourth, what one sees in an object may be more or less closely related to the object in which one sees it. Scruton says: 'I can see some of the bathers in Cézanne's picture (National Gallery London) as either moving or at rest, and my understanding of the picture governs the aspect that I choose'.[13] By contrast, one can hear Vaughan

---

10. Roger Scruton, *Art and Imagination* (London: Methuen, 1974), p. 112.

11. See his essays for example on Radical Interpretation and Language and Reality in his *Inquiries into Truth and Interpretation* (Oxford University Press, 1984).

12. *The Sovereignty of Good* (London: RKP, 1970).

13. *Op. cit.*, p. 112.

Williams's 'Lark Ascending' as very English without taking its Englishness as at all essential to the music. This example, incidentally, brings out another point of considerable importance. One may not be able to fill out what it is for a piece of music to sound very English. As Scruton says: 'There need not be a thought which both fully specifies the intellectual content of "seeing x as y" and which can be itself described independently of this experience... We do not seem able to capture the content of what is seen in the form of a proposition that is, as it were, simultaneously believed'.[14]

This kind of position on the perception of beauty--I do not attribute this particular version to anyone--makes beauty an aspect of a thing. It does not have the property of beauty--there is no such property--it presents as a thing of beauty. In the light of what I said just now, this may mean that, first, one can do something to perceive the object as beautiful; second, one's apprehension of its beauty may be sensorily immediate or more considered; third, one may be moved by or merely cognitively aware of the beauty of the thing; and fourth, one's response to the object may be either cognitively scrupulous or, on the other hand, inspirational, and in both cases not able to be fully encapsulated in a simple proposition.

These variations affect the relation between how something is perceived and the first-order features of what is perceived but do not settle the question of the appropriateness of what is seen in the object to the object in which it is seen. Even if this question involves only comparisons between different presentations of something rather than that between any one presentation and the thing itself-- comparisons between Waltzing Mathilda as a national anthem and as a charac- teristic Australian song, for example--even so, such presentations require the constraints of plausibility and open up the possibility of aspect blindness, as Wittgenstein called it: the first because the aspect under which something is perceived may be due to mere whimsy, and the second because in the extreme case one simply might not know how to perceive anything as, say, patriotic. Since there is here no fact of the matter beyond consensus, whether one is being too fanciful or not fanciful enough can only be determined by a theory of inter- pretation for the particular case, following Davidson,[15] or by drawing on Witt- genstein's agreement in judgement within a shared form of life, which stands behind it. The form of life is important for locating and being confident of one's own perspective from which one ascribes under the principle of charity intelli- gible attitudes to others; without it, first person authority is merely solipsistic. But without one's first person perspective, there is no place to begin.

Sharing a form of life ensures that we speak the same language to the extent

---

14. Roger Scruton, *Art and Imagination* (London: Methuen, 1974), p. 118, p. 119.

15. *Inquiries into Truth and Interpretation* (Oxford University Press, 1984).

that we do and when the subject matter is specific the language and the practices and skills associated with it become expert. Consequently the attitudes we take into the application of a theory of interpretation are themselves properly informed. We know how to take things of beauty and expect others to know that too, saying, for example: give it some time, see it from here, focus on that mass, look at the balletic line, attend to the fact of the images, let it lie on the middle palate, think Bartok; and thus open ourselves to critical discourse.

Knowing the meaning is being able to disagree about truth but it is not an easy matter to determine how much disagreement is consistent with knowing the language. Too much disagreement collapses, in the end, into unstatable difference. But that then, from one's own point of view, raises the question of whether one can understand the other at all. One is able to do so only if one can translate the other's utterances and gestures into one's own language, which reestablishes what looks like disagreement again, but now disagreement unshared unless one teaches the other one's language. These difficulties persist between idiolects within a natural language community. It used to be reasonably common to hear otherwise knowledgeable and intelligent people say of Picasso's or Miro's late paintings: my child could have done that, or even, my child can do better than that. How could a person who said that be credited with any knowledge of what is going on, with knowing the relevant language? How could one not see Matisse's blue dancers or Henry Moore's great pieces, especially in the open landscape, or Mies' city squares or Mozart's arias or Epstein's primitive sculptures as beautiful? But we know that that is of course possible. We do not need much imagination to ascribe to others tastes, likes, dislikes, interests, backgrounds, and the relativities of time, place, social class, society and education that would make such failures of perception intelligible. But that is not the end of the matter. What is important here is that they not remain failures of perception; something can be done to enable another to perceive the beauty that one perceives, to make available to the other as objects of attention the relevant features of the thing. That might be hard or relatively easy but even in the event of total failure, real aspect blindness remains merely presumptive. The argument for this sort of aesthetic objectivity is again from Wittgenstein's shared form of life and the variety of public activities we engage in. Beauty is something we share and can come to share.

The difficulties with objectivity would appear to be compounded in the case of love. If love stands to the beauty that calls it forth as beauty stands to the features of the thing which makes it so, love is in danger of vanishing into complete relativization. But, equally, if there is something about a thing that makes it a thing of beauty, there is something about the beauty perceived that makes the lover love the one in whom it shines. In both cases, what it is about the object will not be captured completely in the form of a proposition, partly because there is no substitute for the experience itself, and for the rest because the features attended to do not merely add up to the beauty or the love--what is experienced is experienced as a whole. But it is not the case that nothing can be said, even if with love and perhaps with beauty too, what is said is prefaced by an acknowledgment of our susceptibility to the features or beauty in question. One might and sometimes does wonder what one person sees in another but the common presumption is that there must be something, that the fact of their love is part of an intelligible world, which fact is taken as such to be explained.

Beauty had better not be wholly in the eye of the beholder if sense is to be made of any lover's perception of the beloved. Cleopatra makes sense. So, unless we indulgently say that everybody loves somebody sometime, which gives up on interpretation, there had best be some good enough reasons for love in any particular case. Plato suggests that the other's beauty is there to be seen. The question is what conditions have to be satisfied for us to see it and whether, given a susceptibility condition of the kind we take for granted in our under-standing of each other in these matters, those conditions might be disclosed as sufficient for the lover's desire for the beloved. If they are not, the perception is incomplete and whether it is love at all is put in question; if they are, the object of love is clearly lovable and the love intelligible. The problem here is a general one within Davidson's mature theory. Concede, as he came to, that there are as many propositional attitudes as there seem to be and not just the one--belief. Then the constraints on the intelligible ascription of propositional attitudes to others are not so clear. One cannot ascribe to others beliefs that are unintelligi-ble to oneself and it is relatively easy to see what an unintelligible belief is. It is much harder to determine what an unintellgible desire or hope might be. In order to be intelligible does one have to imagine circumstances in which one would share it? The same problem comes up with someone's being lovable. I'll return to this problem at the end.

It is significant that it is not easy to discover examples of loves which we find from the start unintelligible. We are free with our promissory notes in our perception of love's possibility. Take the unlikely love between Othello and Desdemona, unlikely, that is, to the Venetian nobles: how is it possible that:

> A maid so tender, fair and happy,
> So opposite to marriage that she shunn'd
> The wealthy curled darlings of our nation,
> Would ever have, to occur a general mock,
> Run from her guardage to the sooty bosom
> Of such a thing as thou...[16]

Admittedly that is her father speaking. But Othello says:

---

16. *Othello*, Act I, Sc. II, William Shakespeare.

> She loved me for the dangers I had passed,
> And I loved her, that she did pity them.[17]

One does not for a moment hesitate to accept their love. It is entirely intelligible that Desdemona is 'consecrate' to Othello's 'honours and his valiant parts', and intelligible too that Othello should fall for a sympathetic and attractive daughter of the magnificoes with a bit of vim.[18] But really what are their perceptions of each other? His beauty includes suffering his trials and winning through, hers that she feels for him in that. There is nothing unintelligible here though the problem is whether these perceptions of beauty are sufficient for the more than erotic love it will turn out Othello and Desdemona will need.

The question now is: what is analogous in the case of the lovable to the features one takes and makes as objects of attention in the case of a thing of beauty; where does one stand when one perceives the other as lovable, when one finds it entirely intelligible that the lover should love the beloved? And is failure even possible here? It would certainly seem so. Construe Dolabella as discounting Cleopatra's hyperboles; his answer is that she is wrong to think that there was ever or might be such an Antony as she describes. Had he bestrid the oceans he would have won the battle; had he dropped realms like plates from his pocket, Egypt would still be his and hers. We are besieged by lovers' stories about the marvels of their beloveds. What is interesting is that we are mostly indulgent in listening to these stories though Dolabella is not, but that is because he is Caesar's man and concerned with Cleopatra's immediate future. Our indulgence is of a piece with our accepting the fact that people love each other and beginning from there. The world will always welcome lovers, as we heard in *Casablanca*.

But the question is whether our indulgence is in the point of truth or fondness. It is fondness when it is the lovers' susceptibility that strikes us--that they should be so carried away, that they should have become so vulnerable, or, which proves the point, the contrary, when we think with irritation that the lovers have been unwise and silly to have allowed themselves to become besotted with each other. Our indulgence in lovers' stories is in point of truth only when there are some truths that we can both see and see that the lover has exaggerated or focussed upon or become fixated by. But more than this: our indulgence suggests that we can understand why someone should be so taken with them even if we are not, otherwise indulgence would be out of place-- indulgence is a logically inappropriate attitude to take to plain error. So lovers' stories are intelligible and the object of love therefore intelligibly lovable.

The difference between the lover who loves and we who do not lies in our

---

17. *Ibid.*, Act I, Sc. III.

18. As Paul Fahey put it to me.

not, for various reasons, being susceptible to the beauty we see, if we see it, or to our not perceiving the other as in fact beautiful though we see how they might be so seen. Our not being susceptible may of course have as much to do with our circumstances and present position or with our impression that there is no likelihood of reciprocity, as with our physical or psychological constitution. Of course difficulties remain about seeing the first order properties of those in question as properly describable in the fulsome terms we are familiar with but such seeing is not unintelligible even if it is only shared in imagination. It is to the point to apply to this kind of perception what was said above about the perception of beauty in general: that it is more or less under the control of the will, more or less sensorily immediate, more or less affecting, and more or less inspirational. In the normal course, observers will hardly *share* the lover's perspective on the one beloved, else jealousy would be so common that the phenomenon would have to be reconceptualized.

III

Apart from the desire to possess and be possessed by the beloved, there are two other desires which muddy the waters of love's truths. The first is the desire to be right in one's perceiving the other as beautiful and the second is the desire to make the good things come true--not to be confused with the desire for the good since we are here with Plato's lovers of sights and sounds. I argued in Part I that, though internally related, what love descried in the beloved was not mediated by the desire engendered by those perceptions. The desire to possess and be possessed is not a ground of the perception of the beloved's beauty. But even if this is so there is a complicating desire to be right about one's perception and to be seen to be justified in the desires one consequently has. This may not mediate the original perception but it very soon becomes enmeshed in the immediate outcome so that, looking on, one may observe that the lover grows too fond and falls into illusion. An aspect fleetingly glimpsed as a possibility, perhaps, becomes constitutive of an object one wants so to be seen and enhanced by. Here is just the point for self-deception and its classical explanation too: the desire to have it so sustains the belief that it is so.

The other desire involves what might look like a bit of 'propter hocery'. It is perhaps a version of 'though we cannot make our sun stand still, yet we shall make him run', and when one has, it looks as if he always had. Less Marvellously, if lovers are lucky, they make their dreams come true, which is a way of validating what they dreamt of in the first place. The beginnings of love need the dreams of its development. Without beliefs in its natural ripening love looks like being doomed from the start. The truth of one's original perception, therefore, and the genuineness of the desires it engended depends in part on one's efforts to make the sequel support them. So how can one take as true at any one time lovers' declarations which are also declarations of intentions to make them true?

This second is no difficulty. When nineteenth century suitors were asked to declare their intentions, they were not thereby understood as not yet being true in their affections and the perceptions that called them forth. Quite the contrary. This is no more a difficulty here than in any other case of intentional action. That one does or does not succeed entails that one tried, and the truth of the trying claim is neither upheld nor undermined by what transpires by way of success. It is very tempting to say that if all turns out well in love then one must have seen the beloved truly and if it turns out ill one was, sadly, mistaken. But this is a temptation that leads us into error. Seeing and believing is one thing; making it, having it, work out is quite another, otherwise acting would be altogether very much easier than it is.

This returns us to the difficulties with the first kind of desire. But now they can be illuminated by the second. The desire to be and be seen to be right in our perceptions and their consequences is fulfilled by making those consequences manifest. There is nothing wrong with forging connections between subsequent evidence and the prior claim for which it is evidence. One can feel confirmed in one's perception of the other as erotically beautiful because one desires to possess and be possessed by him or her, and does, and is so. Effects are good evidence for their causes.

This appears to pay insufficient attention to self-deception, the permanent possibility of which love seems to exhibit. It cannot be denied that seduction is part of love and that it may succeed by ensnaring, duping, and deceiving the other into illusions of perception and thought. There is a line of argument developed from Freud which concludes that qua lover one is more prone to self-deception than one is qua knower, because self-deception is a defence especially called upon when emotional turbulence threatens one's fragile securities. This argument may indeed be right. The crucial point, however, is that here as elsewhere once the possibility of self-deception is taken seriously by us, it is impossible to extrude it directly. Like scepticism, it cannot be confronted and dismissed. Bas van Fraassen's response[19] is to say that this proves the necessity for courage in carrying on living, courage to live with the thought that despite one's best attempts at, as Russell put it, the solvent influence of critical reflection, one still might be deceiving oneself. This is exactly the point with love too. It might take a fool to fall in love but it had better be a brave fool. Love might invite self-deception more than other conditions but both the problems caused and the solutions needed are no different.

---

19. 'The Peculiar Effects of Love and Desire', *Perspectives on Self-Deception*, ed. McLaughlin and Rorty (University of California Press, 1988).

IV

Now to truth and exaggeration and hyperbole. Intelligibility is only the possibility of truth. Lovers' stories are often exaggerated and their descriptions of the beloved often hyperbolic. But it is not uncommon, I said, for us to meet this with an indulgence that suggests an awareness of truths. I want to argue for this now by discussing the figure of hyperbole and the phenomena of exaggeration.

Fowler[20] has it right (of course): hyperbole is exaggeration as emphasis, not deception. Consequently in hyperbole's exaggeration there is a truth about what is exaggerated and a focussing of attention upon it. By contrast, exaggeration of the size of the trout one has caught or the number of people at the protest or the achievements of those one is proud of, bespeaks deception. But then it is just exaggeration, not hyperbole, which raises the question of how one might tell them apart. The answer lies in how extreme it is. Exaggeration which would have itself taken for the truth has to hide its falsehood. Hyperbole proper does not care how impossible what it depicts seems to be. It wears its falsehood on its face. It forces one to see through it because things cannot be as they are said to be. It spruiks the truth.

There is something very interesting here. It seems that emphatic exaggeration is a test of the reality of what is exaggerated--if one cannot be hyperbolic about it, then it does not exist or is the stuff of fantasy. Emphatic exaggeration involves paying attention which involves identifying over time what one is paying attention to. One can also attend to possibilities, impossibilities, the substance of things hoped for and the like, but when exaggerated these are merely amplified: a certain exaggerated possibility is a different object of thought from the same possibility unexaggerated. There is not one thing that stands to the exaggerated possibility as the Antony of the play stands to Cleopatra's dream of him. One cannot exaggerate a phantasm without making it, like a sense datum, a different one. But the emphatic exaggeration in hyperbolic descriptions simply makes us attend to the thing and its features emphasised by the hyperbole--to Antony's power and generosity, for example. It is an implicit imperative to attend to them and marvel or fear, a recommendation to look at them in a particular way, to see them as beautiful perhaps, as worthy of attention. It is to see them under an aspect, to see the object as a thing of wonder. Hyperbole, of course, also draws attention to the describer and to how things are seen through a lover's eyes, but it could not do that unless there was something to be seen.

So what are the truths disclosed by lovers' descriptions? They are whatever is emphasised in hyperbolic descriptions of the beloved. They might

---

20. *Modern English Usage.*

include as well the thought that the features described make the beloved an object of wonder to anyone who can recognize beauty in another. It is significant that even Caesar's description of Antony at the end of the play makes of him something not unlike what Cleopatra saw. In this case it may be that Antony's qualities do not need emphasis in order to be truly seen but in other cases it may be otherwise. Love's perceptions may discover beauty for us all that we might not have seen. In this way love may see not only truths but truths which would have gone unperceived but for the eyes of love. Where does one stand to see what those eyes see? The hyperboles themselves tell us. They tell us first what to look for: we follow the exaggerations to what is so emphasized; and they show us the aspect under which to see it: to Antony's exuberant enjoyments as perfectly controlled and self-aware displays, for example.

But if hyperbole shows what is true by emphasizing it, it necessarily ignores the rest it does not emphasize. If everything were emphasized nothing would be. So the truths erotic love discloses are not the whole truth. But this is exactly what we should expect. If lovers' views of each other are given by the hyperboles they are prey to, then it is no wonder that erotic loves may not last. One has to live with the whole truth whether one realises it or not, not just those truths one's hyperboles track.

This takes us back finally to the question of what we must suppose in order to be in a position to discover love's truths, to the conditions of their intelligibility. I wondered earlier whether to see another as lovable required that one be able to imagine circumstances in which one shared that love. Clearly in general that is too strong a requirement unless those circumstances include so many changes to oneself that self-knowledge is mocked. Knowing ourselves is partly knowing what we cannot love. What we can find intelligible is that someone else loves the other in question; we can imagine what someone would have to be like in order to love the other. As with the perception of beauty, there is no guarantee of success here, but there is no certainty of failure either.

It might be thought that this is still too strong. Understanding sentences in one's natural language that contain psychological predicates essentially, may presuppose one's familiarity with the relevant public manifestations of the psychological states in question, but it could only require some private experience as well, in this case one's successfully imagining something, if there were something deeply wrong with the Private Language Argument. Perhaps there is: the *feelings* of pain, delight, love, and the like, whose primitive expressions are taken up into the meaning of the words for them, cannot themselves be merely part of the background for meaningful discourse involving them without threatening their status as what is *expressed*; but to include them would appear to undermine the argument itself.

This is to forget, however, the activities, the life, which is the medium in which the whole discourse makes sense. This is a shared life which includes both the feelings and their natural expressions and others' responses to them in their equally natural settings in particular lives, relationships, circumstances. The hyperboles celebrate the feelings of love and remind us of what it is like to *want* to exaggerate the features in question and discover to us the community of love. Our knowledge of love and the intelligibility of any particular instance of it lies not just in the love stories we can tell but in the love stories we can tell each other.[21]

---

21. I am indebted particularly to Paul Fahey, Henry Krips, Yasmin Mahdi, and Roger Lamb for illuminating critical discussions of these matters.

Index

Aesthetic apprehension of particulars,
204, 207
  aspects and, 246
  versus knowledge, 204
Agape, 58-59, 78 (fn 22), 222
  concern for the welfare of the other
    and, 58, 68
  not an emotion, 223
Agent-neutral reasons, 157-158
Agent-relative reasons, 157-158
Alcibiades, 3, 10, 59, 201 (fn 26)
  as Diotima's opponent, 3
Alcmene, 52
Aldrich, Virgil, 246
Anderson, Brom, 106
Annis, David, 92
Antony and Cleopatra, 243, 245
Appiah, K.A., 193 (fn 6)
Aquinas, 69, 78 (fn 24)
Aristophanes, 7, 10, 11, 66-67, 71, 90, 91
  (fn 35)
Aristotle, 28 (fn 8), 29 (fns 9, 10), 30 (fn
  11), 37 (fn 26), 46-47, 57, 67, 82 (fn
  28), 89, 156, 215, 216, 217, 220, 223
  on friendship (*philia*), 215, 216, 217
    and belief, 215
    and desire, 215
Aspects, 246-247
  appropriateness of, 246, 248
  blindness towards, 248, 249
  empirical reality and, 247
  hyperbole and, 254-255
  modes of perception and, 246
  not properties, 246
  propositionally specifying their con-
    tent, 248, 249
  seeing them, 246
    affect and, 247, 252
    belief and, 247, 252

    desire to be right in, 252-253
    holism and, 250
    not mediated by desire, 245, 252
    the will and, 247, 248, 252
Attitudes
  as *de re*, 44
  as universalizable, 24-26
  replicable properties and, 23-24
  take non-propositional objects, 25 (fn
    3)
Auden, W.H., 189
Austin, J. L., 236
Autonomy, 97, 107-09
  addiction and, 108
  authorship and, 107, 110
  doing what one wants and, 108
  'extreme' love and, 111, 112, 113,
    117, 118
  loss of, incompatible with robust
    concern for the beloved, 72, 77-80,
    85
  love and, 107-121
    conflict between, 107
  nature of, 108, 110, 114
  'power preference' and, 110-111
  'preference' and, 109-110, 113, 114
  promoting it in one's lover, 86
  Spinoza's conception of, 98, 101
  Spinoza's evaluation of, 98
  well-being and, 85

Bayley, John, 245
Beautiful
  affect and the, 248
  desire to be right in perceiving the
    other as, 252
  erotic delight in the, 245
    desire to possess and, 245, 252-253
  love of the, 244

and the 'now', 244
   willing to perceive the object as, 248
Beauty, 137, 243-244, 246, 251
   affect and, 248
   as an aspect, 248
   as the occasion of desire in love, 246,
      250
   not a property, 248
   not wholly in the eye of the beholder,
      250
   objectivity and, 249
   our delight in, 244-245
   the 'now' and, 244
Being lovable, 250-251, 255
   imagination and, 250, 252, 255
   perceiving this in others, 251, 255
      affect and, 252
      the will and, 252
Bellah, Robert, 85 (fn 30)
Bisexuality, 203 (fn 34)
Bloom, Allan, 65
'Bondage'
   concealment of, by pleasure, 112
   escaping from it (Spinoza), 100, 101
   first-order desire and, 109, 113
   Spinoza's conception of, 98, 101
'Bondage-love', 93-106, 112-113
   as destructive, 93, 95
   as evil, 93
   as intense, 93, 105, 106
   as obsessive, 93, 95-97
   as pathological, 93
   as unrequited, 93
   being 'in love' and, 106
   definition of, 94
   emancipation of women and, 96, 105
   feelings of helplessness and, 95
   nostalgia for, 94, 105
   overcoming it, 97-105
   self-deception and, 96
   significance of, 106
   unconscious desires and, 94, 105-106
   unrealistic demands and, 95, 97
   value of, 105-106
Breuer, 104
Burleigh, Walter, 60
Butler, Judith, 202

Calhoun, Cheshire, 201-202

Campbell, Sue, 203 (fn 37)
Carrington, Dora, 6-11, 13-16, 18-20
Categories
   liberating, 202, 203
   multiplication of, 203, 207
   oppressive, 203
   required for self-knowledge, 202, 207
Categorization, 200-204
   hegemony and, 201, 206
   individuals resistant to, 202, 204
   prescriptive onus and, 200, 206
   suffering and, 200
Chodorow, Nancy, 73 (fn 13)
Chomsky, N., 195
Clarke, Stanley, 227 (fn 5)
Cocking, Dean, 152 (fn 30)
Commitment
   degrees of, 31
   friendship and, 28
   limited character of in friendship, 29-
      30
   limited character of in love, 30, 30 (fn
      13)
   love and, 27-28, 30
   obligation and, 28
   universalizability and, 27, 31
Compulsion, 97, 103, 108, 109
Cyrano de Bergerac 225-227, 230-241

Davidson, Donald, 247, 248, 250
Dawkins, R., 197 (fns 16, 18), 198 (fn 21)
de Beauvoir, Simone, 62, 75
Deigh, John, 212, 213, 224 (fn 17)
   on primitive emotions, 212, 213
Dennett, Daniel, 213
Descartes, 57, 150 (fn 27)
Desire, 131-134
   as occasioned by beauty in love, 246,
      250
   as inertial, 118
   changes in, 118
   conflict and, 112
   emotion and, 221
   enjoying it, 111
   evaluation of one's own, 109, 113,
      115, 118, 119
   for desire in the other, 112
   for pleasure, 111
   hopeless, 118

invasive, 140-152
   as impossible to fulfil, 144
   as predatory, 142, 148
   as solipsistic, 143
   control and, 143-144, 148
   not reciprocal, 142
   possession and, 141-144, 147, 148
   Proust and, 141-145, 147
  invasive *v.* reductive, 140, 143, 149
  love as, 109, 215-224
  manipulation of, 109
  mutual, 112
  orders of, 108
  'preference' and, 109-110
  reductive *v.* invasive, 140, 143, 149
  sexual, 111-112, 125, 132, 133, 135-139
   imagination and, 125
   Kant on 'unnatural', 125
   possession and, 139, 245
  to be indispensable to the beloved, 194
  to possess the good (Plato), and love, 66, 68
  to satisfy desire of the other, 111, 113
  triumph of pain over, 112
  unconscious, 94, 105-106
  uninvited, 109, 119
  weighting, 113
de Sousa, Ronald, 52, 56 (fn 17), 111 (fn 6), 225, 226, 227 (fn 5), 228 (fn 6), 242 (fn 18), 244 (fn 2)
Dewey, John, 235
Diamond, Cora, 207
Dickens, Charles, 58
'Digitality'
  essence of, 190
  paradigms and, 190
  Plato and, 190, 195
  resemblance and, 190-191
   as a three-term relation, 190
'Digitization', 191-200
Dilman, I., 37 (fn 25)
Diotima, 66, 201 (fn 26)
Diotiman optimism, 2
Diotiman order, 3
Dobzhansky, T., 199 (fn 25)
Donne, John, 192
Dworkin, Andrea, 135, 136, 139

Ecclesiastes, 99
Emotion
  belief-desire theory of, 209
  cognitivist theories of, 226-230, 239
  component theory of, 209
  desire and, 214
  evaluative theory of, 209
  expressive action, and, 226-231, 236
  love and, 209-224
  perceptual models of, 227-230, 239
  primitive, 212-213
Emotions
  appraisal-based intentionality of, 227, 229
  belief-based intentionality of, 209, 210, 212-214, 218, 227-229
  belief-based rationality of, 209, 210, 212, 213, 218
  can take propositional objects, 25 (fn 3)
  contrary, 100
  expression-based intentionality of, 227-231, 242
  knowledge of the good and, 99
  passions (Spinoza) and, 100, 101, 102
  perception-based intentionality of, 227-229
  theoretical aim in understanding, 214
Essence anxiety, 193-194, 205
Essentialism, 193

Fairness, 154-155, 156
Farrell, Daniel, 166 (fn 2), 171 (fn 4)
Farrell, Linda, 188 (fn 15)
Fahey, Paul, 251 (fn 18), 256 (fn 21)
Fear
  belief and, 210, 211-212
  groundless, 213
  inner experience and, 212
  irrational, 212
  of snakes, 212-213
Firestone, Shulamith, 73 (fn 14), 75 (fn 18)
Fisher, Helen, 198 (fn 22)
Fisher, Mark, 68, 70-71, 73, 76, 86, 87-90, 91 (fn 35)
Fodor, J., 195
Frankfurt, Harry, 108

Freud, 72 (fn 12), 97, 104, 165, 165 (fn
  1), 246, 253
Fried, Charles, 84 (fn 29)
Friendship, 28-29, 30, 127-129
  allowing oneself to be known and, 128
  as explanatory, 156
  as remedy for solipsism, 127
  belief and, 215
  commitment and, 28-29
  concern for welfare and, 128, 215, 217
  constancy in, 29
  contrary obligations and, 29 (fn 10),
    30
  desire and, 215
  duty to seek out (Kant), 127-128
  honesty and, 130
  Kant on, 127-130, 147
  knowing oneself and, 128, 129, 151
  obligation and, 28-29
  possible with more than one, 29
  Proust on, 147
  reciprocity and, 128, 129, 214, 215
  reciprocity characteristic of, 128, 129
  respect and, 128, 130
  trust and, 29, 29 (fn 9), 129, 149
  with many, as desirable, 30
Fromm, Erich, 68, 74 (fn 15)
Fungibility, 52, 244
  tokens and, 55

Gallois, André, 47
Gardella, Peter, 71 (fn 10)
Gaylin, Willard, 68, 71 (fn 11), 91 (fn 35)
Genesis, 66, 91 (fn 35)
Gibbard, Allan, 187 (fn 14)
Gilligan, Carol, 73 (fn 13)
Goldman, Alan H., 37 (fn 26)
Good
  love of the, 244
    and the future, 244
Goodman, Nelson, 204 (fn 39)
Gordon, Robert, 228 (fn 5)
Green, O.H., 210 (fns 1, 2, 3)
Gregory, D., 203 (fn 34)

Hamlyn, D. W., 46
Hardwig, John, 84 (fn 29)
Hart, H.L., 192 (fn 5)
Hatred, 224

Spinoza's conception of, 104
Hegel, 57, 67-68, 69, 71, 73, 74 (fn 16),
  76, 78, 91 (fn 35)
Herman, Barbara, 133, 135-140
Higgins, K., 57 (fn 18), 62 (fn 26)
Holton, Richard, 141 (fn 22)
Hume, 187 (fn 14)
Hunter, J.F.M., 68, 80-81, 90, 91 (fn 35)
Hurka, Tom, 63
Hyperbole, 254-256
  aspects and, 254-255
  emphasis and, 254-255
  focus and, 254-255
  love's endurance and, 255
  truth and, 254-255

Individuality
  categorization and, 200-204
  love and, 207
  negativity and, 202
  relations and, 57
  the repeatable and, 10, 12, 13
  the unique and, 9
Intensity, 222, 244 (See also entries under
  'Bondage love' and 'Jealousy')
Intentional objects, 134
  specifying them, 225-242
Irigary, Luce, 134 (fn 12)

Jackson, Frank, 160 (fn 7)
Jacobsen, Rockney, 242 (fn 18)
Jagger, Alison, 225-226, 228, 235 (fn 13)
Jealousy, 45, 45 (fn 38), 165-188, 191,
  205, 245, 252
  anger and, 165, 167, 172, 174, 178,
    179
    relevant object of, 174-175
  anguish and, 165
  as explanatory of behaviour, 167
  as 'illness', 184-185
  beloved as possession and, 165
  definition of, 166
    arguments against this, 169-171,
      173-175
  desire and, 165-188
    norms of appropriate, 186
  desire to be 'favored' and, 166, 168,
    170, 172-182, 183, 184-185
    puzzling nature of such desire, 180-

182, 183-184, 185
despair and, 167
devastation and, 185
distinct feeling of, 171-172
envy and, 170-171
exclusivity and, 167, 174, 183
fear and, 165, 178
Freud and, 165
grief and, 165, 172
infantilism and, 165
intensity of feeling and, 165, 172, 178, 179, 181-183, 186-187
   norms of, 186
   urgency of desire and, 184 (fn 13)
loss and, 165, 172-173, 178, 185
Othello and, 167, 172, 185
panic and, 167, 178
personal insecurity and, 176-179, 184 (fns 12, 13), 184-185
   urgency of desire and, 184 (fns 12, 13)
professional, 167-168, 173
rage and, 167, 178, 179
'romantic', 167, 169, 173, 180-183, 185
sexual, 167, 169, 173, 180-183, 185
   biological basis of desires involved in, 181, 183
   violence and, 181 (fn 10), 185
sexual exclusivity and, 166 (fn 2), 173, 174, 180-181, 182, 183
sibling, 168
suspicion and, 167
three parties to, 170
Jeffrey, Richard, 108 (fn 4)
Justification
   as involving abstraction, 159, 161

Kant, 67, 73, 107, 125-140, 142, 145, 147, 152, 245
   feminist critique of, 130 (fn 7)
   feminist incarnations of, 135
   on duty to seek out friendship, 127
   on friendship, 127-128
   on human body, 138, 139
   on reciprocity of friendship, 129
   on reciprocity of love, 128
   on self-knowledge, 128, 130
   on self-love, 127

   on sexual love, 126, 132-133, 135
   on 'union love', 67, 73
   on 'unnatural' sexual desire, 125
   von Herbert, Maria, and, 130
Kennett, Jeanette, 152 (fn 30)
Kern, Jerome, 211
Kierkegäard, 58, 78-79
Kindness, 154-155, 156
'Know thyself', 128, 149, 151
Korsgaard, Christine, 129, 130, 133, 137 (fn 17), 138-141, 148, 149
Kraut, Robert, 53-56, 61, 111 (fn 6), 227 (fn 5), 232 (fn 10)
Kripke, S., 55 (fn 13), 56
Krips, Henry, 256 (fn 21)
Kundera, M., 196 (fn 15)

Lamb, Roger, 60 (fn 24), 63, 92, 105 (fn 36), 106, 121, 126 (fn 5), 140 (fn 19), 163 (fn 8), 178 (fn 9), 184 (fn 12), 188 (fn 15), 224 (fn 17), 242 (fn 18), 256 (fn 21)
Langton, Rae, 126 (fn 3), 130 (fn 6), 134 (fn 12), 136 (fn 15), 140 (fn 20), 150 (fn 28)
Language
   empiricist view of its acquisition, 195-196
   innatist view of its acquisition, 195-196
Lawrence, D. H., 137 (fn 17)
Lehrer, Keith, 47, 97 (fn 7), 106, 108 (fn 4), 109 (fn 5)
Leibniz, 57
Liking someone, 31
   rationality and, 31-32
   universalizability of, 31-32
Linden, R.R., 203 (fn 35)
Love
   action and, 59-60
   admiration and, 10, 35-36
   allowing oneself to be known and, 130
   'analog', 189
   Aristophanic view of, 10, 66-67, 71, 90
   as agapic, 223
   as attitude, 25, 25 (fn 3), 214
   as binding, 192
   as desire, 215-224

Love *(cont.)*
  as endlessly variable, 193, 201
  as excusing partiality, 162
  as explanatory, 155-156, 158-159, 227
    then requiring rigid reference to the
      beloved, 158-159
  as friendship, 130
  as informative about oneself, 13, 130,
    148-150 (Proust), 151, 151 (Proust),
    152
  as justificatory, 155, 159-163
  as liberating, 192
  as motive for actions, 221-222, 227
  as 'personal', 34, 40
  as remedy for solipsism, 127, 129,
    204, 245
  as self-interested, 68
  as set of desires, 209, 215-217
  as subjective pleasure (Proust), 146-
    147
  as universal value, 159-163
  aspiration and, 10, 12
  autonomous, 113-120
    advantages of, 118-119
    as contradictory, 116
    as respectful of the preferences of
      the beloved, 113
    autonomous preference and, 114-
      116
    control and, 119
    'extreme' love and, 118
    insecurity and, 119
    mutual, 115-116, 119
    reason and, 119, 157
    scope of, 117, 120
    trust and, 119
  autonomy and, 107-121
  beauty and, 193, 243-244, 246
  belief and, 210-215, 216, 220, 226,
    243, 252
  belief-based intentionality and, 211
  belief-based rationality and, 211
  benevolent concern for the beloved
    and, 65-92, 79, 89, 130, 216
    Aristotle and, 68
    Christianity and, 68
  commitment and, 27-28, 30
  commitment of, 155-156, 159
  commitment to, 155-156, 159

  completeness in, 59-61, 63
  conative theory of, 215-224
    desire for association basic to, 216-
      217
  constancy and, 46, 47, 53, 55, 62, 211,
    218, 219, 220, 223
  conventional character of, 153, 235,
    235 (fn 13), 236, 241-242
  cultural character of, 153, 235, 235 (fn
    13), 236, 241-242
  de dicto, 53
  de re, 53, 55-56
  desire and, 245-246, 252-253
  desire for association basic in, 216-217
  desire for development in, 252
  desire to possess and, 245, 252-253
  desire to possess the good (Plato) and,
    66, 68
  desires and, 209, 215-217
    rational structure of these, 216-217,
      220
  difficulty of a general understanding
    of, 3-4
  'digital', 189-191
    paradigms and, 190
  duties of beneficence and, 79
  egalitarian, 120-121
  emotion and, 209-224
  'essence anxiety' and, 193
  essence of, 193-194, 204-205
  exclusivity and, 36-38, 193, 211, 218,
    220, 223, 245
  expression-based intentionality of,
    232-242
    avowals and, 237, 238
    performatives and, 236, 240
  expressive action, and 226-227, 232-
    236
    avowals as, 233-236
  'extreme', 111-114, 117, 118
    definition of, 111
    its conflict with autonomy, 111,
      112-113, 118
    magic of, 111
    mutual desire to satisfy desire and,
      112
    reciprocity of desire in, 111-112
    transcending it, 113-114
  extreme romantic view of, 10

Love *(cont.)*
   forms of, 114-116, 195, 210, 222-224
      unilateral, 114-115
   friendship and, 130, 214
   functionalism and, 52-56
   gendered views of, 73-74
   haecceity in conception of proper, 35,
      47
   high positive evaluation entailed by,
      244
   'human' (Kant), 133, 142, 147
   idealization and, 194, 206, 211
   ill-formed, 226, 231, 233-234, 236
   individuality and, 207
   institution of, 153
   intensity of, 222, 244
   intentionality of, 217-219, 225-242
      as a function of constitutive
         desires, 218
   its arousal, 12, 111
   its history, 7, 13, 20, 55, 56
   its object, 14, 20, 42 (fn 32), 50-51,
      201, 204, 231, 244
      as the object of a loving practice,
         240 (fn 17)
      failing to individuate it, 226, 231
      non-propositional specification of,
         218
   its particularity, 25-47
   its truths, 243-256 (esp. 254-256)
      as revealed in hyperbole, 254-255
      not the whole truth, 255
   its universalizability, 25-47
      practical problems of that, 26
   jealousy and, 191, 245, 252 (See also
      separate entry under 'Jealousy')
      desiring the beloved's good and,
         191
   knowledge of, and narrative, 245
   loyalty and, 20, 53, 56, 62-63, 153
   lust and, 244, 246
   moral discourse and, 153-163
   morality and, 116
   narrative writing about it, 4-5, 18
   nonautonomous, 117
   nonrepeatable properties and, 7, 20, 51
   not transferable, 43, 54
   not valuing it, 162
   obligation and, 28, 79

   of the beautiful, 244
   of the good, 244
   of wine, 224
   orderly life and, 3
   pain and, 191-192, 205
   paradoxes of paradigms of, 191-194,
      205
   patriotism and, 32-33, 224
   philosophical writing about it as
      determinative, 17
   Plato's account normative, 15
   possession and, 62, 135, 245, 252
   rationality and, 25-47, 51-52, 61
   rationality of, 219-220
   'rational structure' of, 216
   'real', 193, 205, 206, 207
   reciprocity and, 50, 58-63, 128, 130,
      194, 214, 215, 216, 217, 223, 245
   repeatable properties and, 11, 12, 14,
      34, 34 (fn 19), 50-51, 59, 210, 211
      their priority, 20
   respect and, 113, 132
   roles in, 196, 207
   seduction and, 253
   self-, 127
   self-deception and, 245, 252, 253
   self-sacrifice and, 65, 78, 83, 153
   self-surrender and (Kant), 130, 138
   sex and, 192, 205-206, 216, 223
   sexual, 111, 131-133
      delight and, 131
      Kant on, 126, 130, 135
      solipsism in, 126, 133
   sexual desire and, 111-112, 132
   solipsism and, 123-152
   Spinoza's conception of, 104
   surviving its loss, 5, 13, 17, 20
   'tough', 114, 115
   transcending it, 3
   transformative character of, 194
   trust and, 130
   understanding of value and, 3
   union view of, 66-92
   unrequited, 59-60, 108, 118, 245
   value and, 154, 159-163
   virtue and, 154-159
   what is desired in, 244-245, 252-253
      and illusion, 252
      and self-deception, 252

Love *(cont.)*
  wishes and, 217
  writing about it, 8-9
Loved individuals
  as instantiations of a universal, 3
  as replaceable, 2, 34, 38 (fn 27), 41, 51
  beauty of, 12, 244, 246
    a sign of cherished values, 12
    revealed by lovers' perceptions,
      255
  belief in their goodness, 10
  lovers' beliefs about, 210-211
  lovers' descriptions of, 254
    and hyperbole, 254-256
  lovers' desires with respect to, 244,
    245, 252
    their effect on what is perceived in,
      244, 245
  lovers' perceptions of, 243-245
    as beautiful, 244-246, 251
    aspects and, 243, 247
    exaggeration and, 243, 251, 254
    seeing-as and, 243-244
    their effect on what is desired in
      love, 244-245
  Plato on, 2, 3, 49, 51, 52, 244
  uniqueness of, 7, 201
Lovers
  advertising for, 13, 16
  as friends (Kant), 131
  as self-help gangs of two, 162
  as useful (Proust), 148-151
  autonomy of, 65-92
  law and order and, 207
  more than one desirable, 30
  our indulgence of, 251
  partiality of, 153
  pursuing the good for one's, 65
  their bodies, 137
  theory of interpretation for, 243-244,
    246, 247, 248, 249
    beauty and, 243, 246
    susceptibility condition and, 246,
      250, 252
  union of, 65-92, 111
  virtual, 125
  well-being of, 81
  wishing the best for one's, 65

Loves
  as individual (*v.* social) realities, 204
  similar, 13
  unintelligible, 250-251
Loyalty, 53, 56, 62-63, 153
Lucretius, 206
Lumsden, C.J., 199

MacKinnon, Catherine, 126, 135
  on pornography, 126
Mahdi, Yasmin, 256 (fn 21)
Marriage, 199 (fn 22)
  Kant on, 133, 135 (fn 13)
Masochism, 118
Matthen, Mohan, 63
Matthew, 66 (fn 2)
Maugham, Somerset, 93-94, 96, 101-102
May, Rollo, 71 (fn 10)
Maynard-Smith, J., 197 (fn 17), 205 (fn
  40)
McIntyre, R., 44 (fn 37)
McTaggart, J., 34 (fn 19)
Mill, John Stuart, 72 (fn 11), 79 (fn 25)
Miller, Henry, 137 (fn 17)
Millett, Kate, 137 (fn 17)
Montaigne, 36 (fn 23), 65 (fn 1), 66-67,
  70, 79-80, 84, 90, 91
Morgan, Kathryn Pauly, 62 (fn 26), 198
Motherby, Elizabeth, 132 (fn 10)
Mullen, P., 165 (fn 1), 178 (fn 8)
Murdoch, Iris, 247
Mutuality, 50 (fn 3), 60, 112

Nagel, T., 43 (fns 34, 35), 50 (fn 3), 157
  (fn 3)
Narcissism, 244
Neely, Wright, 108 (fn 4)
Nissenbaum, Helen Fay, 227 (fn 5)
Nominalism, 50-52
Nozick, Robert, 43 (fn 34), 52-53, 56-58,
  61, 68, 72-77, 81-86, 91 (fn 35), 194
Nussbaum, Martha C., 2 (fns 1, 2), 34 (fns
  17, 18), 144 (fn 24), 145, 151, 201 (fn
  26), 204 (fn 38), 245

'Objectification', 135, 136
'Oedipus complex', 97, 104, 105
Otello (Verdi), 167, 172

Othello (Shakespeare), 167, 172, 185,
250-251
Ovid, 99

Parfit, Derek, 157 (fn 3)
Parker, Dorothy, 95 (fn 4)
Passion
    best type of
        as essential part of best human life,
        12
        enables knowledge of the beloved,
        12
        recognition of values and, 12
        understanding of values and, 16
    its arousal, 12, 119
    preference for, 119-120
    rational aspiration and, 3
    Spinoza on, 100, 101, 102, 104
Patriotism, 32-33, 224
    exclusivity and, 33
    loyalty and, 33
Patsakos, George, 106
Performative utterances, 236
Perry, John, 159 (fn 5)
Persons
    as objects of appetite, 126, 132-133,
    134-140
    treating them as things, 124, 126, 133,
    134, 135-136, 139, 148-150
Pettit, Philip, 156 (fn 2), 158 (fn 4), 160
    (fn 6), 163
Philia, 89
    concern for the welfare of the other
    and, 68, 215. 216, 217
Pitt-Kethley, Fiona, 246
Pity
    definitely directed, 44
    de re attitude, 44
Plato, 2, 3, 15, 49-50, 52, 58 (fn 22), 61,
    66, 68, 190, 193, 201 (fn 26), 244, 250
Pleasure, 111-112
Pornography, 135 (fn 13)
    solipsism and, 126, 150 (fn 28)
'Preference'
    autonomous, 114-117
        autonomous love and, 114-117
    autonomy and, 109-110
    degrees of, 120-121
    nature of, 109
        the 'power *p*', 110-111
            not externally grounded, 110, 117
            self-referential character of, 110
        to be loved autonomously, 119
        weighting, 120-121
Pride
    belief and, 210
Private Language Argument, 255
Properties
    alteration in the *p* of individuals, 53,
    55, 62
    nonreplicable within a world, 23 (fn 1)
        special historical relationships and,
        23 (fn 1)
    replicable within a world, 23, 23 (fn 1)
        attitudes and, 23-24
Proust, 133, 136 (fn 15), 141-152
Psychoanalysis, 190

Queer theory, 200-204
Quine, W.V.O., 195

Raine, Craig, 246 (fn 6)
Rapaport, Elizabeth, 73 (fn 14)
Rape, 50 (fn 3)
Rawls, John, 222
Reasons
    agent-neutral, 157
    agent-relative, 157
Reciprocity, 50, 58-63, 130, 194, 214,
    215, 216, 217, 223, 245
    as *telos* of love, 59
    characteristic of moral relations, 128
    completeness in love and, 59-61, 63
    intense in friendship, 128
Reference, rigid and non-rigid, 157-158
Reich, Peter, 195
Rejection, 108
Relations
    Leibniz on, 57
Repeatable properties
    as love's object, 14, 231
Representation and reproduction
    analog, 189 (fn 2)
    digital, 189 (fn 2), 190-191
        degradation and, 190
        drawback of, 190
        paradigms and, 190

Respect
  as universalizable, 26
Rich, A., 201 (fn 28)
Richards, J.R., 193 (fn 6)
Rorty, Amelie, 37 (fn 25), 38 (fn 26), 46-
  47, 52 (fn 6), 53, 59, 63, 111 (fn 6), 226,
  227 (fn 5), 227-228, 228 (fns 6, 7), 229
  (fn 8)
Rostand, Edmond, 226 (fn 3)
Rotkin, Karen, 189-190
Rubin, Lillian, 73
Russell, Bertrand, 146 (fn 26), 253
Ryle, Gilbert, 233

Sartre, 50 (fn 3), 61-62, 107, 134 (fn 12)
Scheler, Max, 25 (fn 4)
Schueler, Fred, 106
Scruton, Roger, 25 (fn 4), 39 (fn 29), 42
  (fns 31, 32), 43 (fn 34), 81 (fn 27), 246-
  248
Self-control, 94, 95, 100, 102
Sen, Amartya, 157 (fn 3)
Sex (See also entries under 'Desire, sex-
  ual' and 'Love, sexual')
  love and, 192
  virtual, 126
Shand, Alexander, 221
Sibling incest, 199-200
Singer, Irving, 81 (fn 27)
Singular reference, 55-56, 60
Skinner, B.F., 195
Smith, D. W., 44 (fn 37)
Smith, Michael, 156 (fn 2), 160 (fn 7)
Soble, Alan, 42 (fn 33), 43 (fn 36), 47,
  50 (fn 3), 73 (fn 14), 211-212
Soifer, Eldon, 60 (fn 23), 63
Solipsism, 123-131
  attitudinal, 123-127
  epistemic, 134, 143, 144-145, 147
  escape from, 127-131
  love as a remedy for, 127
  moral, 134, 143, 144-145, 147, 149-
    150
  pornography and, 126
  sexual, 125-126, 133
Solomon, Robert, 57 (fns 18, 19), 62 (fn
  26), 81 (fn 27), 193-194
Song of Solomon, 131, 134 (fn 11), 137
  (fn 16)

Spelman, E., 193 (fn 6)
Spinoza, 94, 97-104
  autonomy, his conception of, 98
  autonomy, his evaluation of, 98
  clear and distinct ideas, 98, 100, 101
    and control, 100
    and passions, 100, 101
  controlling the passions, 100, 101,
    104, 105
  emotion, his conception of, 100
  knowledge of the good
    and a sense of personal weakness,
     100
    and emotion, 99
    insufficient for its attainment, 99
    reason and, 103
  suicide and, 103
  valuational relativism, and 98
  virtue, his conception of, 102-103
    and power, 103
Stocker, Michael, 156 (fn 1)
Swift, Jonathan, 221

Talleyrand, 198
Taylor, Charles, 187 (fn 14)
Taylor, Gabrielle, 215
Teller, Paul, 51 (fn 4), 63
Thalberg, Irving, 24 (fn 3)
Tillich, Paul, 68
Tormey, Alan, 229 (fn 8)
Transferability of attitudes, 43
  replaceability of object and, 43
Tropes, 51

Union view of love,
  Aristophanes and, 66-67, 71, 90, 91
    (fn 35)
  Aristotle and, 57, 67
  autonomy and, 72, 73, 75-77, 85-86,
    88, 90, 111
  concern for others and, 67
  concern ('robust') for the welfare of
    the beloved and, 68-92, esp. 77-80 &
    81-86, 87, 90, 91
  de Beauvoir, Simone, and 75
  Descartes and, 57
  duties to others and, 79
  exhaustion and, 67, 79
  'extreme love' (*cp.*), 111-112

Fisher, Mark, and, 68, 70-71, 73, 76,
  87-90, 91 (fn 35)
Fromm, Erich, and 68, 70
Gaylin, Willard, and 68, 71 (fn 11)
Genesis and, 66, 91 (fn 35)
Hegel and, 57, 67-68, 69-70, 71, 73,
  76, 90, 91 (fn 35)
Hunter, J.F.M., and, 68, 80-81, 90, 91
  (fn 35)
Kant and, 67, 73. *Cp.* 129, 130
Kierkegäard and, 78-79
loss of self and, 67
Matthew and, 66 (fn 2)
May, Rollo, and, 71
Montaigne and, 66-67, 70, 79, 80, 84,
  90, 91
Nozick, Robert, and, 56-58, 68, 72-77,
  81-86, 91 (fn 35)
paradox and, 70, 75, 83, 85, 89-90
Paul and, 66 (fn 2), 69
Plato and, 66
reciprocity in, 88
self-interest and, 68-69, 78, 80, 82-83,
  86, 90, 91
selfishness and, 77-79, 84-85
self-sacrifice and, 78, 83-85
solipsism and, 80
Tillich, Paul, and, 68
Wojtyla, Karol, and 68, 77
Universalizability
  commitment and, 27, 31
Universalizable attitudes
  particular objects and, 41-43
  replaceability and, 43-44
  transferability and, 43-44

Value, 159-163
  lovers and the pursuit of, 13

Values
  as revisable, 16
  recognition of one's own involves
    passion, 12
van Fraassen, Bas, 145 (fn 24), 253
Vannoy, R., 192 (fn 4)
Virtues, 154-159
  as explanatory, 153-155
  as justificatory, 153-155
  moral and epistemic, 145
Vlastos, G., 34 (fn 17), 49
von Herbert, Maria, 130

'We', 56-58, 66, 69-70, 72, 74-75, 77,
  81, 83, 85, 90
  autonomy and, 75, 77
White, G., 165 (fn 1), 178 (fn 8)
Williams, Bernard, 35 (fn 20)
Wilmot, John. 192
Wilson, Edward O., 199
Winterson, Jeanette, 125-126, 136 (fn 15)
Wittgenstein, 243, 246, 247, 248, 249
Wodehouse, P.G., 211
Wojtyla, Karol, 68, 77
Wolf-whistle, 50 (fn 3)
Wollheim, R., 246
Women,
  emancipation of, 96
  objectification of, 126, 135, 136
  treated as chattel, 62
Writing
  about love, 18
  its ruthlessness toward life, 9

Yeats, 46

Ziff, Paul, 195 (fn 13)

About the Book and Editor

Philosophers have turned their attention in recent years to many previously unmined topics, among them love and friendship. In this collection of new essays in philosophical and moral psychology, philosophers turn their analytic tools to a topic perhaps most resistant to reasoned analysis: erotic love. Also included is one previously published paper by Martha Nussbaum.

Among the problems discussed are the role that qualities of the beloved play in love, the so-called union theory of love, intentionality and autonomy in love, and traditional issues surrounding jealousy and morality.

Roger E. Lamb is a lecturer in philosophy at the University of Queensland. He received his doctorate from the University of Rochester and specializes in the philosophy of the emotions.